discover
IRELAND

FIONN DAVENPORT
CATHERINE LE NEVEZ, ETAIN O'CARROLL,
RYAN VER BERKMOES, NEIL WILSON

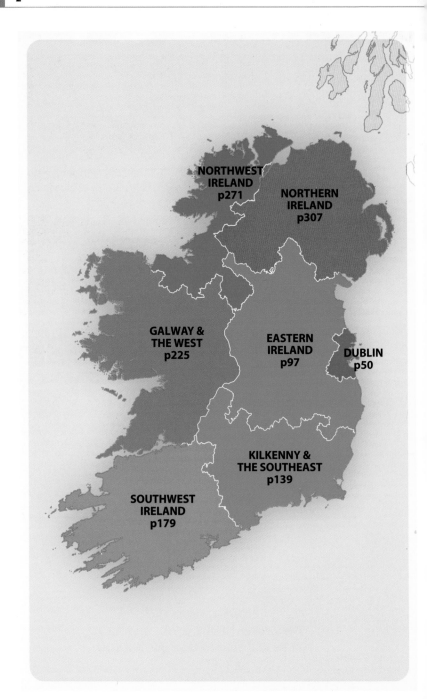

NORTHWEST
IRELAND
p271

NORTHERN
IRELAND
p307

GALWAY &
THE WEST
p225

EASTERN
IRELAND
p97

DUBLIN
p50

KILKENNY &
THE SOUTHEAST
p139

SOUTHWEST
IRELAND
p179

DISCOVER IRELAND

Dublin (p50) Great pubs, fabulous museums and big-city amenities with a small-town feel – that's a capital!

Eastern Ireland (p97) Ancient history and modern distractions, all found only a stone's throw from Dublin.

Kilkenny & the Southeast (p139) A medieval gem at the heart of Ireland's warmest corner, with culture and cuisine to boot.

Southwest Ireland (p179) Want the picture-postcard version of Ireland? Don't look any further than Cork and Kerry.

Galway & the West (p225) The mainstays for visitors, from the Burren to the Aran Islands – and don't forget Connemara.

Northwest Ireland (p271) Donegal and Sligo rarely get the attention their beauty deserves, but that's no bad thing.

Northern Ireland (p307) Once troubled, now thriving, Northern Ireland is showing the world its wonderful plumage.

⬊ CONTENTS

THE ANTRIM COAST p331

Go beyond the Giant's Causeway and explore one of Ireland's most scenic coastlines

WEST BELFAST p323

Regenerating Belfast is staking its claim as Ireland's hottest party town

BRÚ NA BÓINNE p124

Walk the dark tunnel into prehistory at these magnificent neolithic passage graves

DERRY p335

Ancient history and terrific pubs in one of the country's most fascinating cities

LEGEND

Freeway
Primary Road
Secondary Road
Railway

0 ___ 50 km
0 ___ 30 miles

ELEVATION

700m
500m
300m
200m
100m
0

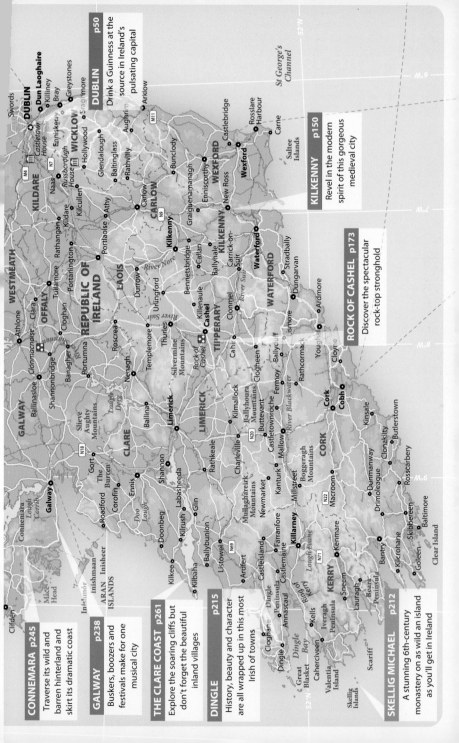

CONNEMARA p245
Traverse its wild and barren hinterland and skirt its dramatic coast

GALWAY p238
Buskers, boozers and festivals make for one musical city

THE CLARE COAST p261
Explore the soaring cliffs but don't forget the beautiful inland villages

DINGLE p215
History, beauty and character are all wrapped up in this most Irish of towns

SKELLIG MICHAEL p212
A stunning 6th-century monastery on as wild an island as you'll get in Ireland

ROCK OF CASHEL p173
Discover the spectacular rock-top stronghold

KILKENNY p150
Revel in the modern spirit of this gorgeous medieval city

DUBLIN p50
Drink a Guinness at the source in Ireland's pulsating capital

↘ THIS IS IRELAND

For such a tiny country, Ireland gets a pretty big billing. Hundreds of songs sing its praises, telling of a green landscape brushed with rain, a wild coastline tormented by a windblown sea… Hang on, can this idyll actually be *real*?

Of course it is. Those songs may be sung with greatest fervour by the hyphenated Irish whose ancestors left Ireland's starving shores in their ragged millions, never to return or forget, but the images still endure. It doesn't really matter that Ireland has long since outgrown its forty shades of green and all of the other shamrock-laden clichés that never really did it justice.

Ireland may have modernised dramatically, but some things never change. From the lonely, wind-lashed wilderness of Donegal to the postcard landscapes of West Cork, Ireland has retained that staggering beauty that has flummoxed all but the greatest poets; spend a day absorbing the brooding beauty of Connemara or brave the raging Atlantic on a crossing to Skellig Michael and we guarantee you'll struggle to find the words to describe how intoxicating the experience is.

Because, despite the trappings of modernity, Ireland remains one of the world's most beautiful countries, and worth every effort you make to explore it. And we mean, of course, the whole island, including the North – for so long scarred by conflict but now finally engaged in the process of recovery and able to once again parade its stunning self to a world that for so long only heard about the province on the evening news.

> 'Ireland's staggering beauty has flummoxed all but the greatest poets'

Contemporary Ireland is a land of compelling contradictions, the inevitable consequence of marrying modernity and all its noisy demands with the island's age-old charms. Yes, everyone might appear to be in a hurry, but thankfully there's still time for a slow day and plenty of room for a history so old that much of it is made up, with myths and little people thrown in to fill the gaps.

⬂IRELAND'S TOP
25 EXPERIENCES

⬎ THE PUB

1

Whether it's an old traditional boozer or a sleek designer bar, virtually every Irish person has a local, because the **pub** (p382) is where the country's social heart beats, and where you'll find out what makes this country tick – and of course drink some fine beer in the process!

↘ THE BIG SMOKE

Known colloquially in Ireland as 'the Big Smoke', **Dublin** (p50) is the island's largest city. It has blossomed into a proper metropolis over the last two decades, with all of the distractions and dressings of a major international capital, but in doing so has managed that rare skill of retaining the friendliness, intimacy and feel of a provincial town.

↘ TRADITIONAL MUSIC

Let your inevitable love affair with Europe's most vibrant folk music begin by sitting in on a traditional *seisiún* (music session); you won't be asked to play, but you won't be able to stop your feet from tapping or your hands from clapping. They occur all over the country, but are best enjoyed in the traditional heartland of **County Clare** (p230).

1 NEIL SETCHFIELD; 2 RICHARD CUMMINS; 3 DOUG MCKINLAY

1 Traditional pub, County Galway; 2 Base of the Spire (p76), O'Connell St, Dublin; 3 Musicians at a *seisiún*, Dublin

⚓ CONNEMARA

Welcome to one of the most stunning corners of Europe: **Connemara** (p245). This kaleidoscope of rusty bogs, lonely valleys and enticing seaside hamlets laid across a patchwork of narrow country roads punctuated by the odd, inviting country pub evokes the timelessness of the very best of Irish scenery, unsullied by centuries of history and transformation.

4

5

⚓ GLENDALOUGH

Wicklow's nickname is the 'Garden of Ireland', but there's nothing genteel or tame about the wild beauty of the monastic ruins of **Glendalough** (p114), which are strung along a glacial valley on the edge of two stunning lakes and surrounded by some of the best walking in the country.

⭦ A ROUND OF GOLF

If Scotland is the home of golf, then Ireland is where golf goes on holiday: there are over 300 courses around the country, but the best are along the coastline, which is dotted with some truly exceptional links; especially try just outside **Sligo** (p285) and along the northern coast of **Donegal** (p297, p301, p302 and p305).

6

4 GARETH MCCORMACK; 5 JOHN ELK III; 6 HOLGER LEUE

4 Connemara coast (p245), County Galway; 5 St Kevin's Kitchen (p116), Glendalough, County Wicklow; 6 Golf course, County Cavan

⟲ CLONMACNOISE

The once enormous ecclesiastical city of Clonmacnoise (p250) may be long past its pre-medieval prime, but these magnificent ruins overlooking the River Shannon still pay a fine tribute to its former glory, when scholars from all over Europe came to study – giving credence to Ireland's reputation as the 'isle of saints and scholars'.

7

8

⬎ CITY OF THE TRIBES

Storied, sung-about and snug, Galway city (p238) is one of Ireland's great pleasures, so much so that it's full of people who came, saw and still haven't managed to leave. Wandering the tuneful streets and alleys and refuelling in any of the great pubs will keep you busy for a month's worth of nights.

⬎ BRÚ NA BÓINNE

9

The vast, striking neolithic necropolis of Brú na Bóinne (p124) in County Meath is 600 years older than the Egyptian pyramids, a thousand years older than Stonehenge and as magnificent an example of prehistoric genius as you'll find anywhere in the world. A visit here is a must, especially for the simulated winter sunrise that illuminates the main burial chamber.

7 JOHN ELK III; 8 RICHARD CUMMINS; 9 TONY WHEELER

7 Clonmacnoise (p250), County Offaly; 8 River Corrib, Galway city (p238); 9 Newgrange passage tomb (p125), Brú na Bóinne, County Meath

⬅ DINGLE

10

Everybody has heard of Dingle (p214) and it seems everybody wants to go there. But this is one place that transcends the crowds with its allure. Sure, you may be stuck behind a tour bus, but this rocky, striated land that seems to dissolve into the sea has a history as compelling as its beauty.

⬅ GHOSTS OF VINEGAR HILL

The panoramic views from Vinegar Hill (p163), just outside Enniscorthy in County Wexford, are reason enough to head up to its summit. But it's a totally different experience after visiting **11** the town's National 1798 Rebellion Centre (p162), which brings the battle into human scale and gives those who lost their lives here a presence that's almost palpable.

⬏ UNCORK THE REBEL CAPITAL

12

An appealing waterfront location, some of the best food you'll find anywhere in the country, lively craic and a vibrant 'Dublin? Where?' dynamic make Ireland's second city, Cork (p190), hard to resist. Surprises abound on its busy, narrow streets that weave around the River Lee and its canals.

13

⬊ ROCK OF CASHEL

The Rock of Cashel (p173) never ceases to startle when first seen rising from the otherwise mundane plains of Tipperary. And this ancient fortified home of kings is just the tip of the iceberg for moody and forlorn ruins hidden away in the surrounding green expanse.

10 RICHARD CUMMINS; 11 MAURICE SAVAGE/ALAMY; 12 OLIVER STREWE; 13 JOHN ELK III

10 Dingle Peninsula (p214), County Kerry; 11 Memorial to the 1798 Rebellion, Vinegar Hill (p163), County Wexford; 12 Olive stall, Cork city (p190); 13 Rock of Cashel (p173), County Tipperary

14

↘ BLACK TAXI TOUR

Learn about Northern Ireland's recent troubled history as you tour the political murals and peace lines of West Belfast's divided neighbourhoods of the Falls and the Shankill in the back of a **black taxi** (p325), leavened with a touch of black humour from the wise-cracking driver.

↘ RING TO RULE THEM

Yes, it's popular. Yes, it's always choked with bus traffic, especially in summer. But there's about a thousand reasons why the **Ring of Kerry** (p209) is the tourist charm bracelet it is, and you'll find most of them as you move counter-clockwise around the Iveragh Peninsula, just west of Killarney.

15

14 DAMIAN TULLY/ALAMY; 15 MARK DAFFEY

14 Black taxi passing Republican murals along Falls Rd, West Belfast (p323), Northern Ireland; 15 Jaunting cars travelling through Gap of Dunloe (p207), County Kerry

⬦ THE MARBLE CITY

Fulfil your fantasies of historic Ireland by soaking up **Kilkenny city's** (p150) iconic, incredible 12th-century castle; its narrow, winding medieval alleyways lined with colourfully painted shopfronts; its cultural events, including its famous comedy bash and arts festival; cracking traditional music sessions; and, of course, its superb beer.

16

17

⬎ SURFING THE NORTHWEST

Northwest Ireland a surfer's paradise? You'd better believe it, or better still, check it out at the likes of **Strandhill** (p286) and **Easkey** (p288), County Sligo, or further north at the Donegal resorts of **Rossnowlagh** (p293) and **Bundoran** (p292), the latter of which hosts the annual Irish Surfing Championships.

⬎ SLIEVE LEAGUE

18

The Cliffs of Moher may be more famous and get all the tourist kudos, but the sea cliffs at **Slieve League** (p294) in County Donegal are taller – the highest in Europe, in fact. Sail beneath them aboard a diminutive 12-seater boat, or head up to the top to see its stark, otherworldly rock face sloping into the Atlantic Ocean.

16 RICHARD CUMMINS; 17 GARETH MCCORMACK; 18 SIMON GREENWOOD

16 High St, Kilkenny city (p150), County Kilkenny; 17 Surfing off of Ireland's west coast; 18 Sea cliffs at Slieve League (p294), County Donegal

↘ ANTRIM COASTAL WALK

Put on your walking boots, load your rucksack with sandwiches and tea and set off along one of Ireland's finest coastal walks, stretching for 16 scenic kilometres between the swaying rope bridge of **Carrick-a-Rede** (p333) and the grand geological flourish of the **Giant's Causeway** (p332), Northern Ireland's most popular attraction.

19

20

⌁ CASTLES & STATELY HOMES

The Anglo-Norman stamp is best seen in the country's collection of handsome Palladian mansions, from the magnificence of County Wicklow's Russborough House (p118) and its incredible collection of art to the exuberance of Castletown House (p122) in County Kildare, once the home of Ireland's richest man.

19 JOHN SONES; 20 RICHARD CUMMINS;

19 Carrick-a-Rede rope bridge (p333), County Antrim, Northern Ireland; 20 Long Gallery, Castletown House (p122), County Kildare

21

⬐ IT'S QUIET IN ARDMORE

The quiet seaside village of **Ardmore** (p169) in County Waterford is blessed by the wide, ranging arc of a superb beach; a magnificent headland that makes for a fabulous hike; and one of the finest boutique hotels in the country. And all of this beauty remains largely undiscovered!

⬐ CLARE COAST

The coast of **County Clare** (p261) alternates long beaches with soaring cliffs but the real appeal lies inland, in the myriad tiny villages where traditional Irish culture persists, oblivious to the demands of tourism. Everyone might have heard of Doolin, but they really need to hear about places like Kilfenora, Ennistymon, Corofin…

22

↘ LOUGHCREW CAIRNS

23

Brú na Bóinne might get all the palaver, but the thirty-odd Stone Age passage graves of Loughcrew (p134) are no less deserving of your attention, if only because the setting is so beautiful and peaceful. There's no museum, but there's also no entrance fee – and no swarms of tourists.

24

↘ THE DERRY AIR

Northern Ireland's second city might have a disputed name, but no one will dispute that Derry/Londonderry (p335) is worth a visit for its superb – and intact – city walls and fascinating neighbourhoods, especially the Bogside, a hardscrabble district that has borne the brunt of violence but still comes up smiling.

21 Ardmore (p169), County Waterford; 22 Cliffs of Moher (p261), County Clare; 23 Loughcrew Cairns (p134), County Meath; 24 Peace monument, Derry (p335), Northern Ireland

⤵ A PROPER IRISH MEAL

Blessed with a bounty of local produce, Ireland's homegrown cuisine has finally come of age, offering up some outstanding dishes to tease and surprise even the most discerning palate. There's a fine meal to be had almost anywhere, but Ireland's gourmet capital is unquestionably County Cork – especially the villages of western Cork (p196).

25

FOODFOLIO/ALAMY

Traditional Irish stew (p348)

⬊ IRELAND'S TOP
ITINERARIES

IRELAND IN A NUTSHELL

FIVE DAYS DUBLIN TO KILLARNEY

Five days only? Well, you'd better get cracking if you want to get the most out of the country. You won't linger too long anywhere, but if you manage it correctly, you'll leave with the country's top highlights in your memory and on your memory card.

❶ DUBLIN

A one-day whistle-stop tour of the **capital** (p50) should include visits to **Trinity College** (p69) and the **Book of Kells** (boxed text, p70), the **National Museum – Archaeology & History** (p71) and the **Guinness Storehouse** (p75), although make sure you also sample a pint of Guinness in one of the city's collection of superb **pubs** (p88).

❷ GALWAY

On day two, cross the island and make for the capital of the west, **Galway city** (p238) – a journey that should take no longer than three hours. Once settled in, take a drive into Connemara: you won't get far, but the drive to **Oughterard** (p246) will give you more than a taste of Connemara's stunning beauty. In the late afternoon, return to Galway and soak in the city's aesthetic delights: a meal followed by a drink (or four) and a live *céilidh* (session of traditional music and dancing) in a traditional old pub like **Tig Cóilí** (p241).

LEFT: RICHARD CUMMINS; RIGHT: OLIVIER CIRENDINI

Left: St Stephen's Green (p73), Dublin; Right: Trinity College (p69), Dublin

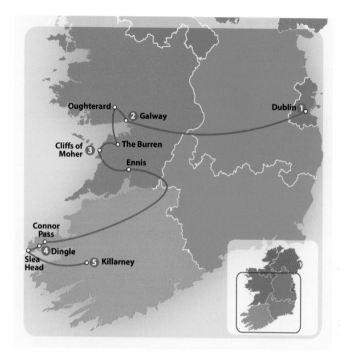

❸ CLIFFS OF MOHER

On day three, go south, through the **Burren** (p260) towards the **Cliffs of Moher** (p261), where the crowds are a small price to pay for some of the most stunning views you'll see anywhere. A good base for the evening is **Ennis** (p253), County Clare's largest town, where you'll find decent hotels and some excellent music bars – we recommend **Cíaran's Bar** (p254), unassuming by day but livened up by trad music at night.

❹ DINGLE

Moving south again, cross into County Kerry through the beautiful **Connor Pass** (p218) and make for **Dingle** (p215), on its eponymous peninsula. The town itself has plenty to keep you there, but it would be a shame to miss the peninsula itself, especially **Slea Head** (p219) and its stunning prehistoric monuments – not to mention the views!

❺ KILLARNEY

On day five, head south once more to storied **Killarney** (p202), which you should use as a base for the equally renowned Ring of Kerry, a much-trafficked loop around the Iveragh Peninsula. By day's end you should feel exhausted and need another holiday; the good news is that there's plenty more to see and do in Ireland when you next return.

TIP TO TOE

10 DAYS DERRY TO WEXFORD

Explore the heart of Ireland from tip to toe, from the country's wild northwestern corner to the sunny southeast, home of a thousand traditional Irish holidays. You might skip out on some of the country's best-trodden tourist attractions, but the reward is a look at Ireland's authentic heart.

❶ DERRY

Begin in Northern Ireland's second city, **Derry** (p335), by walking the **city walls** (p337) and exploring the fascinating **Bogside** (p338) neighbourhood, home to the **People's Gallery** (p339). On day two, cross into County Donegal and explore the **Inishowen Peninsula** (p302) before settling down for the night in **Dunfanaghy** (p296).

❷ SLIGO

As you move down Donegal's stunning coastline, check out the monastic ruins of **Glencolumbcille** (p294) and the extraordinary sea cliffs at **Slieve League** (p294). The landscape softens as you cross into County Sligo, where you should visit the **Carrowmore Megalithic Cemetery** (p285) before checking in at your hotel in **Sligo town** (p282). The next day, treat yourself to either a round of golf at the stunning **County Sligo Golf Course** (p285) and/or a **seaweed bath** (p287) in Enniscrone.

SIMON GREENWOOD

Slieve League, County Donegal (p294)

❸ GALWAY

Skirt Connemara's (p245) eastern edge as you travel southeast to Galway city (p238), and then strike out for Clonmacnoise (p250), probably Ireland's most important monastic site. From here, head through the heart of the midlands to Cashel (p172), County Tipperary, whose own collection of ruins gives Clonmacnoise a real run for its money.

❹ KILKENNY

Marvellously medieval Kilkenny city (p150) is only an hour away, and it makes a superb base from which to explore the surrounding countryside. Don't forget to visit the city's stunning castle (p152) before exploring nearby Thomastown (p155) and Jerpoint Abbey (p156).

❺ WEXFORD

For generations County Wexford has been a popular seaside destination, but its attractions aren't merely balneological. Using Wexford town (p157) as a base, explore the Irish National Heritage Park (p158), which should put you in the right frame for a visit to Enniscorthy (p162) and the National 1798 Rebellion Centre (p162). Or chill out in lovely Kilmore Quay (p158), a working fishing village, from which you can also explore the Saltee Islands bird sanctuary (p158).

THE LONG WAY ROUND

TWO WEEKS DUBLIN TO DUBLIN

This tourist trail takes you past some of Ireland's most famous attractions and through spectacular countryside. It's only about 500km in length, so you could manage it in three days, but what would be the point of rushing? You won't be disappointed on this route.

❶ DUBLIN

Start your loop in **Dublin** (p50), visiting the main attractions before heading north to the mind-blowing neolithic necropolis at **Brú na Bóinne** (p124), built before the Great Pyramids were even a twinkle in Pharaoh's eye. Continue north to **Mellifont Abbey** (p137), Ireland's first Cistercian abbey, before crossing the border into Northern Ireland.

❷ BELFAST

After arriving in **Belfast** (p320), take a **black taxi tour** (p325) and visit both the Falls and Shankill Roads – separated by a 'peace wall' – in order to get a real sense of the sectarian divide. Head northwest along the Antrim coast to the Unesco World Heritage site of the **Giant's Causeway** (p332), best enjoyed at sunset.

❸ SLIGO

Continue around the stunning coastline of north Donegal, stopping at gorgeous **Dunfanaghy** (p296) then on to beautiful **Glenveagh National Park** (p299). Head south through the monastic ruins of

LEFT: EOIN CLARKE; RIGHT: WAYNE WALTON

Left: Folk dancing, Inishmór, Aran Islands (p243); Right: Dún Aengus fort, Inishmór

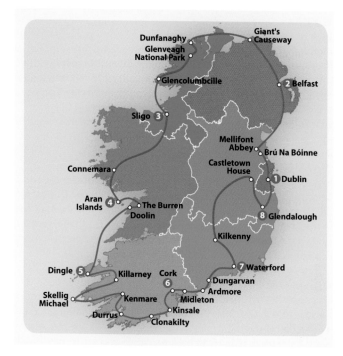

Glencolumbcille (p294) and into lively **Sligo town** (p282), where you can climb the Stone Age passage grave **Carrowkeel** (p287) for panoramic views of Lough Arrow.

❹ ARAN ISLANDS

Make your way to the southwest via **Connemara** (p245), visiting at least one of the **Aran Islands** (p242) as you go – Inishmór, with its magnificent Stone Age forts, is the biggest and most popular, but for a slice of traditional island life you're better off on Inisheer or Inishmaan. Wonder at the moonlike karst landscape of the **Burren** (p260) and check out some lively traditional music in **Doolin** (p262) before crossing into County Kerry.

❺ DINGLE

Explore the **Dingle Peninsula** (p215) from your base in **Dingle** (p214). Go through **Killarney** (p202) to experience the modern Irish tourist machine at full tilt on your way round the **Ring of Kerry** (p209), but step offshore and into a different century with a visit to **Skellig Michael** (p212). Make your camp in handsome **Kenmare** (p213).

❻ CORK

Explore the windswept remoteness of the **Beara Peninsula** (p201), then verify Cork's foodie credentials by buying some cheese in **Durrus** (p199) and some black pudding in **Clonakilty** (p198) before visiting **Kinsale** (p196) to sample some fine dining. Explore Ireland's second city, **Cork** (p190), taking in some high-quality art at the **Crawford Municipal Art Gallery** (p190) and some comestibles at the magnificent **English Market** (p194). From Cork, head east to **Midleton** (p195) for a picnic and a visit to the **Old Jameson Distillery** (p195).

❼ WATERFORD

Explore the oft-ignored beauty of County Waterford from the handsome seaside village of **Ardmore** (p169), then take a trip to **Dungarvan Castle** (p168) to see its unusual 12th-century shell. In **Waterford city** (p164), visit the **Waterford Museum of Treasures** (p164) and the **Waterford Crystal Visitor Centre** (p164), then head northwards to **Kilkenny city** (p150) for a visit to **St Canice's Cathedral** (p150).

❽ GLENDALOUGH

Visit **Castletown House** (p122) in County Kildare before cutting east through the Wicklow Mountains to visit stunning **Glendalough** (p114), a collection of monastic ruins in the middle of **Wicklow Mountains National Park** (p108). Head back to Dublin and settle into a well-deserved pint of Guinness at the **Long Hall** (p89).

RICHARD CUMMINS

Stone fort, Ring of Kerry (p209)

↘ PLANNING YOUR TRIP

IRELAND'S BEST...

ANCIENT MONUMENTS

- **Brú Na Bóinne** (p124) Passage graves older than the pyramids.
- **Clonmacnoise** (p250) Once one of Europe's greatest universities... before universities even existed.
- **Rock of Cashel** (p173) Thousand-year-old castle, abbey and cathedral.
- **Skellig Michael** (p212) Monastic settlement clinging to a rock.
- **Glendalough** (p114) Beautiful monastic ruins in the serenest of settings.

MUSEUMS

- **Chester Beatty Library** (p70) Extraordinary collection of religious books and precious artefacts.
- **National 1798 Rebellion Centre** (p162) The history of rebellion in bloody and magnificent detail.

- **Dunbrody Heritage Ship** (p161) Full-scale replica of a 19th-century 'famine ship'.
- **Ulster Folk Museum** (p328) The fascinating lives of ordinary people of the 18th and 19th centuries.
- **Skibbereen Heritage Centre** (p199) Want to know what the Famine was like?

TRADITIONAL PUBS

- **John Mulligan's** (p89) The classic Dublin pub.
- **C Ní Cairbre** (p136) A rural country pub in the middle of a big town.
- **Jimmy O'Brien's** (p202) No better place in Ireland to learn the lore of Gaelic football.
- **Tig Cóilí** (p241) Where trad musicians go to drink.
- **Olde Glen Bar and Restaurant** (p301) A perfect boozer in a remote corner of the country.

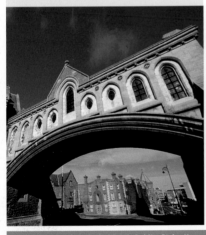

LEFT: RICHARD CUMMINS; RIGHT: OLIVIER CIRENDINI

Left: Christ Church Cathedral (p73), Dublin; Right: Neon signs near O'Connell St (p76), Dublin

⬇ SCENIC DRIVES

- **Sky Road** (p247) A spectacular Connemara loop.
- **Ring of Kerry** (p209) Ireland's most popular drive.
- **The Healy Pass** (p202) Spectacular border crossing between Cork and Kerry.
- **Lough Inagh Valley** (p246) In the shadow of the brooding Twelve Bens.
- **Glen Gesh Pass** (p295) A touch of the Alps in Donegal.

⬇ ACTIVITIES

- **Climb Croagh Patrick** (p267) A three-hour climb rewarded with superb views and even a touch of spiritual enlightenment.
- **Catch a Donegal Wave** (p274) Test your skills and try your luck on The Peak, Ireland's most famous wave.
- **Cooking in Cork** (p196) Learn the nuances of fine Irish cuisine at the country's most famous cooking school.
- **Catch a Fish** (p158) Tackle the sea with some angling off the coast of Kilmore Quay.
- **Tee off in Sligo** (p285) Go for par on one of Ireland's most beautiful links, in the shadow of Benbulben.

⬇ FESTIVALS

- **Kilkenny Arts Festival** (p153) Medieval Kilkenny shows its artistic side.
- **Cat Laughs Comedy Festival** (p153) Comics from the world over descend upon Kilkenny every year for fits and giggles.
- **Willie Clancy Irish Music Festival** (p259) You'll hear some of the best traditional music in the world at this annual festival on the Clare coast.
- **Wexford Festival Opera** (p157) The high art of lyric opera is celebrated in the sunny southeast.
- **Galway International Oyster Festival** (p240) Locally fished oysters washed down with Guinness to a lively musical soundtrack.

⬇ WALKS

- **Mourne Mountains** (p329) The most scenic walks in Northern Ireland are around these famed mountains.
- **Glendalough** (p114) Fabulous walks around this monastic site are part of the 73-mile Wicklow Way.
- **Killarney National Park** (p205) You've seen these views on a thousand postcards – now you can see them for yourself.
- **Dublin City Centre** (p65) Who says you need greenery for a good walk? Try Dublin's Georgian architecture instead.
- **Ardmore Cliffs** (p170) Walk part of the ancient St Declan's Way across green fields and beside stunning cliff views.

PLANNING YOUR TRIP

THINGS YOU NEED TO KNOW

THINGS YOU NEED TO KNOW

➘ AT A GLANCE

- **ATMs** Widely available in towns and cities.
- **Credit cards** Major cards accepted practically everywhere.
- **Currency** The euro (Republic); the pound sterling (Northern Ireland)
- **Language** English spoken everywhere; Irish spoken in Gaeltacht areas.
- **Tipping** Not required, but 10–15% expected for good service.
- **Visas** Not required for most Western nationalities.

➘ ACCOMMODATION

- **B&Bs** Ubiquitous and varying in standard. Many rural ones accept only cash (p389).
- **Guesthouses** Expanded family homes with the comfort of a boutique hotel. Most accept credit cards (p389).
- **Hotels** Ranging from local pubs to five-star castles; priced accordingly. Business chain hotels are clean, comfortable and characterless (p389).

➘ ADVANCE PLANNING

- **Two months ahead** Book accommodation and any special activities.
- **One month ahead** Book your rental car and reservations for top-end restaurants.
- **Two weeks ahead** Confirm opening times and prices for visitor attractions.

- **One week ahead** Check the weather forecast (but plan for it to be wrong).

➘ BE FOREWARNED

- **Public holidays** Banks and businesses close on bank holidays; *everything* (including pubs) closes on Good Friday and Christmas Day in the Republic; not much opens on 26 December and New Year's Day. Avoid Northern Ireland on 12 July, the climax of the Loyalist marching season.
- **Pub restrictions** Under 16s aren't allowed in pubs after 7pm, even if accompanied by parents (enforced less strictly in rural areas).
- **Traffic jams** A fact of life in big towns and cities during rush hours.

➘ COSTS

- **Under €100/£100 per day** Allows for budget B&Bs and restaurants.
- **€100/£100 to €200/£200** Double room in a midrange hotel or B&B, with cash left over for attractions, transport and a decent evening meal.
- **More than €200/£200** Allows you to travel, eat and sleep in style, visit every attraction and engage in any activity.

➘ EMERGENCY NUMBERS

- **999** Ambulance, fire and police for both the Republic and Northern Ireland.

⬛ GETTING AROUND

- **Air** Besides the main hubs (p405), Donegal, Kerry, Knock and Waterford have regional airports (p409).
- **Bus** Bus Éireann (p411) has the most extensive network; local operators offer regular – and often cheaper – regional services.
- **Train** The train network is limited and expensive, but the easiest way to travel between major urban centres (p414).
- **Car** Your own car will let you reach those out-of-the-way spots; petrol is expensive and traffic can be challenging (p411).

⬛ GETTING THERE & AWAY

- **Fly** The Republic's main international airports are Dublin (p93), Cork (p193) and Shannon (p405).

Belfast (p326) has two airports, while Derry (p341) serves other UK cities.
- **Boat** There are ferries to/from France and ferry and fast boats to/from the UK (p407).

⬛ TECH STUFF

- **Cameras** Memory cards readily available; print film sold in big towns and cities.
- **DVD** Region 2/PAL.
- **Weights, distances & measures** The Republic uses metric; Northern Ireland uses the imperial system.
- **Electricity** 220v/50Hz.
- **Mobiles/cell phones** GSM 900/1800 system.
- **Plugs** Three flat-pin plug in both the Republic and Northern Ireland.

RICHARD CUMMINS

Luas public transport, Dublin

PLANNING YOUR TRIP

THINGS YOU NEED TO KNOW

↘ TRAVEL SEASONS

- **High season** June to late August.
- **Shoulder seasons** Easter (mid-March to early April) to the end of May; September to October.
- **Low season** November to mid-March.
- **School holidays** Christmas, Easter, summer; mid-term breaks in October and February.
- **Other considerations** St Patrick's Festival (around 17 March) is one of the year's biggest celebrations.

↘ WHAT TO BRING

- **Good walking shoes** Rubber soles and weatherproof uppers an advantage.
- **Rain jacket** It really could rain at any minute.
- **UK/Ireland electrical adapter** Those three-pin plugs are quite devilish!

- **A good sense of humour** The Irish express affection by making fun of each other – and you.
- **A hollow leg** How else can you last the night in a pub?

↘ WHEN TO GO

- **Spring** Quieter sights, but the weather is notoriously fickle.
- **Summer** The high season has traffic, crowds, higher prices, booked-out hotels and often uncooperative weather.
- **Autumn** The weather is still good and summer crowds have gone.
- **Winter** Cold and wet, but peaceful and quiet. Many rural attractions and accommodation are closed.

GARETH MCCORMACK

Lough Corrib, County Galway (p266)

GET INSPIRED

❧ BOOKS

- **Dubliners** (James Joyce, 1914) Classic short stories about Joyce's hometown.
- **The Book of Evidence** (John Banville, 1989) Psychological portrait of a killer, based on real-life events.
- **The Butcher Boy** (Patrick McCabe, 1992) Boy retreats into a violent fantasy world as his small-town world collapses.
- **Paddy Clarke Ha Ha Ha** (Roddy Doyle, 1993) Booker Prize winner about the trials of a Dublin child.
- **All the Names Have Been Changed** (Claire Kilroy, 2009) Life of a Trinity student in the 1990s.
- **Amongst Women** (John McGahern, 1990) Masterpiece about the tyranny within an Irish family.

❧ FILMS

- **Bloody Sunday** (Paul Greengrass, 2002) Superb film about the events of 30 January 1972.
- **The Dead** (John Huston, 1987) Joyce's fantastic *Dubliners* story.
- **My Left Foot** (Jim Sheridan, 1989) Daniel Day-Lewis as cerebral palsy sufferer and artist Christy Brown.
- **Once** (John Carney, 2007) Oscar-winning sweet story about a busker and a girl.
- **The Crying Game** (Neil Jordan, 1992) A classic, exploring violence, gender and the IRA.
- **The Magdalene Sisters** (Peter Mullan, 2002) Harrowing portrayal of life in the infamous Magdalene laundries.

❧ TRADITIONAL MUSIC

- **The Quiet Glen** (Tommy Peoples) Virtuoso fiddler in the Donegal style of trad music.
- **Paddy Keenan** (Paddy Keenan) One of the greatest uillean pipers.
- **Compendium: The Best of Patrick Street** (Various artists) Veterans of some of Irish music's most popular groups come together.
- **The Chieftains 6: Bonaparte's Retreat** (The Chieftains) Our favourite by this extraordinary Irish group.
- **Old Hag You Have Killed Me** (The Bothy Band) The second album from one of the best-loved traditional groups.

❧ WEBSITES

- **Blather** (www.blather.net) Irreverent commentary on all things Irish.
- **Entertainment Ireland** (www.entertainmentireland.ie) Countrywide listings for clubs, theatres, festivals, cinemas, museums and more.
- **Fáilte Ireland** (www.discoverireland.ie) The Republic's tourist information site has practical info and a huge accommodation database.
- **Irish Election** (www.irishelection.com) Great Irish political blogging.
- **Irish Times** (www.irishtimes.com) Ireland's newspaper of record.
- **Lonely Planet** (www.lonelyplanet.com) Comprehensive travel information and advice.
- **Northern Ireland Tourism** (www.discovernorthernireland.com) Official tourist information site, with activities and accommodation.

PLANNING YOUR TRIP

GET INSPIRED

PLANNING YOUR TRIP

CALENDAR

CALENDAR

| JAN | FEB | MAR | APR |

CONOR CAFFREY

St Patrick's Day parade, Dublin

◥ FEBRUARY

**JAMESON DUBLIN
INTERNATIONAL FILM FESTIVAL**
The island's biggest film festival – with local flicks, arty international films and advance releases of mainstream movies – runs during the last two weeks of the month. See p81.

◥ MARCH

ST PATRICK'S DAY   17 MAR
Ireland marks St Patrick's Day (www .stpatricksday.ie) by erupting into one giant celebration. The biggest party is in Dublin (p81), where the streets reverberate to a cacophony of parades, fireworks and light shows for five days around 17 March. Over 250,000 attend. Cork, Armagh and Belfast also have parades; elsewhere festivities are less ostentatious.

**WORLD IRISH DANCING
CHAMPIONSHIPS**
About 4000 dancers from all over the globe compete in this competition (www.worldirishdancing.com) in late March or early April. The location varies from year to year; in 2009 it took place in the USA for the first time, but it normally occurs in Ireland.

◥ APRIL

**CIRCUIT OF IRELAND
INTERNATIONAL RALLY
EASTER WEEKEND**
Known locally as the Circuit (www .circuitofireland.net), this rally car race, held over the Easter weekend, begins and ends in Northern Ireland, but takes in chunks of the Republic, too.

↘ MAY

CORK INTERNATIONAL CHORAL FESTIVAL
One of Europe's premier choral festivals (www.corkchoral.ie), with the winners going on to the Fleischmann International Trophy Competition. It's held over four days from the first Monday of May.

NORTH WEST 200
Ireland's most famous road race (www.northwest200.org) is also the country's biggest outdoor sporting event: 150,000-plus people line the triangular route to cheer on some of the biggest names in motorcycle racing. Held in mid-May; see p311.

OLIVIER CIRENDINI
Hurling stick and ball (p377)

FLEADH NUA
Absorb a week of traditional music as Ennis, County Clare hosts one of the country's most important festivals during the third week of the month. See p254.

CAT LAUGHS COMEDY FESTIVAL
Kilkenny gets very, very funny from late May into early June for the country's best comedy festival, attracting the cream of local and international talent. See p153.

↘ JUNE

WEXFORD FESTIVAL OPERA
Ireland's premier festival of classical music and opera runs for two weeks in early June. See p157.

NEIL SETCHFIELD
Traditional Irish dancing

CALENDAR

| JAN | FEB | MAR | APR |

BLOOMSDAY   **16 JUN**
Edwardian dress and breakfast of 'the inner organs of beast and fowl' are but two of the elements of this Dublin festival celebrating 16 June, the day on which Joyce's *Ulysses* takes place – the real highlight is retracing Leopold Bloom's daily steps. See p83.

◥ JULY

WILLIE CLANCY IRISH MUSIC FESTIVAL
A superb festival of six days of intense traditional music workshops, gigs and pub sessions in **Miltown Malbay** (p259), County Clare; the best players in the world generally show up.

GALWAY ARTS FESTIVAL
The country's most important arts festival (www.galwayartsfestival.ie) sees Galway city go mental for the last two weeks of the month, with lots of music, drama and merriment. See p240.

◥ AUGUST

FÉILE AN PHOBAIL WEST BELFAST
Europe's largest community arts festival (www.feilebelfast.com) takes place on Falls Rd in West Belfast over two weeks in early August.

PUCK FAIR   **10-12 AUG**
Three days of what must be one of the quirkiest festivals in Europe has Killorglin, County Kerry, celebrating the crowning of a goat amid plenty of mayhem. See p210.

FLEADH CHEOIL NA HÉIREANN
The mother of all Irish music festivals (www.comhaltas.ie) attracts in excess

EOIN CLARKE

Galway Arts Festival

| MAY | JUN | JUL | AUG | SEP | OCT | NOV | DEC |

of 250,000 revellers to whichever town is playing host; it usually takes place over a week towards the end of the month.

☑ SEPTEMBER

ALL-IRELAND FINALS
The finals of the hurling and Gaelic football championships (www.gaa.ie) are held, respectively, on the second and fourth Sundays of the month, with 80,000-plus thronging into Dublin's Croke Park for the biggest sporting days of the year.

DUBLIN FRINGE FESTIVAL
Comedy and alternative fringe theatre precede the main Dublin Theatre Festival and are often a hell of a lot more fun. Runs for two weeks from late September to early October. See p82.

☑ OCTOBER

DUBLIN THEATRE FESTIVAL
The cream of Irish theatre festivals sees all manner of theatrics at venues throughout the capital. Runs for two weeks in mid-October; see p81.

BELFAST FESTIVAL AT QUEENS
Northern Ireland's top arts festival (www.belfastfestival.com) attracts performers from all over the world; on offer is everything from visual arts to dance. Held mid- to late October.

RICHARD CUMMINS

Puck Fair

CORK JAZZ FESTIVAL
Over the last weekend of the month the city goes mad for all kinds of jazz in one of the country's most popular festivals (www.corkjazzfestival.com).

☑ DECEMBER

CHRISTMAS   25 DEC
This is a quiet affair in the countryside, though on 26 December the ancient custom of Wren Boys is reenacted – most notably in the town of Dingle, County Kerry – as groups of children dress up and go about singing hymns.

GREATER DUBLIN

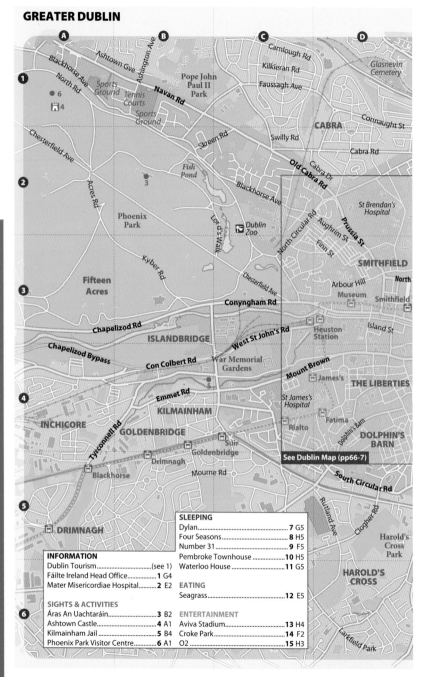

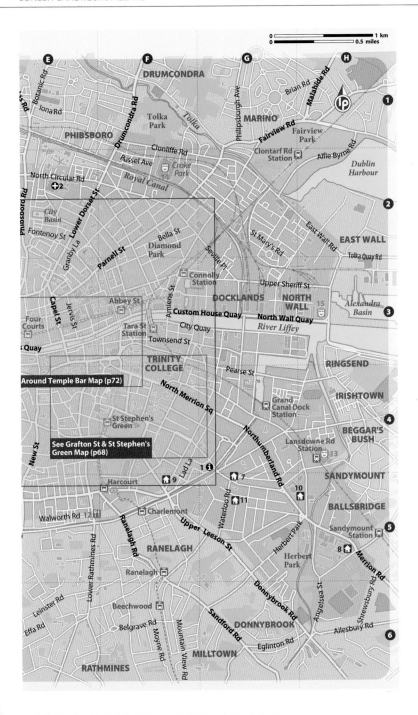

DUBLIN HIGHLIGHTS

1 DUBLIN RESTAURANTS

BY MICEAL MURRAY, MANAGER OF L'GUEULETON

In the last couple of years there's been an exciting reinterpretation of what was once seen as middle-of-the-road, midpriced casual dining. A lot of restaurants have reimagined their menus and are offering some pretty tasty versions of standard fare. In fact, I'd say we're quite spoilt for choice!

⬊ MICEAL MURRAY'S DON'T MISS LIST

❶ GRUEL
Gruel's (p86) kitsch decor and hearty cuisine is only part of why this place is so successful. The staff are all so familiar and friendly it always feels like you're in somebody's house rather than a restaurant. But in the end it comes down to food, and here it's always good.

❷ COPPINGER ROW
This is a pretty new **restaurant** (☎ 01-672 9884; www.coppingerrow.com; Coppinger Row; mains €12-16; ⏱ noon-11pm Tue-Sat,

1-8pm Sun) so it's hard to judge its success, but so far, so very good. It's a smart place that's always buzzing, whether for lunch or for dinner.

❸ MERMAID CAFÉ
It's one of the city centre's most respected midrange **restaurants** (p88), but what really works for me is the rustic approach to cooking: tasty ingredients cooked solidly without too much fuss. I also love the room, the affable service and the eccentric wine list.

Clockwise from top: Menu at the Winding Stair (p88); Traditional Irish breakfast; Outdoor restaurants on Ann St; A couple dining at Gruel (p86)

DUBLIN

DUBLIN HIGHLIGHTS

Edam + Salad
- Bram Stoker   € 4·25   € 4·
Garlic Salami + Salad
The Power & The Glory   € 4·25   € 4
Whisky Salami + Salad
- The bare Necessities   € 3·60   € 3
Banana + honey
- The Old man and the Sea € 4·25   € 4
Tuna, Celery, Onion and mayo

AT BUSY TIMES FOO

❹ WINDING STAIR

In a beautiful Georgian building on the quays, this was once my favourite bookshop cafe in town, but the **restaurant** (p88) that's replaced it is so good that I don't resent its passing! Its main strength is its strict policy of sourcing all its ingredients locally and producing high-end comfort food.

❺ THE HOUSE

I generally wouldn't travel to the suburbs for a restaurant, but **The House** (p108) is an exception. Howth is a surprising little oasis of food, and the barest nod to Middle Eastern cuisine gives House something a little special besides the excellent salads, homecooked lunches and the brilliant brunch.

❶ Gruel
❷ Coppinger Row
❸ Mermaid Café
❹ Winding Stair

⬦ THINGS YOU NEED TO KNOW

Top tip Book ahead for Friday or Saturday dining **Best avoid** Temple Bar's restaurants may be popular, but they're not very good **Did you know?** The most Dublin of dishes is coddle: layers of sliced sausage and bacon with potatoes, onions and barley. **For full details on dining in Dublin, see p86.**

DUBLIN HIGHLIGHTS

DUBLIN

DUBLIN HIGHLIGHTS

2 | CHESTER BEATTY LIBRARY

BY MICHAEL RYAN, DIRECTOR OF THE CHESTER BEATTY LIBRARY

The Chester Beatty Library – Ireland's Museum of the Book – was originally the private library of its founder, Alfred Chester Beatty. Its treasures are remarkable, and since it became a fully public institution in 1969 it has become one of Ireland's national cultural icons. I've been fortunate enough to have been its director since 1992.

◣ MICHAEL RYAN'S DON'T MISS LIST

❶ SACRED TRADITIONS GALLERY

The Sacred Traditions Gallery on the 2nd floor exhibits sacred texts, illuminated manuscripts and miniature paintings from the great religions and systems of belief represented in the collections – Christianity, Islam and Buddhism – with smaller displays on Confucianism, Taoism, Sikhism and Jainism.

❷ THE ISLAMIC COLLECTION

The collection of Qur'ans dating from the 9th to the 19th centuries – the

library has over 270 of them – is the best example of illuminated Islamic texts in the world and the centrepiece of the collection. They derive primarily, though not exclusively, from the Arab worlds of Iran, Turkey and India, and include some of the greatest documents of Islamic art and culture.

❸ THE ARTS OF THE BOOK EXHIBITION

This permanent exhibition was installed in 2008 and contains spectacular displays of illustrated manuscripts

Clockwise from top: Gardens outside Chester Beatty Library (p70); Entrance exterior; Eastern Religions display; Interior staircase; Old hymnbook on display

and printed books from many different cultures, including Egyptian Books of the Dead and beautifully illuminated European medieval manuscripts, as well as one of the finest collection of Chinese jade books in the world.

❹ THE EAST ASIAN EXHIBITION
Of particular beauty in the Artistic Traditions Gallery on the 1st floor are rare Burmese and Thai manuscripts on the life of the Buddha; a devotional text in the handwriting of Qianlong, the great 18th-century Emperor of China; and an amazing printed document from 8th-century Japan.

❺ SILK ROAD CAFÉ
Cafes aren't usually a highlight of a museum visit, but this is the exception –

the food is suitably Middle Eastern, and of a very high standard. There are daily specials like *djaj mehshi:* chicken stuffed with spices, rice, dried fruit, almonds and pine nuts, and served with okra and Greek yoghurt. For dessert, there's Lebanese baklava and coconut kataif. All dishes are halal and kosher.

↘ THINGS YOU NEED TO KNOW
Best time to visit Any day but Monday, when we're closed **How long will I need?** A couple of hours **Top tips** Take a breather on the rooftop Japanese Garden **Tours** Free guided tours are offered throughout the day **For full details on the Chester Beatty Library, see p70.**

DUBLIN HIGHLIGHTS

DUBLIN

DUBLIN HIGHLIGHTS

3

↘ TRINITY COLLEGE

Ireland's most prestigious university is also its most beautiful, a 16-hectare master-piece of Victorian architecture and landscaping. **Trinity College** (p69) was chartered in 1592 by Queen Elizabeth I so that Dublin's youth would not be 'infected with popery'; it remained exclusively Protestant until 1793. No such exclusions exist today, cementing its reputation as one of the world's best universities.

4

↘ IRISH MUSEUM OF MODERN ART

Whatever you happen to think of modern art (inner genius revealed or 'my kid could do that'), a visit to the **Irish Museum of Modern Art** (p74) in Kilmainham should leave you thoroughly satisfied – if not for the magnificent range of contemporary art hanging on its walls, then for the exquisite surroundings of its building, styled after Les Invalides in Paris and also once used as a hospital for veterans.

DUBLIN

DUBLIN HIGHLIGHTS

5

↘ KILMAINHAM JAIL

Ireland's tempestuous and torturous path to independence is vividly documented in this former **prison** (p75), whose list of (reluctant) residents reads like a roll call of Irish patriots and revolutionaries. A visit here is as close to Irish history as you can get in Dublin, especially when standing in the yard where the leaders of the 1916 Easter Rising were executed.

6

↘ A PINT OF PLAIN

Go on, admit it: there's a good likelihood that you came to Dublin in the hope of tasting the magic that is Guinness, in its native home. The **Guinness Storehouse** (p75), on the grounds of the famous brewery, isn't a bad place to start, but a pint is best enjoyed in the surroundings of a good pub – try **John Mulligan's** (p89) or **Kehoe's** (p89) on for size.

7

↘ DUBLIN GREENERY

From the well-trodden paths of **St Stephen's Green** (p73) to the elegant folds of **Merrion Square** (p73), Dublin's green spaces are more than just places to breathe some fresh air: they're the ideal spots to appreciate the grandeur of the Georgian experiment. But if you want real green, go west and lose yourself in the massive expanse of **Phoenix Park** (p78).

3 & 6 OLIVIER CIRENDINI; 4 & 5 MARTIN MOOS; 7 JONATHAN SMITH

3 Trinity College (p69); 4 Courtyard, Irish Museum of Modern Art (p74); 5 Kilmainhaim Jail (p75); 6 Gravity Bar, Guinness Storehouse (p75); 7 St Stephen's Green (p73)

DUBLIN'S BEST...

⬎ THINGS FOR FREE

- Dublin's four national **museums** are all free to visit.
- Have a picnic in **St Stephen's Green** (p73).
- Explore the wonders of the **Chester Beatty Library** (p70).
- Window-shopping on **Grafton Street** (p65) won't cost a penny.
- **Phoenix Park** (p78) has sport, walks, museums and a herd of red deer.

⬎ SPOTS TO WET YOUR BEAK

- **Grogan's Castle Lounge** (p89) For a decent pint and a chat.
- **Anseo** (p90) For beats and beatniks.
- **Cobblestone** (p90) For fiddles and bodhráns.
- **O'Donoghue's** (p90) For mixing with Dubliners.
- **Bar With No Name** (p90) To see and be seen.

⬎ UNIQUELY DUBLIN

- **Bloomsday** (p83) Get Edwardian every 16 June.
- **Guinness Storehouse** (p75) Home of the world's most famous beer.
- **Ha'Penny Bridge** (p70) Get a snap of Dublin's most iconic bridge.
- **Merrion Square** (p73) The perfect Georgian square.
- **St Patrick's Cathedral** (p74) Visit Jonathan Swift's tomb.

⬎ GEORGIAN CLASSICS

- **Leinster House** (p71) Ireland's parliament was once the city's most handsome residence.
- **Four Courts** (p78) One of architect James Gandon's greatest works.
- **Custom House** (p76) James Gandon's first Irish masterpiece.
- **The Merrion** (p84) This historical building is a top Dublin hotel.
- **Áras an Uachtaráin** (p78) The official residence of the President inspired the White House.

RICK GERTHARTER

Custom House (p76) beside the River Liffey, Dublin

THINGS YOU NEED TO KNOW

⬊ VITAL STATISTICS

- **Population** 1.3 million
- **Area** 921 sq km

⬊ NEIGHBOURHOODS IN A NUTSHELL

- **Grafton Street & Around** (p65) The affluent heart of the city, just south of the River Liffey.
- **The Liberties & Kilmainham** (p73) The oldest neighbourhood in town, traditional and thriving.
- **O'Connell Street & Around** (p75) The grandest street in the city, just north of the river.
- **Docklands** (p76) Once-grimy docks get the Cinderella treatment.
- **Smithfield & Phoenix Park** (p77) Northside quays lead west to Europe's largest enclosed park.

⬊ ADVANCE PLANNING

- **Two months before** Sort your hotel room.
- **Two weeks before** Work on your hollow leg.
- **One week before** Make restaurant reservations.

⬊ RESOURCES

- **Visit Dublin** (www.visitdublin.com) The main event.
- **Dublin Links** (www.dublinks.com) One-stop guide for all manner of goings-on.

- **Overheard in Dublin** (www.over heardindublin.com) Proof that people are funnier than scriptwriters.
- **Le Cool** (www.lecool.com/cities/dublin) Listings, reviews and events.
- **The Dubliner** (www.thedubliner.ie) Gossip and other salacious features.

⬊ EMERGENCY NUMBERS

- **Police/Fire/Ambulance** (☎ 999)
- **Samaritans** (☎ 1850 609 090)

⬊ GETTING AROUND

- **Bus** Good for sightseeing; not good for traffic.
- **Walk** The easiest way to get around town.
- **Cycle** If you're not overly worried about cars.
- **Luas** The best way to visit the southern suburbs.

⬊ BE FOREWARNED

- **Sightseeing** Cut costs on entrance charges and skip the queues with the **Dublin Pass** (boxed text, p64).
- **Restaurants** You'll need to book for top-end establishments.
- **Public Transport** You'll need exact change if you're getting a bus.
- **Rounds System** In the pub, you take it in turns to buy rounds of drinks for your party.

DUBLIN

THINGS YOU NEED TO KNOW

DISCOVER DUBLIN

Prosperous or not, Dublin has always been unflappable in its commitment to the belief that you don't need piles of money to enjoy yourself. Still, the transformation of the last few years – the most radical in its thousand-plus year history – has raised some challenging questions for many Dubliners, who welcomed the city's fortunes but were suspicious of the crass commercialism that came with it.

But it's done wonders for the city too. Dubliners take it as a given that their city is a multicultural melting pot where Russians shop for tinned caviar, Nigerian teenagers discuss the merits of hair extensions and Koreans hawk phone cards from their cars. They're confident their city is so hip that travellers from all over the world can't wait to get there and indulge in the many pleasures it has to offer.

Because pleasure is something Dublin knows all about – from its music, art and literature to the legendary nightlife that has inspired those same musicians, artists and writers, Dublin knows how to have fun and does it with deadly seriousness. As you'll soon find out.

DUBLIN IN...

Two Days

Kick-start your day with breakfast at Honest to Goodness (p86) in the wonderful George's St Arcade (Map p68), then ramble through the arcade's stalls and funky stores. A stone's throw away is Trinity College (p69) and the Book of Kells (see the boxed text, p70). Head up to Grafton Street (p65) to catch the buskers and splurge in Dublin's most exclusive shops. Round it off with a cocktail, dinner and outdoor movie on the terrace at Eden (p87), one of Dublin's trendiest restaurants, in the Temple Bar (p69) area. The next day marvel at the art of the Chester Beatty Library (p70) before strolling up to the Guinness Storehouse (p75) for a tour that ends with a glass of 'plain' in the Gravity Bar, with stunning, 360-degree views of the city.

Four Days

Follow the two-day itinerary, then wander around the designer clothing shops in Temple Bar and grab a bite at L'Gueuleton (p87), then go on the Dublin Literary Pub Crawl (p81). The following day head up the coast to the pretty village of Howth (p108). On your return, gather your strength with a fine meal at Town Bar & Grill (p88) before taking in a gig at Vicar Street (p91).

DUBLIN

HISTORY

The Celts went about their merry way for 1000 years or so, but it wasn't until the Vikings showed up that Dublin was urbanised in any significant way. By the 9th century, raids from the north had become a fact of Irish life, and some of the fierce Danes chose to stay rather than simply rape, pillage and depart.

Fast-forward another 1000 years, past the arrival of the Normans in the 12th century and the slow process of subjugating Ireland to Anglo-Norman (then British) rule, a process in which Dublin generally played the role of bandleader. Roads were widened, landscaped squares laid out and new town houses were built, all in a proto-Palladian style that soon became known as Georgian (after the kings then on the English throne).

The Georgian boom came to a sudden and dramatic halt after the Act of Union in 1801, when Ireland was formally united with Britain and its separate parliament closed down. As Dublin entered the 20th century, it was a dispirited place plagued by poverty, disease and more social problems than anyone cared to mention.

When the new state finally started doing business, Dublin was an exhausted capital. Despite slow and steady improvements, the city – like the rest of Ireland – continued to be plagued by rising unemployment, high emigration rates and a general stagnation that hung about the place like an impenetrable cloud. Dubliners made the most of the little

HISTORY

CLOCKWISE FROM TOP: OLIVIER CIRENDINI; JOHN SONES; OLIVIER CIRENDINI; RICHARD CUMMINS

Clockwise from top: Old Guinness bottles at the Guinness Storehouse (p75); Trinity College (p69); Sunset sailing Dublin's harbour; Street mosaic at the entrance to Temple Bar (p69)

DUBLIN

ORIENTATION

they had, but times were tough. Then, in the 1960s, a silver lining appeared in the shape of an economic boom: Dublin went suburban and began the outward expansion that continues unabated today.

A boom ain't a miracle, however, and Dublin trudged along for another couple of decades with pretty much the same age-old problems (high unemployment, emigration) and some new ones (drug addiction, gangland criminality) before everything began to change in 1994 and a terrible beauty known as the Celtic Tiger was born. Fifteen years later, Dublin is a place transformed, a capital in more than name and a city that has finally taken its rightful place as one of the most vibrant in Europe.

ORIENTATION

Small and compact, the city centre (which has traditionally been defined as within the boundaries of the Royal Canal, to the north, and the Grand Canal, to the south) has a clear focus and is a walker's delight. It is split in two by the unremarkable River Liffey, which traditionally marks a psychological and social break between the affluent southside and the poorer northside.

South of the river, over O'Connell Bridge, is the Temple Bar area and the expanse of Trinity College. Nassau St, along the southern edge of the campus, and pedestrianised Grafton St are the main shopping streets. North of the Liffey are O'Connell St and, just off it, Henry St, the major shopping thoroughfares. Most of the northside's B&Bs are on Gardiner St, which becomes rather run-down as it continues north.

INFORMATION
MEDICAL SERVICES
Should you experience an immediate health problem, contact the casualty section (emergency room) of the nearest public hospital; in an emergency, call an ambulance (☎ 999). There are no 24-hour pharmacies in Dublin; the latest any stay open is 10pm.

Grafton Medical Centre (Map p68; ☎ 01-671 2122; www.graftonmedical.ie; 34 Grafton St; ⏰ 8.30am-6.30pm Mon-Thu, to 6pm Fri) One-stop shop with male and female doctors, physiotherapists and a tropical medicine bureau.

Mater Misericordiae Hospital (Map pp52-3; ☎ 01-830 1122; Eccles St) Northside city centre, off Lower Dorset St.

St James's Hospital (Map pp66-7; ☎ 01-453 7941; James St) Southside.

MONEY
There are currency-exchange counters at Dublin airport in the baggage-collection area, and on the arrival and departure floors. The counters are open 5.30am to 11pm.

First Rate (Map p72; ☎ 01-671 3233; 1 Westmoreland St; ⏰ 8am-9pm Mon-Fri, 9am-9pm Sat, 10am-9pm Sun Jun-Sep, 9am-6pm Mon-Sat Oct-May)

THE DUBLIN PASS
If you're planning some heavy-duty sightseeing, you'll save a packet by investing in the **Dublin Pass** (adult/child 1-day €35/19, 2-day €55/31, 3-day €65/39, 6-day €95/49). Not only do you gain free entry into 27 attractions, but you can skip whatever queue there is by presenting your card; it also includes free transfer to and from the airport on the Aircoach (see p94). The card is available from any of the Dublin Tourism offices (p65).

Grafton Street

ANN CECIL

DUBLIN

DANGERS & ANNOYANCES

TOURIST INFORMATION
Dublin Tourism (www.visitdublin.com);
Dublin Airport (arrivals hall; ☽ 8am-10pm);
Dun Laoghaire (Dun Laoghaire ferry terminal;
☽ 10am-1pm & 2-6pm Mon-Sat); O'Connell St
(Map pp66-7; 14 Upper O'Connell St; ☽ 9am-5pm
Mon-Sat); Wilton Tce (Map pp52-3; Wilton Tce;
☽ 9.30am-noon & 12.30-5.15pm Mon-Fri)
Dublin Tourism Centre (Map p72; ☎ 01-605
7700; www.visitdublin.com; St Andrew's Church,
2 Suffolk St; ☽ 9am-7pm Mon-Sat, 10.30am-3pm
Sun Jul & Aug, 9am-5.30pm Mon-Sat Sep-Jun)
Dublin's main tourist office. There's a
booking fee of €4.50 for serviced accommodation or €7.50 for self-catering
accommodation, and a 10% deposit that
is refunded through your hotel bill.
Fáilte Ireland head office (Map pp52-3;
☎ 1850 230 330; www.ireland.ie; Wilton Tce;
☽ 9am-5.15pm Mon-Fri)

DANGERS & ANNOYANCES
Dublin's city centre is generally safe, even
if petty crime of the bag-snatching, pick-
pocketing and car-break-in variety can be
a low- to mid-level irritant.

The only consistent trouble in Dublin
is alcohol-related: where there are pubs
and clubs there are worse-for-wear revellers looking to get home and/or get laid,
and sometimes the frustrations of getting
neither can result in a trip to the casualty
department of the nearest hospital – hospitals are clogged to bursting with drink-
related cases throughout the weekend.

SIGHTS
GRAFTON STREET & AROUND
Dublin's most celebrated shopping street
is the elegant, pedestrianised spine of the
southern city centre: at its northern end is
Trinity College, the country's oldest and
most beautiful university, which stretches
its leafy self across a healthy chunk of
south-city real estate. A few steps northwest is the area called Temple Bar, where
bacchanalia and bohemia scrap it out for
supremacy – when the sun sets, Bacchus
is king. Grafton St's southern end runs into
the main entrance to St Stephen's Green,

DUBLIN

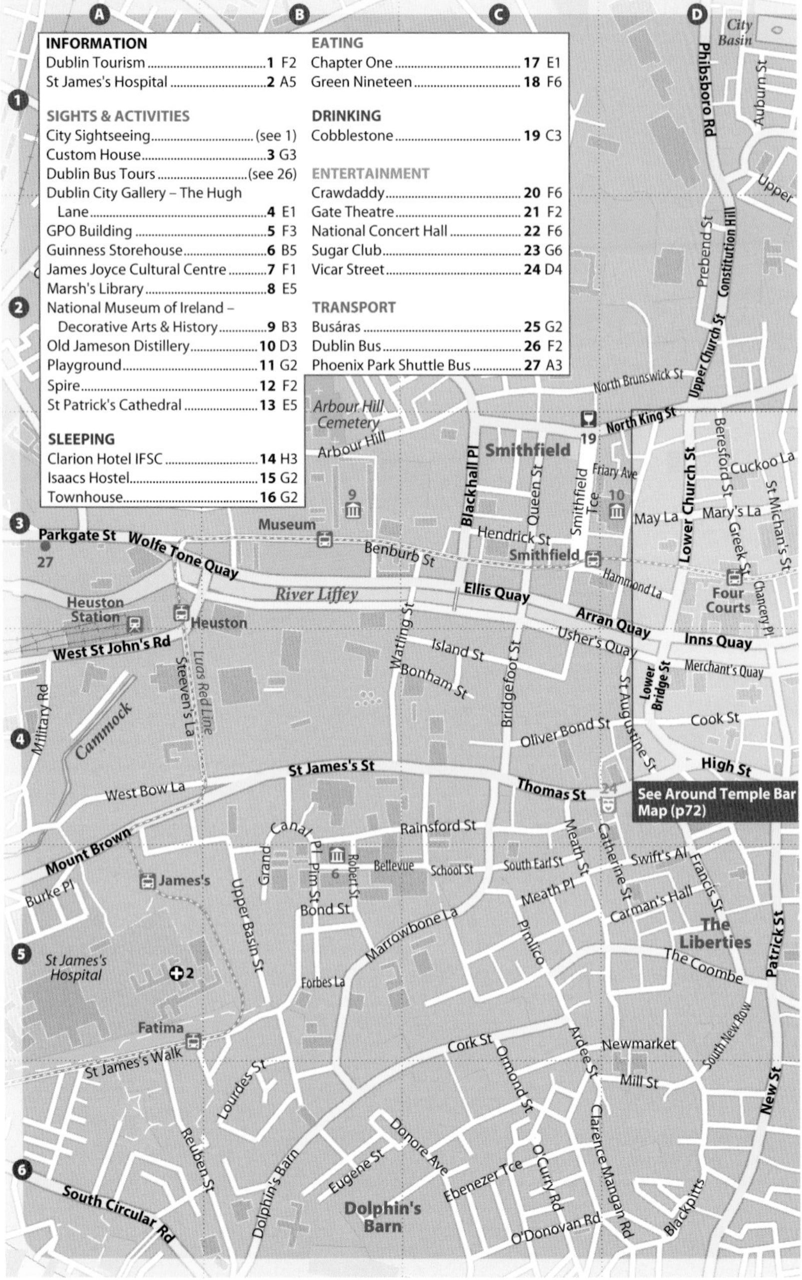
A
B
C
D
1
2
3
4
5
6
INFORMATION
Dublin Tourism 1 F2
St James's Hospital 2 A5
SIGHTS & ACTIVITIES
City Sightseeing (see 1)
Custom House 3 G3
Dublin Bus Tours (see 26)
Dublin City Gallery – The Hugh Lane 4 E1
GPO Building 5 F3
Guinness Storehouse 6 B5
James Joyce Cultural Centre 7 F1
Marsh's Library 8 E5
National Museum of Ireland – Decorative Arts & History 9 B3
Old Jameson Distillery 10 D3
Playground 11 G2
Spire 12 F2
St Patrick's Cathedral 13 E5
SLEEPING
Clarion Hotel IFSC 14 H3
Isaacs Hostel 15 G2
Townhouse 16 G2
EATING
Chapter One 17 E1
Green Nineteen 18 F6
DRINKING
Cobblestone 19 C3
ENTERTAINMENT
Crawdaddy 20 F6
Gate Theatre 21 F2
National Concert Hall 22 F6
Sugar Club 23 G6
Vicar Street 24 D4
TRANSPORT
Busáras 25 G2
Dublin Bus 26 F2
Phoenix Park Shuttle Bus 27 A3
City Basin
Phibsboro Rd
Auburn St
Upper
Prebend St
Constitution Hill
Upper Church St
North Brunswick St
North King St
Arbour Hill Cemetery
Arbour Hill
Smithfield
Blackhall Pl
Queen St
Smithfield Tce
Friary Ave
Beresford St
Cuckoo La
St Michan's St
Lower Church St
May La
Mary's La
Greek St
Hendrick St
Museum
Parkgate St
Wolfe Tone Quay
Benburb St
Hammond La
Four Courts
Chancery Pl
River Liffey
Ellis Quay
Arran Quay
Inns Quay
Heuston Station
Heuston
West St John's Rd
Watling St
Island St
Usher's Quay
Merchant's Quay
Bonham St
Bridgefoot St
St Augustine St
Lower Bridge St
Cook St
Military Rd
Cammock
Steeven's La
Luas Red Line
Oliver Bond St
High St
St James's St
Thomas St
See Around Temple Bar Map (p72)
West Bow La
Mount Brown
Grand Canal Pl
Rainsford St
Pim St
Robert St
Bellevue
School St
South Earl St
Meath St
Catherine St
Swift's Al
Francis St
Burke Pl
James's
Upper Basin St
Bond St
Marrowbone La
Meath Pl
Carman's Hall
Pimlico
The Liberties
Patrick St
St James's Hospital
Forbes La
The Coombe
Fatima
South New Row
St James's Walk
Cork St
Ormond St
Ardee St
Newmarket
Mill St
Lourdes St
New St
Reuben St
Donore Ave
Clarence Mangan Rd
Dolphin's Barn
Eugene St
Ebenezer Tce
O'Curry Rd
South Circular Rd
Dolphin's Barn
O'Donovan Rd
Blackpitts

DUBLIN

DUBLIN

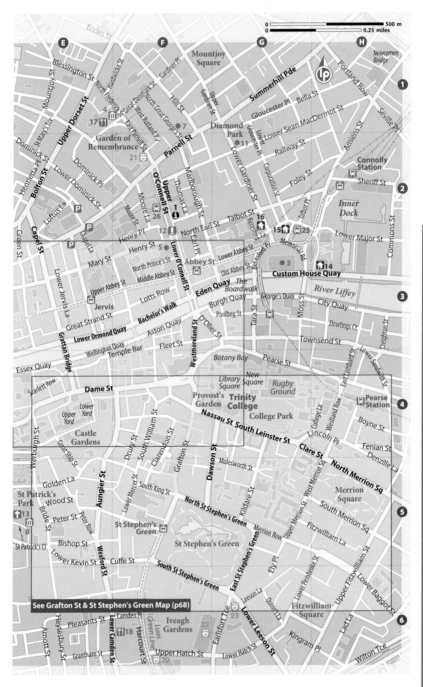

See Grafton St & St Stephen's Green Map (p68)

GRAFTON ST & ST STEPHEN'S GREEN

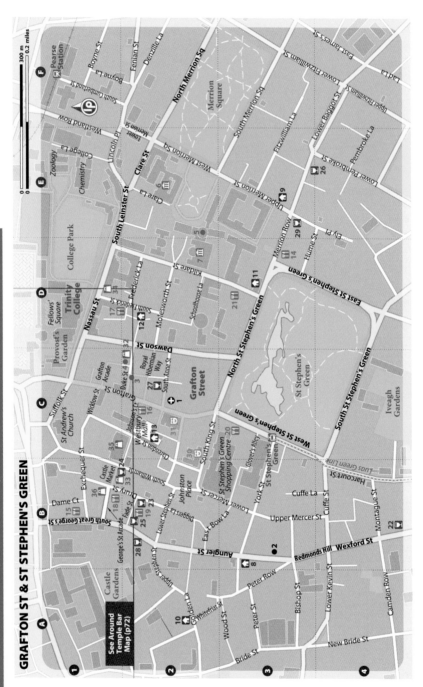

See Around
Temple Bar
Map (p72)

Dublin's perennially popular green lung; surrounding and beyond it is the capital's exquisite Georgian heritage, a collection of galleries, museums, and private and public buildings as handsome as any you'll see in Europe.

TRINITY COLLEGE

On a summer's evening, when the bustling crowds have gone for the day, there's hardly a more delightful place in Dublin than the grounds of Ireland's most prestigious **university** (Map pp66-7; ☎ 01-896 1000, walking tours 01-896 1827; tour €5, incl Long Room €10; ☼ tours every 40min 10.15am-3.40pm Mon-Sat, 10.15am-3pm Sun mid-May–Sep), a masterpiece of architecture and landscaping beautifully preserved in Georgian aspic. Not only is it Dublin's most attractive bit of historical real estate, but it's also home to one of the world's most famous – and most beautiful – books, the gloriously illuminated Book of Kells. There is no charge to wander the gardens on your own between 8am and 10pm.

Trinity's greatest treasures are kept in the Old Library's stunning 65m **Long Room** (☎ 01-896 2320; East Pavilion, Library Colonnades; adult/student/child €9/8/free; ☼ 9.30am-5pm Mon-Sat year-round, noon-4.30pm Sun Oct-Apr, 9.30am-4.30pm Sun May-Sep), which houses about 250,000 of the library's oldest volumes,

including the breathtaking **Book of Kells** (see the boxed text, p70). Your entry ticket includes admission to temporary exhibitions on display in the East Pavilion.

TEMPLE BAR

There's been many a wild night had within the cobbled precincts of Temple Bar (Map p72), Dublin's most visited neighbourhood, a maze of streets and alleys sandwiched between Dame St and the Liffey, running from Trinity College to Christ Church Cathedral. But it's not all booze and infamy: you can browse for vintage clothes, check out the latest art installations, get your nipples pierced and nibble on Mongolian barbecue. In good weather you can watch outdoor movies in one square or join in a pulsating drum circle in another – just a few slices of life in Dublin's Cultural Quarter.

Meeting House Square (Map p72) is one of the real success stories of Temple Bar. On one side is the excellent **Gallery of Photography** (Map p72; ☎ 01-671 4653; admission free; ☼ 11am-6pm Mon-Sat), hosting temporary exhibitions of contemporary local and international photographers. Staying with the photography theme, the other side of the square is home to the **National Photographic Archive** (Map p72; ☎ 01-671 0073; admission free; ☼ 11am-6pm

DUBLIN

SIGHTS

INFORMATION								
Grafton Medical Centre	**1**	C2	Trinity Lodge	**12**	D2	Grogan's Castle Lounge	**24**	B1
National Map Centre	**2**	B3	Westbury Hotel	**13**	C2	Hogan's	**25**	B2
						James Toner's	**26**	E4
SIGHTS & ACTIVITIES			EATING			Kehoe's	**27**	C2
Davy Byrne's	**3**	C2	Bang	**14**	D3	Long Hall	**28**	B2
Dublin Footsteps Walking Tour	(see 16)		Café Bardeli	**15**	B1	O'Donoghue's	**29**	E3
Dublin Literary Pub Crawl	**4**	C2	Café Bardeli	**16**	C2			
Leinster House	**5**	E2	Dunne & Crescenzi	**17**	D1	ENTERTAINMENT		
National Gallery	**6**	E2	Honest to Goodness	**18**	B1	Gaiety Theatre	**30**	C2
National Museum of Ireland –			L'Gueuleton	**19**	B2	HMV	**31**	C2
Archaeology & History	**7**	D2	Restaurant Patrick					
			Guilbaud	(see 9)		SHOPPING		
SLEEPING			Thornton's	**20**	C3	Cathach Books	**32**	C2
Avalon House	**8**	B3	Town Bar & Grill	**21**	D3	Costume	**33**	B1
Merrion	**9**	E3				Kilkenny Shop	**34**	D1
Radisson Blu Royal Hotel	**10**	A2	DRINKING			Powerscourt Townhouse		
Shelbourne	**11**	D3	Anseo	**22**	B4	Shopping Centre	**35**	C1
			Bar With No Name	**23**	B2	Stokes Books	**36**	B1

DUBLIN

SIGHTS

THE BOOK OF KELLS

More than half a million visitors stop in each year to see Trinity's top show-stopper, the world-famous **Book of Kells**. This illuminated manuscript, dating from around AD 800 and thus one of the oldest books in the world, was probably produced by monks at St Colmcille's Monastery on the remote island of Iona, off the western coast of Scotland. Repeated looting by marauding Vikings forced the monks to flee to the temporary safety of Kells, County Meath, in AD 806, along with their masterpiece. Around 850 years later, the book was brought to the college for safekeeping and has remained there since.

To really appreciate the book, you can get your own reproduction copy for a mere €22,000. Failing that, the library bookshop stocks a plethora of souvenirs and other memorabilia, including Otto Simm's excellent *Exploring the Book of Kells* (€12.95), a thorough guide with attractive colour plates, and a popular DVD-ROM (€31.95) showing all 800 pages. Kids looking for something a little less stuffy might enjoy the animated *The Secret of Kells* (2009), which is more fun than accurate in its portrayal of how the gospel was actually put together.

Mon-Sat, 2-6pm Sun), a magnificent resource for anyone interested in a photographic history of Ireland. On Saturdays it hosts a popular **food market**.

To the east, buildings on interesting **Eustace Street** (Map p72) include the 1715 Presbyterian Meeting House, now the **Ark** (Map p72; ☎ 01-670 7788; www.ark.ie; 11A Eustace St), an excellent children's cultural centre.

Merchant's Arch leads to the **Ha'penny Bridge** (Map p72), named after the ha'penny (half-penny) toll once needed to cross. The **Stock Exchange** (Map p72) is on Anglesea St, in a building dating from 1878.

DUBLIN CASTLE

The centre of British power in Ireland for most of 800 years, **Dublin Castle** (Map p72; ☎ 01-645 8813; www.dublincastle.ie; Cork Hill) sits atop Cork Hill, behind City Hall. It was originally built on the orders of King John in 1204, but it's more higgledy-piggledy palace than castle. Only the **Record Tower**, completed in 1258, survives from

the original Norman construction. Parts of the castle's foundations remain and a visit to the excavations is the most interesting part of the castle tour. The moats, now completely covered by more modern developments, were once filled by the River Poddle. The castle is also home to one of Dublin's best museums, the Chester Beatty Library (below).

The castle's beautiful **State Apartments** – easily the standout attraction – are still used for government business, so **tours** (full tour adult/student/child €4.50/3.50/2, undercroft & Chapel Royal only adult/student/child €3.50/2.50/free; ☼ every 20min, 10am-4.45pm Mon-Fri, 2-4.45pm Sat & Sun) are tailored around meetings and conferences; if the State Apartments are unavailable the discounted tour takes in only the undercroft and the Chapel Royal.

CHESTER BEATTY LIBRARY

The world-famous **Chester Beatty Library** (Map p72; ☎ 01-407 0750; www.cbl.ie; Dublin Castle, Cork Hill; admission free; ☼ 10am-5pm Mon-Fri, 11am-5pm Sat, 1-5pm Sun year-round,

closed Mon Oct-Apr) houses the collection of mining engineer Sir Alfred Chester Beatty (1875–1968), bequeathed to the Irish State on his death. And we're immensely grateful for Chester's patronage: spread over two floors, the breathtaking collection includes more than 20,000 manuscripts, rare books, miniature paintings, clay tablets, costumes and other objects of artistic, historical and aesthetic importance. The library runs tours at 1pm on Wednesdays and at 3pm and 4pm on Sundays.

NATIONAL MUSEUM OF IRELAND – ARCHAEOLOGY & HISTORY

Designed by Sir Thomas Newenham Deane and completed in 1890, the star attraction of this branch of the **National Museum of Ireland** **(Map p68; ☎ 01-677 7444; www.museum.ie; Kildare St; admission free; 10am-5pm Tue-Sat, 2-5pm Sun)** is the Treasury, home to the finest collection of Bronze Age and Iron Age gold artefacts in the world, and the world's most complete collection of medieval Celtic metalwork.

NATIONAL GALLERY

A magnificent Caravaggio and a breathtaking collection of works by Jack B Yeats – William Butler's kid brother – are the main reasons to visit the **National Gallery** **(Map p68; ☎ 01-661 5133; www.nationalgallery.ie; West Merrion Sq; admission free; 9.30am-5.30pm Mon-Wed, Fri & Sat, 9.30am-8.30pm Thu, noon-5.30pm Sun)**, but not the only ones. Its excellent collection is strong in Irish art, but there are also high-quality collections of every major European school of painting. There are free tours at 3pm on Saturdays and at 2pm, 3pm and 4pm on Sundays.

LEINSTER HOUSE

Dublin's grandest Georgian home, built by Richard Cassels between 1745 and 1748 for the very grand James Fitzgerald, earl of Kildare, is now the seat of both houses of the Oireachtas na Éireann (Irish Parliament) – the Dáil (Lower House) and Seanad (Upper House). Originally called Kildare House, it was changed to **Leinster**

HANNAH LEVY

Marsh's Library

IF YOU LIKE...

If you're a fan of the **Chester Beatty Library** (left) we think you'll enjoy perusing the collections at these literary spots:

- **Cathach Books** **(Map p68; ☎ 01-671 8676; www.rarebooks.ie; 10 Duke St)** A rich and remarkable collection of secondhand Irish-interest books, including 1st editions.
- **Marsh's Library** **(Map pp66-7; ☎ 01-454 3511; www.marshlibrary.ie; St Patrick's Close; adult/child/student €2.50/free/1.50; 10am-1pm & 2-5pm Mon & Wed-Fri, 10.30am-1pm Sat)** One of the city's most beautiful open secrets is this barely visited antique library with a look and atmosphere that has hardly changed since it opened its doors to awkward scholars in 1707. It's just around the corner from St Patrick's Cathedral.
- **Stokes Books** **(Map p68; ☎ 01-671 3584; 19 George's St Arcade)** Dusty little bookshop that specialises in historical books, old and new, from Ireland and elsewhere.

DUBLIN

AROUND TEMPLE BAR

AROUND TEMPLE BAR

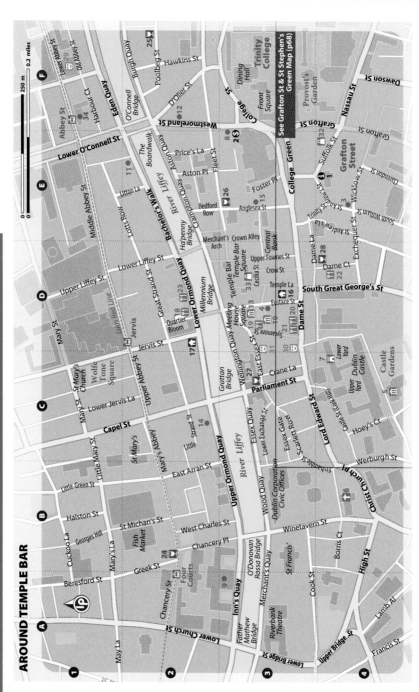

Name	No.	Grid
INFORMATION		
Dublin Tourism Centre	**1**	E4
First Rate	**2**	E3
SIGHTS & ACTIVITIES		
1916 Easter Rising Walk	**3**	E4
Ark	**4**	D3
Chester Beatty Library	**5**	C4
Christ Church Cathedral	**6**	B4
Dublin Bus Tours	(see 1)	
Dublin Castle	**7**	C4
Dublin Musical Pub Crawl	(see 26)	
Dublin Rock'n'Roll Writers Bus Tour Stop	**8**	E3
Four Courts	**9**	A3
Gallery of Photography	**10**	D3
Gray Line Dublin Tour	(see 1)	
Gray Line Dublin Tour	**11**	E2
Harrisons	**12**	F2
National Photographic Archive	**13**	D3
Ormond Quay Hotel	**14**	C2
Pat Liddy Walking Tours	(see 1)	
Stock Exchange	**15**	E3
SLEEPING		
Irish Landmark Trust	**16**	D3
Morrison Hotel	**17**	D2
EATING		
Bar Italia	**18**	D2
Eden	**19**	D3
Gruel	**20**	D3
Mermaid Café	**21**	D3
Odessa	**22**	D4
Silk Road Café	(see 5)	
Winding Stair	**23**	D2
DRINKING		
Hughes' Bar	**24**	B2
John Mulligan's	**25**	F2
Oliver St John Gogarty's	**26**	E3
Porterhouse	**27**	C3
Stag's Head	**28**	D4
ENTERTAINMENT		
Abbey Theatre	**29**	F1
Ark	(see 4)	
Olympia Theatre	**30**	D3
Peacock Theatre	(see 29)	
Project Arts Centre	**31**	D3
SHOPPING		
Avoca Handweavers	**32**	E4
Claddagh Records	**33**	D3
TRANSPORT		
Iarnród Éireann Travel Centre	**34**	F1

House (**Map p68; ☎ 01-618 3000, tour information 01-618 3271; www.oireachtas.ie; Kildare St; admission free; observation gallery 2.30-8.30pm Tue, 10.30am-8.30pm Wed, 10.30am-5.30pm Thu Nov-May, tours 10.30am, 11.30am, 2.30pm & 3.30pm Mon-Fri when parliament is not in session**) after the earl assumed the title of Duke of Leinster in 1766.

When Parliament is sitting, visitors are admitted to an observation gallery. You'll get an entry ticket from the Kildare St entrance on production of some identification. Bags can't be taken in, nor can notes or photographs be taken. Free guided tours are available (by appointment) on weekdays when parliament is not in session.

ST STEPHEN'S GREEN

While enjoying the nine gorgeous, landscaped hectares of Dublin's most popular square, consider that once upon a time **St Stephen's Green** (**Map p68; admission free; dawn-dusk**) was an open common used for public whippings, beatings and hangings. Activities in the green have quieted since then and are generally confined to the lunchtime picnic-and-stroll variety. Still, on a summer's day it is the favourite retreat of office workers, lovers and visitors alike, who come to breathe a little fresh air, feed the ducks and cuddle on the grass.

MERRION SQUARE

St Stephen's Green may win the popularity contest, but tranquil **Merrion Square** (**Map p68; admission free; dawn-dusk**) is our choice for favourite city park. Surrounding the well-kept lawns and beautifully tended flower beds are some of Dublin's most exceptional Georgian frontages, with fine doors, peacock fanlights, ornate door knockers and foot scrapers (used by gentlemen to scrape mud from their boots before venturing indoors).

THE LIBERTIES & KILMAINHAM

CHRIST CHURCH CATHEDRAL

The mother of all of Dublin's churches is **Christ Church Cathedral** (**Church of the Holy Trinity; Map p72; ☎ 01-677 8099; www.cccdub.ie; Christ Church Pl; adult/senior/student €6/4/3; 9.45am-4.15pm Mon-Sat, 12.30-2.30pm Sun Sep-May, 9.45am-6.15pm Mon-Tue & Fri, to 4.15pm Wed-Thu & Sat, 12.30-2.30pm & 4.30-6.15pm Sun Jun–mid-Jul, 9.45am-6.15pm Mon-Fri, to 4.15pm Sat, 12.30-2.30pm & 4.30-6.15pm Sun mid-Jul–Aug**), just south of the river and west of Temple Bar. It was founded in 1030 on what was then the southern edge of Dublin's Viking settlement.

Interior, St Patrick's Cathedral

RICHARD CUMMINS

Throughout much of its history, Christ Church vied for supremacy with nearby St Patrick's Cathedral (below) but, like its neighbour, it fell on hard times in the 18th and 19th centuries – earlier, the nave had been used as a market and the crypt had housed taverns – and was virtually derelict by the time restoration took place. Today, both Church of Ireland cathedrals are outsiders in a largely Catholic nation.

ST PATRICK'S CATHEDRAL

It was at this **cathedral** (Map pp66-7; ☎ 01-475 4817; www.stpatrickscathedral.ie; St Patrick's Close; adult/senior & student/child €5.50/4.50/free; ☺ 9am-6pm Mon-Sat, 9-11am, 12.45-3pm & 4.15-6pm Sun Mar-Oct, 9am-6pm Mon-Fri, 9am-5pm Sat, 10-11am & 12.45-3pm Sun Nov-Feb), reputedly, that St Paddy himself dunked the Irish

heathens into the waters of a well, so the church that bears his name stands on one of the earliest Christian sites in the city. There's been a church here since the 5th century, but the present building dates from 1190 or 1225 (opinions differ) and has been altered several times, most notably in 1864 when the flying buttresses were added. **St Patrick's Park**, the expanse of green beside the cathedral, was a crowded slum until it was cleared and razed in the early 20th century.

Like Christ Church Cathedral (p73), the building has suffered a rather dramatic history of storm and fire damage. Oliver Cromwell, during his 1649 conquest of Ireland, used St Patrick's as a stable for his army's horses. Jonathan Swift, author of *Gulliver's Travels*, was dean of the cathedral from 1713 to 1745, but prior to its restoration it was very neglected. Entering the cathedral from the southwestern porch, you'll find, just on your right, the graves of Swift and his long-time companion Esther Johnson, aka Stella. On the wall nearby are Swift's own Latin epitaphs for the two of them, and a bust of Swift.

IRISH MUSEUM OF MODERN ART

Ireland's most important collection of modern and contemporary Irish art is housed in the elegant, airy expanse of the Royal Hospital at Kilmainham, which in 1991 became the **Irish Museum of Modern Art** (IMMA; Map pp52-3; ☎ 01-612 9900; www.imma.ie; Military Rd; admission free; ☺ 10am-5.30pm Tue-Sat, noon-5.30pm Sun).

The gallery's 4000-strong collection includes works by artists such as Picasso, Miró and Vasarely, as well as works by more contemporary artists, including Iran do Espírito Santo, Philip Taaffe and Kathy Prendergast. The gallery displays ever-changing shows from its own works, and hosts regular touring exhibitions.

There are free guided tours (2.30pm Wednesday, Friday and Sunday) of the museum's exhibits throughout the year, but we strongly recommend the free seasonal heritage tours (hourly from 11am to 4pm Tuesday to Saturday, and from 1pm to 4pm Sunday) of the building itself, which run from July to September. To get there catch bus 24, 79 or 90 from Aston Quay.

KILMAINHAM JAIL

If you have *any* desire to understand Irish history – especially the juicy bits about resistance to English rule – then a visit to **Kilmainham Jail** (Map pp52-3; ☎ 01-453 5984; www.heritageireland.com; Inchicore Rd; adult/student/child €6/2/2; ☽ 9.30am-5pm Apr-Oct, 9.30am-4pm Mon-Sat, 10am-4pm Sun Nov-Mar) is an absolute must. This threatening grey building, built between 1792 and 1795, has played a role in virtually every act of Ireland's painful path to independence.

The uprisings of 1798, 1803, 1848, 1867 and 1916 ended with the leaders' confinement here. Robert Emmet, Thomas Francis Meagher, Charles Stewart Parnell and the 1916 Easter Rising leaders were all visitors, but it was the executions in 1916 that most deeply etched the jail's name into the Irish consciousness.

An excellent audiovisual introduction to the building is followed by a thought-provoking tour through the eerie prison, the largest unoccupied building of its kind in Europe. The tour finishes in the gloomy yard where the 1916 executions took place.

To get here, catch bus 23, 51, 51A, 78 or 79 from Aston Quay.

O'CONNELL STREET & AROUND

After decades of playing second fiddle to Grafton St and the other byways of the southside, the northside's grandest thoroughfare is finally getting its mojo

Entrance sign, Guinness Storehouse

DUBLIN

SIGHTS

↘ GUINNESS STOREHOUSE

The most popular visit in town is the beer-lover's Disneyland, a multimedia bells-and-whistles homage to the country's most famous export and the city's most enduring symbol. The **Guinness Storehouse**, the only part of the massive, 26-hectare St James's Gate Brewery open to the public, is a suitable cathedral in which to worship the black gold; shaped like a giant pint of Guinness, it rises seven impressive storeys high around a stunning central atrium. At the top is the head, represented by the **Gravity Bar**, with a panoramic view of Dublin.

To get to the Storehouse, take bus 21A, 78 or 78A from Fleet St, or the Luas Red Line to James's.

Things you need to know: Map pp66-7; ☎ 01-408 4800; www.guinness -storehouse.com; St James's Gate Brewery; adult/child/student under 18yr/student over 18yr & senior €15/5/9/11; ☽ 9.30am-5pm Sep-Jun, 9.30am-7pm Jul & Aug)

back, even if it hasn't quite recaptured the grandeur that once made it Dublin's finest avenue.

O'CONNELL STREET

It's amazing what a few hundred million euros and a new vision will do to a street plagued by years of neglect, a criminally blind development policy and a history as a hothouse of street trouble. It's difficult to fathom why O'Connell St (Map pp66-7), once so proud and elegant, could have been so humbled that the street's top draws were amusement arcades and fast-food outlets.

Thankfully, Dublin City Council is committed to a thorough reappraisal of the street's appearance: a lot done, more to do. The first project was the impressive Spire (the Monument of Light; Map pp66-7), which graced the spot once occupied by a statue of Admiral Nelson (who disappeared in explosive fashion, thanks to the IRA, in 1966). Other projects have seen the widening of the pavements and the limiting of traffic, although the street will truly be grand when the plethora of fast-food joints are given the elbow.

GENERAL POST OFFICE

Talk about going postal. The GPO building (Map pp66-7; ☎ 01-705 7000; www.anpost.ie; O'Connell St; ☒ 8am-8pm Mon-Sat) will forever be linked to the dramatic and tragic events of Easter Week 1916, when Pádraig Pearse, James Connolly and the other leaders of the Easter Rising read their proclamation from the front steps and made the building their headquarters. The building – a neoclassical masterpiece designed by Francis Johnston in 1818 – was burnt out in the subsequent siege, but that wasn't the end of it. There was bitter fighting in and around the building during the Civil War of 1922; you can still see the pockmarks of the struggle in the Doric columns. Since its reopening in 1929 it has lived through quieter times, but its central role in the history of independent Ireland has made it a prime site for everything from official parades to personal protests.

DUBLIN CITY GALLERY – THE HUGH LANE

Whatever reputation Dublin has as a repository of world-class art owes a lot to the simply stunning collection at the Hugh Lane Gallery (Map pp66-7; ☎ 01-874 1903; www.hughlane.ie; 22 North Parnell Sq; admission free; ☒ 10am-6pm Tue-Thu, 10am-5pm Fri & Sat, 11am-5pm Sun), which is not only home to works by some of the brightest stars in the modern and contemporary art world both foreign and domestic, but is where you'll find one of the most singular exhibitions to be seen anywhere: the actual studio of one of the 20th century's truly iconic artists, Francis Bacon.

All of the big names of French Impressionism and early-20th-century Irish art are here. Sculptures by Rodin and Degas, and paintings by Corot, Courbet, Manet and Monet sit alongside works by Irish greats Jack B Yeats, William Leech and Nathaniel Hone.

DOCKLANDS
CUSTOM HOUSE

Architect James Gandon (1743–1823) announced his arrival on the Dublin scene with the stunning, glistening white building that is the Custom House (Map pp66-7), one of the city's finest Georgian monuments. It was constructed between 1781 and 1791, in spite of opposition from city merchants and dockers at the original Custom House, upriver in Temple Bar.

The best complete view of a building that stretches 114m along the Liffey is obtained from across the river, though a close-up inspection of its many fine details is also worthwhile. The building is topped

DUBLIN

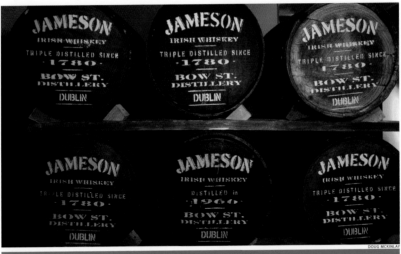

Barrels at the Old Jameson Distillery

DOUG MCKINLAY

SIGHTS

by a copper dome with four clocks. Atop stands a 5m-high statue of Hope.

SMITHFIELD & PHOENIX PARK
NATIONAL MUSEUM OF IRELAND – DECORATIVE ARTS & HISTORY

So much for the austere life of a soldier. Until it was decommissioned over a decade ago, Collins Barracks, built in 1704 on the orders of Queen Anne, was the largest military barracks in the world. In 1997 the early neoclassical grey stone building on the Liffey's northern bank was given a sparkling, modern makeover and now houses the decorative arts and history collection of the **National Museum of Ireland** (Map pp66-7; ☎ 01-677 7444; www. museum.ie; Benburb St; admission free; ☼ 10am-5pm Tue-Sat, 2-5pm Sun).

The exhibits are good, but the building is stunning: at its heart is the huge central square surrounded by arcaded colonnades and blocks linked by walking bridges. While wandering about the plaza, imagine it holding up to six regiments in formation. The whole shebang is the work

of Thomas Burgh (1670–1730), who also designed the Old Library in Trinity College (p69).

Inside the imposing exterior lies a treasure trove of artefacts ranging from silver, ceramics and glassware to weaponry, furniture and folk-life displays. Some of the best pieces are gathered in the 'Curator's Choice' exhibition, a collection of 25 objects hand-picked by different curators, displayed with an account of why they were chosen.

OLD JAMESON DISTILLERY

Smithfield's biggest draw is the **Old Jameson Distillery** (Map pp66-7; ☎ 01-807 2355; www.jameson.ie; Bow St; adult/child/student €13.50/8/10; ☼ tours every 35min 9am-5.30pm), a huge museum devoted to *uisce beatha* (the water of life). To its more serious devotees, that is precisely what whiskey is, although they may be put off by the slickness of the museum, which shepherds visitors through a compulsory tour of the re-created factory and into the ubiquitous gift shop.

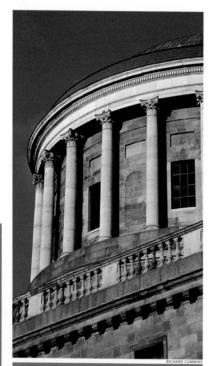

RICHARD CUMMINS

Four Courts building

If you're buying whiskey, go for the stuff you can't buy at home, such as the excellent Red Breast or the super exclusive Midleton, a very limited reserve that is appropriately expensive.

FOUR COURTS

Appellants quake and the accused may shiver, but visitors are only likely to be amazed by James Gandon's imposing **Four Courts** (Map p72; ☎ 01-872 5555; Inn's Quay; admission free; ⏰ 9am-5pm Mon-Fri), Ireland's uppermost courts of law. Gandon's Georgian masterpiece is a mammoth structure incorporating a 130m-long facade and a collection of statuary. The Corinthian-columned central block, connected to flanking wings with enclosed quadrangles, was begun in 1786 and not

completed until 1802. The original four courts (Exchequer, Common Pleas, King's Bench and Chancery) all branch off the central rotunda.

Visitors are allowed to wander through the building, but not to enter courts or other restricted areas. In the lobby of the central rotunda you'll see bewigged barristers conferring and police officers handcuffed to their charges.

PHOENIX PARK

Measuring 709 glorious hectares, **Phoenix Park** (Map pp52-3; admission free) is Europe's largest city park: a green lung that is more than double the size of New York's Central Park (a paltry 337 hectares), and larger than all of London's major parks put together. Here you'll find gardens and lakes; pitches for all kinds of British sports from soccer to cricket to polo (the dry original one, with horses); the second-oldest zoo in Europe; a castle and visitor centre; the headquarters of the Garda Síochána (police); the Ordnance Survey offices; and the homes of both the president of Ireland and the US ambassador, who live in two exquisite residences more or less opposite each other. There's even a herd of some 500 fallow deer.

The deer were first introduced by Lord Ormond in 1662, when lands once owned by the Knights of Jerusalem were turned into a royal hunting ground. In 1745 the viceroy Lord Chesterfield threw it open to the public and it has remained so ever since. (The name 'Phoenix' has nothing to do with the mythical bird; it is a corruption of the Irish *fionn uisce,* meaning 'clear water'.)

The residence of the Irish president, **Áras an Uachtaráin** (Map pp52-3; ☎ 01-617 1000; Phoenix Park; admission free; ⏰ guided tours hourly 10.30am-4.30pm Sat) was built in 1751 and enlarged in 1782, then again in 1816, this time by noted Irish architect Francis Johnston, who added the Ionic portico. From 1782 to 1922 it was the residence of the British viceroys or lord lieutenants. After independence it became the home of Ireland's governor general until Ireland cut ties with the British Crown and created the office of president in 1937.

Tickets for the tour can be collected from the **Phoenix Park Visitor Centre** (Map pp52-3; ☎ 01-677 0095; adult/concession/family €2.75/1.25/7; ☼ 10am-6pm daily Apr-Sep, 10am-5pm daily Oct, 10am-5pm Mon-Sat Nov & Dec, 10am-5pm Sat & Sun Jan-Mar), the converted former stables of the papal nunciate, now devoted to the park's history and ecology over the last 3500 years.

Take bus 10 from O'Connell St, or bus 25 or 26 from Middle Abbey St to get to Dublin's beloved playground. The best way to get around the park is to hop on the new **Phoenix Park Shuttle Bus** (Map pp66-7; adult/child €2/1; ☼ hourly 7am-5pm Mon-Fri, 10am-5pm Sat & Sun), which goes from just outside the main gate on Parkgate St and loops around to the visitor centre.

DUBLIN FOR CHILDREN

There are reasonably sized playgrounds on Gardiner St (Map pp66-7) and in St Stephen's Green (p73), where you can also feed the ducks. The Iveagh Gardens (Map p68) doesn't have a playground but has a waterfall and small maze, and is a lovely quiet space to relax while your children play.

The **Ark** (Map p72; ☎ 01-670 7788; www.ark.ie; 11A Eustace St) is a children's cultural centre that organises plays, exhibitions and workshops for four- to 14-year-olds. You really need to book in advance for events.

You could spend the entire day at the **National Aquatic Centre** (Map p110; ☎ 01-646 4300; www.nationalacquaticcentre.ie; Snugborough Rd, Blanchardstown; adult/child & student €14/12; ☼ 6am-10pm Mon-Fri, 9am-8pm Sat & Sun), and if you don't the kids will certainly try to, as they glide from slide to slide and pool to pool.

Lambert Puppet Theatre (☎ 01-280 0974; www.lambertpuppettheatre.com; Clifton Lane, Monkstown) stages puppet shows for

JONATHAN SMITH

Cricket match at Phoenix Park

DUBLIN

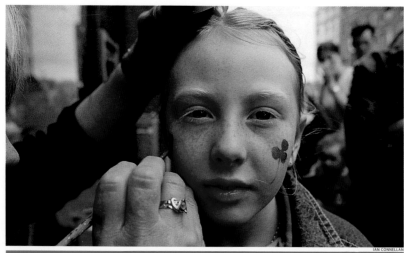
Face-painting at St Patrick's Festival

IAN CONNELLAN

TOURS

the over-threes in Monkstown, 10km south of Dublin. Take bus 7, 7A, 8, 46A, 46X or 746 to get there.

The National Museum (p71 & p77) and the Irish Museum of Modern Art (p74) run fun, educational programs for children at weekends. A nice spot for a picnic is **Newbridge House** (Map p110; ☎ 01-843 6534; Donabate; adult/child €3.50/2; 🕙 10am-5pm Tue-Sat, 2-6pm Sun Apr-Sep, 2-5pm Sat & Sun Oct-Mar), with its large traditional farm, which has cows, pigs and chickens, a large park and an adventure playground. It's northeast of Swords at Donabate, 19km from the centre. You can get here on the Suburban Rail service (€2.70, 30 minutes), which departs hourly from either Connolly or Pearse Station in the city centre.

TOURS

Dublin is an easy city to see on foot, so a guided walking tour is an ideal way to double up on a bit of culture and exercise. For longer tours or a cushier ride, there are numerous themed citywide bus tours,

and several companies also do day trips further afield.

BUS TOURS

City Sightseeing (Map pp66-7; www.city-sightseeing.com; Dublin Tourism, 14 Upper O'Connell St; adult/child/family €15.50/7/38; 🕙 every 8-15min 9am-6pm) City Sightseeing's time-tested hop-on, hop-off open-top tours. Allow 1½ hours.

Dublin Bus Tours (www.dublinbus.ie; tours €15-25; 🕙 tours daily) O'Connell St (Map pp66-7; ☎ 01-872 0000; 59 Upper O'Connell St); Suffolk St (Map p72; Dublin Tourism Centre, St Andrew's Church, 2 Suffolk St) Offers a variety of tours, including Dublin City Tour, Ghost Bus Tour, Coast and Castles Tour, and South Coast and Gardens Tour.

Dublin Rock'n'Roll Writers Bus Tour (Map p72; ☎ 01-620 3929; www.dublinrocktours.ie; 3 Westmoreland St; tours €15; 🕙 noon, 2pm, 4pm & 6pm Wed-Sun) Dublin's rich rock legacy is explored audiovisually from the comfort of a kitted-out tour bus. The bus stop is outside O'Brien's sandwich shop on Westmoreland St; the tour lasts about 90 minutes.

Gray Line Dublin Tour (☎ 01-872 9010; www.irishcitytours.com; adult/child/student/senior/family €15.50/7/13/13/38; ⌚ every 15min 9.30am-5.30pm, to 6.30pm Jul & Aug) Bachelor's Walk (Map p72; 33 Bachelor's Walk); Suffolk St (Map p72; Dublin Tourism Centre, St Andrew's Church, 2 Suffolk St) Another hop-on, hop-off tour (1½ hours) of the city's primary attractions.

WALKING TOURS

1916 Easter Rising Walk (Map p72; ☎ 01-676 2493; www.1916rising.com; International Bar, 23 Wicklow St; adult/child €12/free; ⌚ 11.30am Mon-Sat, 1pm Sun Mar-Oct) A recommended two-hour tour run by graduates of Trinity College, it takes in parts of Dublin that were directly involved in the Easter Rising. Leaves from the International Bar.

Dublin Footsteps Walking Tours (Map p68; ☎ 01-496 0641; Bewley's Bldg, Grafton St; adult €10; ⌚ 10.30am Mon, Wed, Fri & Sat Jun-Sep) Departing from Bewley's on Grafton St, these excellent two-hour tours weave Georgian, literary and architectural Dublin into a fascinating walk.

Dublin Literary Pub Crawl (Map p68; ☎ 01-670 5602; www.dublinpubcrawl.com; The Duke, 9 Duke St; adult/student €12/10; ⌚ 7.30pm Mon-Sat, noon & 7.30pm Sun Apr-Nov, 7.30pm Thu-Sun Dec-Mar) An award-winning 2½-hour walk-and-performance tour led by two actors, exploring pubs with literary connections. There's plenty of drink taken, which makes it all the more popular; get to the Duke pub by 7pm to reserve a spot.

Dublin Musical Pub Crawl (Map p72; ☎ 01-478 0193; www.discoverdublin.com; Oliver St John Gogarty's, 58-59 Fleet St; adult/student €12/10; ⌚ 7.30pm Apr-Oct, 7.30pm Thu-Sat Nov-Mar) The story of Irish traditional music and its influence on contemporary styles is explained and demonstrated by two expert musicians in a number of Temple Bar pubs. Tours meet upstairs at Oliver St John Gogarty's and take 2½ hours.

James Joyce Walking Tour (Map pp66-7; ☎ 01-878 8547; James Joyce Cultural Centre, 35 North Great George's St; adult/student €10/8; ⌚ 2pm Tue, Thu & Sat) Excellent 1¼-hour walking tours of northside attractions associated with James Joyce, departing from James Joyce Cultural Centre.

Pat Liddy Walking Tours (Map p72; ☎ 01-831 1109; www.walkingtours.ie; Dublin Tourism Centre, St Andrew's Church, 2 Suffolk St; adult €6-22, child €5-20) Award-winning themed tours of the city by well-known Dublin historian Pat Liddy, ranging from the 75-minute Dublin Experience to the two-hour Great Guinness Walk, which includes a queue-skipping tour of the Guinness Storehouse. Check the website for details of tour options and times. All tours depart from the Dublin Tourism Centre.

FESTIVALS & EVENTS

Jameson Dublin International Film Festival (☎ 01-872 1122; www.dubliniff.com) Local flicks, arty international films and advance releases of mainstream movies make up the menu of the city's film festival, which runs over two weeks in mid-February.

St Patrick's Festival (☎ 01-676 3205; www.stpatricksfestival.ie) The mother of all festivals; 600,000-odd gather to 'honour' St Patrick over four days around 17 March on city streets and in venues.

Dun Laoghaire Festival of World Cultures (☎ 01-271 9555; www.festivalofworldcultures.com) Colourful multicultural music, art and theatre festival on the last weekend of August.

Dublin Theatre Festival (☎ 01-677 8439; www.dublintheatrefestival.com) This

DUBLIN

SLEEPING

Bloomsday mural at the James Joyce Cultural Centre

RICHARD CUMMINS

well-established international theatre festival is held over a fortnight in late September.

Dublin Fringe Festival (☎ 01-872 9016; www.fringefest.com) Comedy and alternative fringe theatre from late September to early October.

SLEEPING

You can pay anything from €80 to €200 for a quality guesthouse or midrange hotel, while the city's top digs usually start their rates at €200; at the other end of the scale, a hostel bed will cost anything from €18 to as much as €34. (Note that hostel rates don't include breakfast; exceptions are noted.)

GRAFTON STREET & AROUND

You can't get more central than the relatively small patch of real estate just south of the Liffey, which has a good mix of options ranging from backpacker hostels to the fanciest hotels. Bear in mind that the location comes with a price.

Avalon House (Map p68; ☎ 01-475 0001; www.avalon-house.ie; 55 Aungier St; dm/s/d €18/30/60; 💻 🛜) Before there was tourism, this hostel in a gorgeous Victorian building catered to the thin trickle of adventurers who landed in Dublin. The lounges are great for hanging out, the Bald Barista serves a sublime cappuccino and there's free wi-fi.

our pick **Number 31** (Map pp52-3; ☎ 01-676 5011; www.number31.ie; 31 Leeson Close; s/d/tr from €115/150/225) This elegant slice of accommodation paradise, designed for his own use by modernist architect Sam Stephenson (of Central Bank fame – or infamy), is unquestionably the most unique of Dublin's hotels. Separated by a beautiful garden, its 21 bedrooms are split between the chichi coach house and the more gracious Georgian house, where rooms are individually furnished with French antiques and big beds. Gourmet breakfasts are served in the conservatory. Children under 10 are not permitted.

Trinity Lodge (Map p68; ☎ 01-617 0900; www.trinitylodge.com; 12 South Frederick St; s/d from €130/170; ⊚) Martin Sheen's grin greets you on entering this cosy, award-winning guesthouse. Not that he's ditched movies for hospitality: he just enjoyed his stay (and full Irish breakfast, presumably) at this classically refurbished Georgian pad so much that he let them take a mugshot. Room 2 has a lovely bay window.

Radisson Blu Royal Hotel (Map p68; ☎ 01-898 2900; www.radissonblu.ie/royalhotel -dublin; Golden Lane; r €160-220; P ⊠ ⊚) The stunning Dublin flagship of this well-respected Scandinavian group is an excellent example of how sleek lines and muted colours can combine beautifully with luxury to make for a memorable

night's stay: from the hugely impressive public areas (the bar alone is worth the visit) to the sophisticated bedrooms – each with flat-screen digital TVs embedded in the wall, to go along with all of the other little touches – this is bound to be one of the most popular options for the business traveller.

Irish Landmark Trust (Map p72; ☎ 01-670 4733; www.irishlandmark.com; 25 Eustace St; 1 night/weekend/week €400/800/2000) If you're travelling in a group, instead of renting a bunch of doubles in a hotel that you'll barely remember a week after you've gone home, why not go for this fabulous 18th-century heritage house, gloriously

BLOOMSDAY

It's 16 June. There's a bunch of weirdos wandering around the city dressed in Edwardian gear and talking nonsense in dramatic tones. They're not mad – at least not clinically – they're only Bloomsdayers committed to commemorating James Joyce's epic *Ulysses,* which anyone familiar with the book will tell you (and that doesn't necessarily mean that they've *read* the bloody thing) takes place over the course of one day.

Although Ireland treated Joyce like a literary pornographer while he was alive, the country (and especially Dublin) can't get enough of him today. In general, events are designed to follow Leopold Bloom's progress around town, and in recent years festivities have expanded to continue over four days around 16 June. On Bloomsday proper you can kick things off with breakfast at the James Joyce Cultural Centre (Map pp66-7), where the 'inner organs of beast and fowl' come accompanied by celebratory readings.

In the morning, guided tours of Joycean sites usually leave from the GPO Building (Map pp66-7) and the James Joyce Cultural Centre. Lunchtime activity focuses on **Davy Byrne's** (Map p68; Duke St), Joyce's 'moral pub', where Bloom paused to dine on a glass of burgundy and a slice of gorgonzola. Street entertainers are likely to keep you amused through the afternoon as you take guided walks and watch animated readings from *Ulysses* and Joyce's other books; there's a reading at **Ormond Quay Hotel** (Map p72; Ormond Quay) at 4pm and **Harrisons** (Map p72; Westmoreland St) in the late afternoon.

Events also take place in the days leading up to and following Bloomsday. The best source of information about what's on in any particular year is the **James Joyce Cultural Centre** (www.jamesjoyce.ie) or the free *Dublin Event Guide*, close to the date.

restored to the highest standard by the Irish Landmark Trust charity? You'll have this unique house all to yourselves. It sleeps up to seven in its double, twin and triple bedrooms. Furnished with tasteful antiques, authentic furniture and fittings (including a grand piano in the drawing room), this kind of period rental accommodation is something really special.

Westbury Hotel (Map p68; ☎ 01-679 1122; www.doylecollection.com; Grafton St; s/d from €170/260; P ☐) The Westbury sits snugly on a small street just off Grafton St, which suits the high-powered business people and visiting celebs that favour the hotel's finer suites, where they can watch TV from the Jacuzzi before retiring to a four-poster bed. Mere mortals tend to make do with the standard rooms, which are perfectly appointed but lack the sophisticated grandeur promised by the luxurious public spaces.

Merrion (Map p68; ☎ 01-603 0600; www.merrionhotel.com; Upper Merrion St; r from €455; P ☐ ☒) This is a resplendent five-star hotel set in a terrace of beautifully restored Georgian town houses. Try to get a room in the old house (which has the largest private art collection in the city) – rather than the newer wing – to sample the hotel's truly elegant comforts. Located opposite government buildings, its marble corridors are patronised by visiting dignitaries and the odd celeb. Even if you don't stay, come for the superb afternoon tea (€34), with endless cups of tea served out of silver pots near a raging fire.

Shelbourne (Map p68; ☎ 01-676 6471; www.theshelbourne.ie; 27 North St Stephen's Green; r from €200; P ☐ ☜) Dublin's most iconic hotel has long been the best address in town – it was good enough for the framers of the Irish Constitution – but since a major refurbishment and its acquisition by the Marriott group there has been steady grumbling that the hotel is not quite at the top of its five-star game. It *looks* pretty impressive, especially the Lord Mayor's Lounge, where afternoon tea is still one of the best experiences in town.

O'CONNELL STREET & AROUND

There are a few elegant hotels around O'Connell St, but the real draw round these parts is just to the east on Gardiner St, Dublin's B&B row. Caveat emptor: the further north you go along Gardiner St the dodgier the lodgings and the neighbourhood get, so we've kept our inclusions to the southern end of the street, below Mountjoy Sq.

our pick **Isaacs Hostel** (Map pp66–7; ☎ 01-855 6215; www.isaacs.ie; 2-5 Frenchman's Lane; dm/d from €14/62; ☜) Located in a 200-year-old wine vault, this popular, grungy hostel with loads of character is the place to head if you want one of the cheapest beds in town – without sacrificing the basics of health and hygiene. Global nomads will feel right at home.

Townhouse (Map pp66–7; ☎ 01-878 8808; www.townhouseofdublin.com; 47-48 Lower Gardiner St; s/d/tr from €70/115/132) The ghostly writing of Irish-Japanese author Lafcadio Hearn may have influenced the Gothic-style interior of his former home. Some rooms in the new wing are larger, with balconies overlooking the small Japanese garden.

Morrison Hotel (Map p72; ☎ 01-887 2400; www.morrisonhotel.ie; Lower Ormond Quay; r from €135, ste from €285; ☐) Fashion designer John Rocha's loosely Oriental style is evident in the Zen-like furnishings, but extras such as iMac computers, iPod docking stations and Aveda goodies clinch it for us. For a few euro extra, nab a far superior studio den (€415) in the new wing: there's a balcony and enough space to throw a party. This could be the most affordable posh hotel in town.

O'Connell Street (p75)

JOHN ELK III

DOCKLANDS

Clarion Hotel IFSC (Map pp66-7; ☎ 01-433 8800; www.clarionhotelifsc.com; Custom House Quay; r €265, ste €395-1000; ⓟ ⊠ ⌨ ⌗ ⌖) This swanky business hotel in the heart of the Irish Financial Services Centre has beautiful rooms decorated in contemporary light oak furnishings and a blue-and-taupe colour scheme that is supposed to relax the mind after a long day of meetings. We prefer to relax with a swim in the Sanovitae health club downstairs.

BEYOND THE GRAND CANAL

You'll get more for your euro in the largely stylish digs dotted throughout the southern city suburb of Ballsbridge, a 30-minute walk from the city centre or a short ride on bus 5, 7, 7A, 8, 18 or 45.

Waterloo House (Map pp52-3; ☎ 01-660 1888; www.waterloohouse.ie; 8-10 Waterloo Rd; s/d €70/120; ⓟ ⌗) A short walk from St Stephen's Green, this lovely guesthouse is spread over two ivy-clad Georgian houses off Baggot St. Rooms are tastefully decorated with high-quality furnishings in authentic Farrow & Ball Georgian colours, and all have cable TV and kettles.

our pick Pembroke Townhouse (Map pp52-3; ☎ 01-660 0277; www.pembroketown house.ie; 90 Pembroke Rd; s €90-195, d €115-290; ⓟ ⌗) This superluxurious town house is a perfect example of what happens when traditional and modern combine to great effect. A classical Georgian house has been transformed into a superb boutique hotel, with each room carefully crafted and appointed to reflect the best of contemporary design and style, right down to the modern art on the walls and the handy lift to the upper floors.

Dylan (Map pp52-3; ☎ 01-660 3001; www. dylan.ie; Eastmoreland Pl; r from €200; ⊠ ⌨ ⌗) A genuine contender for favourite celebrity stopover, the Dylan's designer OTT look – baroque meets Scandinavian sleek by way of neo-art nouveau and glammed-up 1940s art deco – has nevertheless been a big hit, a reflection perhaps of a time when too much was barely enough for the glitterati who signed contracts over cocktails before retiring to the crisp Frette

DUBLIN

linen sheets in the snazzily appointed rooms upstairs.

Four Seasons (Map pp52-3; ☎ 01-665 4000; www.fourseasons.com; Simmonscourt Rd; r from €225; P ☐ ⌗ ☎) The muscular, no-holds-barred style of American corporate innkeeping is in full force at this huge hotel that has sought to raise the hospitality bar. The spa is superb, and the lit basement pool a treat. For many, this is the best hotel in town. We're suckers for a slightly more demure luxury, so we'll stick it in the top three. It's in the grounds of the Royal Dublin Society Showground.

EATING

EATING

The transformation of Dublin from culinary backwater to gourmet metropolis has resulted in a city with more restaurants than it knows what to do with, and a population whose palates have grown increasingly sophisticated on a diet of dishes from around the world – a far cry from the days when the joke held true that Irish food was wonderful until it was cooked.

The most concentrated restaurant area is Temple Bar, but apart from a handful of good places, the bulk of eateries offer bland, unimaginative fodder and cheap set menus for tourists. Better food and service can usually be found on either side of Grafton St, while the top-end restaurants are clustered around Merrion Sq and Fitzwilliam Sq.

GRAFTON STREET & AROUND

Gruel (Map p72; ☎ 01-670 7119; 68a Dame St; breakfast €4, lunch €4.50-8, brunch €5-12, dinner mains €9-15; ⊙ 7am-9.30pm Mon-Fri, 10.30am-10.30pm Sat & Sun) For its regulars, Gruel is the best dish in town, whether it's for the superfilling, tasty lunchtime roast-in-a-roll – a rotating list of slow-roasted organic meats stuffed into a bap (large bread roll)

and flavoured with homemade relishes – or the exceptional evening menu, where pasta, fish and chicken are given an exotic once-over. It doesn't accept bookings.

our pick **Honest to Goodness** (Map p68; ☎ 01-677 5373; George's St Arcade; mains €6; ⊙ 9am-6pm Mon-Sat, noon-4pm Sun) Wholesome sandwiches (made with freshly baked bread), tasty soups and a near-legendary Sloppy Joe, all made on the premises using produce sourced from local farmers, have earned this lovely spot in the George's St Arcade a bevy of loyal fans who want to keep it all to themselves.

Dunne & Crescenzi (Map p68; ☎ 01-677 3815; 14-16 South Frederick St; mains €9-12; ⊙ 9am-7pm Mon & Tue, to 10pm Wed-Sat) This exceptional Italian eatery delights its regulars with a basic menu of rustic pleasures: panini, a single pasta dish and a superb plate of mixed antipasti drizzled in olive oil.

Café Bardeli (Map p68; www.cafebardeli.ie; mains €9-13; ⊙ 7am-11pm) Grafton St (☎ 01-672 7720; Bewley's Bldg, Grafton St); South Great George's St (☎ 01-677 1646; 12-13 South Great George's St) With three branches in the city – including a spectacular one in Dublin's most beloved cafe, Bewley's of Grafton St – the folks behind Bardeli have hit the nail firmly on the head: great crispy pizzas with imaginative toppings such as spicy lamb and tzatziki, fresh homemade pastas, and salads such as broccoli, feta and chickpea that you'll dream about for days.

Green Nineteen (Map pp66-7; ☎ 01-478 9626; 19 Lower Camden St; mains €10-12; ⊙ 10am-11pm Mon-Sat, noon-6pm Sun) The newest addition to Camden St's growing corridor of cool is this sleek restaurant that specialises in locally sourced, organic grub – without the fancy price tag.

Silk Road Café (Map p72; ☎ 01-407 0770; Chester Beatty Library, Dublin Castle; mains around €11; ⊙ 11am-4pm Mon-Fri) The menu

Four Courts building (p78) and the O'Donovan Rossa Bridge

SEAN CAFFREY

is about two-thirds vegetarian, with house specialities of Greek moussaka and spinach lasagne complementing the deep-fried chickpeas and hummus starters. For dessert, there's Lebanese baklava and coconut *kataïfi* (angel-hair pastry), or you could opt for the juiciest dates this side of Tyre. All dishes are halal and kosher.

L'Gueuleton (Map p68; ☎ 01-675 3708; 1 Fade St; mains €12-25; 🕑 noon-3pm & 6-11.30pm Mon-Sat) Dubliners have a devil of a time pronouncing the name (which means 'the Gluttonous Feast' in French) and have had their patience tested with the no-reservations, get-in-line-and-wait policy, but they just can't get enough of this restaurant's take on French rustic cuisine, which makes twisted tongues and sore feet a small price to pay.

Odessa (Map p72; ☎ 01-670 7634; 13 Dame Ct; mains €13-25) Odessa's lounge atmosphere, with comfy sofas and retro standard lamps, has long attracted the city's hipsters, who flock here for homemade burgers, steaks or daily fish specials.

Weekend brunch is *extremely* popular: you have been warned.

Seagrass (Map pp52-3; ☎ 01-478 9595; 30 South Richmond St; mains €15-22; 🕑 6-11pm) Utterly unassuming from the outside, this is one of Dublin's best new openings of the last couple of years: the locally sourced, roughly Mediterranean menu (baked seafood penne, pan-fried lambs' livers and a bacon-and-cabbage risotto are typical) is uniformly excellent, the dining room is quietly elegant and the service absolutely perfect.

Eden (Map p72; ☎ 01-670 5372; Meeting House Sq; mains €15-28; 🕑 noon-2.30pm & 6-10.30pm Mon-Fri, noon-3pm & 6-11pm Sat & Sun) Eden is the epitome of Temple Bar chic with its trendy waitstaff, minimalist surroundings, high ceiling, hanging plants and terrace opening onto Meeting House Sq. But the food is the real star: unfussy modern Irish cuisine using organic seasonal produce, complemented by a carefully chosen wine list.

Bang (Map p68; ☎ 01-676 0898; www.bang restaurant.com; 11 Merrion Row; mains €16-36;

🕑 12.30-3pm & 6.30-10.30pm Mon-Sat) The modern European grub – carefully created by chef Lorcan Cribbin (ex-Ivy in London, don't you know) – is sharp, tasty and very much in demand. Reservations are a must, even for lunch.

Town Bar & Grill (Map p68; ☎ 01-662 4724; 21 Kildare St; mains €18-28; 🕑 noon-11pm Mon-Sat, to 10pm Sun) On any given night, you're likely to share this low-ceilinged basement dining room with a selection of Ireland's most affluent and influential people, who conduct their oh-so-important affairs barely above a murmur. But the slight stuffiness of the place is swept aside by the simply mouth-watering food, which ranges from lamb's liver to slow-rotated rabbit or sweet pepper-stuffed lamb.

Mermaid Café (Map p72; ☎ 01-670 8236; 22 Dame St; mains €18-31; 🕑 12.30-2.30pm & 6-11pm Mon-Sat, 12.30-3pm & 6-9pm Sun) The Mermaid is an American-style bistro with natural wood furniture and abstract canvases on its panelled walls. Its informal atmosphere, pure food and friendly staff make it difficult to get a table without booking.

Thornton's (Map p68; ☎ 01-478 7000; www.thorntonsrestaurant.com; 128 St Stephen's Green; midweek 2-/3-course lunch €25/38, dinner mains €45; 🕑 12.30-2pm & 7-10pm Tue-Sat) Kevin Thornton may have lost one of his two Michelin stars a few years ago, but he has proved somewhat defiantly that Michelin's loss was his customers' gain, and his mouth-watering interpretation of modern French cuisine is as superb as ever, with faultless service in a gorgeous room overlooking St Stephen's Green.

Restaurant Patrick Guilbaud (Map p68; ☎ 01-676 4192; www.restaurantpatrickguilbaud.ie; 21 Upper Merrion St; 2-/3-course set lunch €38/50, dinner mains €38-50; 🕑 12.30-2.30pm & 7.30-10.30pm Tue-Sat) With two Michelin stars on its resumé, this elegant restaurant is one of the best in Ireland, and head chef Guillaume Lebrun does his best to ensure that it stays that way. Next door to the Merrion Hotel, Guilbaud has French haute cuisine that is beautifully executed and served in delectable surroundings.

O'CONNELL STREET & AROUND

Bar Italia (Map p72; ☎ 01-874 1000; 28 Lower Ormond Quay; mains €9-18; 🕑 10.30am-11pm Mon-Sat, 1-9pm Sun) One of a new generation of eateries that's showing the more established Italian restaurants how the Old Country *really* eats, Bar Italia's specialities are its ever-changing pasta dishes, homemade risottos and excellent Palombini coffee.

Winding Stair (Map p72; ☎ 01-873 7320; 40 Lower Ormond Quay; mains €22-27; 🕑 noon-4pm & 6-10pm Tue-Sat, 1-10pm Sun) The wonderful Irish menu – creamy fish pie, bacon and organic cabbage, steamed mussels, and Irish farmyard cheeses – coupled with an excellent wine list make for a memorable meal.

Chapter One (Map pp66-7; ☎ 01-873 2266; www.chapteronerestaurant.com; 18 North Parnell Sq; mains €33-35; 🕑 12.30-2pm Tue-Fri, 6-11pm Tue-Sat) Southside snobs who think fine cuisine ends at the Liffey's edge have never had the pleasure of savouring the classic French cuisine in the best restaurant north of the river, situated in the lovely vaulted basement of the Dublin Writers Museum. That's probably because getting a table here can take months, which is what happens when Monsieur Michelin bestows one of his stars upon you. You'll have to book in advance, but the three-course pre-theatre special (€37.50; served before 7pm) is excellent.

DRINKING

It'll hardly come as a surprise that there are some good pubs in Dublin – it's probably one of the main reasons you came here in the first place – but first-time visitors may be taken aback by the protagonist's role the pub has in virtually every Dubliner's social life.

TRADITIONAL PUBS

Grogan's Castle Lounge (Map p68; ☎ 01-677 9320; 15 South William St) A city-centre institution, Grogan's has long been a favourite haunt of Dublin's writers, painters and others from the bohemian, alternative set. An odd quirk of the pub is that drinks are marginally cheaper at the stone-floor bar than in the carpeted lounge, even though they're served by the same bar!

John Mulligan's (Map p72; ☎ 01-677 5582; 8 Poolbeg St) Outside the eastern boundary of Temple Bar, John Mulligan's is another pub that has scarcely changed over the years. It featured as the local in the film *My Left Foot* and is also popular with journalists from the nearby newspaper offices. Mulligan's was established in 1782 and has long been reputed to have the best

Guinness in Ireland, as well as a wonderfully varied collection of regulars.

Stag's Head (Map p72; ☎ 01-679 3701; 1 Dame Ct) At the intersection of Dame Ct and Dame Lane, just off Dame St, the Stag's Head was built in 1770 and remodelled in 1895. It's sufficiently picturesque to have featured in a postage-stamp series depicting Irish pubs.

Long Hall (Map p68; ☎ 01-475 1590; 51 South Great George's St) Luxuriating in full Victorian splendour, this is one of the city's most beautiful and best-loved pubs. Check out the elegant chandeliers and the ornate carvings in the woodwork behind the bar. The bartenders are experts at their craft – an increasingly rare experience in Dublin these days.

Kehoe's (Map p68; ☎ 01-677 8312; 9 South Anne St) This is one of the most atmospheric pubs in the city centre and a real favourite with all kinds of Dubliners. It has a beautiful Victorian bar, a wonderful snug, and plenty of other little nooks and crannies. Upstairs, drinks are served in

OLIVER STREWE

Interior, the Stag's Head

DUBLIN

DRINKING

what was once the publican's living room. And it looks it!

James Toner's (Map p68; ☎ 01-676 3090; 139 Lower Baggot St) With its stone floor, Toner's is almost a country pub in the heart of the city, and the shelves and drawers are reminders that it once doubled as a grocery store. Not that its suit-wearing business crowd would ever have shopped here…

LIVE MUSIC PUBS

Hughes' Bar (Map p72; ☎ 01-872 6540; 19 Chancery St) Directly behind the Four Courts, this bar has nightly, if impromptu, sessions that often result in a closed door – that is, they go on long past official closing time. The pub is also a popular lunchtime spot with barristers working nearby.

Cobblestone (Map pp66-7; ☎ 01-872 1799; North King St) This pub is on the main square in Smithfield, an old northside marketplace. There's a great atmosphere in the cosy upstairs bar, where the nightly music sessions – both traditional and up-and-coming folk and singer-songwriter acts – are superb.

Oliver St John Gogarty's (Map p72; ☎ 01-671 1822; 58-59 Fleet St) You can hear live traditional music nightly at this busy Temple Bar pub, which caters to a mostly tourist crowd.

O'Donoghue's (Map p68; ☎ 01-661 4303; 15 Merrion Row) The most famous traditional music bar in Dublin, O'Donoghue's is where world-famous folk group the Dubliners started off in the 1960s. On summer evenings a young, international crowd spills out into the courtyard beside the pub.

BARS

Anseo (Map p68; ☎ 01-475 1321; 28 Lower Camden St) Unpretentious, unaffected and incredibly popular, this cosy alternative bar is a favourite with those who live by

the credo that to try too hard is far worse than not trying at all. Wearing cool like a loose garment, the punters thrive on the mix of chat and terrific music.

Bar With No Name (Map p68; ☎ 01-675 3708; 3 Fade St) A low-key entrance just next to L'Gueuleton leads upstairs to one of the nicest bar spaces in town – three huge rooms in a restored Victorian townhouse plus a sizeable heated patio area for smokers. There's no sign or a name – folks just refer to it as the bar with no name or, if you're a real insider, Number 3.

Hogan's (Map p68; ☎ 01-677 5904; 35 South Great George's St) Hogan's is a gigantic boozer spread across two floors. A popular hangout for young professionals, it gets very full at the weekend with folks eager to take advantage of its late licence.

Porterhouse (Map p72; ☎ 01-679 8847; 16-18 Parliament St) Dublin's first microbrewery is our favourite Temple Bar watering hole. Especially popular with foreign residents and visitors, the Porterhouse sells only its own stouts and beers – and they're all excellent.

ENTERTAINMENT
LIVE MUSIC

Bookings can be made either directly at the venues or through **HMV** (Map p68; ☎ 01-679 5334; 65 Grafton St) or **Ticketmaster** (☎ 0818 719 300, 01-456 9569; www.ticketmaster.ie), but they charge between 9% and 12.5% service charge *per ticket,* not per booking, on credit-card bookings.

CLASSICAL MUSIC & OPERA VENUES

National Concert Hall (Map pp66-7; ☎ 01-417 0000; www.nch.ie; Earlsfort Tce) Ireland's premier orchestral hall hosts a variety of concerts year-round, including a series of lunchtime concerts from 1.05pm to 2pm on Tuesdays, June to August.

DUBLIN

Traditional music played at O'Donoghue's

DOUG MCKINLAY

ENTERTAINMENT

Gaiety Theatre (Map p68; ☎ 01-677 1717; www.gaietytheatre.com; South King St) This popular Dublin theatre hosts a program of classical concerts and opera.

ROCK & POP VENUES
Crawdaddy (Map p66-7; ☎ 01-478 0225; www.pod.ie; 35A Harcourt St) Named after the London club where the Stones launched their professional careers in 1963, Crawdaddy is an intimate bar/venue that specialises in putting on rootsy performers, from African drum bands to avant-garde jazz artists and flamenco guitarists.

O2 (Map pp52-3; ☎ 01-819 8888; www.theo2.ie; East Link Bridge, North Wall Quay) Formerly the Point Depot, a complete overhaul of what was once a rail terminal (built in 1878) has resulted in this superb new venue with a capacity of around 10,000. The acoustics are sublime and the performing acts picked out of the very top drawer: Beyoncé, Britney and Neil Young are just some of the names that played here in 2009.

Olympia Theatre (Map p72; ☎ 01-677 7744; Dame St) This pleasantly tatty place features everything from disco to country on Friday nights; the eclectic 'Midnight at the Olympia' runs from midnight to 2am on Friday.

Sugar Club (Map pp66-7; ☎ 01-678 7188; 8 Lower Leeson St) There's live jazz, cabaret and soul music at weekends in this comfortable new theatre-style venue on the corner of St Stephen's Green.

Vicar Street (Map pp66-7; ☎ 01-454 5533; www.vicarstreet.com; 58-59 Thomas St) Smaller performances take place at this intimate venue, near Christ Church Cathedral. It has a capacity of 1000, spread between table-serviced group seating downstairs and a theatre-style balcony. It has a varied program of performers, with a strong emphasis on folk and jazz.

SPORT
Croke Park (Map pp52-3; ☎ 01-836 3222; www.crokepark.ie; Clonliffe Rd) Hurling and Gaelic football games are held from February to November at Europe's fourth-largest

DUBLIN

ENTERTAINMENT

Powerscourt Townhouse Shopping Centre

TONY WHEELER

stadium (capacity around 82,000), north of the Royal Canal in Drumcondra; see www.gaa.ie for schedules. Catch bus 19 or 19A to get there.

Aviva Stadium (Map pp52-3; ☎ 01-647 3800; www.avivastadium.ie; 11-12 Lansdowne Rd) The beloved Lansdowne Road stadium, the home of Irish rugby and international soccer, has been razed, rebuilt and renamed after its most prominent sponsor. The 50,000-capacity ground is scheduled to open in 2010.

THEATRE

Dublin's theatre scene is small but busy. Bookings can usually be made by quoting a credit-card number over the phone and tickets collected just before the performance.

Abbey Theatre (Map p72; ☎ 01-878 7222; www.abbeytheatre.ie; Lower Abbey St) It's scheduled to move to a purpose-built location in the Docklands, but for now Ireland's national theatre still resides in a large concrete box by the river. It puts on new Irish works, as well as revivals of classic Irish plays by writers such as WB Yeats, JM Synge, Sean O'Casey, Brendan Behan and Samuel Beckett. Tickets for evening performances cost up to €25, except on Monday, when they're cheaper. The smaller **Peacock Theatre** (Map p72; ☎ 01-878 7222) is part of the same complex and stages more fringe work.

Ark (Map p72; ☎ 01-670 7788; 11A Eustace St) A 150-seat venue that stages shows for kids aged between five and 13.

Gaiety Theatre (Map p68; ☎ 01-677 1717; www.gaietytheatre.com; South King St) Opened in 1871, this theatre is used for modern plays, TV shows, musical comedies and revues.

Gate Theatre (Map pp66-7; ☎ 01-874 4045; www.gatetheatre.ie; 1 Cavendish Row) To the north of the Liffey, the Gate Theatre specialises in international classics and older Irish works with a touch of comedy by playwrights such as Oscar Wilde, George Bernard Shaw and Oliver Goldsmith, although newer plays are sometimes staged too. Prices vary according to what's on, but they're usually around €20.

Project Arts Centre (Map p72; ☎ 1850 260 027; www.project.ie; 39 East Essex St) This centre puts on excellent productions of experimental plays by up-and-coming Irish and foreign writers.

SHOPPING

British and US chains dominate the high street and major shopping centres but there are also numerous small, independent shops selling high-quality, locally made goods. Irish designer clothing and streetwear, handmade jewellery, unusual homewares and crafts, and cheeses to die for are readily available if you know where to look.

Powerscourt Townhouse Shopping Centre (Map p68; ☎ 01-679 4144; 59 South William St) This absolutely gorgeous and stylish centre is in a carefully refurbished Georgian town house, originally built between 1741 and 1744. These days its best known for its cafes and restaurants but it still does a top-end, selective trade in high fashion, art, exquisite handicrafts and other chichi sundries.

Costume (Map p68; ☎ 01-679 5200; 10 Castle Market) From casuals to sparkly full-length dresses, Costume specialises in stylish contemporary women's wear from young European designers. Its own Costume label sits alongside pieces by Isabel Marant, Anna Sui, Jonathan Saunders and Irish label Leighlee.

Avoca Handweavers (Map p72; ☎ 01-677 4215; 11-13 Suffolk St) This contemporary craft shop is a treasure trove of interesting Irish and foreign products. The colourful shop is chock-a-block with woollen knits, ceramics, handcrafted gadgets and a wonderful toy selection – and not a tweed cap in sight.

Claddagh Records (Map p72; ☎ 01-677 0262; 2 Cecilia St) This shop sells a wide range of Irish traditional and folk music.

Kilkenny Shop (Map p68; ☎ 01-677 7066; 6 Nassau St) This shop has a wonderful selection of finely made Irish crafts, featuring clothing, glassware, pottery, jewellery, crystal and silver from some of Ireland's best designers.

GETTING THERE & AWAY
AIR

Dublin Airport (Map p110; ☎ 01-814 1111; www.dublinairport.com), 13km north of the centre, is Ireland's major international gateway airport, with direct flights from Europe, North America and Asia.

BOAT

Dublin has two ferry ports: the **Dun Laoghaire ferry terminal** (☎ 01-280 1905; Dun Laoghaire), 13km southeast of the city, serves Holyhead in Wales and can be reached by DART to Dun Laoghaire, or bus 7, 7A or 8 from Burgh Quay or bus 46A from Trinity College; and the **Dublin Port terminal** (Map p110; ☎ 01-855 2222; Alexandra Rd), 3km northeast of the city centre, which serves Holyhead and Liverpool.

Buses from Busáras (below) are timed to coincide with arrivals and departures: for the 9.45am ferry departure from Dublin Port, buses leave Busáras at 8.30am. For the 9.45pm departure, buses depart from Busáras at 8.30pm. For the 1am sailing to Liverpool, the bus departs from Busáras at 11.45pm. All bus trips cost adult/child €2.50/1.25.

See p407 for details of ferry journeys.

BUS

Busáras (Map pp66-7; ☎ 01-836 6111; www.buseireann.ie; Store St), the main bus station, is just north of the river behind Custom House, and serves as the main city stop for **Bus Éireann** (www.buseireann.ie).

For information on fares, frequencies and durations to various destinations in

DUBLIN

SHOPPING

the Republic and Northern Ireland, see p411.

TRAIN

For general train information, contact **Iarnród Éireann Travel Centre** (Map p72; ☎ 01-836 6222; www.irishrail.ie; 35 Lower Abbey St; ☒ 9am-5pm Mon-Fri, 9am-1pm Sat). **Connolly Station** (Map pp66-7; ☎ 01-836 3333), just north of the Liffey and the city centre, is the station for trains to Belfast, Derry, Sligo and other northern destinations. **Heuston Station** (Map pp66-7; ☎ 01-836 5421), just south of the Liffey and well west of the centre, is the station for Cork, Galway, Killarney, Limerick, Wexford, Waterford and other destinations west, south and southwest of Dublin. See p414 for more information.

GETTING AROUND
TO/FROM THE AIRPORT

There is no train service to/from Dublin airport, but there are several bus and taxi options.

BUS

Aircoach (☎ 01-844 7118; www.aircoach.ie; one way/return €7/12) Private coach service with two routes from the airport to 18 destinations throughout the city, including the main streets of the city centre. Coaches run every 10 to 15 minutes between 6am and midnight, then hourly from midnight until 6am.
Airlink Express Coach (☎ 01-872 0000, 873 4222; www.dublinbus.ie; adult/child €6/3) Bus 747 runs every 10 to 20 minutes from 5.45am to 11.30pm between the airport, the central bus station (Busáras; p93) and the Dublin Bus office on Upper O'Connell St; bus 748 runs every 15 to 30 minutes from 6.50am to 10.05pm between the airport and Heuston and Connolly Stations.

Dublin Bus (Map pp66-7; ☎ 01-872 0000; www.dublinbus.ie; 59 Upper O'Connell St; adult/child €2.20/1) A number of buses serve the airport from various points in Dublin, including buses 16A (Rathfarnham), 746 (Dun Laoghaire) and 230 (Portmarnock); all cross the city centre on their way to the airport.

TAXI

There is a taxi rank directly outside the arrivals concourse. A taxi should cost about €20 from the airport to the city centre, including a supplementary charge of €2.50 (not applied going to the airport). Make sure the meter is switched on.

BICYCLE

In September 2009, Dublin City Council launched **DublinBikes** (www.dublinbikes.ie), a pay-as-you-go bike scheme, similar to the Parisian Vélib' system, with 450 bikes at 40 stations spread throughout the city centre. Cyclists must purchase a €10 Smart Card (as well as put down a credit-card deposit of €150) – either online or at any of the stations – before 'freeing' a bike for use, which is then free for the first 30 minutes and €0.50 for each half-hour thereafter.

PUBLIC TRANSPORT
BUS

The office of **Dublin Bus** (Map pp66-7; ☎ 01-872 0000; www.dublinbus.ie; 59 Upper O'Connell St; ☒ 9am-5.30pm Mon-Fri, 9am-2pm Sat) has free single-route timetables of all its services.

Buses run from around 6am (some start at 5.30am) to 11.30pm. Fares are calculated according to stages: one to three stages costs €1.15; four to seven stages, €1.60; eight to 13 stages, €1.80; and 14 to 23 stages, €2.20. You must use exact change for tickets when boarding buses; anything more and you will be given a receipt for reimbursement, which is possible only at the Dublin Bus main office.

JONATHAN SMITH

Irish Museum of Modern Art (p74)

LUAS

The **Luas** (www.luas.ie; ⊙ 5.30am-12.30am Mon-Fri, from 6.30am Sat, 7am-11.30pm Sun) light-rail system has two lines: the Green Line (trains run every five to 15 minutes), which connects St Stephen's Green with Sandyford in south Dublin via Ranelagh and Dundrum; and the Red Line (trains run every 20 minutes), which runs from Lower Abbey St to Tallaght via the north quays and Heuston Station. There are ticket machines at every stop or you can buy tickets from newsagencies throughout the city centre; a typical short-hop fare will cost you €1.90.

NITELINK

These late-night buses run from the College St, Westmoreland St and D'Olier St triangle (at Trinity College's northwest corner), covering most of Dublin's suburbs. Buses leave at 12.30am and 2am Monday to Wednesday, and every 20 minutes between 12.30am and 3.30am Thursday to Saturday. Tickets start at €4.

TRAIN

The **Dublin Area Rapid Transport** (DART; ☎ 01-836 6222; www.irishrail.ie) provides quick train access to the coast as far north as Howth (about 30 minutes) and as far south as Greystones in County Wicklow. Pearse Station (Map pp66-7) is convenient for central Dublin south of the Liffey, and Connolly Station for north of the Liffey. There are services every 10 to 20 minutes, sometimes even more frequently, from around 6.30am to midnight Monday to Saturday; services are less frequent on Sunday. Dublin to Dun Laoghaire takes about 15 to 20 minutes. A one-way DART ticket from Dublin to Dun Laoghaire or Howth costs €2.20; to Bray it's €2.50.

There are also suburban rail services north as far as Dundalk, inland to Mullingar and south past Bray to Arklow.

You can get fare-saver passes from www.dublinbus.ie or at the Dublin Tourism Office (p65). Some examples: **Adult (Bus & Rail) Short Hop (€10.20)** Valid for unlimited one-day travel on

Georgian doorways near Merrion Square (p73)

OLIVIER CIRENDINI

Dublin Bus, DART, Luas and suburban rail travel, but not Nitelink or Airlink.

Bus/Luas Pass (1/7 days €7/29) One-day unlimited travel on both bus and Luas.

Family (Bus & Rail) Short Hop (€15.60) Valid for travel for unlimited one-day travel for a family of two adults and four children aged under 16 on all bus and rail services except for Nitelink, Airlink, ferry services and tours.

Rambler Pass (1/3/5 days €6/13.30/20) Valid for unlimited travel on all Dublin Bus and Airlink services, but not Nitelink.

TAXI

From 8am to 10pm, taxi fares begin with a flagfall of €4.10, followed by around €1 per kilometre thereafter; from 10pm to 8am, it's €4.45 flagfall and €1.35 per kilometre. Extra charges include €1 for each extra passenger and €2 for telephone bookings; there is no charge for luggage.

Taxis can be hailed on the street and found at **taxi ranks** around the city, including O'Connell St, College Green (in front of Trinity College) and St Stephen's Green at the end of Grafton St. There are numerous taxi companies that will dispatch taxis by radio. Some options:

City Cabs (☎ 01-872 2688)

National Radio Cabs (☎ 01-677 2222)

Phone the **Garda Carriage Office** (☎ 01-475 5888) if you have any complaints about taxis or queries regarding lost property.

EASTERN IRELAND

EASTERN IRELAND

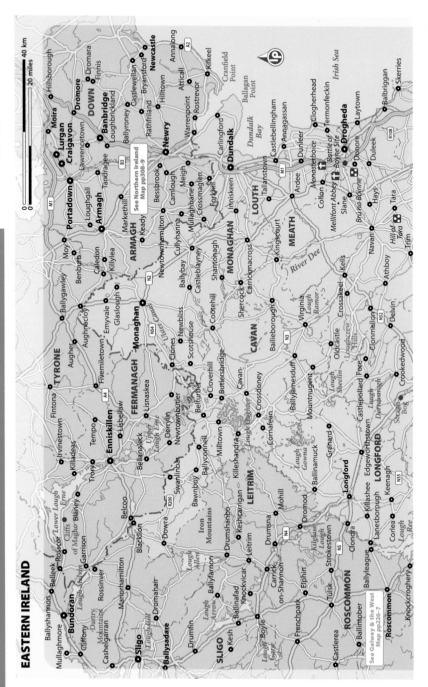

See Northern Ireland Map pp308-9

See Galway & the West Map pp226-7

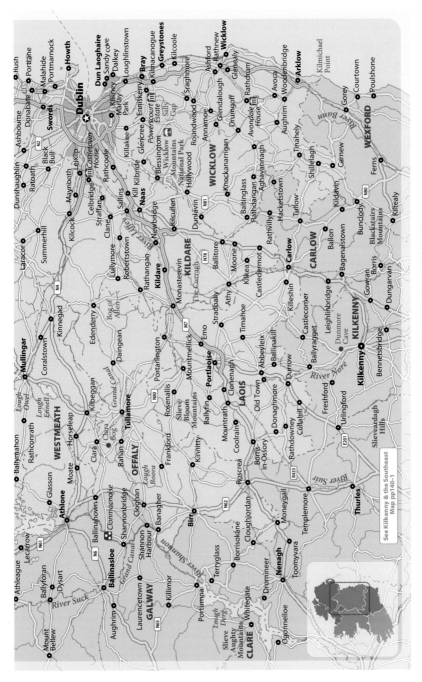

EASTERN IRELAND HIGHLIGHTS

1   BRÚ NA BÓINNE

BY MARY GIBBONS, HERITAGE TOUR SPECIALIST

Newgrange and its surrounding tombs of Knowth and Dowth – known in Irish mythology as Brú na Bóinne, it was the home of the god Dagda and his wife Bóinne (the River Boyne), and later the burial place of the pagan kings of Tara – are one of only three World Heritage sites in Ireland.

➘ MARY GIBBONS' DON'T MISS LIST

❶ GREAT STONE CIRCLE

The great stone circle surrounding Newgrange (p125) is the largest of its kind in Ireland; although only 12 are left, there were once 35-odd standing stones. It's believed to have been an astronomical calendar, with shadows dividing the year into times of planting and harvest.

❷ THE KERBSTONES

The decorated kerbstones built into the outside of the great passage tomb are part of a neolithic art tradition which spanned over a thousand years. The most magnificent is found at the entrance, forming a symbolic barrier between the living and the dead; a second decorated stone is diametrically opposite, perhaps marking a 'symbolic exit'.

❸ THE PASSAGE

The 19m stone tunnel passage that leads into the mound has some of the most beautifully executed neolithic art anywhere in the world. Individual decorated stones alternate with undecorated ones. Just before the inner chamber is

Clockwise from top: Newgrange (p125), Tomb interior, Knowth (p126); Newgrange; Carved kerbstone, Newgrange; Visitors witnessing winter solstice at Newgrange

one of the most famous pieces of neolithic art in Ireland: a triple spiral framed by triple lines in a chevron pattern.

❹ THE INNER CHAMBER

The inner chamber, rediscovered in 1699 by one of the victors of the Battle of the Boyne, is a corbelled, cruciform-shaped space over 6m high, with three heavily decorated recesses; one has a triple spiral regarded by Dr Geraldine Stout, the foremost authority on Newgrange, as 'the most exquisite carving to be found in the entire corpus of European megalithic art'.

❺ THE WINTER SOLSTICE EVENT

For 17 minutes of magic on the morning of 21 December, the light of the rising sun funnels through a light-box above the main passage entrance and illuminates the passageway and the main chamber to reveal one of the world's most extraordinary prehistoric art galleries. At other times of the year visitors witness an inspiring recreation of this singular event.

↘ THINGS YOU NEED TO KNOW

Best time to visit Midweek outside of the summer months **Advance planning** Enter the Winter Solstice lottery before 25 September to have a chance of winning one of 50 tickets to the once-in-a-lifetime event **Resources** www.heritageireland.ie **For full details, see 124.**

EASTERN IRELAND HIGHLIGHTS

2

⬐ GLENDALOUGH

The simply extraordinary monastic remains at Glendalough (p114) are reason enough to make the visit, but once you're there you'll see why St Kevin chose this particular spot to set up shop: nestled in a tree-dotted glacial valley and bordered by two lakes, Glendalough is without a doubt one of the most beautiful corners of the whole country.

3

⬐ MONASTERBOICE

Most Irish monastic sites are soaked in atmosphere, but Monasterboice (p138) has an extra-special hue. The ancient church ruins, the near-perfect round tower and the exquisite high crosses dotted around a grass-covered cemetery make this site at the end of a country lane one of Ireland's most beautiful. Best of all, it doesn't get nearly as many visitors as its competitors.

4

⬎ MELLIFONT ABBEY

Of Ireland's one-time powerful abbeys, none is more evocative of its past than Mellifont Abbey (p137), built by the Cistercians and once their most magnificent domicile: a home for 400 monks and a motherhouse for 21 lesser monasteries spread throughout the country. The ruins are beautiful, and the adjacent rushing stream gives the whole place a romantic feel.

5

⬎ POWERSCOURT ESTATE

For a sense of how well the powerful and mighty Anglo-Normans lived, wander the magnificent Italianate gardens of Powerscourt Estate (p111), soak up the superb views of nearby Sugarloaf and then peek inside the former home of the Power family. This isn't how the other half lived, but how the other half *per cent* lived.

6

⬎ CASTLETOWN HOUSE

William Conolly was Speaker of the Irish House of Commons and, conveniently, Ireland's richest man, so he commissioned construction of the breathtaking Castletown House (p122), near Maynooth, County Kildare. Its classical Palladian style would influence the architects of the soon-to-be-constructed Washington, DC.

2 STEPHEN SAKS; 3, 5 & 6 RICHARD CUMMINS; 4 EOIN CLARKE

2 St Kevin's Kitchen, Glendalough (p116), County Wicklow; 3 Monasterboice (p138), County Louth; 4 Mellifont Abbey (p137), County Louth; 5 Powerscourt Estate (p111), County Wicklow; 6 Castletown House (p122), County

EASTERN IRELAND

EASTERN IRELAND'S BEST...

EASTERN IRELAND'S BEST...

⚑ BEAUTY SPOTS

- **Sally Gap** (p113) Cut across the Wicklow Mountains.
- **Avondale House** (p120) Where Parnell would retreat to.
- **Powerscourt Estate** (p111) The most beautiful garden in Ireland?
- **Hill of Tara** (p128) Ireland's most sacred turf.
- **Loughcrew Cairns** (p134) Superb views from the top of the hill.

⚑ GOURMET EXPERIENCES

- **The House** (p108) If only home dining was this good.
- **Organic Life/Marc Michel** (p120) All organic, from farm to food.
- **Rathsallagh House** (p118) Luxury, quality and style in a fine Palladian mansion.
- **Eastern Seaboard Bar & Grill** (p136) Drogheda's finest eatery.
- **Ballyknocken House** (p120) Learn to cook like a gourmet chef.

⚑ HISTORICAL SPOTS

- **Battle of the Boyne Site** (p128) King James got whupped here by King William of Orange in 1690.
- **Hill of Tara** (p128) Home of the High Kings.
- **Monasterboice** (p138) One of Ireland's most important monasteries.
- **Avondale House** (p120) Charles Parnell's country pile.
- **Russborough House** (p118) A thieves' paradise?

⚑ THINGS FOR FREE

- **Glendalough** (p114) Monastic magic in the valley.
- **Battle of the Boyne Site** (p128) The eye of Irish history's storm.
- **Mellifont Abbey** (p137) Handsome ruins of a mighty Cistercian abbey.
- **Monasterboice** (p138) Visit the marvellous high crosses.
- **Loughcrew Cairns** (p134) Little-visited neolithic passage graves.

MARTIN MOOS

Powerscourt Estate (p111)

THINGS YOU NEED TO KNOW

⤷ VITAL STATISTICS

- **Area** 6567 sq km
- **Population** 537,775
- **Best time to go** Summer or autumn

⤷ AREAS IN A NUTSHELL

- **County Dublin** (p108) Howth is Dublin's loveliest harbour village.
- **County Wicklow** (p108) Savage scenery, monastic calm and stately homes next to the Dublin suburbs.
- **County Kildare** (p123) Wealthy, genteel and full of really expensive racehorses.
- **County Meath** (p124) Pastoral landscape replete with both ancient and more recent history.
- **County Louth** (p135) The 'Wee County' is packed with historic sites and prehistoric ruins.

⤷ ADVANCE PLANNING

- **Ten months before** Put your name into the Winter Solstice lottery at Brú na Bóinne.
- **One month before** Sort out your accommodation.
- **Two weeks before** Check out the weather forecast. Then ignore it.

⤷ RESOURCES

- **Wicklow National Park** (www .wicklownationalpark.ie) All the info on the national park, including walks and visits to Glendalough.

- **Heritage Ireland** (www.heritage ireland.ie) The Heritage Service is responsible for Glendalough, Brú na Bóinne and other sites of historical and archaeological importance.
- **Bus Eireann** (www.buseireann.ie) Official site for the national bus service, which is handy for getting around the region.
- **Battle of the Boyne** (www.battleof theboyne.ie) All the info on one of the most decisive battles of Irish history.

⤷ GETTING AROUND

- **Bus** Good bus networks cover most of the East Coast.
- **Train** Good service along the coast only – fine for coastal Wicklow and up to Drogheda.
- **Car** The best way of getting around; watch out for commuter traffic!

⤷ BE FOREWARNED

- **Crowds** Be prepared for summer crowds and traffic jams, especially in the Wicklow Mountains and the N11 south through Wicklow.
- **School Tours** Brú na Bóinne is not just spectacular, but educational and very popular with school outings.
- **Weather** The Wicklow Mountains ain't high, but they can get very cold. Come prepared.

EASTERN IRELAND

THINGS YOU NEED TO KNOW

EASTERN IRELAND ITINERARIES

IN & OUT FROM DUBLIN Three Days

Happily, all of the attractions mentioned in this chapter are but an easy hop from the capital, which you can use as a base for your explorations. Start southward, in the Wicklow Mountains, taking in (1) Glendalough (p114) and (2) Powerscourt Estate (p111), both of which can be visited in the morning – most organised tours take in both. In the afternoon, venture southward to Rathdrum and pay a visit to (3) Avondale House (p120), which you can get to by public transport. On the second day explore the magnificent (4) Brú na Bóinne (p124), leaving a visit to (5) Castletown House (p122) until day three.

HISTORY & HEDONISM Five Days

This five-day route explores the rich heritage that surrounds Dublin but doesn't forget that with all that learning must come a little bit of fun. When you've done exploring (1) Glendalough (p114) and (2) Powerscourt Estate (p111), head south into Southern Wicklow to set up luxurious camp at (3) Brook Lodge (p121). If you fancy a more hands-on rest, put on the apron at (4) Ballynocken House (p120) and learn the essentials of Irish gourmet cooking. After a couple of days of R&R, cross into County Kildare to (5) Maynooth (p123), visiting St Patrick's College before pitching your tent at Carton House (p123), home to two exquisite golf courses. You can spend the rest of your time here, or if the golf bug has bitten, get over to the nearby (6) K Club (p123) in Straffan, and imagine that you too are playing in the Ryder Cup.

SHADES OF GREEN One Week

Sure, you can rush through the counties surrounding the capital, but if you have the time, linger a while and appreciate sometimes subtle – but often dramatic – changes in scenery. To the north, Counties Meath and Louth are flecked with rich pastures across rolling hills; you can best appreciate these from the once blood-soaked (1) Battle of the Boyne site (p128) – now just gentle fields on either side of the river – but you'll really know what we mean by standing atop the (2) Hill of Tara (p128) to survey the rich archaeological expanse of what was once known as the 'Middle Kingdom'. Next, explore the flatter pastures of County Kildare, long known as horse country for the sheer number of stud farms in the area. All this gentleness, however, is but preparation for the drama that occurs once you cross the border into Wicklow. Here, the gorse-and-bracken mountains rise up steeply, creating an often forbidding wall that can be crossed only through the likes of

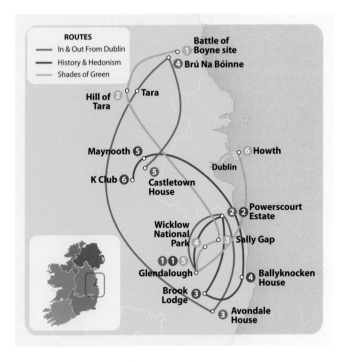

ROUTES
- In & Out From Dublin
- History & Hedonism
- Shades of Green

Battle of
❶ Boyne site
❹ Brú Na Bóinne
Tara
Hill of ❷ Tara
Maynooth ❺   ❻ Howth
❺   Dublin
K Club ❻ Castletown
House
❷ ❷ Powerscourt
Estate
Wicklow
National
Park ❹   ❸ Sally Gap
❶❶❺
Glendalough   ❹ Ballyknocken
House
Brook
Lodge ❸
❸ Avondale
House

the (3) Sally Gap (p113). You could spend a couple of days within the confines of the (4) Wicklow National Park (p108), within which you'll find (5) Glendalough (p114). Return back to Dublin and make your way to (6) Howth (p108); climb to the top of the hill and survey the capital as you've never seen it before.

DISCOVER EASTERN IRELAND

Dublin is surrounded by a handful of counties that offer a variety of experiences. To the south is Wicklow, the 'Garden of Ireland': the magnificent gorse-and-bracken spine of rugged mountain that runs down its middle hides some stunning glacial valleys, ancient ruins and some of the country's finest Georgian buildings. Southwest is pastoral Kildare, the home of Irish horse racing and some of the richest farmland in the country – what it lacks in drama and history it more than makes up for in beautiful countryside.

Northwest is Meath, once one of the five provinces of ancient Ireland. The 'Middle Kingdom' attracted Ireland's first settlers, who left behind the Boyne Valley's magnificent neolithic monuments. Further north is Louth, the 'Wee County' – it may be small, but it packs a scenic punch: the ruins of Mellifont and Monasterboice are but two of the county's big attractions.

Before you head for the hills, spare a thought for Dublin's suburbs themselves: amid the grey concrete are some wonderful little seaside villages.

COUNTY DUBLIN

HOWTH

The pretty fishing village of Howth (Binn Éadair; Map p110), built on steep steps that run down to the waterfront, is a popular excursion from Dublin and has developed as a residential suburb of the city. The most desirable properties are on the hill above the village, located on a bulbous head that juts into the northern edge of Dublin Bay. The views from the top are magnificent. Although the harbour's role as a shipping port has long gone, Howth is a major fishing centre and yachting harbour.

EATING

ourpick **The House** (☎ 01-839 6388; www. thehouse-howth.ie; 4 Main St; mains €16-22; ☺ 9am-3pm Mon-Fri, 11.30am-3pm & 6-11pm Sat & Sun) One of our favourite new openings in Dublin is this wonderful spot on the main street leading away from the harbour. In the handsome, airy dining room you can feast on dishes like crunchy Bellingham blue cheese polenta or wild Wicklow venison stew, as well as a fine selection of fish.

GETTING THERE & AWAY

The easiest and quickest way to get to Howth from Dublin is on the DART, which whisks you there in just over 20 minutes for a fare of €2.20. For the same fare, buses 31 and 31A from Lower Abbey St in the city centre run as far as the Summit, 5km to the southeast of Howth.

COUNTY WICKLOW

NATIONAL PARKS

Wicklow Mountains National Park covers more than 170 sq km of mountainous blanket bogs and woodland. Plans to extend it will eventually see virtually all of the higher ground stretching the length of the mountains fall under the protection

DETOUR: SANDYCOVE & JAMES JOYCE MUSEUM

About 12km southeast of Dublin is **Sandycove** (Map p110), with a pretty little beach and a **Martello tower** – built by British forces to keep an eye out for a Napoleonic invasion – now housing the **James Joyce Museum** (☎ 01-280 9265; www.visitdublin.com; Joyce Tower, Sandycove; adult/child/student €6.70/4.20/5.70; ⏰ 10am-1pm & 2-5pm Mon-Sat, 2-6pm Sun Apr-Oct, by appointment only Nov-Mar). This is where the action begins in James Joyce's epic novel *Ulysses*. The museum was opened in 1962 by Sylvia Beach, the Paris-based publisher who first dared to put *Ulysses* into print, and has photographs, letters, documents, various editions of Joyce's work and two death masks of Joyce on display.

Below the Martello tower is the **Forty Foot Pool**, an open-air, sea-water bathing pool that took its name from the army regiment, the Fortieth Foot, that was stationed at the tower until the regiment was disbanded in 1904. At the close of the first chapter of *Ulysses*, Buck Mulligan heads off to the Forty Foot Pool for a morning swim. A morning wake-up here is still a local tradition, winter or summer. In fact, a winter dip isn't much braver than a summer one since the water temperature varies by only about 5°C (9°F). Basically, it's always bloody cold.

Pressure from female bathers eventually opened this public stretch of water – originally nudist and for men only – to both sexes, despite strong opposition from the 'forty foot gentlemen'. They eventually compromised with the ruling that a 'Togs Must Be Worn' sign would apply after 9am. Prior to that time nudity prevails and swimmers are still predominantly male.

The DART train runs from Dublin to Sandycove (€2.30, 27 minutes).

of the national park, which will cover more than 300 sq km.

Most of Ireland's native mammal species can be found within the confines of the park. Large herds of deer roam on the open hill areas, though these were introduced in the 20th century as the native red-deer population became extinct during the first half of the 18th century. The uplands are the preserve of foxes, badgers and hares. Red squirrels are usually found in the pine woodlands – look out for them around the Upper Lake.

The bird population of the park is plentiful. Birds of prey abound, the most common being peregrine falcons, marlins, kestrels, hawks and sparrowhawks. Hen harriers are a rarer sight, though they too live in the park. Moorland birds found in the area include meadow pipits and skylarks. Less common birds such as whinchats, ring ouzels and dippers can be spotted, as can red grouse, whose numbers are quickly disappearing in other parts of Ireland. For information, call in or contact the **National Park Information Point** (Map p114; ☎ 0404-45425; www.wicklownationalpark.ie; Bolger's Cottage, Miners' Rd, Upper Lake, Glendalough; ⏰ 10am-6pm May-Sep, to dusk Sat & Sun Oct-Apr), off the Green Rd that runs by the Upper Lake, about 2km from the Glendalough Visitor Centre. There's usually someone on hand to help, but if you find it closed the staff may be out running guided walks. *Exploring the Glendalough Valley* (Heritage Service;

COUNTY DUBLIN

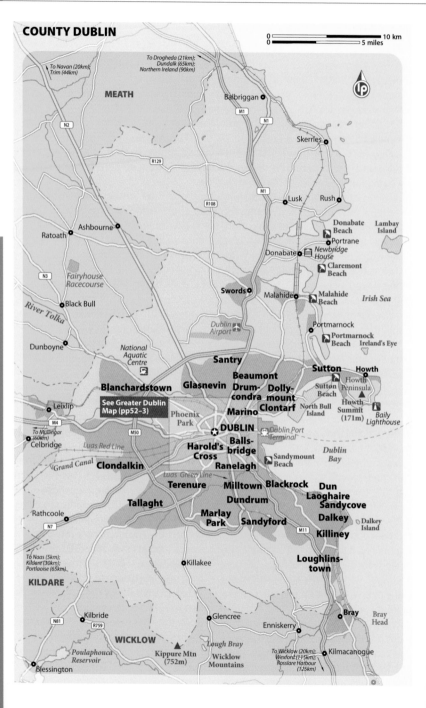

€2) is a good booklet on the trails in the area.

WICKLOW MOUNTAINS

As you leave Dublin and cross into Wicklow, the landscape changes – dramatically. From Killakee, still in Dublin, the Military Rd begins a 30km southward journey across vast sweeps of gorse-, bracken- and heather-clad moors, bogs, and mountains dotted with small corrie lakes.

The peaks are marvellously desolate and as raw as only nature can be. Between the mountains are a number of deep glacial valleys, most notably Glenmacnass, Glenmalure and Glendalough; while corrie lakes such as Lough Bray Upper and Lower, gouged out by ice at the head of the glaciers, complete the wild topography.

The narrow Military Rd winds its way through the most remote parts of the mountains, offering some extraordinary views of the surrounding countryside. The best place to join it is at Glencree (from Enniskerry). It then runs south through the Sally Gap, Glenmacnass Valley and Laragh, then on to Glenmalure Valley and Aghavannagh.

ENNISKERRY & POWERSCOURT ESTATE

pop 2672

Found at the top of the '21 Bends', as the winding R117 from Dublin is known, the handsome village of Enniskerry is home to art galleries and the kind of all-organic gourmet cafes that would treat you as a war criminal if you admitted to eating battery eggs. Such preening self-regard is a far cry from the village's origins, when Richard Wingfield, earl of nearby Powerscourt, commissioned a row of terraced cottages for his labourers in 1760. These days, you'd want to have laboured pretty successfully to get your hands on one of them.

The village is lovely, but the main reason for its popularity is the magnificent 64-sq-km **Powerscourt Estate** (☎ 01-204 6000; www.powerscourt.ie; adult/child/student €8/5/7; ☑ 9.30am-5.30pm Feb-Oct, to 4.30pm Nov-

Walking near the Wicklow Mountains

EOIN CLARKE

Jan), which gives contemporary observers a true insight into the style of the 18th-century super-rich. The main entrance is 500m south of the village square.

The estate has existed more or less since 1300, when the LePoer (later anglicised to Power) family built themselves a castle here. The property changed Anglo-Norman hands a few times before coming into the possession of Richard Wingfield, newly appointed Marshall of Ireland, in 1603 – his descendants were to live here for the next 350 years. In 1731 the Georgian wunderkind Richard Cassels (or Castle) was given the job of building a Palladian-style mansion around the core of the old castle. He finished the job in 1743, but an extra storey was added in 1787 and other alterations were made in the 19th century.

Easily the biggest drawcards of the whole pile are the simply magnificent 20-hectare formal gardens and the breathtaking views that accompany them. Originally laid out in the 1740s, the gardens were redesigned in the

19th century by Daniel Robinson, who had as much fondness for the booze as he did for horticultural pursuits: he liked (needed?) to be wheeled around in a wheelbarrow after a certain point in the day. Perhaps this influenced his largely informal style, which resulted in a magnificent blend of landscaped gardens, sweeping terraces, statuary, ornamental lakes, secret hollows, rambling walks and walled enclosures replete with more than 200 types of trees and shrubs, all beneath the stunning natural backdrop of the Great Sugarloaf Mountain to the southeast. Tickets come with a map laying out 40-minute and hour-long tours of the gardens.

A 7km walk to a separate part of the estate takes you to the 130m **Powerscourt Waterfall** (adult/child/student €5/3.50/4.50; 9.30am-7pm May-Aug, 10.30am-5.30pm Mar-Apr & Sep-Oct, to 4.30pm Nov-Jan). It's the highest waterfall in Britain and Ireland, and is most impressive after heavy rain. You can also get to the falls by road, following the signs from the estate. A nature trail has been

GREG GAWLOWSKI

Powerscourt Estate

laid out around the base of the waterfall, taking you past giant redwoods, ancient oaks, beech, birch and rowan trees. There are plenty of birds in the vicinity, including the chaffinch, cuckoo, chiffchaff, raven and willow warbler.

TOURS

All tours that take in Powerscourt start in Dublin.

Bus Éireann (☎ 01-836 6111; www.buseireann.ie; Busáras; adult/child/student €28.80/22.50/25.20; ☼ 10am mid-Mar–Oct) A whole-day tour that takes in Powerscourt and Glendalough (all admissions included), departing from Busáras (Map pp66-7).

Dublin Bus Tours (Map pp66-7; ☎ 01-872 0000; www.dublinbus.ie; 59 Upper O'Connell St; adult/child €25/12; ☼ 11am) A visit to Powerscourt is included in the four-hour South Coast & Gardens tour, which takes in the stretch of coastline between Dun Laoghaire and Killiney before turning inland to Wicklow and on to Enniskerry. Admission to the gardens is included.

Gray Line Tours (☎ 01-872 9010; www.irishcitytours.com; Gresham Hotel, O'Connell St; adult/student/child €35/32/25; ☼ 10am Fri-Sun) Incorporating Wicklow's big hits – Powerscourt, Glendalough and the lakes and a stop at Avoca, then takes in Dun Laoghaire and Dalkey (includes admission to Glendalough Visitor Centre and Powerscourt, but not coffee).

EATING

Johnnie Fox (☎ 01-295 5647; www.jfp.ie; Glencullen; Hungry Fisherman's seafood platter €29.95; ☼ noon-10pm) Busloads of tourists fill the place nightly throughout the summer, mostly for the knees-up, faux-Irish floorshow of music and dancing. But there's nothing contrived about the seafood, which is so damn good we'd happily sit through yet another chorus of *Danny Boy* and even consider joining in the jig. The pub is 3km northwest of Enniskerry in Glencullen.

GETTING THERE & AWAY

Enniskerry is 18km south of Dublin, just 3km west of the M11 along the R117. **Dublin Bus** (☎ 01-872 0000, 01-873 4222) service 44 (€2.20, every 20 minutes) takes about 1¼ hours to get to Enniskerry from Hawkins St in Dublin. Alternatively, you can take the DART train to Bray (€2.75) and catch bus 185 (€1.60, hourly) from the station, which takes an extra 40 minutes.

Getting to Powerscourt House under your own steam is not a problem (it's 500m from the town), but getting to the waterfall is tricky. **Alpine Coaches** (☎ 01-286 2547; www.alpinecoaches.ie) runs a shuttle service between the DART station in Bray, the waterfall (€6 return) and the house (€4.50). Shuttles leave Bray at 11.05am (11.30am July and August), 12.30pm, 1.30pm (and 3.30pm September to June) Monday to Saturday, and 11am, noon and 1pm Sunday. The last departure from Powerscourt House is at 5.30pm.

SALLY GAP

One of the two main east-west passes across the Wicklow Mountains, the Sally Gap is surrounded by some spectacular countryside. From the turn-off on the lower road (R755) between Roundwood and Kilmacanogue near Bray, the narrow road (R759) passes above the dark and dramatic Lough Tay, whose scree slopes slide into **Luggala** (Fancy Mountain). This almost fairy-tale estate is owned by one Garech de Brún, member of the Guinness family and founder of Claddagh Records, a leading producer of Irish traditional and folk music. The small River Cloghoge links Lough Tay with Lough Dan just to the south. It then heads up to the Sally

Gap crossroads, where it cuts across the Military Rd and heads northwest for Kilbride and the N81, following the young River Liffey, still only a stream.

GLENDALOUGH

pop 280

If you've come to Wicklow, chances are that a visit to Glendalough (Gleann dá Loch, 'Valley of the Two Lakes') is one of your main reasons for being here. And you're not wrong, for this is one of the most beautiful corners of the whole country and the epitome of the kind of rugged, romantic Ireland that probably drew you to the island in the first place.

The substantial remains of this important monastic settlement are certainly impressive, but the real draw is the splendid setting: two dark and mysterious lakes tucked into a deep valley covered in for-

est. It is, despite its immense popularity, a deeply tranquil and spiritual place, and you will have little difficulty in understanding why those solitude-seeking monks came here in the first place.

HISTORY

In AD 498 a young monk named Kevin arrived in the valley looking for somewhere to kick back, meditate and be at one with nature. He pitched up in what had been a Bronze Age tomb on the southern side of the Upper Lake and for the next seven years slept on stones, wore animal skins, maintained a near-starvation diet and – according to the legend – became bosom buddies with the birds and animals. Kevin's ecofriendly lifestyle soon attracted a bunch of disciples, all seemingly unaware of the irony that they were flocking to hang out with a hermit who wanted to

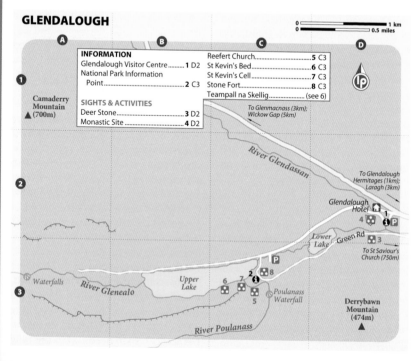

GLENDALOUGH

INFORMATION		
Glendalough Visitor Centre	**1** D2	
National Park Information		
Point	**2** C3	

SIGHTS & ACTIVITIES		
Deer Stone	**3** D2	
Monastic Site	**4** D2	

Reefert Church	**5** C3	
St Kevin's Bed	**6** C3	
St Kevin's Cell	**7** C3	
Stone Fort	**8** C3	
Teampall na Skellig	(see 6)	

0 — 1 km
0 — 0.5 miles

Camaderry Mountain ▲ (700m)

River Glendassan

To Glenmacnass (3km);
Wickow Gap (5km)

To Glendalough
Hermitages (1km);
Laragh (3km)

Glendalough Hotel

To St Saviour's
Church (750m)

Green Rd

Lower Lake

Waterfalls

River Glenealo

Upper Lake

Poulanass Waterfall

Derrybawn Mountain (474m) ▲

River Poulanass

EASTERN IRELAND

COUNTY WICKLOW

live as far away from other people as possible. Over the next couple of centuries his one-man operation mushroomed into a proper settlement and by the 9th century Glendalough rivalled Clonmacnoise (p250) as the island's premier monastic city. Thousands of students studied and lived in a thriving community that was spread over a considerable area.

Inevitably, Glendalough's success made it a key target of Viking raiders, who sacked the monastery at least four times between 775 and 1071. The final blow came in 1398, when English forces from Dublin almost completely destroyed it. Efforts were made to rebuild and some life lingered on here as late as the 17th century, when, under renewed repression, the monastery finally died.

ORIENTATION & INFORMATION

At the valley entrance, before the Glendalough Hotel, is the **Glendalough Visitor Centre** (☎ 0404-45325; www.heritage ireland.ie/en/MidlandsEastCoast/Glendalough VisitorCentre; adult/child & student €3/1; ◷ 9.30am-6pm mid-Mar–Oct, to 5pm Nov–mid-Mar). It has a high-quality 17-minute audiovisual presentation called *Ireland of the Monasteries*, which does exactly what it says on the tin.

SIGHTS

UPPER LAKE

The original site of St Kevin's settlement, **Teampall na Skellig** is at the base of the cliffs towering over the southern side of the Upper Lake and is accessible only by boat; unfortunately, there's no boat service to the site and you'll have to settle for looking at it across the lake. The terraced shelf has the reconstructed ruins of a church and early graveyard. Rough wattle huts once stood on the raised ground

STEPHEN SAKS
Round tower and ruins, Glendalough

nearby. Scattered around are some early grave slabs and simple stone crosses.

Just east of here and 10m above the lake waters is the 2m-deep artificial cave called **St Kevin's Bed**, said to be where Kevin lived. The earliest human habitation of the cave was long before St Kevin's era – there's evidence that people lived in the valley for thousands of years before the monks arrived. In the green area just south of the car park is a large circular wall thought to be the remains of an early Christian **stone fort** (caher).

Follow the lakeshore path southwest of the car park until you come to the considerable remains of **Reefert Church** above the tiny River Poulanass. It's a small, plain, 11th-century Romanesque nave-and-chancel church with some reassembled

Round tower and graveyard, Glendalough

JOHN ELK III

arches and walls. Traditionally, Reefert (literally 'Royal Burial Place') was the burial site of the chiefs of the local O'Toole family. The surrounding graveyard contains a number of rough stone crosses and slabs, most made of shiny mica schist.

Climb the steps at the back of the churchyard and follow the path to the west and you'll find, at the top of a rise overlooking the lake, the scant remains of **St Kevin's Cell**, a small beehive hut.

LOWER LAKE

While the Upper Lake has the best scenery, the most fascinating buildings lie in the lower part of the valley east of the Lower Lake, huddled together in the heart of the ancient **monastic site**.

Just round the bend from the Glendalough Hotel is the stone arch of the **monastery gatehouse**, the only surviving example of a monastic entranceway in the country. Just inside the entrance is a large slab with an incised cross.

Beyond that lies a **graveyard**, which is still in use. The 10th-century **round tower** is 33m tall and 16m in circumference at the base. The upper storeys and conical roof were reconstructed in 1876. Near the tower, to the southeast, is the **Cathedral of St Peter and St Paul** with a 10th-century nave. The chancel and sacristy date from the 12th century.

At the centre of the graveyard to the south of the round tower is the **Priest's House**. This odd building dates from 1170 but has been heavily reconstructed. It may have been the location of shrines of St Kevin. Later, during penal times, it became a burial site for local priests – hence the name. The 10th-century **St Mary's Church**, 140m southwest of the round tower, probably originally stood outside the walls of the monastery and belonged to local nuns. It has a lovely western doorway. A little to the east are the scant remains of **St Kieran's Church**, the smallest at Glendalough.

Glendalough's trademark is **St Kevin's Kitchen** or Church at the southern edge of the enclosure. This church, with a miniature round towerlike belfry, protruding sacristy and steep stone roof, is a masterpiece. How it came to be known as a kitchen is a mystery as there's no indication that it was anything other than a church. The oldest parts of the building date from the 11th century – the structure has been remodelled since but it's still a classic early Irish church.

At the junction with Green Rd as you cross the river just south of these two churches is the **Deer Stone** in the middle of a group of rocks. Legend claims that when St Kevin needed milk for two orphaned babies, a doe stood here waiting to be milked. The stone is actually a *bullaun* (a stone used as a mortar for grinding medicines or food). Many such stones are thought to be prehistoric, and they were widely regarded as having supernatural properties: women who bathed their faces with water from the hollow were supposed to keep their looks forever. The early churchmen brought the stones into their monasteries, perhaps hoping to inherit some of their powers.

The road east leads to **St Saviour's Church**, with its detailed Romanesque carvings. To the west, a nice woodland trail leads up the valley past the Lower Lake to the Upper Lake.

TOURS

If you don't fancy discovering Glendalough under your own steam, there are a couple of tours that will make it fairly effortless. They both depart from Dublin.

Bus Éireann (Map pp66-7; ☎ 01-836 6111; www.buseireann.ie; Busáras; adult/child/student €28.80/22.50/25.20; ☺ departs 10am mid-Mar–Oct) Includes admission to the visitor centre and a visit to Powerscourt Estate in this whole-day tour which returns to Dublin at about 5.45pm. The guides are good but impersonal.

Wild Wicklow Tour (☎ 01-280 1899; www.discoverdublin.ie; adult/student & child €28/25;

☺ departs 9am) Award-winning tours of Glendalough, Avoca and the Sally Gap that never fail to generate rave reviews for atmosphere and all-round fun, but so much craic (chit-chat) has made a casualty of informative depth. The first pick-up is at the Dublin Tourism office, but there are a variety of pick-up points throughout Dublin; check the point nearest you when booking. The tour returns to Dublin about 5.30pm.

SLEEPING

our pick **Glendalough Hermitages** (☎ 0404-45140, for bookings 0404-45777; www.hermitage.dublindiocese.ie; St Kevin's Parish Church, Glendalough; s/d €45/70) In an effort to recreate something of the contemplative spirit of Kevin's early years in the valley, St Kevin's Parish Church rents out five *cillíns* (hermitages) for folks looking to take time out from the bustle of daily life and reflect on more spiritual matters. In keeping with more modern needs, however, there are a few more facilities than were present in Kevin's cave. Each hermitage is a small bungalow consisting of a bedroom, a bathroom, a small kitchen area and an open fire supplemented by a storage heating facility. The whole venture is managed by the local parish, and while there is a strong spiritual emphasis here, it is not necessarily a Catholic one. Visitors of all denominations and creeds are welcome, so long as their intentions are reflective and meditative; backpackers looking for a cheap place to bed down are not. The hermitages are in a field next to St Kevin's Parish Church, about 1km east of Glendalough on the R756 to Laragh.

GETTING THERE & AWAY

St Kevin's Bus (☎ 0404-481 8119; www.glendaloughbus.com) departs from outside the

Mansion House on Dawson St in Dublin at 11.30am and 6pm Monday to Saturday, and 11.30am and 7pm Sunday (one way/return €13/20, 1½ hours). It also stops at the Town Hall in Bray. Departures from Glendalough are at 7.15am and 4.30pm Monday to Saturday. During the week in July and August the later bus runs at 5.30pm, and there is an additional service at 9.45am.

BLESSINGTON

pop 4018

There's little to see in Blessington; it's basically made up of a long row of pubs, shops and 17th- and 18th-century town houses. It's the main town in the area, and as such makes a decent exploring base.

SIGHTS

Magnificent **Russborough House** (**☎ 045-865 239; www.russborough.ie; Blessington; adult/child/student €10/5/8; 10am-6pm May-Sep, Sun & bank holidays only Apr & Oct, closed rest of year**) is one of Ireland's finest stately homes, a Palladian pleasure palace built for Joseph Leeson (1705-83), later the first Earl of Milltown and, later still, Lord Russborough. It was built between 1741 and 1751 to the design of Richard Cassels, who was at the height of his fame as an architect. Poor old Richard didn't live to see it finished, but the job was well executed by Francis Bindon. Now, let's get down to the juicy bits.

The house remained in the Leeson family until 1931. In 1952 it was sold to Sir Alfred Beit, the eponymous nephew of the co-founder of the de Beers diamond-mining company. Uncle Alfred was an obsessive art collector, and when he died his impressive haul – which includes works by Velázquez, Vermeer, Goya and Rubens – was passed on to his nephew, who brought it to Russborough House.

In 1974 the IRA decided to get into the art business by robbing 16 of the paintings. They were eventually all recovered, but 10 years later the notorious Dublin criminal Martin Cahill (aka the General) masterminded another robbery, this time for Loyalist paramilitaries. The sorry story didn't conclude there. In 2001 two thieves took the direct approach and drove a jeep through the front doors, making off with two paintings worth nearly €4 million, including a Gainsborough that had been stolen, and recovered, twice before. And then, to add abuse to the insult already added to injury, the house was broken into again in 2002, with the thieves taking five more paintings, including two by Rubens. Incredibly, however, both hauls were quickly recovered.

The admission price includes a 45-minute tour of the house, which is decorated in typical Georgian style, and all the important paintings, which, given the history, is a monumental exercise in staying positive. Whatever you do, make no sudden moves.

SLEEPING & EATING

our pick **Rathsallagh House & Country Club** (**☎ 045-403 112; www.rathsallaghhousehotel.com; Dunlavin; mains €33-42, s/d from €135/260**) About 20km south of Blessington, this fabulous country manor, converted from Queen Anne stables in 1798, is more than just a fancy hotel. Luxury is par for the course here, from the splendidly appointed rooms to the exquisite country-house dining (the food here is some of the best you'll eat anywhere in Ireland) and the marvellous golf course that surrounds the estate. Even the breakfast is extraordinary: it has won the National Breakfast Award three times. Is there anything Irish tourism doesn't have an award for?

GETTING THERE & AWAY

Blessington is 35km southwest of Dublin on the N81. There are regular daily services by **Dublin Bus** (☎ 01-872 0000, 01-873 4222); catch bus 65 from Eden Quay in Dublin (€4.50, 1½ hours, every 1½ hours). **Bus Éireann** (☎ 01-836 6111; www.buseireann. ie) operates express bus 005 to and from Waterford, with stops in Blessington two or three times daily; from Dublin it's pick-up only, and from Waterford drop-off only.

THE COAST

KILMACANOGUE & THE GREAT SUGARLOAF

pop 839

At 503m, it's not even Wicklow's highest mountain, but the Great Sugarloaf is one of the most distinctive peaks in Ireland, its conical tip visible for many miles around. The mountain towers over the small village of Kilmacanogue, on the N11 about 4km south of Bray, which would barely merit a passing nod were it not for the presence of the mother of all Irish craft shops just across the road from the village.

Avoca Handweavers (☎ 01-286 7466; www.avoca.ie; Main St) is one hell of an operation, with seven branches nationwide and an even more widespread reputation for adding elegance and style to traditional rural handicrafts. Operational HQ is in a 19th-century arboretum, and its showroom will leave you in no doubt as to the company's incredible success.

Shopping for pashminas and placemats can put a fierce hunger on you, and there's no better place to satisfy it than at the shop's huge and always-busy **restaurant** (mains €12-18; ☻ 9.30am-5.30pm), which puts a premium on sourcing the very best ingredients for its dishes. It is best known for its beef-and-Guinness casserole, but vegetarians are very well catered for as well. Many of the recipes are available in the two volumes of the *Avoca Cookbook*, both on sale for €45 for two.

Bus Éireann (☎ 01-836 6111; www.bus eireann.ie) operates bus 133 from Dublin to Wicklow town and Arklow, with stops in

FEARGUS COONEY

The Great Sugarloaf

DETOUR: BALLYKNOCKEN HOUSE

As fine a country home as you could ever hope to find, **Ballyknocken House & Cookery School** (☎ 0404-69274; www.ballyknocken.com; Glenealy, Ashford; s/d from €69/118, 3-/4-course dinner €35/45) is a beautiful ivy-clad Victorian home, 5km south of Ashford on the R752 to Glenealy. Each of the bedrooms is carefully appointed with original furnishings and en-suite bathrooms, some with stencilled Victorian claw-foot tubs, which lends the whole place an air of timeless elegance that is becoming increasingly difficult to find. The old milking parlour on the farm grounds has been converted into a tidy two-bedroom loft that sleeps up to six people. Besides the home itself, the big draw is Catherine Fulvio's **cooking classes** (€110) which run throughout the year; check the website for details.

Kilmacanogue (one way/return €3.60/5.80, 30 minutes, 10 daily).

EATING

our pick **Organic Life/Marc Michel** (☎ 01-201 1882; Tinna Park, Kilpedder; mains around €17; ⏱ 10am-5pm, restaurant noon-4pm) Our favourite spot in all of Wicklow is this superb organic restaurant attached to the Organic Life shop in the town of Kilpedder, about 2km south of the Greystones turn-off on the N11. All of the vegetables are grown in the fields surrounding you (Ireland's first organically certified farm), while the beef served in the superb burger is bought from a local cattle rancher. The only pity is that it's only open for lunch.

SOUTHERN WICKLOW
RATHDRUM
pop 2123

The quiet village of Rathdrum at the foot of the Vale of Clara comprises little more than a few old houses and shops, but in the late 19th century it had a healthy flannel industry and a poorhouse. It's not what's in the town that's of interest to visitors, however, but what's just outside it.

SIGHTS

> Woe be to the man by whom the scandal cometh…It would be better for him that a millstone were tied about his neck and that he were cast into the depth of the sea rather than that he should scandalise one of these, my least little ones.
>
> JAMES JOYCE, *A PORTRAIT OF THE ARTIST AS A YOUNG MAN*

Joyce's fictional dinner-table argument wasn't about a murderer or any such criminal, but about Charles Stewart Parnell (1846–91), the 'uncrowned king of Ireland' and unquestionably one of the key figures in the Irish independence movement. **Avondale House**, a marvellous 209-hectare estate, dominated by a fine Palladian **mansion** (☎ 0404-46111; adult/student & child €6.50/6; ⏱ 11am-6pm May-Aug, Sat & Sun only Apr, by appointment only rest of year), designed by James Wyatt in 1779, was his birthplace and Irish headquarters. Of the house's many highlights, the most impressive are the stunning vermilion-coloured library (Parnell's favourite room) and beautiful dining room.

From 1880 to 1890, Avondale was synonymous with the fight for Home Rule, which was brilliantly led by Parnell until 1890 when a member of his own Irish Parliamentary Party, Captain William O'Shea, sued his wife Kitty for divorce and named Parnell as co-respondent. Parnell's affair with Kitty scandalised this 'priest-ridden' nation, and the ultraconservative clergy declared that Parnell was 'unfit to lead' – despite the fact that as soon as the divorce was granted the two lovers were quickly married. Parnell resigned as leader of the party and withdrew in despair to Avondale, where he died the following year.

Surrounding the house are 200 hectares of forest and parkland, where the first silvicultural experiments by the Irish Forestry Service (Coillte) were conceived, after the purchase of the house by the state in 1904. These plots, about half a hectare in size, are still visible today, flanking what many consider to be the best of Avondale's many walking trails, the Great Ride. You can visit the park during daylight hours year-round.

SLEEPING & EATING

our pick **Brook Lodge & Wells Spa** (☎ 0402-36444; www.brooklodge.com; Macreddin; r/ste from €260/330; P 🛜) The favourite chill-out spot for Dublin's high-flyers is this luxurious country house about 3km west of Rathdrum in the village of Macreddin. The 39 standard rooms set a pretty high tone, with four-poster and sleigh beds dressed in crisp Frette linen. But the suites sing an altogether more harmonious tune, each a minimalist marvel that wouldn't seem out of place in a New York boutique hotel – massive beds, flat-screen plasma TVs, top-of-the-range sound system and every other style sundry. The accommodation is pure luxury, but it's the outstanding spa that keeps guests coming back for more. Mud and flotation chambers, Finnish and aroma baths, *hammam* (Turkish bath) massages and a full range of Decléor and Carita treatments make this one of the top spas in the country. Your credit card will never have nestled in softer hands.

STEPHEN SAKS

Avondale House

GARETH BYRNE/ALAMY

Castletown House

CASTLETOWN HOUSE

In a country full of elegant Palladian mansions, it's no mean feat to be considered the grandest of the lot, but Castletown House, near Maynooth, simply has no peer. It is Ireland's largest and most imposing Georgian estate, and a testament to the vast wealth enjoyed by the Anglo-Irish gentry during the 18th century.

The house was built between the years 1722 and 1732 for William Conolly (1662–1729), speaker of the Irish House of Commons, and, at the time, Ireland's richest man. Born into relatively humble circumstances in Ballyshannon, County Donegal, Conolly made his fortune through land transactions in the uncertain aftermath of the Battle of the Boyne in 1690 (see p356).

The interior is as opulent as the exterior suggests, especially the Long Gallery, replete with family portraits and exquisite stucco work by the Francini brothers. (In the US, Thomas Jefferson became a Palladian acolyte and much of official Washington, DC is in this style.)

As always seems the way with these grand projects, Conolly didn't live to see the completion of his wonder-palace. His widow, Katherine, continued to live at the unfinished house after his death in 1729, instigating many of the improvements made after the main structure was completed in 1732.

Castletown house remained in the family's hands until 1965, when it was purchased by Desmond Guinness. In 1994 Castletown House was transferred to state care and today it is managed by the Heritage Service.

Buses 120 and 123 run from Dublin to Celbridge (€3.50, 30 minutes, every half-hour Monday to Friday, hourly Saturday, six buses Sunday).

What you need to know: ☎ 01-628 8252; www.castletownhouse.ie; Celbridge; adult/child €4.50/3.50; ⏱ 10am-6pm Mon-Fri, from 1pm Sat & Sun Easter-Sep, 10am-5pm Mon-Fri, from 1pm Sun Oct

GETTING THERE & AWAY

Bus Éireann (☎ 01-836 6111; www.buseireann .ie) service 133 goes to Rathdrum from Dublin (one way/return €6.90/9.50, 1¾ hours, 10 daily) on its way to Arklow.

Iarnród Éireann (☎ 01-836 6222) serves Rathdrum from Dublin on the main Dublin to Rosslare Harbour line (one way/return €15.50/19.50, 1½ hours, five daily).

COUNTY KILDARE
MAYNOOTH

pop 10,715

Much of Maynooth's (Maigh Nuad) life comes from the university (National University of Ireland Maynooth; NUIM), which gives this tree-lined town with stone-fronted houses and shops a dynamism that belies its country-town appearance. It's within easy reach of Dublin by public transport, thanks as much to the university as to the legions of barristers and other swells that make the town their home.

SIGHTS
ST PATRICK'S COLLEGE

Turning out Catholic priests since 1795, **St Patrick's College & Seminary** (☎ 01-628 5222; www.maynoothcollege.ie; Main St) was founded to ensure that aspiring priests wouldn't skip off to seminary school in France and get infected with strains of republicanism and revolution. It became a Pontifical University in 1898 (granting control of the college's theological courses to the Holy See) but in 1910 it joined the newly established National University of Ireland (NUI), which governed the university's non-theological studies. Nevertheless, the student body remained exclusively clerical until 1966, when lay students were finally admitted. A restructuring of the NUI in 1997 made

St Patrick's College independent of the bigger university, which now has more than 6500 students; there are only a few dozen studying for the priesthood.

ACTIVITIES
GOLF

On the edge of town, **Carton House** (☎ 01-651 7720; www.cartonhousegolf.ie; green fees Sun-Wed €90, Thu-Sat €110) is home to two outstanding 18-hole championship courses designed by Colin Montgomery and Mark O'Meara respectively.

SLEEPING

Carton House (☎ 01-505 2000; www.carton house.com; r from €150; P 🖳 🛜 🐩) It really doesn't get any grander than this vast, early-19th-century estate set on over 400 hectares of lavish grounds. The interiors belie the Palladian exterior and are stylishly minimalist. As you'd expect, the beautiful rooms come equipped with all the latest high-tech gadgetry. To reach the hotel, follow the R148 east towards Leixlip along the Royal Canal.

GETTING THERE & AWAY

Dublin Bus (☎ 01-873 4222; www.dublinbus .ie) runs a service to Maynooth (€3.10, one hour) leaving several times an hour from Pearse St in Dublin.

Maynooth is on the main Dublin-Sligo line, with regular trains in each direction: to Dublin (€2.70, 35 minutes, one to four per hour); to Sligo (€35, two hours 40 minutes, four per day).

STRAFFAN

pop 439

Two of Ireland's top golf courses can be found at the **K Club** (Kildare Hotel & Country Club; ☎ 01-601 7200; www.kclub.com; Straffan; r from €200; P 🖳 🛜 🐩), a Georgian estate and golfers' paradise. Inside there are 92 well-appointed rooms and lots of public spaces for having a drink and lying about your exploits outside. There are two golf courses: one, with Arnold Palmer's design imprimatur, is one of the best in Ireland and hosted the PGA European Open until 2008; the second course opened in 2003. Like everywhere else, the K Club is suffering the effects of the recession and has lowered its green fees from a prohibitive €250 to a more interesting €100. Not bad for the course where, in 2006, Europe won its third Ryder Cup in a row.

Bus Éireann (☎ 01-836 6111; www.bus eireann.ie) runs buses from Dublin (one way/return €3.80/5.80, 30 minutes, every half hour, six buses Sunday).

COUNTY MEATH
BRÚ NA BÓINNE
The vast neolithic necropolis known as Brú na Bóinne (the Boyne Palace) is one of the most extraordinary sites in Europe and shouldn't be missed. A thousand years older than Stonehenge, this is a powerful and evocative testament to the mind-boggling achievements of prehistoric humans.

The complex was built to house the remains of those who were at the top of the social heap and its tombs were the largest artificial structures in Ireland until the construction of the Anglo-Norman castles 4000 years later. The area consists of many different sites, with the three principal ones being Newgrange, Knowth and Dowth.

Over the centuries the tombs decayed, were covered by grass and trees, and were plundered by everybody from Vikings to Victorian treasure hunters, whose carved initials can be seen on the great stones of Newgrange. The countryside around the tombs is littered with countless other ancient tumuli (mounds) and standing stones.

ORIENTATION & INFORMATION
In an effort to protect the tombs and preserve the mystical atmosphere around them, all visits to Brú na Bóinne must start at the **Brú na Bóinne visitor centre** (☎ 041-988 0300; www.heritageireland.ie; Donore; adult/child visitor centre €3/2, visitor centre, Newgrange & Knowth €11/6; 🕙 9am-6.30pm May, 9am-7pm Jun-Sep, 9.30am-5pm Oct-Apr) from where a shuttle bus will take you to the tombs. Happily, this is a superb interpretive centre, its spiral design echoing that of Newgrange. The centre houses an extraordinary series of interactive exhibits on prehistoric Ireland and its passage tombs, and has regional tourism information, a good cafe and a bookshop.

You should allow plenty of time to visit Brú na Bóinne. Plan on an hour's visit for the interpretive centre alone, two hours if you wish to include a trip to Newgrange or Knowth, and a half day to see all three in one go (Dowth is not open to tourists).

In summer, particularly on weekends, and during school holidays, the place gets very crowded, and you will not be guaranteed a visit to either of the passage tombs. There are only 750 tour slots and on peak days 2000 people show up. Tickets are sold on a first-come, first-served basis (no advance booking) so the best advice is to arrive early in the morning or visit midweek and be prepared for a wait.

The important thing to note is that if you turn up at either Newgrange or Knowth first, you'll be sent to the visitor centre. Tours depart from a bus stop that you reach by walking across a spiral bridge over the River Boyne, and the buses take just a few minutes to reach the sites. Technically you can walk the 4km to either site from the visitor centre, but

JOE FOX/ALAMY

Newgrange

you're discouraged from doing so as you might get mowed down on the very narrow lanes by the tour bus you've chosen not to take.

The visitor centre is on the south side of the river. It's 2km west of Donore and 6km east of Slane, where bridges cross the river from the N51.

SIGHTS
NEWGRANGE

Even from afar, you know that Newgrange (adult/child incl visitor centre €6/3) is something special. Its white, round stone walls topped by a grass dome look otherworldly, and just the size is impressive: 80m in diameter and 13m high. But underneath it gets even better. Here lies the finest Stone Age passage tomb in Ireland, and one of the most remarkable prehistoric sites in Europe. It dates from around 3200 BC, predating the Pyramids by some six centuries. No one is quite sure of its original purpose. It could have been a burial place for kings or a centre for ritual – although the tomb's precise

alignment with the sun at the time of the winter solstice also suggests it was designed to act as a calendar.

The name derives from 'New Granary' (the tomb did in fact serve as a repository for wheat and grain at one stage), although a more popular belief is that it comes from the Irish for 'Cave of Gráinne', a reference to a popular Celtic myth. *The Pursuit of Diarmuid and Gráinne* tells of the illicit love between the woman betrothed to Fionn McCumhaill (or Finn McCool), leader of the Fianna, and Diarmuid, one of his most trusted lieutenants. When Diarmuid was fatally wounded, his body was brought to Newgrange by the god Aengus in a vain attempt to save him, and the despairing Gráinne followed him into the cave, where she remained long after he died. This suspiciously Arthurian tale (sub in Lancelot and Guinevere for Diarmuid and Gráinne) is undoubtedly a myth, but it's still a pretty good story. Newgrange also plays another role in Celtic mythology as the site where the hero Cúchulainn was conceived.

Over time, Newgrange, like Dowth and Knowth, deteriorated and was at one stage even used as a quarry. The site was extensively restored in 1962 and again in 1975.

A superbly carved kerbstone with double and triple spirals guards the tomb's main entrance, but the area has been reconstructed so that tourists don't have to clamber in over it. Above the entrance is a slit, or roof box, which lets light in. Another beautifully decorated kerbstone stands at the exact opposite side of the mound. Some experts say that a ring of standing stones encircled the mound, forming a great circle about 100m in diameter, but only 12 of these stones remain, with traces of some others below ground level.

Holding the whole structure together are the 97 boulders of the kerb ring, designed to stop the mound from collapsing outwards. Eleven of these are decorated with motifs similar to those on the main entrance stone, although only three have extensive carvings.

The white quartzite that decorates the tomb was originally obtained from Wicklow, 70km to the south. In an age before horse and wheel, it was transported by sea and then up the River Boyne, and there is also some granite from the Mourne Mountains in Northern Ireland. Over 200,000 tonnes of earth and stone also went into the mound.

You can walk down the narrow 19m passage, lined with 43 stone uprights (some of them engraved), which leads into the tomb chamber about one-third of the way into the colossal mound. The chamber has three recesses, and in these are large basin stones that held cremated human bones. As well as the remains, the basins would have held funeral offerings of beads and pendants, but these were stolen long before the archaeologists arrived.

Above, the massive stones support a 6m-high corbel-vaulted roof. A complex drainage system means that not a drop of water has penetrated the interior in 40 centuries.

At 8.20am on the winter solstice (sometime between 19 and 23 December), the rising sun's rays shine through the roof box above the entrance, creep slowly down the long passage and illuminate the tomb chamber for 17 minutes. There is little doubt that this is one of the country's most memorable, even mystical, experiences. There is a simulated winter sunrise for every group taken into the mound, but to be in with a chance of witnessing the real thing add your name to the list that is drawn by lottery every 1 October.

KNOWTH

Northwest of Newgrange, the burial mound of **Knowth** (adult/child incl visitor centre €5/3; ⏰ Easter-Oct) was built around the same time and seems set to surpass its better-known neighbour in both its size and the importance of the discoveries made here. It has the greatest collection of passage-grave art ever uncovered in Western Europe, and has been under excavation since 1962.

The excavations soon cleared a passage leading to the central chamber, which at 34m is much longer than the one at Newgrange. In 1968, a 40m passage was unearthed on the opposite side of the mound. Although the chambers are separate, they're close enough for archaeologists to hear each other at work. Also in the mound are the remains of six early Christian souterrains (underground chambers) built into the side. Some 300 carved slabs and 17 satellite graves surround the main mound.

Knowth burial mound

RICHARD CUMMINS

Human activity at Knowth continued for thousands of years after its construction, which accounts for the site's complexity. The Beaker folk, so called because they buried their dead with drinking vessels, occupied the site in the Bronze Age (c 1800 BC), as did the Celts in the Iron Age (c 500 BC). Remnants of bronze and iron work from these periods have been discovered. Around AD 800 to 900, it was turned into a *ráth* (earthen ring fort), a stronghold of the very powerful O'Neill clan. In 965, it was the seat of Cormac MacMaelmithic, later Ireland's high king for nine years, and in the 12th century the Normans built a motte-and-bailey (raised mound with a small castle) here. The site was finally abandoned in about 1400.

Further excavations are likely to continue for at least the next decade so you may see archaeologists at work when you visit.

DOWTH

The circular mound at Dowth is similar in size to Newgrange – about 63m in diameter – but is slightly taller at 14m high. It has suffered badly at the hands of everyone from road builders and treasure hunters to amateur archaeologists, who scooped out the centre of the tumulus in the 19th century. For a time, Dowth even had a tearoom ignobly perched on its summit. Relatively untouched by modern archaeologists, Dowth shows what Newgrange and Knowth looked like for most of their history. Because it's unsafe, Dowth is closed to visitors, though the mound can be viewed from the road between Newgrange and Drogheda. Excavations began in 1998 and will continue for years to come.

Dowth has two entrance passages leading to separate chambers (both sealed), and a 24m early Christian underground passage at either end, which each connect up with the western passage. This 8m-long passage leads into a small cruciform chamber, in which a recess acts as an entrance to an additional series of small compartments, a feature unique to Dowth. To the southwest is the entrance to a shorter passage and smaller chamber.

North of the tumulus are the ruins of **Dowth Castle** and **Dowth House**.

TOURS
Brú na Bóinne is one of the most popular tourist attractions in Ireland, and there are oodles of organised tours transporting busloads of eager tourists to the visitor centre. Most depart from Dublin.

The **Mary Gibbons Tours** (☎ 01-283 9973; www.newgrangetours.com; tour €35) are highly recommended. Tours depart from numerous Dublin hotels, beginning at 9.30am Monday to Saturday, and take in the whole of the Boyne Valley including Newgrange and the Hill of Tara. The expert guides offer a fascinating insight into Celtic and pre-Celtic life in Ireland, and you'll get access to Newgrange even on days when all visiting slots are filled.

Bus Éireann (☎ 01-836 6111; www.bus eireann.ie; adult/child €30/25; ☺ Mon-Thu, Sat & Sun mid-Mar–Sep) runs Newgrange and the Boyne Valley tours departing from **Busáras** (Map pp66-7; Store St) in Dublin at 10am, returning at approximately 5.45pm.

GETTING THERE & AWAY
From Drogheda, **Bus Éireann** (☎ 041-983 5023) runs a service that drops you off at the entrance to the visitor centre (€3.50, 20 minutes, five daily).

Newgrange Shuttlebus (☎ 1800-424 252; www.overthetoptours.com; return ticket €18) runs one or two trips daily to the Brú na Bóinne visitor centre from central Dublin. Book in advance.

BATTLE OF THE BOYNE SITE
More than 60,000 soldiers of the armies of King James II and King William III fought on this patch of farmland on the border of Counties Meath and Louth in 1690. In the end, William prevailed and James

sailed off to France. Today the **battle site** (☎ 041-980 9950; www.battleoftheboyne.ie; adult/child €4/2; ☺ 10am-6pm May-Sep, 9.30am-5pm Oct-Apr, last admission 1hr before closing) is part of the Oldbridge Estate farm. The visitor centre offers a short show about the battle, original and replica weaponry of the time and a laser model of the battlefield. Self-guided walks through the parkland and battle site are eerily low-key, allowing ample time to think about the events that saw Protestant interests remain in Ireland. The site, 3km north of Donore, is signposted off the N51.

TARA
The **Hill of Tara** is Ireland's most sacred stretch of turf, an entrance to the underworld and a place at the heart of Irish history, legend and folklore. It was the home of the mystical druids, the priest-rulers of ancient Ireland, who practised their particular form of Celtic paganism under the watchful gaze of the all-powerful goddess Maeve (Medbh). Later it was the ceremonial capital of the high kings – 142 of them in all – who ruled until the arrival of Christianity in the 6th century. It is also one of the most important ancient sites in Europe, with a Stone Age passage tomb and prehistoric burial mounds that date back up to 5000 years.

Although little remains other than humps and mounds of earth on the hill, its historic and folkloristic significance is immense. However, preservation and history have run headlong into the demands of sprawl and convenience in the Tara Valley with controversy around the construction of a new motorway. A battle between government and campaigners over the proposed route has been raging for years and work had to be halted on the first day of digging in 2007 when an ancient site that could rival Stonehenge was uncovered. Despite pleas from eminent historians and archaeologists around the world, the government looks set to ignore calls for a new route that would completely avoid the area and plough ahead with its controversial plans for the M3. For updates, visit www.tarawatch.org.

HISTORY

The Celts believed that Tara was the sacred dwelling place of the gods and the gateway to the otherworld. The passage grave was thought to be the final resting place of the Tuatha dé Danann, the mythical fairyfolk – who were real enough, but instead of pixies and brownies, they were earlier Stone Age arrivals on the island.

As the Celtic political landscape began to evolve, the druids' power was usurped by warlike chieftains who took kingly titles; there was no sense of a united Ireland, so at any given time there were countless *rí tuaithe* (regional kings) controlling many small areas. The king who ruled Tara, though, was generally considered the big shot, the high king, even though his direct rule didn't extend too far beyond the provincial border. The most lauded of all the high kings was Cormac MacArt, who ruled during the 3rd century.

The most important event in Tara's calendar was the three-day harvest *feis* (festival) that took place at Samhain, a precursor to modern Halloween. During the festival, the high king pulled out all the stops: grievances would be heard, laws passed and disputes settled amid an orgy of eating, drinking and partying.

When the early Christians hit town in the 5th century, they targeted Tara straight away. Although the legend has it that St Patrick lit the paschal fire on the Hill of Slane, some people believe that Patrick's incendiary act took place on Tara's sacred hump. The arrival of Christianity marked the beginning of the end for Celtic pagan civilisation, and the high kings began to desert Tara, even though the kings of Leinster continued to be based here until the 11th century.

In August 1843, Tara saw one of the greatest crowds ever to gather in Ireland.

EOIN CLARKE

Winter solstice sunrise hits the entrance stone of Newgrange (p125)

Daniel O'Connell, the 'Liberator' and the leader of the opposition to union with Great Britain, held one of his monster rallies at Tara, and up to 750,000 people came to hear him speak.

INFORMATION

A former Protestant church (with a window by the well-known artist Evie Hone) is home to the **Tara Visitor Centre** (☎ 046-902 5903; www.heritageireland.ie; adult/child €3/1; ⏰ 10am-6pm mid-May–mid-Sep, last admission 5pm), where a 20-minute audiovisual presentation about the site is shown. Entrance to Tara is free and the site itself is always open. There are good explanatory panels by the entrance.

SIGHTS
RATH OF THE SYNODS

The names applied to Tara's various humps and mounds were adopted from ancient texts, and mythology and religion intertwine with the historical facts. The Protestant church grounds and graveyard spill onto the remains of the Rath of the Synods, a triple-ringed fort where some of St Patrick's early synods (meetings) supposedly took place. Excavations of the enclosure suggest that it was used between AD 200 and 400 for burials, rituals and living quarters. Originally the ring fort would have contained wooden houses surrounded by timber palisades.

During a digging session in the graveyard in 1810, a boy found a pair of gold torcs (crescents of beaten gold hung around the neck), which are now in the National Museum in Dublin. Later excavations discovered Roman glass, shards of pottery and seals, showing links with the Roman Empire even though the Romans never extended their power into Ireland.

The poor state of the enclosure is due in part to a group of British 'Israelites' who in the 1890s dug the place up looking for the Ark of the Covenant, much to the consternation of the local people. The Israelites' leader claimed to see a mysterious pillar on the enclosure, but unfortunately it was invisible to everyone else. After they failed to uncover anything, the invisible pillar moved to the other side of the road but, before the adventurers had time to start work there, the locals chased them away.

ROYAL ENCLOSURE

To the south of the church, the Royal Enclosure is a large, oval Iron Age hill fort, 315m in diameter and surrounded by a bank and ditch cut through solid rock under the soil. Inside the Royal Enclosure are several smaller sites.

MOUND OF THE HOSTAGES

This bump in the northern corner of the enclosure is the most ancient known part of Tara and the most visible of its remains. Supposedly a prison cell for hostages of the 3rd-century king Cormac MacArt, it is in fact a small Stone Age passage grave dating from around 1800 BC that was later used by Bronze Age people. The passage contains some carved stonework, but is closed to the public.

The mound produced a treasure trove of artefacts, including some ancient Mediterranean beads of amber and faience (glazed pottery). More than 35 Bronze Age burials were found here, as well as a mass of cremated remains from the Stone Age.

CORMAC'S HOUSE & THE ROYAL SEAT

Two other earthworks found inside the enclosure are Cormac's House and the Royal Seat. Although they look similar, the Royal Seat is a ring fort with a house site in the centre, while Cormac's House is a barrow (burial mound) in the side of

GARETH MCCORMACK

Sunset over the River Boyne

the circular bank. Cormac's House commands the best views of the surrounding lowlands of the Boyne and Blackwater Valleys.

Atop Cormac's House is the phallic Stone of Destiny, originally located near the Mound of the Hostages, which represents the joining of the gods of the earth and the heavens. It's said to be the inauguration stone of the high kings, although alternative sources suggest that the actual coronation stone was the Stone of Scone, which was removed to Edinburgh, Scotland, and used to crown British kings. The would-be king stood on top of the Stone of Destiny and, if the stone let out three roars, he was crowned. The mass grave of 37 men who died in a skirmish on Tara during the 1798 Rising is next to the stone.

ENCLOSURE OF KING LAOGHAIRE

South of the Royal Enclosure is the Enclosure of King Laoghaire, a large but worn ring fort where the king, a contemporary of St Patrick, is supposedly bur-

ied dressed in his armour and standing upright.

BANQUET HALL

North of the churchyard is Tara's most unusual feature, the Banquet Hall. This rectangular earthwork measures 230m by 27m along a north-south axis. Tradition holds that it was built to cater for thousands of guests during feasts. Much of this information comes from the 12th-century *Book of Leinster* and the *Yellow Book of Lecan*, which even includes drawings of the hall.

Opinions vary as to the site's real purpose. Its orientation suggests that it was a sunken entrance to Tara, leading directly to the Royal Enclosure. More recent research, however, has uncovered graves within the compound, and it's possible that the banks are in fact the burial sites of some of the kings of Tara.

GRÁINNE'S FORT

Gráinne was the daughter of King Cormac who was betrothed to Fionn McCumhaill

EASTERN IRELAND

COUNTY MEATH

Trim Castle

STEPHEN SAKS

(Finn McCool) but eloped with Diarmuid, one of the king's warriors, on her wedding night, becoming the subject of the epic *The Pursuit of Diarmuid and Gráinne*. Gráinne's Fort and the northern and southern **Sloping Trenches** off to the northwest are burial mounds.

TOURS

The **Mary Gibbons Tours** (☎ 01-283 9973; www.newgrangetours.com; tour €35) to Brú na Bóinne take in the whole of the Boyne Valley, including the Hill of Tara.

Bus Éireann (☎ 01-836 6111; www.bus eireann.ie; adult/child €30/25; ☼ Mon–Thu, Sat & Sun mid-Mar–Sep) tours to Newgrange and the Boyne Valley include a visit to Tara on certain days.

GETTING THERE & AWAY

Tara is 10km southeast of Navan, just off the Dublin-Cavan road (N3). **Bus Éireann** (☎ 01-836 6111) services linking Dublin and Navan pass within 1km of the site (€8.20, 40 minutes, hourly Monday to Saturday and four times on Sunday). Ask the driver

to drop you off at the Tara Cross, where you take a left turn off the main road and follow the signs.

TRIM

pop 1375

Dominated by its mighty castle and littered with atmospheric ruins, the quiet town of Trim was an important settlement in medieval times. Five city gates surrounded a busy jumble of streets, and as many as seven monasteries were established in the immediate area.

Today, Trim's history is everywhere, with ruins scattered about the town. The streets, still lined with tiny old workers cottages, are seeing a few new developments aimed at realising the area's huge tourism potential.

SIGHTS
TRIM CASTLE

This remarkably preserved edifice was Ireland's largest Anglo-Norman fortification and is proof of Trim's medieval importance. Hugh de Lacy founded the truly impressive **Trim Castle** (King John's Castle; ☎ 046-943 8619; www.heritageireland.ie; adult/child €4/2, grounds only €3/1; ⏰ 10am-6pm Easter-Oct, 9.30am-5pm Sat & Sun Nov-Easter, last admission 1hr before closing) in 1173, but Rory O'Connor, said to have been the last high king of Ireland, destroyed this motte and bailey within a year. The building you see today was begun around 1200 and has hardly been modified since.

Throughout Anglo-Norman times the castle occupied a strategic position on the western edge of the Pale, the area where the Anglo-Normans ruled supreme; beyond Trim was the volatile country where Irish chieftains and lords fought with their Norman rivals and vied for position, power and terrain. By the 16th century, the castle had begun to fall into decline and in 1649, when the town was taken by Cromwellian forces, it was severely damaged.

In 1996, the castle briefly returned to its former glory as a location for Mel Gibson's *Braveheart,* in which it served as a 'castle double' for the castle at York. A small booklet sold at the castle gives a fuller insight into its history and acts as a handy guide for touring the grounds.

The castle's grassy 2-hectare enclosure is dominated by a massive stone keep, 25m tall and mounted on a Norman motte. Inside are three levels, the lowest divided by a central wall. Just outside the central keep are the remains of an earlier wall.

The principal outer-curtain wall, some 500m long and for the most part still standing, dates from around 1250 and includes eight towers and a gatehouse. It also has a number of sally gates from which defenders could exit to confront the enemy. The finest stretch of the outer wall runs from the River Boyne through Dublin Gate to Castle St. Within the northern corner was a church and, facing the river, the Royal Mint, which produced Irish coinage (called 'Patricks' and 'Irelands') into the 15th century.

In 1971, excavations done in the castle grounds revealed the remains of 10 headless men, presumably hapless criminals who fell foul of Edward IV's 1465 decree that anyone who had robbed or 'who was going to rob' should be beheaded, their heads mounted on spikes and publicly displayed as a warning to other thieves.

In the car park is a Russian cannon, a trophy from the Crimean War, which bears the tsarist double-headed eagle.

SLEEPING

Trim Castle Hotel (☎ 046-948 3000; www .trimcastlehotel.com; Castle St; s/d from €165/180; Ⓟ ⌨ 🛜) This stylish new boutique hotel is part of a development that is spiffing up an area close to the castle. The 68 rooms here have wi-fi and a compact but comfortable modern design. Check for special offers online.

EATING & DRINKING

Brogan's Beacon (☎ 046-943 1237; www.bro gans.ie; High St; mains €13-19; ⏰ noon-9pm) This popular restaurant serves country-style comfort food for adoring locals. The menu is fairly predictable with hearty chicken, salmon and pasta dishes, the odd risotto and the usual array of steaks and burgers. It won't win any awards, but may just satisfy a niggling craving. There's also a bar menu for lighter snacks.

Marcy Regan's (David's Lad; ☎ 046-943 6103; Lackanash Rd, Newtown, Trim; ⏰ Thu-Tue) This small, traditional pub beside St Peter's Bridge claims to be Ireland's second-oldest. It's a no-frills kind of place just steeped in old-world atmosphere. There's often a trad music session on Friday nights.

Celtic high cross, Monasterboice (p138)

EOIN CLARKE

GETTING THERE & AWAY

Bus Éireann runs a bus at least once an hour between Dublin and Trim (€10.30, 70 minutes). Buses stop on New Rd just beyond the bridge.

LOUGHCREW CAIRNS

With all the hoopla over Brú na Bóinne, the amazing Stone Age passage graves strewn about the Loughcrew Hills are often overlooked. There are 30-odd tombs here but they're hard to get to and relatively few people ever bother, which means you can enjoy this moody and evocative place in peace.

It's well worth making the effort to get to the three hills, Carnbane East (194m), Carnbane West (206m) and Patrickstown (279m) – although the last has been so ru-

ined by 19th-century builders that there's little to see other than splendid views of the surrounding countryside.

Like Brú na Bóinne, the graves were all built around 3000 BC, but, unlike their better-known and better-excavated peers, the Loughcrew tombs were used at least until 750 BC. As at Newgrange, larger stones in some of the graves are decorated with spiral patterns. Some of the graves look like large piles of stones, while others are less obvious, their cairn having been removed. Archaeologists have unearthed bone fragments and ashes, stone balls and beads.

The cairns are west of Kells, along the R154, near Oldcastle.

CARNBANE EAST

Carnbane East has a cluster of sites; **Cairn T** (☎ 049-854 1240; www.heritageireland. ie; admission free; 🕙 10am-6pm mid-Jun–Aug; P) is the biggest at about 35m in diameter and has numerous carved stones. One of its outlying kerbstones is called the Hag's Chair, and is covered in gouged holes, circles and other markings. You need the gate key to enter the passageway and a torch to see anything in detail. It takes about half an hour to climb Carnbane East from the car park. From the summit on a reasonably clear day, you should be able to see the Hill of Tara to the southeast, while the view north is into Cavan, with Lough Ramor to the north, and Oldcastle and Lough Sheelin to the northwest.

In summer, access to Cairn T is controlled by the Heritage Service, which also provides guides. But locals are passionate about the place and at any time of the year you can arrange for guides who will not only show you Cairn T but take you to some of the other cairns as well. Enquire at the Kells tourist office.

CARNBANE WEST

From the car park, it takes about an hour to reach Carnbane West's summit, where Cairns D and L, both some 60m in diameter, are located. Cairn D has been disturbed in an unsuccessful search for a central chamber. Cairn L, to the northeast, is also in poor condition, but you can enter the passage and chamber, which has numerous carved stones and a curved basin stone in which human ashes were placed.

Cairn L is administered by the Heritage Service, which only gives out the key to those with an authentic research interest.

COUNTY LOUTH

DROGHEDA

pop 28,973

Ongoing development and a rising population of commuters have begun to breathe new life into Drogheda, a historic fortified town straddling the River Boyne. A clutch of fine old buildings, a handsome cathedral and a riveting museum give it plenty of cultural interest, while its wonderful old pubs, fine restaurants, good transport and numerous sleeping options make it an excellent base for

EASTERN IRELAND

COUNTY LOUTH

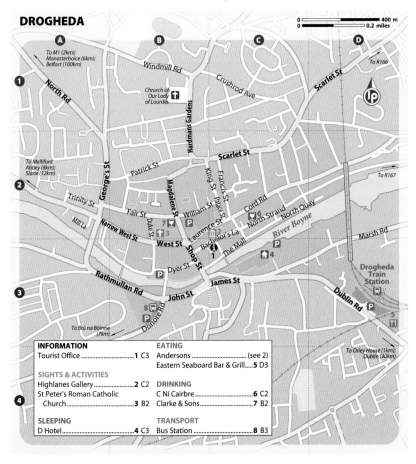

DROGHEDA

INFORMATION		EATING	
Tourist Office	**1** C3	Andersons	(see 2)
		Eastern Seaboard Bar & Grill	**5** D3
SIGHTS & ACTIVITIES			
Highlanes Gallery	**2** C2	DRINKING	
St Peter's Roman Catholic		C Ní Cairbre	**6** C2
Church	**3** B2	Clarke & Sons	**7** B2
SLEEPING		TRANSPORT	
D Hotel	**4** C3	Bus Station	**8** B3

exploring the world-class attractions that surround it.

INFORMATION

Tourist office (☎ 041-983 7070; www.drogheda.ie; Mayoralty St; ⏰ 9am-5pm Mon-Fri, 9am-4.30pm Sat) Located on the northern side of the river, just off the docklands.

SIGHTS

ST PETER'S ROMAN CATHOLIC CHURCH

The shrivelled little head of the martyr St Oliver Plunkett (1629–81) is the main draw of the 19th-century **Catholic church** (West St), which is actually two churches in one: the first, designed by Francis Johnston in classical style and built in 1791; and the newer addition, built in the Gothic style visible today. Plunkett's head – from which the rest of him was separated following his hanging in 1681 – is kept in a glittering brass-and-glass case in the north transept.

HIGHLANES GALLERY

This impressive **gallery** (☎ 041-980 3311; www.highlanes.ie; Laurence St; admission free; ⏰ 10am-6pm Mon-Sat, to 8pm Thu, noon-5pm Sun) is set in a beautifully converted 19th-century monastery. All the visual arts can be found here, as well as a good permanent collection of paintings. There are regular special exhibitions and the entire complex is worth a look – as is the view down to the Boyne. Attached is a well-stocked shop featuring the best of Louth craftwork.

SLEEPING

D Hotel (☎ 041-987 7700; www.thed.ie; Scotch Hall, Marsh Rd; s/d from €70/130; 🅿 💻 🛜) Slick, hip and unexpected, this is Drogheda's top dog when it comes to accommodation. The luxurious but minimalist rooms

are bathed in light and decked out with designer furniture and cool gadgets. There's a stylish bar and restaurant and great views of the city. Book in advance online and you could nab a fantastic deal.

Orley House (☎ 041-983 6019; www.orleyhouse.com; Bryanstown, Dublin Rd; r from €80; 🅿) This spick-and-span B&B has large comfortable rooms and a warm welcome for families. It's a well-run place with excellent service and hearty breakfast served in a sun-filled conservatory. Orley House is about 2km out of town on the Dublin road.

EATING

Andersons (☎ 041-980 3295; Highlanes Gallery, Laurence St; meals €5-10; ⏰ 10am-6pm Mon-Sat, noon-5pm Sun; 🛜) Located in the impressive new Highlanes Gallery, this modern cafe serves a tempting range of soups, salads, sandwiches and wraps, as well as continental-style platters of luscious cheeses and cured meats. There's free wi-fi.

Eastern Seaboard Bar & Grill (☎ 041-980 2570; 1 Bryanstown Centre, Dublin Rd; mains €9-16; ⏰ noon-10pm Mon-Sat, to 8pm Sun; 🛜) Despite the swish, contemporary design, this popular new eatery manages to exude a warm, relaxed atmosphere with plenty of quirky details adding to its allure. The menu features all American classics from sweet potato fries to burgers and New England clam chowder. Book ahead, it's been packed since opening.

DRINKING & ENTERTAINMENT

our pick **C Ní Cairbre** (Carberry's; ☎ 041-984 7569; North Strand) A national treasure, this pub has been owned by the same family since 1880. Old newspaper clippings and long-faded artwork cover most surfaces and it's a great place to catch some traditional music. You might find a ses-

Thatched cottage near Drogheda

EOIN CLARKE

sion going on any night of the week but Tuesday nights and Sunday afternoons are your best bet.

Clarke & Sons (☎ 041-983 6724; Peter St) This wonderful old boozer is right out of a time capsule. The unrestored wooden interior features snugs and leaded-glass doors that read Open Bar. The pints just taste better at this corner classic.

GETTING THERE & AWAY
BUS
Drogheda is only 48km north of Dublin, on the main M1 route to Belfast. The bus station is just south of the river on the corner of Rathmullan Rd and Donore Rd. This is one of the busiest bus routes in the country, and **Bus Éireann** (☎ 041-983 5023) regularly serves Drogheda from Dublin (€6, one hour, one to four hourly). Drogheda to Dundalk is another busy route (€5, 30 minutes, hourly).

From Drogheda you can get a bus that drops you off at the entrance of the Brú na Bóinne visitor centre (€2, 15 minutes, four to six daily).

TRAIN
The **train station** (☎ 041-983 8749) is just south of the river and east of the town centre, off Dublin Rd. Drogheda is on the main Belfast-Dublin line (Dublin €15, 35 minutes; Belfast €27.50, 1½ hours), and there are six express trains (and many slower ones) each way, with five on Sunday. This is the best line in Ireland, with excellent on-board service.

AROUND DROGHEDA
MELLIFONT ABBEY
In its Anglo-Norman prime, **Mellifont Abbey** (☎ 041-982 6459; www.heritageireland. ie; Tullyallen; adult/child €3/2; ✆ visitor centre 10am-6pm May-Sep; Ⓟ) was the Cistercians' first and most magnificent centre in the country. Although the ruins are highly evocative and well worth exploring, they still don't do real justice to the site's former splendour.

In the mid-12th century, Irish monastic orders had grown a little too fond of the good life and were not averse to a bit of corruption. In 1142, Malachy, Bishop of

Down (later canonised for his troubles), was at the end of his tether and he invited a group of hard-core monks from Clairvaux in France to set up shop in a remote location, where they would act as a sobering influence on the local clergy. The Irish monks didn't quite get on with their French guests, and the latter soon left for home. Still, the construction of Mellifont – the name comes from the Latin *mellifons* (honey fountain) – continued, and within 10 years, nine more Cistercian monasteries were established. Mellifont was eventually the mother house for 21 lesser monasteries, and at one point as many as 400 monks lived here.

Mellifont not only brought fresh ideas to the Irish religious scene, it also heralded a new style of architecture. For the first time in Ireland, monasteries were built with the formal layout and structure that was being used on the Continent. Only fragments of the original settlement remain, but the plan of the extensive monastery can easily be traced.

The visitor centre next to the site describes monastic life in detail. The ruins themselves are always open and there's good picnicking next to the rushing stream. The abbey is about 1.5km off the main Drogheda-Collon road (R168). A back road connects Mellifont with Monasterboice. There is no public transport to the abbey.

MONASTERBOICE

Crowing ravens lend just the right atmosphere to **Monasterboice** (admission free; ☼ sunrise-sunset; Ⓟ), an intriguing monastic site containing a cemetery, two ancient church ruins, one of the finest and tallest round towers in Ireland, and two of the best high crosses. The site can be reached directly from Mellifont via a winding route along narrow country roads.

Down a leafy lane and set in sweeping farmland, Monasterboice has a special atmosphere, particularly at quiet times. The original monastic settlement here is said to have been founded in the 5th or 6th century by St Buithe, a follower of St Patrick, although the site probably had pre-Christian significance. St Buithe's name somehow got converted to Boyne, and the river is named after him; it's said that he made a direct ascent to heaven via a ladder lowered from above. An invading Viking force took over the settlement in 968, only to be comprehensively expelled by Donal, the Irish high king of Tara, who killed at least 300 of the Vikings in the process.

The high crosses of Monasterboice are superb examples of Celtic art. The crosses had an important didactic use, bringing the gospels alive for the uneducated, and they were probably brightly painted originally, although all traces of colour have long disappeared.

The **round tower**, minus its cap, is over 30m tall, and stands in a corner of the complex. Records suggest the tower interior went up in flames in 1097, destroying many valuable manuscripts and other treasures. It's closed to the public.

There's a small gift shop outside the compound in summer. There are no set hours but come early or late in the day to avoid the crowds. It's just off the M1 motorway, about 8km north of Drogheda.

↘ KILKENNY & THE SOUTHEAST

KILKENNY & THE SOUTHEAST

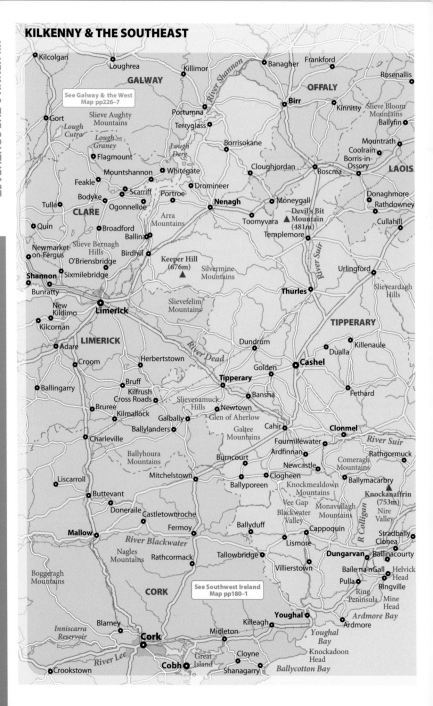

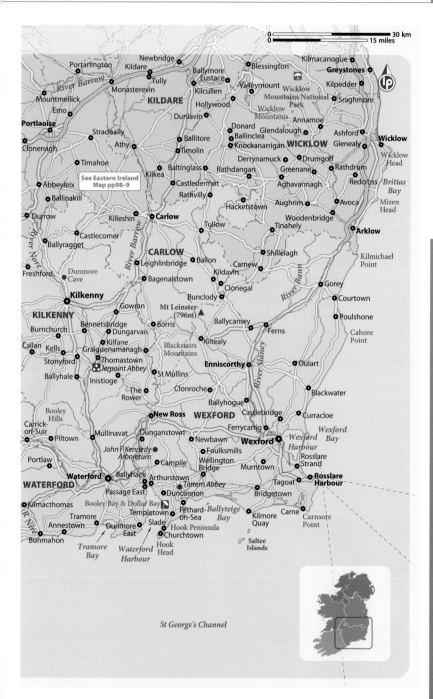

KILKENNY & SOUTHEAST HIGHLIGHTS

1 DUNGARVAN

BY PAUL FLYNN, HEAD CHEF AT THE TANNERY RESTAURANT & COOKERY SCHOOL

Obviously my primary interest is food and how it's prepared, but what I love most about Dungarvan is that its blossoming reputation as a foodie hub is more than well deserved – it's a real town rather than one dressed and dollied up for tourism.

PAUL FLYNN'S DON'T MISS LIST

❶ DUNGARVAN FARMERS MARKET
The Dungarvan Farmers Market (p169) helps engender a real sense of community as growers and customers come together to talk about produce, the weather and everything else! I love browsing the stalls – the best of what local growers have to offer.

❷ WATERFORD FESTIVAL OF FOOD
The Waterford Festival of Food (p168) has a terrific food fair, a host of cooking workshops and demonstrations, and plenty of talks by local producers at their farms, which is about as close to the source as you can get. It takes place during the third weekend in April.

❸ NUDE FOOD
Nude (p168) is the antithesis of what I call 'chefiness', which is all about drips, splodges and towers. Here you get big bowls of great food – impeccably sourced and put together in a wonderful way. As I often say to students, I

Clockwise from top: Waterford Festival of Food (p168); Heirloom tomatoes; Atlantic mackerel; Local produce stall at street market; Kerr's Pink potatoes

CLOCKWISE FROM TOP: GEORGE MUNDAY/ALAMY; OLIVER STREWE; OLIVER STREWE; OLIVER STREWE; OLIVER STREWE

spent 15 years trying to be a chef, and then the next 10 learning how to be a cook.

❹ CLIFF HOUSE HOTEL

OK, so it's not technically in Dungarvan, but Ardmore isn't too far away and the **Cliff House Hotel** (p170) should be in any list of top picks for the southeast – a great restaurant in a wonderful and elegant boutique hotel that has managed to make the most of the views and location.

❺ THE TANNERY RESTAURANT & COOKERY SCHOOL

The secret to my success is in my garden. Having the garden attached to the **cooking school** (p168) gives it soul. The economic downturn means

more people want to grow their own produce; we also help local special-needs schools set up gardens. A lot of people want to be celebrity chefs for the sake of it, but the ones I really admire, like Jamie Oliver and Rick Stein, are the ones who stand for something. I want to give something back.

⬃ THINGS YOU NEED TO KNOW

Best time to visit Summers are busiest, but autumn is quieter, cheaper and often has the best weather **Advance planning** If you're planning a cooking course you'll need to book months in advance **Resources** www.dungarvan tourism.com is the official website

KILKENNY & SOUTHEAST HIGHLIGHTS

⬊ KILKENNY CITY

Forget Galway, ignore Cork and don't even bother with Dublin. Kilkenny (p150) can stake its claim as Ireland's best city because it combines a stunning medieval historical centre of winding streets and notable buildings with a rich heritage of arts and culture – best expressed in the myriad festivals it hosts – and a throbbing nightlife that draws them in from far afield.

⬊ ROCK OF CASHEL

Surely a highlight of any trip to Ireland, the iconic and much-photographed Rock of Cashel (p173) is one of the country's most spectacular archaeological sites. For over a thousand years the rock's sturdy walls have protected a fabulous castle, an atmospheric (if roofless) abbey, a perfectly preserved round tower and the country's finest example of a Romanesque chapel.

4

⬎ NATIONAL 1798 REBELLION CENTRE

Ireland's history is rich in drama, struggle and tragedy, expressed poignantly in the National 1798 Rebellion Centre (p162), located in Enniscorthy, County Wexford. Near Vinegar Hill, site of the bloodiest battle of the 1798 Rebellion, this centre reconstructs the struggle for Irish independence in memorable, moving fashion.

5

⬎ SOUTHEASTERN KITCHENS

Although not quite as renowned as next-door County Cork, the southeast has been developing its own rep for gourmet excellence, thanks in part to pioneering chefs such as Paul Flynn in Dungarvan (p168) and Kevin Dundon in Arthurstown (p161), who have taken advantage of the southeast's fine local produce.

6

⬎ WALKS ON HOOK HEAD

Hook Head (p160), one of the southeast's most beautiful headlands, offers hypnotic horizons beyond the world's oldest working lighthouse. There are superb walks on both sides of the head; you'll battle raging winds, freak waves and blowholes on the western side – all part of the adventure that makes this area so special.

2 Parliament St, Kilkenny city (p150); 3 Rock of Cashel (p173), County Tipperary; 4 National 1798 Rebellion Centre (p162), County Wexfod; 5 Irish chef preparing a meal; 6 Hook Head lighthouse (p160), County Wexford

KILKENNY & SOUTHEAST'S BEST...

BEAUTY SPOTS

- **Kilmore Quay** (p158) Small fishing village that's all atmophere.
- **Hook Head** (p160) Brave the winds for beauty.
- **Ardmore Cliffs** (p169) Stunning views from the clifftop.
- **Nire Valley** (p172) Beautiful stretch of north County Waterford.
- **Rock of Cashel** (p173) Best viewed from just north of town.

FESTIVALS

- **Kilkenny Arts Festival** (p153) Second-largest festival of its kind in Ireland.
- **Kilkenny Rhythm & Roots** (p153) Ireland's biggest music festival.
- **Cat Laughs Comedy Festival** (p153) Acclaimed gathering of international comics.
- **Wexford Festival Opera** (p157) The best in the country.
- **Waterford Festival of Food** (p168) The best of the region's produce.

HISTORIC NOTABLES

- **Kilkenny Castle** (p152) One of the country's most important heritage sites.
- **Dunbrody Heritage Ship** (p161) Full-scale replica of a 19th-century 'famine ship'.
- **Rothe House** (p153) Perfect example of 16th-century Tudor home.
- **Jerpoint Abbey** (p156) Fine Cistercian ruin.
- **Irish National Heritage Park** (p158) Nine thousand years of Irish history in one spot!

LOCAL ACTIVITIES

- Try **sea angling** (p158) off the coast of Kilmore Quay.
- Walk **St Declan's Way** (p170), even as far as the Rock of Cashel.
- Try **fly fishing** (p172) in the Rivers Nire or Suir, County Waterford.
- Take a **cooking course** (p161 & p168) with either of the region's top chefs.

STEPHEN SAKS

Portal tomb dolmen replica, Irish National Heritage Park (p158)

THINGS YOU NEED TO KNOW

⇘ VITAL STATISTICS

- Area 7147 sq km
- Population 377,617
- Best time to go Autumn

⇘ AREAS IN A NUTSHELL

- County Kilkenny (p150) Handsome farming county dominated by the eponymous city.
- County Wexford (p157) The paragon of the traditional holiday destination in the sunny southeast.
- County Waterford (p164) A bustling capital city surrounded by diverse countryside and an often beautiful coastline.
- County Tipperary (p172) A rich historical tradition in one of Ireland's more prosperous farming counties.

⇘ ADVANCE PLANNING

- Five months before Book hotels and tickets if you're attending any of the big festivals in Kilkenny or Wexford.
- One month before Book your hotel and make a reservation if you want to take a cooking course.
- Two weeks before Cram in a little bit of Irish history, especially about Ireland's monastic tradition and its long struggle against the English!

⇘ RESOURCES

- Wexford Festival Opera (www.wexfordopera.com) This festival is much sought after.
- Wexford Live (www.wexlive.com) Gigs, theatres, exhibitions etc.
- Sailing Ireland (www.sailingireland.ie) Details of sailing charters.
- Discover Ireland (www.discoverireland.ie/southeast) Official tourist website.
- Kilkenny Tourist (www.kilkennytourist.com) What to see and do in Kilkenny and its environs.

⇘ GETTING AROUND

- Bus Good bus networks cover most of the area, but it's a slow way of exploring.
- Train The main towns are linked, but not necessarily to each other.
- Car The region's beauty is off the beaten path; you'll need a car to get there.

⇘ BE FOREWARNED

- Crowds Kilkenny gets slammed during the major festivals.
- Weather Statistically speaking, the southeast is the warmest region of Ireland, which doesn't necessarily mean it's warm. Come prepared.
- Hurling The sport of choice in the southeast, especially in Kilkenny, whose rivalry with Waterford and Wexford is passionate!

KILKENNY & THE SOUTHEAST ITINERARIES

KILKENNY BUZZ Three Days

Between the city's superb collection of pubs, the gorgeous medieval layout and its collection of world-class festivals, (1) **Kilkenny city** (p150) could keep you busy for months, never mind the three days you've allotted here. Still, to make the best of your time, make a beeline on day one to **Kilkenny Castle** (p152), which has been central to the major developments of Irish history since its construction in 1192. The basement **Butler Gallery** (p152) is small but usually chock-full of top-class international and local art. Be sure to look inside **St Canice's Cathedral** (p150) – which gave the city its name – and **Rothe House** (p153) before visiting the **Black Abbey** (p153), named after the dark robes of the Dominican monks who founded it. On day two, spread your wings and make for the antique shops of (2) **Thomastown** (p155) and the nearby ruins of **Jerpoint Abbey** (p156). On day three, make the trek across the border into County Tipperary and feast your eyes on the rock-top stronghold of (3) **Cashel** (p173). All the while, don't forget to sample Kilkenny's superb collection of great pubs!

SOUTHEASTERN COASTLINER Five Days

In five days you can explore the best of the coastline counties of Wexford and Waterford. Start in (1) **Wexford Town** (p157), using it as a base to visit the (2) **Irish National Heritage Park** (p158), before heading south (bypassing Rosslare Harbour altogether) towards the traditional fishing village of (3) **Kilmore Quay** (p158), from which you can visit the bird sanctuary on the (4) **Saltee Islands** (p158). On day three, continue westward around the Hook Peninsula, stopping off to sample some of Kevin Dundon's excellent fare at (5) **Dunbrody Country House** (p161). Cross the border into County Waterford and visit (6) **Waterford city** (p164), making sure not to miss the excellent **Waterford Museum of Treasures** (p164) and the ever-popular **Waterford Crystal Visitor Centre** (p164). On day four, keep going west and make for (7) **Dungarvan** (p168) or (8) **Ardmore** (p169), on the border with County Cork. Here there are some fine walks and some excellent restaurants.

SOUTHEASTERN TREASURES One Week

The southeast may be a well-trodden holiday destination, but it is also packed with heritage attractions that link the visitor to Irish history and its extraordinary cultural legacy. (1) Kilkenny city (p150) is an obvious destination for its central role in Irish history, but across the border in County Tipperary the heritage twins of (2) Cahir (p176), with its im-

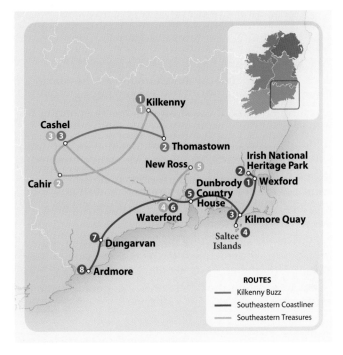

pressive 12th-century castle, and the unforgettable (3) Cashel (p172) testify to Ireland's rich Norman and monastic heritages, respectively. Moving southward through the Comeragh Mountains into County Waterford, travel eastward through the Nire Valley to (4) Waterford city (p164) and its host of superb treasures before moving northeast to (5) New Ross (p161) in County Wexford, home of the Dunbrody Famine Ship (p161), a faithful reconstruction of the boats that transported many a starving emigrant to the New World. The local Kennedy clan made such a trip – and went on to make a name for themselves in the US – and the Kennedy Homestead (p162) has been restored as a reminder of Irish–American ties.

DISCOVER KILKENNY & THE SOUTHEAST

Counties Wexford, Waterford and Kilkenny are (along with the southern chunk of Tipperary) collectively referred to as the 'sunny southeast'. This being Ireland the term is, of course, relative. But due to the moderating effect of the Gulf Stream, it *is* the country's warmest, driest region.

Although sun-lounger time might be limited, the coastal counties of Wexford and Waterford are wreathed with wide, sandy beaches, along with thatched fishing villages, genteel seaside towns and remote, windswept peninsulas littered by wrecks – as well as a swashbuckling history of marauding Vikings, lighthouse-keeping monks and shadowy knights' sects.

Deeper inland, the gently meandering River Barrow borders along verdant County Kilkenny, whose namesake city is home to a mighty castle, a magnificent cathedral, narrow, winding medieval lanes and cracking pubs – not to mention the hip eateries, happening clubs and a host of festivals that give this spirited little city a worldly sophistication.

COUNTY KILKENNY
KILKENNY CITY
pop 8661

Kilkenny (Cill Chainnigh) is the Ireland of many visitors' imaginations. Its majestic riverside castle, tangle of 17th-century passageways, centuries-old pubs with traditional live music and rows of colourful old-fashioned shopfronts all have a timeless appeal, as does its splendid medieval cathedral. But Kilkenny is also awash with contemporary eateries, and is a hotbed of arts, crafts and cultural activities.

Kilkenny's architectural charm owes a huge debt to the Middle Ages, when the city was a seat of political power. It's also sometimes called the 'marble city' because of the local black limestone, which resembles a slate-coloured marble and is used on floors and in decorative trim all over town.

INFORMATION
Tourist office (☎ 056-775 1500; www.discoverireland.ie; Rose Inn St; 9am-7pm Mon-Sat, 11am-5pm Sun Jul & Aug, 9.15am-1pm & 2-5pm Mon-Sat Sep-Jun) County Kilkenny's only tourist office, stocking excellent guides and walking maps, is set in Shee Alms House, built in local stone in 1582 by local benefactor Sir Richard Shee to provide help for the poor.

SIGHTS
ST CANICE'S CATHEDRAL
Soaring over the north end of the centre is Ireland's second-largest medieval cathedral (after St Patrick's in Dublin), **St Canice's Cathedral** (☎ 056-776 4971; www.stcanicescathedral.ie; St Canice's Pl; adult/child €4/3, combo ticket with Rothe House €6; 9am-6pm Mon-

Sat, 2-6pm Sun Jun-Aug, 10am-1pm & 2-5pm Mon-Sat, 2-5pm Sun Apr-May & Sep, 10am-1pm & 2-4pm Mon-Sat, 2-4pm Sun Oct-Mar). This Gothic edifice with its iconic round tower has had a long and fascinating history. Legend has it that the first monastery was built here in the 6th century by St Canice, Kilkenny's patron saint. Records show that a wooden church on the site was burned down in 1087.

The existing structure was raised between 1202 and 1285, but then endured a series of catastrophes and resurrections. The first disaster, the collapse of the church tower in 1332, was the consequence of Dame Alice Kyteler's conviction for witchcraft. Her maid was also convicted, and her nephew, William Outlawe, was implicated. The unfortunate maid was burned at the stake, but Dame Alice escaped to London and William spared himself by offering to re-roof part of St Canice's Cathedral with lead tiles. His new roof proved too heavy, however, bringing the church tower down with it.

In 1650, Cromwell's forces defaced and damaged the church, using it to stable their horses. Repairs began in 1661

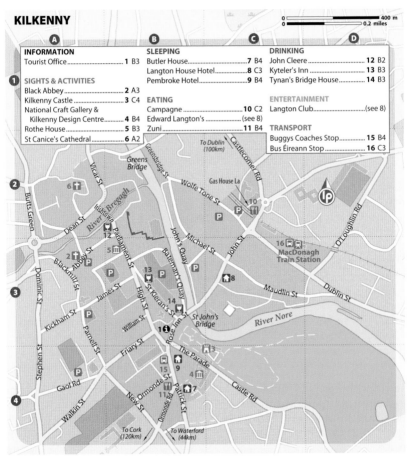

KILKENNY

0 — 400 m
0 — 0.2 miles

INFORMATION		
Tourist Office	**1**	B3

SIGHTS & ACTIVITIES		
Black Abbey	**2**	A3
Kilkenny Castle	**3**	C4
National Craft Gallery &		
Kilkenny Design Centre	**4**	B4
Rothe House	**5**	B3
St Canice's Cathedral	**6**	A2

SLEEPING		
Butler House	**7**	B4
Langton House Hotel	**8**	C3
Pembroke Hotel	**9**	B4

EATING		
Campagne	**10**	C2
Edward Langton's	(see 8)	
Zuni	**11**	B4

DRINKING		
John Cleere	**12**	B2
Kyteler's Inn	**13**	B3
Tynan's Bridge House	**14**	B3

ENTERTAINMENT		
Langton Club	(see 8)	

TRANSPORT		
Buggys Coaches Stop	**15**	B4
Bus Éireann Stop	**16**	C3

RICHARD CUMMINS

Kilkenny Castle

⬎ KILKENNY CASTLE

Rising above the Nore, Kilkenny Castle is one of Ireland's most visited heritage sites. The first structure on this strategic site was a wooden tower built in 1172 by Richard de Clare (aka Strongbow), the Anglo-Norman conqueror of Ireland. In 1192, Strongbow's son-in-law, William Marshall, erected a stone castle with four towers, three of which survive. The castle was bought by the powerful Butler family in 1391; their descendants lived there until 1935. Maintaining such a structure became a big financial strain, so most of the furnishings were sold at auction and the castle handed over to the city in 1967 – for the princely sum of £50.

Regular 40-minute guided tours focus on the Long Gallery, in the wing of the castle nearest the river. The gallery, which showcases stuffy portraits of the Butler family members over the centuries, is an impressive hall with high ceilings vividly painted with Celtic and Pre-Raphaelite motifs.

The castle basement is also home to the Butler Gallery, one of the country's most important art galleries outside Dublin. Small exhibitions featuring the work of contemporary artists are held throughout the year. Also in the basement, the castle kitchen houses a popular summertime cafe. You can head directly to either the Butler Gallery or the cafe without paying the tour admission price.

Things you need to know: Kilkenny Castle (☎ 056-772 1450; www.kilkennycastle .ie; adult/child €6/2.50; ☺ 9am-5.30pm Jun-Aug, 9.30am-5.30pm Apr-May & Sep, to 5pm Mar, to 4.30pm Oct-Feb); Butler Gallery (☎ 056-776 1106; www.butlergallery.com; admission free)

and are still ongoing. The beautiful roof in the nave was completed in 1863. Also worth a look is a model of Kilkenny as it was in 1642 – things haven't changed that much.

Outside the cathedral, a 30m-high round tower (adult/child €3/2.50; ☺ Apr-Oct) rises amid an odd array of ancient tombstones and is the oldest structure within the grounds. It was built sometime between AD 700 and 1000 on the site of an earlier Christian cemetery. Apart from missing its crown, the round tower is in excellent condition and those aged over 12 can admire a fine view from the top.

ROTHE HOUSE
Ireland's best surviving example of a 16th-century merchant's house is the Tudor **Rothe House** (☎ 056-772 2893; www .rothehouse.com; Parliament St; adult/child €5/4, combo ticket with cathedral €6; ⏱ 10.30am-5pm Mon-Sat, 3-5pm Sun Apr-Oct, 10.30am-4.30pm Mon-Sat Nov-Mar). Built around a series of courtyards, it now houses a museum with local artefacts including a well-used Viking sword found nearby and a grinning head sculpted from a stone by a Celtic artist. The king-post roof of the 2nd floor is a meticulous reconstruction.

BLACK ABBEY
This Dominican **abbey** (Abbey St; ⏱ open daily for Mass) was founded in 1225 by William Marshall and takes its name from the monks' black habits. In 1543, six years after Henry VIII's dissolution of the monasteries, it was turned into a courthouse. Following Cromwell's visit in 1650, it remained a roofless ruin until restoration in 1866. Much of what survives dates from the 18th and 19th centuries, but remnants of more ancient archways are still evident within the newer stonework. Look for the 13th-century coffins near the entrance.

NATIONAL CRAFT GALLERY & KILKENNY DESIGN CENTRE
Contemporary Irish crafts are showcased at this imaginative **gallery** (☎ 056-776 1804; www.ccoi.ie; Castle Yard; admission free; ⏱ 10am-6pm Mon-Sat, plus 11am-6pm Sun Apr-Dec) in the former castle stables that also house the Kilkenny Design Centre. Ceramics dominate, but exhibits often feature furniture, jewellery and weaving from the members of the Crafts Council of Ireland. There are regular classes in pottery and jewellery making.

FESTIVALS & EVENTS
Kilkenny hosts several world-class events throughout the year that attract revellers in the thousands.

Kilkenny Rhythm & Roots (☎ 056-779 0057; www.kilkennyroots.com; ⏱ early May) Over 30 pubs and other venues participate in hosting Ireland's biggest music festival, which has an emphasis on country and 'old-timey' American roots music.

Cat Laughs Comedy Festival (☎ 056-776 3416; www.thecatlaughs.com; ⏱ late May-early Jun) Acclaimed gathering of world-class comics in Kilkenny's hotels and pubs.

Kilkenny Arts Festival (☎ 056-775 2175; www.kilkennyarts.ie; ⏱ mid-Aug) The city comes alive with theatre, cinema, music, literature, visual arts, children's events and street spectacles for 10 action-packed days.

Kilkenny Celtic Festival (www.celticfestival.ie; ⏱ late Sep-early Oct) A week-long celebration of all things trad Irish, especially the language, which spans performances, exhibits, seminars and more.

SLEEPING
Pembroke Hotel (☎ 056-778 3500; www.pembrokekilkenny.com; Patrick St; r from €69; ☎) Wake up to castle views (from some of the 74 rooms) at this new epicentral hotel. The Pembroke's decor has a retro-funky feel, there's a leather-sofa-filled bar onsite, and free parking and use of the swimming and leisure facilities just around the corner.

Black Abbey (p153)

STEPHEN SAKS

Langton House Hotel (☎ 056-776 5133; www.langtons.ie; 67 John St; s €75-125, d €130-200; ℗ 🖳 📶) In the same family since the 1930s, but constantly evolving, this Kilkenny icon has some 30 rooms of varying styles – from clubby, leather-upholstered affairs to futuristic ones with 16-jet, computerised showers complete with double bench-seats, in-shower lighting and an in-shower radio to drown out your singing. There's also a fine restaurant (Edward Langton's; right) and a sophisticated nightclub, the Langton Club.

our pick **Butler House** (☎ 056-772 2828; www.butler.ie; 16 Patrick St; s €120-155, d €170-225; ℗ 🖳 📶) You can't stay in Kilkenny Castle, but this historic mansion is surely the next best thing. Once the home of the earls of Ormonde, who built the castle, these days it houses a boutique hotel with aristocratic trappings including sweeping staircases, marble fireplaces, an art collection and impeccably trimmed gardens. The 13 generously sized rooms are individually decorated, including brand-new bathrooms.

EATING

Zuni (☎ 056-772 3999; www.zuni.ie; 26 Patrick St; lunch mains €7-13, dinner mains €21-27; 🕑 lunch & dinner) Dark leathers contrasting with lighter tables and walls at this one-time theatre provide a stylised backdrop for chef Maria Rafferty's show-stopping cooking in the open kitchen. Irish produce takes on pan-European flavours in dishes like wild Wicklow venison with potato gratin.

Edward Langton's (☎ 056-776 5133; 67 John St; mains €15-28; 🕑 noon-10pm) The restaurant within this enormous, snazzy pub seems able to seat much of the town (certainly most everybody's here for Sunday lunch). The food is quality trad Irish: never-ending bowls of boiled potatoes and desserts like toffee and brown bread pudding with hot butterscotch sauce. Regular dinner-and-show specials for around €40 are popular with locals and tourists alike.

Campagne (☎ 056-777 2858; The Arches, 5 Gashouse Lane; lunch 2-/3-course set menu €24/28, dinner mains €24-29; ✆ lunch Fri & Sun, dinner Wed-Sun) Chef Garrett Byrne has returned home from the capital's Michelin-starred Chapter One restaurant to open this bold, stylish new restaurant in his native Kilkenny. Dubliners now commute to feast on specialities like chestnut and pheasant soup, and goose terrine with apple marmalade.

DRINKING
Tynan's Bridge House (☎ 056-772 1291; St John's Bridge) Looking like it might fall down at any moment, this wonky Georgian pub is the best trad bar in town. To be sure, the 300-year-old building has settled a bit over the years, but then so have many of the customers.

John Cleere (☎ 056-776 2573; 22 Parliament St) One of Kilkenny's finest venues for live music, this long bar has blues, jazz and rock, as well as trad music sessions.

Kyteler's Inn (☎ 056-772 1064; 27 St Kieran's St) Dame Alice Kyteler's (see p151) old house was built back in 1224 and has seen its share of history: the Dame had four husbands, all of whom died in suspicious circumstances, and she was charged with witchcraft in 1323. Today, tourists of all ages whoop it up in the dungeonlike basement.

GETTING THERE & AWAY
BUS
Bus Éireann (☎ 056-776 4933) operates from a shelter about 200m east of John St, adjacent to the train station. Bus Éireann also picks up and drops off passengers on St Patrick's St in the centre of town. There are services to Carlow (€7.40, one hour, 12 daily), Clonmel (€8.10, one hour, 12 daily), Cork (€16.10, three hours, two daily), Dublin (€10.80, 2¼ hours, five daily) and Waterford (€9, one hour, two daily).

JJ Kavanagh & Sons (☎ 056-883 1106; www.jjkavanagh.ie) has regular services to destinations including Carlow town, Portlaoise and Dublin airport, with wi-fi available in some vehicles.

Buggys Coaches (☎ 056-444 1264; www.buggy.ie) runs services to the north of the county.

TRAIN
On the eastern side of the new shopping mall of the same name, **MacDonagh Train Station** (☎ 056-772 2024) has five trains daily to/from Dublin's Heuston Station (from €10, 1¾ hours) and Waterford (from €10, 50 minutes).

CENTRAL KILKENNY
THOMASTOWN & AROUND
pop 1837

The busy N9 runs right through the centre of this small market town but it's worth stopping the car for a short stroll around its compact centre. Named after Welsh mercenary Thomas de Cantwell, Thomastown has some fragments of a medieval wall and the partly ruined 13th-century **Church of St Mary**. Down by the bridge, **Mullin's Castle** is the sole survivor of the 14 castles once here.

Like the rest of Kilkenny, the area has a vibrant craft scene. Look out for **Clay Creations** (☎ 056-772 4977; Low St; ✆ 10am-1pm & 2-5pm Tue-Sat) displaying the quixotic ceramics and sculptures of local artist Brid Lyons.

Just 4km southwest of Thomastown, high-fliers can tee off at the **Mount Juliet** (☎ 056-777 3000; www.mountjuliet.ie; Thomastown; green fees €90-120; Ⓟ ▣) golf course, designed by Jack Nicklaus. Set over 600 wooded hectares, it also has its own equestrian centre, a gym and spa,

Jerpoint Abbey

RICHARD CUMMINS

two restaurants, wine master-classes, and palatial rooms catering to every whim, right down to the pillow menu (accommodation from €169).

In town, the pistachio-and-cream-painted **Blackberry Cafe** (☎ 087 053 7858; Market St, Thomastown; dishes €4.50-7.50; 🕙 9.30am-5.30pm Mon-Fri, 10.30am-5.30pm Sat) does superb thick-cut sandwiches and warming soups (the tomato-and-basil is delicious) served with pumpkin-seed-speckled soda bread. Between noon and 2pm, great-value multicourse hot lunches see the place squeezed-to-bursting.

JERPOINT ABBEY

One of Ireland's finest Cistercian ruins, **Jerpoint Abbey** (☎ 056-24623; www.heritage ireland.ie; Hwy N9; adult/child €2.90/1.30; 🕙 9.30am-6pm Jun-Sep, 9.30am-5.30pm Oct, 10am-4pm Nov, 10am-5pm Mar-May, closed Dec-Feb, last tour 1hr before closing) is about 2.5km southwest of Thomastown on the N9. It was established in the 12th century and has been partially restored. The tower and cloister are late 14th or early 15th

century. Look for the series of often amusing figures carved on the cloister pillars, including a knight. There are also stone carvings on the church walls and in the tombs of members of the Butler and Walshe families. Faint traces of a 15th- or 16th-century painting remain on the northern wall of the church. This chancel area also contains a tomb thought to belong to hardheaded Felix O'Dulany, Jerpoint's first abbot and bishop of Ossory, who died in 1202.

According to local legend, St Nicholas (or Santa Claus) is buried near the abbey. While retreating in the Crusades, the knights of Jerpoint removed his body from Myra in modern-day Turkey and re-buried him in the **Church of St Nicholas** to the west of the abbey. The grave is marked by a broken slab decorated with a carving of a monk.

GETTING THERE & AWAY

There are bus services to Thomastown operated by **Kilbride Coaches** (☎ 051-423 633) and **JJ Kavanagh & Sons** (☎ 056-883

1106; www.jjkavanagh.ie). The train, however, offers the most frequent public transport to and from Thomastown. Five trains daily (four on Sunday) stop on the Dublin–Waterford route via Kilkenny (€7, 12 minutes). The station is located 1km west of town.

COUNTY WEXFORD
WEXFORD TOWN
pop 8931

At first glance, Wexford (Loch Garman) appears to be a sleepy port town where the silted estuary now sees less traffic than Waterford and Rosslare Harbour. However, there are reminders of its glorious Viking and Norman past in the meandering lanes off Main St – as well as some medieval monuments and a world-class opera festival in autumn, held in the city's state-of-the-art new opera house.

INFORMATION
Tourist office (☎ 053-912 3111; Quay front; ⊙ 9am-6pm Mon-Sat Apr-Oct plus 11am-1pm & 2-5pm Sun Jul & Aug, 9.15am-1pm & 2-5pm Mon-Sat Nov-Mar)

FESTIVALS & EVENTS
The **Wexford Festival Opera** (www.wexford opera.com), an 18-day extravaganza, is held at the Wexford Opera House in October/ November. First held in 1951, it's now the country's premier opera event, with rarely performed operas and shows playing to packed audiences. Fringe street theatre, poetry readings and exhibitions give the town a fiesta atmosphere during the festival, and many local bars run amateur song competitions. Although it's advisable to book several months ahead, it's worth checking for last-minute tickets.

SLEEPING
Whites of Wexford (☎ 053-912 2311; www .whitesofwexford.ie; Abbey St; r €98-256; P 🛜 ⏧) With its bars, restaurants and high-tech spa, Whites is a contemporary colossus. The 157 rooms are all metal right-angles, plasma and glass, gazing across the estuary to Curracloe Beach. Public areas and high-end rooms have wi-fi.

Ferrycarrig Hotel (☎ 053-912 0999; www.ferrycarrighotel.ie; Ferrycarrig; r €99-239; P 🛏 🛜 ⏧) Don't let the institutional exterior of this sprawling complex put you off – it's oriented to take advantage of its position on a glorious seal- and swan-inhabited stretch of the River Slaney. All 102 rooms have river views, and most have balconies. A handy 10-minute walk from the Irish National Heritage Park, the Ferrycarrig's restaurants, bars and leisure facilities are family friendly, but one floor of guestrooms is peacefully designated adults-only.

EATING
ourpick **Yard** (☎ 053-914 4083; 3 Lower George St; lunch mains €8-12, dinner mains €18.50-26.50; ⊙ cafe 9am-6pm, restaurant lunch & dinner) The brainchild of the Centenary Stores' owner, this intimate low-lit restaurant opens to an elegant courtyard beneath a canopy of fairy lights. Adventurous contemporary cuisine ranges from oxtail ragout with truffle oil to a chocolate-cola cake.

GETTING THERE & AROUND
BUS
Bus Éireann (☎ 053-912 2522; www.bus eireann.ie) buses leave from O'Hanrahan train station on Redmond Sq and travel to Rosslare Harbour (€4.50, 30 minutes, at least nine daily), Waterford (€7.20, one hour, six daily Monday to Saturday, three Sunday) and Dublin (€13.10, three hours, at least nine daily), normally via

Enniscorthy (€5.80, 25 minutes). Tickets are available across the street at the Mace newsagency.

TRAIN

O'Hanrahan Station (☎ 053-912 2522; **Redmond Pl**) is situated at the northern end of town. Wexford is on the Dublin Connolly Station (€22.50, 2½ hours) to Rosslare Europort (€4.70, 25 minutes) line (via Enniscorthy and Rosslare Strand), and is serviced by three trains daily in each direction.

AROUND WEXFORD TOWN

IRISH NATIONAL HERITAGE PARK

The **Irish National Heritage Park** (☎ 053-912 0733; Ferrycarrig; adult/under 13yr/13-16yr/family incl 90min guided tour €8/4/6.50/20; 9.30am-6.30pm Apr-Sep, 9.30am-5.30pm Oct-Mar) successfully squashes 9000 years of Irish history, up to the Normans, into an entertaining and informative visit. Costumed actors guide you past a re-created Neolithic farmstead, ring fort, stone circle, monastery, *crannóg* (lake settlement on an artificial island), Viking shipyard and Norman castle, while sound effects and smoking fires add to the realism.

The park is 3.5km northwest of Wexford town on the N11. A taxi from Wexford town costs about €7.

KILMORE QUAY

pop 396

Dotted with thatched cottages, Kilmore Quay is a small, working fishing village whose harbour is the jumping-off point for Ireland's largest bird sanctuary, the Saltee Islands (right), which are clearly visible out to sea.

Mussel in on the four-day **Seafood Festival** (☎ 053-912 9918) in mid-July for music, dancing and, of course, tastings.

SIGHTS & ACTIVITIES

To charter a boat for sea angling, contact **Kilmore Quay Boat Charters** (☎ 053-912 9704).

Sailing Ireland (☎ 053-913 9163; www .sailingireland.ie) offers five-day live-aboard courses (from €750 per person) and skippered boat charters (per boat €300/550 per half-day/day).

GETTING THERE & AWAY

The Viking Shuttle Bus, operated by **Wexford Bus** (☎ 053-914 2742; www.wexford bus.com), runs to/from Wexford up to four times daily (€5.50, 45 minutes). **Bus Éireann** (☎ 053-912 2522) service 383 covers the same route on Wednesday and Saturday (two services in each direction).

SALTEE ISLANDS

Once the haunt of privateers, smugglers and 'dyvars pyrates', the **Saltee Islands** (www.salteeislands.info) now have a peaceful existence as one of Europe's most important bird sanctuaries. Over 375 recorded species make their home here, 4km offshore from Kilmore Quay, principally the gannet, guillemot, cormorant, kittiwake, puffin, aux and Manx shearwater. The best time to visit is the spring and early summer nesting season. The birds leave once the chicks can fly, and by early August it's eerily quiet.

Boats make the trip from Kilmore Quay harbour, but docking depends on the wind direction and is often impossible. Contact local boatmen such as **Declan Bates** (☎ 053-912 9684, 087 252 9736; day trip €25), who also runs a 1½-hour trip around the islands (€20).

EOIN CLARKE

Headland, Saltee Islands

HOOK PENINSULA & AROUND

The road shadowing the long, tapering finger of the Hook Peninsula is signposted as the Ring of Hook coastal drive. Around every other bend is a quiet beach, a crumbling fortress, a stately abbey or a seafood restaurant, with the world's oldest working lighthouse flung out at its tip.

Strongbow (Richard de Clare, earl of Pembroke) landed here on his way to capture Waterford in 1169, reputedly instructing his men to land 'by Hook or by Crooke', the latter referring to the nearby settlement of Crooke in County Waterford across the harbour.

TINTERN ABBEY

In better structural condition than its Welsh counterpart, from where its first monks hailed, Ireland's **Tintern Abbey** (☎ 051-562 650; Saltmills; admission free; ⏱ 10am-6pm mid-Jun–Sep, 10am-5pm Oct) is secluded amid 40 hectares of woodland. William Marshal, earl of Pembroke,

founded the Cistercian abbey in the early 13th century after he nearly perished at sea and swore to establish a church if he made it ashore.

Allow some time to explore the **Tintern Trails**, a series of short woodland and coastal tracks around the abbey estate. Free walking maps are available from the tourist office in Fethard-on-Sea.

FETHARD-ON-SEA
pop 326

Continuing south towards the Head, Fethard is the largest village in the area. It's home to the scant ruins of the 9th-century church **St Mogue's** and a 15th-century **castle** (too unstable to walk inside), which belonged to the bishop of Ferns. There's a small community-run **tourist office** (☎ 051-397 502; www.thehook -wexford.com; Main St; ⏱ 9.30am-5pm Mon-Fri) opposite the castle.

About 1km north of town, the quiet little **Ocean Island Camping & Caravan Park** (☎ 051-397 148; camp sites €24; ⏱ Apr-Sep)

KILKENNY & THE SOUTHEAST

COUNTY WEXFORD

Hook Head lighthouse

RICHARD CUMMINS

has a shop, a playground, and laundry and games rooms.

HOOK HEAD & AROUND

The journey from Fethard to Hook Head takes in a hypnotic stretch of horizon, with few houses between the flat, open fields on the tapering peninsula. Views extend across Waterford Harbour and, on a clear day, as far as the Comeragh and Galtee Mountains.

On its southern tip, Hook Head is capped by the world's oldest working **lighthouse** (☎ 051-397 055; adult/child €6/3.50 incl guided tour; ☺ 9.30am-6pm Jun-Aug, 9.30am-5.30pm May & Sep, 9.30am-5pm Nov-Feb, closed mid-late Dec), which was staffed until 1996. It's said that monks lit a beacon on the head from the 5th century and that the first Viking invaders were so happy to have a guiding light that they left them alone. In the early 13th century, William Marshal erected a more permanent structure, which has remained largely unchanged. Traces of the lighthouse keepers' lives remain inside the black-

and-white-striped tower. Access is by half-hour guided tour. The visitor centre has a decent cafe/restaurant.

There are brilliant, blustery **walks** on both sides of the head, but be aware of freak waves and numerous blowholes on the western side of the peninsula. Caves, crevasses and gullies are part of the underwater scenery at diving sites out from the inlet under the lighthouse and from the rocks at the southwestern corner of the head, with a maximum depth of 15m. If it's too rough, try Churchtown, 1km north of the point on the western side of the peninsula. The rocks south of Slade Harbour are another popular area. Contact Ray Forlong at the **Hook Sub Aqua Club** (☎ 087 678 1636; rfurlong@boland cars.ie) for advice.

About 5km northeast of the Hook Head lighthouse, ghostly Loftus Hall (closed to the public), built by the Marquis of Ely in the 1870s, gazes across the estuary at Dunmore East. The English-owned Loftus estate once covered much of the peninsula.

About 3km further on, turning left at a small roundabout brings you to the village of **Slade**, where the most activity is the swirl of seagulls above the ruined castle and harbour.

Across the street from the church, the roadside pub **Templar's Inn** (☎ 051-397 162; Templetown; mains €10-22; ☙ restaurant 12.30-9pm Mar-Oct, noon-8pm Thu-Sun Nov-Mar, pub noon-late daily) opens to a panoramic outdoor terrace overlooking the church, fields and ocean beyond. Inside, the dark-timber interior looks like a wayfarers' tavern, but is a cosy place for a steak or seafood. Owner Nancy is a fount of information on the area.

Just beyond Templetown en route to Duncannon are two small, delightfully secluded beaches: **Dollar Bay** and **Booley Bay**.

SLEEPING & EATING

our pick **Dunbrody Country House Hotel, Restaurant & Cookery School** (☎ 051-389 600; www.dunbrodyhouse.com; Arthurstown; 2-/3-course restaurant meal €52/65, tasting menu with paired wines €80; P ☎) Chef Kevin Dundon is a familiar face on Irish TV, and the author of cookbooks *Full On Irish* and *Great Family Food*. His spa hotel (single/double from €145/240), in a period-decorated 1830s Georgian manor on 120-hectare grounds, is the stuff of foodies' fantasies, with a gourmet restaurant and cooking school (1-/2-day courses €175/320 excluding accommodation).

GETTING THERE & AWAY

West Coast Wexford Rural Transport (☎ 051-389 679; www.wexfordruralbus.com; Ramsgrange Centre, New Ross) has at least one service per week to towns throughout the upper Hook Peninsula. Return fares are €5 to €8; €3 for students and under-16s.

On Monday and Thursday, **Bus Éireann** (☎ 053-912 2522) service 370 runs between Waterford, New Ross, Duncannon, Templetown, Fethard, Wellington Bridge and Wexford. The entire journey takes 2¾ hours. The same bus links Waterford, New Ross and Duncannon from Monday to Saturday (departing in the evening), and Waterford, New Ross, Wellington Bridge and Wexford on Wednesday and Saturday. In all cases there is one service in each direction (none on Sunday).

NEW ROSS

pop 4677

The big attraction at New Ross (Rhos Mhic Triúin), 34km west of Wexford town, is the opportunity to board a 19th-century Famine ship. But New Ross' historical links stretch back much further, to the 12th century, when it developed as a Norman port on the River Barrow. A group of rebels tried to seize the town during the 1798 Rising. They were repelled by the defending garrison, leaving 3000 dead and much of the place in tatters. Today its eastern bank retains some intriguing steep, narrow streets and the impressive ruins of a medieval abbey.

The **tourist office** (☎ 051-421 857; The Quay; ☙ 9am-6pm Apr-Sep, 9am-5pm Oct-Mar) doubles as the entrance to the Dunbrody Heritage Ship, and also has a small cafe and internet terminals (€2 per 20 minutes).

SIGHTS & ACTIVITIES

Émigrés' sorrowful yet often-inspiring stories are brought to life by actors during a 30-minute tour of the **Dunbrody Heritage Ship** (☎ 051-425 239; www.dunbrody.com; The Quay; adult/child €7.50/4.50; ☙ 10am-6pm Apr-Sep, 10am-5pm Oct-Mar), a full-scale replica 1845 Famine ship (also known as a 'coffin ship', due to the high number of passengers who didn't survive the journey). Prior to the tour, a 10-minute film gives you background on the original three-masted barque and the construction of the new one. Admission includes access to the on-site database of Irish emigration to America from 1845 to 1875, containing over two million records.

GETTING THERE & AWAY

Bus Éireann (☎ 053-912 2522) buses depart from Dunbrody Inn on the Quay and travel to Waterford (€5.40, 30 minutes, 11 daily Monday to Saturday, seven Sunday), Wexford (€6.30, 40 minutes, four daily Monday to Friday, three Saturday), Rosslare Harbour (€12.20, one hour, four daily Monday to Saturday, three Sunday) and Dublin (€12.20, three hours, four daily).

AROUND NEW ROSS

About 7km south of New Ross is the **Kennedy Homestead** (☎ 051-388 264; www.kennedyhomestead.com; Dunganstown; adult/child/family €5/2.50/15; ☼ 10am-5pm Jul & Aug, 11.30am-4.30pm Mon-Fri May, Jun & Sep, by appointment rest of year), the birthplace of Patrick Kennedy, the great-grandfather of John F Kennedy who left Ireland for the USA in 1848. When JFK visited the farm in 1963 and hugged the current owner's grandmother, it was his first public display of affection according to his sister Jean. Jean later unveiled the plaque here. The outbuildings have been turned into a museum that examines the Irish American dynasty's history on both sides of the Atlantic.

Containing 4500 species of trees and shrubs in 252 hectares of woodlands and gardens, the **John F Kennedy Arboretum** (☎ 051-388 171; New Ross; adult/child/family €2.90/1.30/7.40; ☼ 10am-8pm May-Aug, 10am-6.30pm Apr & Sep, 10am-5pm Oct-Mar) is the promised land for families on a sunny day. The park, 2km southeast of the Kennedy Homestead, has a small visitor centre, tearooms and a picnic area; a miniature train tootles around in the summer months. **Slieve Coillte** (270m), opposite the park entrance, has a viewing point from where you can see the arboretum and six counties on a clear day.

ENNISCORTHY

pop 3241

County Wexford's second-largest town, Enniscorthy (Inis Coirthaidh), has a warren of steep streets descending from Augustus Pugin's cathedral to the Norman castle and the River Slaney. Enniscorthy is inextricably linked to some of the fiercest fighting of the 1798 Rising, when rebels captured the town and set up camp at Vinegar Hill.

INFORMATION

The **tourist office** (☎ 053-923 4699; Mill Park Rd; ☼ 9.30am-5pm Mon-Fri, noon-4pm Sat & Sun Jun-Aug, 9.30am-4pm Mon-Fri Sep-May), inside the National 1798 Rebellion Centre, can book accommodation (€4).

SIGHTS

Visiting the excellent **National 1798 Rebellion Centre** (☎ 053-923 7198; www .iol.ie/~98com; Mill Park Rd; adult/child €6/3.50; ☼ same hours as tourist office) before climbing Vinegar Hill greatly enhances its impact. The centre's exhibits cover the French and American revolutions that sparked Wexford's abortive uprising against British rule in Ireland, before chronicling what was one of the most bloodthirsty battles of the 1798 Rebellion, and a turning point in the struggle. A month later, British government troops attacked and

Enniscorthy

RICHARD CUMMINS

forced the rebels to retreat, massacring hundreds of women and children in the 'follow-up' operation. Interactive displays include a chessboard with pieces representing key figures in the Rising, and a multiscreen re-creation of the finale atop a virtual Vinegar Hill. It's chilly inside – bring a jacket. From Abbey Sq walk out of town along Mill Park Rd, then take the first right after the school.

To reach **Vinegar Hill** itself, follow the brown sign from Templeshannon on the eastern side of the river. It takes about 45 minutes to walk to the top of the hill (or five minutes to drive). At the summit there's a memorial to the uprising.

During the 1798 Rising, rebels used the **Enniscorthy Castle** as a prison. The stout, four-towered keep was built by the Normans; Queen Elizabeth I awarded its lease to the poet Edmund Spenser for the flattering things he said about her in his epic *The Faerie Queene*. Rather ungratefully, he sold it on to a local landlord. Like everything else in these parts, the castle was attacked by Cromwell in 1649.

Restored to its original glory (check out the star-spangled roof), the dazzling Roman Catholic **St Aidan's Cathedral** (1846) was designed by Augustus Pugin, the architect behind the Houses of Parliament in London.

SLEEPING

Treacy's Hotel (☎ 053-923 7798; www.treacys hotel.com; Templeshannon; r €150; P ⓦ) With spruced-up rooms in streamlined, woodsy colours, Treacy's also scores with two bars, two restaurants (one international, one Thai) and a nightclub. Entertainment includes live bands and Irish dancing, and guests can use the leisure centre opposite for free.

Monart (☎ 053-923 8999; www.monart.ie; The Still; r from €175; P ⓔ) Hidden in woodland 2km west of Enniscorthy, rooms at this discreet spa resort surround a pond. Modern touches such as a glass walkway have been added to the main house without lessening its stately grandeur. You can be sure of peace and quiet, as kids aren't allowed.

GETTING THERE & AWAY

BUS

Bus Éireann (☎ 053-912 2522) stops on the Shannon Quay on the eastern bank of the river, outside the **Bus Stop Shop** (☎ 053-923 3291; ⏰ 9am-10pm) where you can buy tickets. There are nine daily buses to Dublin (€10.50, 2½ hours), and eight to Rosslare Harbour (€9.30, one hour) via Wexford (€5.80, 25 minutes).

TRAIN

The **train station** (☎ 053-923 3488) is on the eastern bank of the river. The one line serves Dublin Connolly Station (€22.50, 2¼ hours), Wexford (€6.50, 25 minutes) and Rosslare Europort (€7.70, 45 minutes) three times daily.

COUNTY WATERFORD
WATERFORD CITY

pop 45,775

Ireland's oldest city, Waterford (Port Láirge), is first and foremost a busy port. Some parts of the city still feel almost medieval though, with narrow alleyways leading off larger streets. A great introduction to the area is Waterford's state-of-the-art museum on the quay-front, which uses multimedia wizardry to convey the city's extensive history.

INFORMATION

Waterford city tourist office (☎ 051-875 823; www.discoverireland.ie/southeast; Merchants Quay; ⏰ 9am-6pm Mon-Sat, 11am-5pm Sun Jul & Aug, 9.30am-5.30pm Mon-Fri, 10am-6pm Sat May & Jun, 9.15am-5pm Mon-Sat Sep-Apr)

SIGHTS & ACTIVITIES

WATERFORD MUSEUM OF TREASURES

The dazzling **Waterford Museum of Treasures** (☎ 051-304 500; www.waterford treasures.com; Hanover St; adult/child €7/3.20; ⏰ 9am-6pm Mon-Sat, 11am-5pm Sun Jun-Aug, 10am-5pm Mon-Sat, 11am-5pm Sun Sep-May) is one of Ireland's widest-ranging and most high-tech museums. An audio-guide leads you through exhibitions navigating the town's 1000-year-strong history. A highlight is the 'Viking longship', a rocking ride narrated by Waterford's Nordic forebears, who call themselves 'children of the raven' but sound more like comedic Scotsmen. You can also attend the marriage of Strongbow and local princess Aoife, who promises to teach her Anglo-Norman lord how the Irish feast.

Though they can feel a little lost under the weight of 21st-century technology, there are some beautiful 'real' exhibits. Golden Viking brooches, jewel-encrusted Norman crosses, the magnificent 1372 Great Charter Roll and 18th-century church silver are among the booty.

WATERFORD CRYSTAL VISITOR CENTRE

The city's famed Waterford Crystal was not immune to Ireland's economic woes. In 2009, the nation was shocked when this civic icon went into receivership. Despite a sit-in by workers, who symbolically kept the furnaces burning, the future of manufacturing here remained uncertain when this book went to press. However, you can still stop by the **Waterford Crystal Visitor Centre** (☎ 051-332 500; www.waterfordvisitorcentre.com; Cork Rd; ⏰ 9am-5pm), 2km south of the centre. In lieu of its previous factory tours, it's due to house a new multimedia 'visitor experience' by the time you're reading this, including live demonstrations. The factory has previously ridden out hard times: the first Waterford glass factory was established at the western end of the riverside quays in 1783 but closed

68 years later because of punitive taxes imposed by the British before its revival last century. Buses 1C and 3C run to the visitor centre from opposite the Clock Tower every 15 minutes (€1.60).

SLEEPING

Granville Hotel (☎ 051-305 555; www.granville-hotel.ie; Meagher Quay; s/d from €80/99; P 🛜) The floodlit 18th-century building overlooking the river is the Granville, one of Ireland's oldest hotels. Brocaded bedrooms maintain a touch of Georgian elegance, as do the public areas, including

a fine restaurant and bar. The hotel has had its share of famous guests: Charles Stewart Parnell gave a speech from a 1st-floor window.

ourpick Waterford Castle (☎ 051-878 203; www.waterfordcastle.com; The Island, Ballinakill; s €245, d €335-450, cottages per night from €300; P 🖥 🛜) Getting away from it all is an understatement at this mid-19th-century turreted castle, which is located on its own 124-hectare island roamed by deer. A free, private car ferry signposted just east of the Waterford Regional Hospital provides around-the-clock

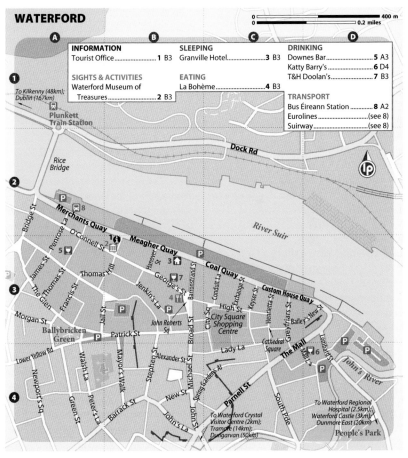

WATERFORD

0 ____ 400 m
0 ____ 0.2 miles

INFORMATION		SLEEPING		DRINKING	
Tourist Office	**1** B3	Granville Hotel	**3** B3	Downes Bar	**5** A3
				Katty Barry's	**6** D4
SIGHTS & ACTIVITIES		EATING		T&H Doolan's	**7** B3
Waterford Museum of		La Bohème	**4** B3		
Treasures	**2** B3			TRANSPORT	
				Bus Éireann Station	**8** A2
				Eurolines	(see 8)
				Suirway	(see 8)

DOUG MCKINLAY
Worker at Waterford Crystal (p164)

access. All 19 castle rooms have claw-foot baths, and some have poster beds. There are also 48 contemporary self-catering cottages on the island. Breakfast is available for €18 to €22, and both guests and nonguests can dine on organic fare in chef Michael Quinn's sublime oak-panelled restaurant (menus from €65), or play a round of golf (green fees midweek/weekend €44/52).

EATING

La Bohème (☎ 051-875 645; 2 George's St; mains €29-32, 7-course tasting menu €75; ☷ dinner Tue-Sat) Down a short flight of steps in the Georgian 'Port of Waterford' vaults, this romantic gem combines French flair with fresh Irish produce, resulting in mains such as mustard-and-honey rack of lamb or seaweed-encrusted scallops, and desserts like Tahitian vanilla crème brûlée.

DRINKING

Downes Bar (☎ 051-874 118; Thomas St; ☷ from 5pm) For a change from stout,

drop into Downes, which has been brewing its No 9 Irish whiskey for over two centuries. Have a dram in its series of character-filled rooms, or buy a bottle to take away.

T&H Doolan's (☎ 051-841 504; 32 George's St) A licensed establishment for over 300 years, Doolan's hosts traditional music every night of the week.

Katty Barry's (☎ 051-855 095; Mall Lane) Don't be discouraged by the plain exterior and side-street location; this small, friendly place serves a smooth Guinness, and has trad sessions every Wednesday.

GETTING THERE & AWAY
BUS

The **Bus Éireann** (☎ 051-879 000) station is on the waterfront at Merchant's Quay. There are frequent daily services to Tramore (€2.70, 30 minutes); Dublin (€12.20, three hours) via Enniscorthy or Carlow; Wexford (€7.20, 1½ hours); Killarney (€21.20, 4¼ hours) via Cork (€17.10, 2¼ hours); and Dungarvan (€10.30, 50 minutes).

Eurolines (☎ 051-879 000; www.eurolines .ie) runs daily buses to London (€58, 13 hours).

Suirway (☎ 051-382 209; www.suirway .com) buses depart to Dunmore East (€4, 30 minutes, at least seven daily Monday to Saturday), Passage East (€4, 30 minutes, at least three daily Monday to Saturday) and Portlaw (€4, 30 minutes, at least four daily Monday to Saturday) from opposite the tourist office, next to the Bus Éireann station.

TRAIN
Plunkett train station (☎ 051-873 401) is north of the river. There are four to six daily services to/from Dublin's Heuston Station (€27 to €34.50, 2¾ hours), Kilkenny (€14.90 to €19, 45 minutes), and Limerick (€34, 2¾ hours) via Limerick Junction or Kildare.

SOUTHEAST COUNTY WATERFORD
This hidden corner of the county makes an easy day trip from Waterford city, but it's also easy to fit in as part of an onward journey.

Some 19km southeast of Waterford, **Dunmore East** (Dún Mór) is strung out along a coastline of red sandstone cliffs full of screaming kittiwakes and concealed coves. In the 19th century, the town was a station for the steam packets that carried mail between England and the south of Ireland. Legacies left from the era include thatched cottages lining the main street and an unusual Doric lighthouse (1825) overlooking the working harbour.

Less than 14km east of Waterford is the estuary village of **Passage East**, from where car ferries yo-yo to Ballyhack in County Wexford. A pretty little fishing village, it's also lined with thatched cottages surrounding its neat harbour.

Although the main roads (and thus public transport) involve returning to Waterford, a little-travelled 11km-long **coast road** wiggles between Dunmore East and Passage East. Single-vehicle-width, steep and poorly signed in parts (don't worry, you won't get lost), it offers mesmerising views of the ocean and undulating fields that you won't see from the main thoroughfares.

Information on the area is available at www.discoverdunmore.com.

SLEEPING & EATING
Haven Hotel (☎ 051-383 150; www.thehaven hotel.com; Dunmore East; s €65, d €110-130; ☺ Mar-Oct; ℗) Built in the 1860s as a summer house for the Malcolmson family, whose coat of arms can still be seen on the fireplaces, the Haven is now run by the Kelly family and remains an elegant retreat with wood-panelled bathrooms and, in two rooms, four-poster beds. Local produce underpins dishes in the restaurant (mains €12.50 to €23, open from 4pm Monday to Saturday and from 12.30pm Sunday) and the low-lit crimson-toned bar (dishes €4.50 to €8.50, open from noon to 4pm).

Parkswood (☎ 051-380 863; www.parks wood.com; Passage East; s €95, d €160-180; ☺ Easter-Nov; ℗ ☏) Storytelling evenings and themed food nights are among the events that take place at this rather pricey but commendably eco-conscious four-room B&B situated on 2.5 hectares on the River Suir. Breakfasts and table d'hôte-style evening meals (€25) are sourced from the gardens, including homemade jams and eggs fresh from the resident hens. Hosts Theresa and Roger can also arrange bike hire for guests (€20 per day).

Bay Cafe (☎ 051-383 900; Dock Rd, Dunmore East; mains €7-11; ⏰ 9am-6pm) With harbour views so good there's a whale-watching guide stuck to its window, this artsy cafe serves interesting twists on local produce like mackerel pâté on homemade brown bread, and Scandinavian-style open-faced seafood sandwiches.

GETTING THERE & AWAY
BUS
Suirway (☎ 051-382 209; www.suirway.com) buses connect Waterford with Dunmore East and Passage East.

DUNGARVAN
pop 7813

With its pastel-shaded buildings ringing the picturesque bay where the River Colligan meets the sea, Dungarvan (Dún Garbhán) resembles Galway in miniature. St Garvan founded a monastery here in the 7th century, but most of the centre dates from the early 19th century when the duke of Devonshire rebuilt the streets around Grattan Sq. Overlooking the bay are a dramatic ruined castle and an Augustinian abbey, as well as lively pubs. The Waterford county town, Dungarvan is also becoming a foodie haven, with outstanding restaurants, a state-of-the-art cooking school and the annual Waterford Festival of Food.

FESTIVALS & EVENTS
The area's abundant fresh produce is celebrated during mid-April's **Waterford Festival of Food** (www.waterfordfestivalof food.ie), featuring cooking workshops and demonstrations, talks by local producers at their farms, and a food fair.

Over the early May bank-holiday weekend, Dungarvan pubs and hotels host the **Féile na nDéise** (www.feilenandeise.com), a lively traditional music and dance festival that attracts around 200 musicians.

SLEEPING
ourpick Powersfield House (☎ 058-45594; www.powersfield.com; Ballinamuck West; s €60-70, d €100-110; ℗) Energetic mother, chef and cooking instructor Eunice Power lives in one half of this Georgian home with her family, and has opened four beautifully decorated rooms in the other for guests. Breakfast is a veritable feast of Eunice's jams, chutneys and other delicacies from her garden, as are her three-course evening meals (€25 to €35, by arrangement). It's a five-minute drive north of town on the road to Clonmel.

EATING
Nude Food (☎ 058-24594; O'Connell St; mains €7.50-14.50; ⏰ 9am-6pm Mon-Wed, 9am-9.30pm Thu-Sat) Jazz provides a soulful soundtrack for sipping Illy coffee or tucking into a wholesome ploughman's platter or veggie burger. Deli items including artisan breads made on the premises, marinated vegetables and salads and organic juices are perfect for a gourmet beach picnic.

ourpick Tannery Restaurant and Cookery School (☎ 058-45420; www.tannery .ie; 10 Quay St; mains €18-29; ⏰ 12.30-2.30pm Tue-Fri & Sun, 6.30-9.30pm Tue-Sat, 6.30-9pm Sun Jul & Aug) An old leather tannery now houses this innovative restaurant, where Paul Flynn (p142) creates seasonally changing dishes like quail and foie gras pie or pan-fried potato gnocchi with red wine butter, followed by roasted fruits with cinnamon custard or warm chocolate mousse with violets. Everything is served so beautifully that it's almost – almost – a shame to eat it. Looking like a futuristic kitchen showroom, Flynn's cooking school (demonstration/class including meal from €60/150) adjoins a fruit, vege-

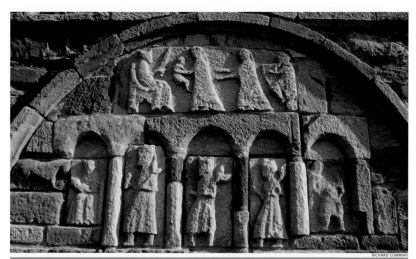
Arcade detail, St Declan's Church (p170), Ardmore
RICHARD CUMMINS

table and herb garden. Some courses include foraging for ingredients, while market gardening classes (from €95) with fun-loving horticulturalist Tim Yorke cover soil preparation, seed germination, bed maintenance and more.

Breads, cheeses, chocolate and hot food to eat on the spot are available at Dungarvan's weekly **farmers market** (www.dungarvanfarmersmarket.com; Grattan Sq; 🕙 9am-2pm Thu).

RING PENINSULA
pop 380

Just 15 minutes' drive from Dungarvan, the Ring Peninsula (An Rinn, meaning 'the headland') is one of Ireland's best-known Gaeltacht areas. En route, views of the Comeragh Mountains, Dungarvan Bay and the Copper Coast drift away to the northeast. At the peninsula's tip, the small working harbour in Helvick Head has a **monument** to the crew of *Erin's Hope*. The crew brought guns from New York in 1867, intending to start a Fenian uprising, but were arrested when they

landed here. Follow signs to An Rinn then Cé Heilbhic, passing Baíle na nGall ('village of strangers'; it was founded by fishermen from elsewhere).

Ex–Waterford Crystal worker Eamonn Terry returned home to the peninsula to set up his own workshop, **Criostal na Rinne** (☎ 058-46174; www.criostal.com; 🕙 by appointment), where you can buy deep-prismatic-cut, full-lead crystal vases, bowls, clocks, jewellery and even chandeliers.

ARDMORE
pop 415

The pretty seaside village of Ardmore may look insignificant, but it's claimed that St Declan set up shop here between 350 and 420. This brought Christianity to southeast Ireland long before St Patrick arrived from Britain. Today's visitors come mainly for its beautiful strand, water sports, and superb places to eat and/or sleep.

Tourist information is available at **Ardmore Pottery** (☎ 024-94152; 🕙 10am-6pm Mon-Sat, 2-6pm Sun May-Oct, by appointment Sat & Sun Nov-Apr).

SIGHTS & ACTIVITIES

In a striking position on a hill above town, the ruins of St Declan's Church stand on the site of St Declan's original monastery alongside a cone-roofed, 29m-high, 12th-century round tower, one of the best examples of these structures in Ireland.

The 94km St Declan's Way mostly traces an old pilgrimage route from Ardmore to the Rock of Cashel (County Tipperary) via Lismore. Catholic pilgrims walk along it on St Declan's Day (24 July).

SLEEPING & EATING

Cliff House Hotel (☎ 024-87800; www.the cliffhousehotel.com; r €225-265, ste €300-450; ⊗ closed Jan; ℗ 🖳 🛜 🐾) Built into the cliff-face, all guestrooms at this ultra-contemporary new edifice overlook the bay, and most have balconies or terraces. Some suites even have two-person floor-to-ceiling glass showers (strategically frosted in places) so you don't miss those sea views. There are also sea views from the indoor swimming pool, outdoor Jacuzzi and spa, the bar (meals €18.50 to €28.50) and the restaurant (menu €62.50). Staff can organise sea kayaking, canoeing, scuba diving, fly-fishing, deep-sea fishing, and rock climbing. Seasonal closures can vary.

White Horses (☎ 024-94040; Main St; lunch mains €8-13, dinner mains €13-24; ⊗ 11am-4pm & 6-11pm Tue-Sun May-Sep, 6-10pm Fri, 11am-4pm & 6-11pm Sat, noon-4pm Sun Oct-Dec & mid-Feb–Apr) Energetically run by three sisters, this smashing bistro serves nourishing fare like fresh seafood chowder or fried brie with tomato chutney on plates handmade in the village. Kids can order half-portions from the adult menu if they fancy something more adventurous than burgers.

GETTING THERE & AWAY

Bus Éireann (☎ 051-879 000) operates two buses daily Monday to Friday, three Saturday and one Sunday from Cork (€13.80, 1¾ hours) to Ardmore. In July and August there are two buses daily Monday to Saturday to Waterford (€15, two hours) via Ring and Dungarvan; on Friday and Saturday only in other months. Buses stop outside O'Reilly's pub on Main St.

LISMORE

pop 790

Today, Lismore's enormous 19th-century castle seems out of proportion to this quiet, elegant town on the River Blackwater. Most of the existing buildings date from the early 19th century, but Lismore once had over 20 churches, many of which were destroyed during 9th- and 10th-century Viking raids. Over the centuries, statesmen and luminaries have streamed through Lismore, the location of a great monastic university founded by St Carthage in the 7th century. King Alfred of Wessex attended the university, Henry II visited the papal legate Bishop Christian O'Conarchy (Gilla Crist Ua Connairche) here in 1171, and even Fred Astaire dropped by when his sister Adele married into the Cavendish family, who own the castle.

INFORMATION

The locally – and enthusiastically – run tourist office (☎ 058-54975; www.lismore heritage.ie; Main St; ⊗ 9.30am-5.30pm Mon-Fri, 10am-5.30pm Sat, noon-5.30pm Sun mid-Mar–Christmas, 9.30am-5.30pm Mon-Fri Jan–mid-Mar) is inside the Lismore Heritage Centre.

SIGHTS

'One of the neatest and prettiest edifices I have seen', commented William

RICHARD CUMMINS
Lismore Castle

Thackeray in 1842 about the striking St Carthage's Cathedral (1679). And that was before the addition of the Edward Burne-Jones stained-glass window, which features all the Pre-Raphaelite hallmarks: an effeminate knight and a pensive maiden against a sensuous background of deep-blue velvet and intertwining flowers. Justice, with sword and scales, and Humility, holding a lamb, honour Francis Currey, who helped to relieve the suffering of the poor during the Famine. Among the cathedral's oddities and wonders are some noteworthy tombs, including the elaborately carved MacGrath family crypt dating from 1557 and fossils in the pulpit.

From the Cappoquin road there are stunning glimpses of the riverside Lismore Castle, which is closed to daytrippers but available for groups to hire. You can visit the 3 hectares of gardens (☎ 058-54424; www.lismorecastle.com; adult/child €8/4; ☉ 11am-4.45pm mid-Mar–Sep), thought to be the oldest in Ireland, divided into the walled Jacobean upper

garden and less formal lower garden. There are brilliant herbaceous borders, magnolias and camellias, and a splendid yew walk where Edmund Spenser is said to have written *The Faerie Queen*. The contemporary sculptures dotting the gardens have been joined by a contemporary art gallery (☎ 058-54061; www.lismorecastlearts.ie) in the west wing of the castle.

SLEEPING & EATING
Lismore House Hotel (☎ 058-72966; www.lismorehousehotel.com; Main St; r €99-139; P ⊗) Directly opposite the heritage centre, Ireland's oldest purpose-made hotel was built in 1797 by the duke of Devonshire. He'd still recognise the exterior, but inside rooms have had a contemporary makeover with sleek dark timber furniture and cream-and-gold fabrics. Breakfast costs extra. You'll often get astounding room rates online (as low as €29 midwinter). The on-site restaurant offers meals from €12.50 to €23.

NORTHERN COUNTY WATERFORD

Some of the most scenic parts of County Waterford are in the north around Ballymacarbry and in the Nire Valley, which runs between the Comeragh and Monavullagh Mountains. While not as rugged as the west of Ireland, with which it shares the same 370-million-year-old red sandstone, this mountain scenery has a stark beauty and doesn't attract much tourist traffic. It's also a great area to catch traditional music and dancing.

SIGHTS & ACTIVITIES

Rolling hills and woodland stuffed with megalithic remains make the county's north a superb area for walkers. The Comeragh Mountains, where there are ridges to trace and loughs to circle, are named after their many *coums* (valleys, often of glacial origin). Coumshingaun and Coum Iarthair – next to Crotty's Lough, and named after an outlaw who lay low in a cave there – are some of Ireland's finest.

Stop for a pint and panino in **Melody's Nire View** (☎ 052-36169; Ballymacarbry), where the genial folk have information on local walks and activities.

Otherwise make sure you're around for the **Nire Valley Walking Festival** (☎ 052-36134), which takes place on the second weekend in October, with guided walks for all, and traditional music in the pubs.

From March to September, the Rivers Nire and Suir are great for **fishing**. Permits (from €30 per day) can be arranged through Hanora's Cottage (right) or the **fly-fishing centre** (☎ 052-36765; www.flyfishing ireland.com; Clonanav, Ballymacarbry), which also has a school and guesthouse, and leads guided trips.

SLEEPING

our pick **Hanora's Cottage** (☎ 052-36134; www.hanorascottage.com; Nire Valley, Ballymacarbry; s/d incl packed lunch €95/170; ⊙ restaurant dinner Mon-Sat; ℗) This 19th-century ancestral home next to Nire Church houses one of the best B&Bs in the country. All 10 rooms have Jacuzzis (try for one overlooking the River Nire swirling under the stone bridge out front). You won't be disturbed by the pattering of little feet as children aren't permitted. Everything in the gourmet restaurant, even the crackers, is made on the premises and gluten-free meals are a speciality (dinner €40 to €50). Take the road east from Ballymacarbry, opposite Melody's; it's signposted 5km further on.

GETTING THERE & AWAY

Bus Éireann (☎ 051-879 000) runs Tuesday services from Ballymacarbry to Dungarvan (€6.80, 45 minutes) at 3pm, and Clonmel in Tipperary (€5.40, one hour) at 9.40am. There are also two buses between Clonmel and Ballymacarbry on Friday afternoon. A taxi from Clonmel to Ballymacarbry costs around €30.

COUNTY TIPPERARY

CASHEL

pop 2500

With one of the finest 1000-year-old castles around looming over town, it's no wonder that Cashel (Caiseal Mumhan) is popular. The iconic Rock of Cashel and the clutch of historical religious buildings that crown its breezy summit seem like a magical extension of the rocky landscape itself. Despite mobs of visitors, Cashel manages to maintain a certain charm as a smallish market town.

INFORMATION

Cashel Heritage Town Centre (☎ 062-62511; www.cashel.ie; Town Hall, Main St; ⏱ 9.30am-5.30pm mid-Mar–Sep, closed weekends Oct–mid-Mar) Helpful staff make this a great place to get information and purchase walking maps. It also has a museum.

SIGHTS

ROCK OF CASHEL

The **Rock of Cashel** (☎ 062-61437; www.heritageireland.com; adult/child €6/2; ⏱ 9am-5.30pm mid-Mar–mid-Oct, to 4.30pm mid-Oct–mid-Mar, last admission 45min before closing) is one of Ireland's most spectacular archaeological sites. The 'Rock' is a prominent green hill, banded with limestone outcrops. It rises from a grassy plain on the outskirts of the town and bristles with ancient fortifications – the word 'cashel' is an anglicised version of the Irish word *caiseal,* meaning 'fortress'. Sturdy walls circle an enclosure that contains a complete round tower, a roofless abbey and the finest 12th-century Romanesque chapel in Ireland. For more

than a thousand years the Rock of Cashel was a symbol of power, and the seat of the kings and churchmen who ruled over the region.

It's a five-minute stroll from the town centre to the rock and you can take some pretty paths including the Bishop's Walk, which ends in the gardens of the Cashel Palace Hotel. Sheep grudgingly allow you to pass. There are a couple of parking spaces for visitors with disabilities at the top of the approach road to the ticket office. The Rock is a major draw for coach parties for most of the year and is extremely busy during July and August. The sweeping views allow you to see a tour bus approaching from any direction like raiding parties. The scaffolding moves from place to place each year as part of the never-ending struggle to keep the Rock caulked.

HISTORY

In the 4th century the Rock of Cashel was chosen as a base by the Eóghanachta clan from Wales, who went on to conquer

RICHARD CUMMINS

Rock of Cashel

KILKENNY & THE SOUTHEAST

COUNTY TIPPERARY

JOHN ELK III

Hall of the Vicars Choral

much of Munster and become kings of the region. For some 400 years it rivalled Tara (p128) as a centre of power in Ireland. The clan was associated with St Patrick, hence the Rock's alternative name of St Patrick's Rock.

In the 10th century, the Eóghanachta lost possession of the rock to the O'Brien (or Dál gCais) tribe, which was under the leadership of Brian Ború. In 1101, King Muircheartach O'Brien presented the Rock to the Church, a move designed to curry favour with the powerful bishops and to end secular rivalry over possession of the Rock with the Eóghanachta, by now known as the MacCarthys. Numerous buildings must have occupied the Rock over the years, but it is the ecclesiastical relics that have survived even the depredations of the Cromwellian army in 1647.

HALL OF THE VICARS CHORAL

The entrance to the Rock of Cashel is through this 15th-century building, once home to the male choristers who sang in

the cathedral. It houses the ticket office. The exhibits in the adjoining undercroft include some very rare silverware, Bronze Age axes and St Patrick's Cross – an impressive, although eroded, 12th-century crutched cross with a crucifixion scene on one face and animals on the other. A replica stands outside, in the castle courtyard. The kitchen and dining hall upstairs contain some period furniture, tapestries and paintings beneath a fine carved-oak roof and gallery. A 20-minute audiovisual presentation on the Rock's history runs every half hour. Showings are in English, French, German and Italian.

CATHEDRAL

This 13th-century Gothic structure overshadows the other ruins. Entry is through a small porch facing the Hall of the Vicars Choral. The cathedral's western location is formed by the **Archbishop's Residence**, a 15th-century, four-storey castle that had its great hall built over the nave. Soaring above the centre of the cathedral is a huge square tower with a turret on the southwestern corner.

Scattered throughout are monuments, panels from 16th-century altar tombs, and coats of arms. If you have binoculars, look for the numerous stone heads on capitals and corbels high above the ground.

ROUND TOWER

On the northeastern corner of the cathedral is an 11th- or 12th-century round tower, the earliest building on the Rock of Cashel. It's 28m tall and the doorway is 3.5m above the ground – perhaps for structural rather than defensive reasons.

CORMAC'S CHAPEL

Even if the Rock of Cashel boasted only Cormac's Chapel, it would still be an outstanding place. This compelling building dates from 1127, and the medieval integrity of its trans-European architecture survives. It was probably the first Romanesque church in Ireland. The style of the square towers that flank it to either side may reflect Germanic influences, but there are haunting similarities in its steep stone roof to the 'boat-hull' shape of older Irish buildings, such as the Gallarus Oratory in County Clare and the beehive huts of the Dingle Peninsula.

The true Romanesque splendour is in the detail of the exquisite doorway arches, the grand chancel arch and ribbed barrel vault, and the outstanding carved vignettes that include a trefoil-tailed grotesque and a Norman-helmeted centaur firing an arrow at a rampaging lion. The chapel's interior is tantalisingly dark, but linger for a while and your eyes will adjust. Inside the main door, on the left, is the sarcophagus said to house King Cormac, dating from between 1125 and 1150. Frescoes once covered the walls, but only vestiges of these survive. The southern

tower leads to a stone-roofed vault and a croft above the nave (no access).

SLEEPING

Hill House (☎ 062-61277; www.hillhousecashel .com; Palmershill; r €60-120; P 💻) It actually could be called Amazing View House, as this Georgian charmer has magnificent views across to the Rock. Set back in gardens, the house is about 400m uphill from Main St. Rooms have a traditional style and come with four-poster beds.

Cashel Palace Hotel (☎ 062-62707; www .cashel-palace.ie; Main St; r from €70-200; P 💻 🛜) The Cashel Palace, a handsome red-brick, late–Queen Anne house, is a local landmark. Fully restored, it has 23 rooms oozing with luxuries like trouser presses (as if you wouldn't have someone else attend to that); some rooms have soaking tubs you'll leave only after you're totally prunified. Built in 1732 for a Protestant archbishop, the rooms are in the gracious main building or quaint mews. The bar is the place to talk about your upcoming hunt.

EATING

ourpick Cafe Hans (☎ 062-63660; Dominic St; mains €10-20; ⏱ noon-5pm Tue-Sat) Competition for the 32 seats is fierce at this casual cafe run by the same family who run Chez Hans (below). There's a terrific selection of salads (the Caesar is always a winner), open sandwiches and fish, shellfish, lamb and vegetarian dishes, with a discerning wine selection and mouthwatering desserts. Get there early or after the rush, or expect to queue.

Chez Hans (☎ 062-61177; www.chezhans .net; Dominic St; 3 courses €40-60; ⏱ 6-10pm Tue-Sat) Since 1968 this former church has been a place of worship for foodies from all over Ireland and, for that matter, the world. Still as fresh and inventive

RICHARD CUMMINS
Cahir

as ever, the superb restaurant gives its blessing to all manner of local foods, which are prepared simply and with elegance. Some of the wines come from Chef Hans' own vineyards in Germany. Book ahead.

GETTING THERE & AWAY
Bus Éireann (www.buseireann.ie) runs eight buses daily between Cashel and Cork (€12, 1½ hours) via Cahir (€4.50, 20 minutes, six to eight daily) and Fermoy. There is one bus daily to Thurles (€6, 30 minutes) where you can connect to trains on the Dublin–Limerick line. The bus stop for Cork is outside the Bake House on Main St. The Dublin stop (€12, three hours, six daily) is opposite. Tickets are available from the nearby Spar shop or you can buy them on the bus.

Bernard Kavanagh (☎ 062-51563; www .bkavcoaches.com) runs one evening service Monday to Saturday to Tipperary (€7, 50 minutes) and a service to Thurles and Clonmel (€7, 30 minutes).

CAHIR
pop 2850
Cahir (An Cathair; pronounced care) is a compact and attractive town that encircles its namesake castle, which doesn't rise to the heights of the Rock of Cashel but does do a good job of looking like every castle you ever tried building at the beach. Towers, a moat and various battlements hit every fortified cliché you can think of – all that's missing is a long-haired maiden in the highest window.

Cahir's town square is lined with pubs and simple cafes. Serene walking paths follow the banks of the River Suir; watch for lazy brown trout. And look for signs marking the Cahir Heritage Trail, which hits a number of buildings that feature from the town's various heydays. You can easily spend a couple of hours wandering about.

INFORMATION
Tourist office (☎ 052-744 1453; www.cahir tourism.ie; Main St; ۞ 9.30am-5pm Mon-Sat Jun-

Sep) Has leaflets and information about the town and region.

SIGHTS

CAHIR CASTLE

Cahir's awesome **castle** (☎ 052-744 1011; www.heritageireland.ie; Castle St; adult/child €3/1; ⏱ 9am-6.30pm mid-Jun–Aug, 9.30am-5.30pm mid-Mar–mid-Jun & Sep–mid-Oct, to 4.30pm mid-Oct–mid-Mar) is feudal fantasy in a big way. A river-island site with moat, rocky foundations, massive walls, turrets and towers, defences and dungeons are all there. This castle is one of Ireland's largest. Founded by Conor O'Brien in 1142, it was passed to the Butler family in 1375. In 1599 it lost the arms race of its day when the Earl of Essex used cannons to shatter the walls, an event explained with a huge model.

The castle was surrendered to Oliver Cromwell in 1650 without a struggle; its future usefulness may have discouraged the usual Cromwellian 'deconstruction'. It is largely intact and formidable still, and was restored in the 1840s and again in the 1960s when it came under state ownership.

A 15-minute audiovisual presentation puts Cahir in context with other Irish castles. The buildings within the castle are sparsely furnished, but there are good displays. The real rewards come from simply wandering through this remarkable survivor of Ireland's medieval past. There are frequent guided tours, and several good printed guides are for sale at the entrance.

SWISS COTTAGE

A pleasant riverside path from behind the town car park meanders 2km south to Cahir Park and the **Swiss Cottage** (☎ 052-744 1144; www.heritageireland.ie; Cahir Park; adult/child €3/1; ⏱ 10am-6pm mid-Apr–mid-Oct), an exquisite, thatched cottage surrounded by roses, lavender and honeysuckle. It's the best thatched fantasy in Ireland, and was built in 1810 as a retreat for Richard Butler, 12th Baron Caher, and his wife. The design was by London architect John Nash, creator of the Royal Pavilion at Brighton and London's Regent's Park. The cottage-orné style emerged during the late 18th and early 19th centuries in England in response to the prevailing taste for the picturesque. Thatched roofs, natural wood and carved weatherboarding were characteristics, and most were built as ornamental features on estates.

There could not be a more lavish example of Regency Picturesque than the Swiss Cottage. It is more of a sizeable house than

RICHARD CUMMINS

Cahir Castle

a cottage and has extensive facilities. The 30-minute (compulsory) guided tours are thoroughly enjoyable, although you may have to wait for one in the busier summer months.

SLEEPING

Tinsley House (☎ 052-744 1947; www.tinsley house.com; The Square; r €40-70; ⊗ May-Sep) This mannered house has a great location and four well-furnished rooms. There's a roof garden and the owner, Liam Roche, is an expert on local history and can recommend walks and other activities.

Cahir House Hotel (☎ 052-744 3000; www .cahirhousehotel.ie; The Square; €60/90; 🖳 🛜) On a prominent corner of the centre, this landmark hotel has a relaxed vibe. The 42 rooms have a rather bold yellow-and-red decor – think of it as a visual wake-up call. A new spa offers a full range of waxing for your debut on the Irish shore.

GETTING THERE & AWAY
BUS
Cahir is a hub for several Bus Éireann routes, including Dublin–Cork, Limerick–Waterford, Galway–Waterford, Kilkenny–Cork and Cork–Athlone. There are eight buses per day Monday to Saturday, and six buses on Sunday to Cashel (€4.50, 20 minutes). Buses stop in the car park beside the tourist office.

TRAIN
From Monday to Saturday, the Limerick Junction–Waterford train stops three times daily in each direction.

SOUTHWEST IRELAND

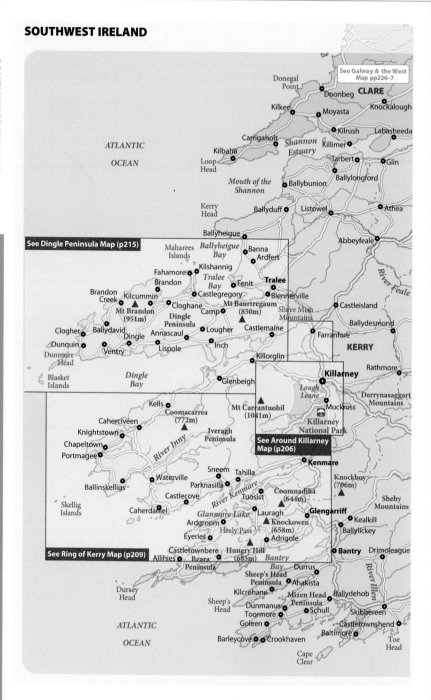

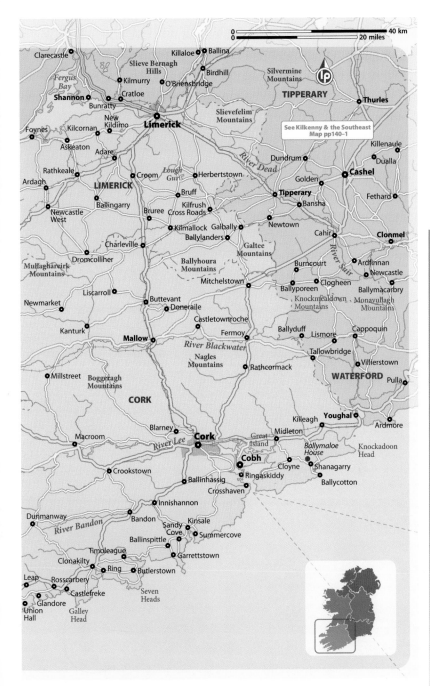

See Kilkenny & the Southeast Map pp140–1

SOUTHWEST IRELAND

SOUTHWEST IRELAND HIGHLIGHTS

SOUTHWEST IRELAND HIGHLIGHTS

1 KILLARNEY & ITS SURROUNDS

BY ALOYSIUS 'WEESHIE' FOGARTY, RADIO PRESENTER AND FORMER KERRY FOOTBALLER

I was born and raised in Killarney, and when people ask me where I'm from, I say, 'I'm from beauty's home.' Where's that, they ask? 'Heaven's Reflect,' I tell them, and it's true: there's no more beautiful place on earth than Killarney and its surrounds.

WEESHIE FOGARTY'S DON'T MISS LIST

❶ KILLARNEY TOWN
Killarney (p202) is one of the top tourist attractions in the world – absolutely buzzing in summer and very cosmopolitan too. It's so busy that every time you step off the sidewalk you're likely to meet a person from anywhere in the world.

❷ KILLARNEY NATIONAL PARK
There's nowhere more special to me than Killarney National Park (p205), which is on the edge of Killarney town

but in a world of its own. The lakes, mountains and stunning views are as beautiful as any I've seen in all my years of travelling. Thank god they're on my doorstep!

❸ JIMMY O'BRIEN'S
It is said that the secret to Ireland is to go into a pub and meet a local. Killarney's pubs are fine pubs indeed, but the best of them is unquestionably Jimmy O'Brien's (p202). It's old, unique and full of wonderful charac-

Clockwise from top: Black Valley, near Killarney National Park (p205); Road signs in Killarney town (p202); Upper Lake, Killarney National Park; Stone fort, Ring of Kerry (p209); Ross Castle (p205)

ALL PHOTOS RICHARD CUMMINS

ters: no matter when you're in there's always someone two stools away who knows twice as much as yourself!

the brown of the autumn, when the Deenagh River ripples through the park into the lakes.

❹ THE RING OF KERRY
Killarney is the doorway to the Ring of Kerry (p209), a circular drive of such stunning beauty that you'd have to travel to Slea Head (p219), at the tip of the Dingle Peninsula, to see its equal. You haven't seen Ireland until you've seen the Ring.

❺ THE CHANGING SEASONS
Killarney is a year-round destination and each season is special. There's the green haze of summer, the rich bloom of spring and the bare frost of winter, when the whole place might be enveloped in snow. But my favourite is

↘ THINGS YOU NEED TO KNOW

Best time to visit Autumn is past the summer crush and still has great weather **Advance planning** The southwest is Ireland's top tourist destination: book accommodation far in advance, especially for summer visits **Resources** Guide Killarney (www.guidekillarney.com), Southwest Tourism (www.corkkerry.ie)

SOUTHWEST IRELAND

SOUTHWEST IRELAND HIGHLIGHTS

SOUTHWEST IRELAND HIGHLIGHTS

2

⬊ KILLARNEY NATIONAL PARK

Nowhere else in Ireland will you find a forest of ancient oaks, two glacial lakes, the island's only herd of native red deer and a couple of stunning buildings. But Killarney National Park (p205) is far, far bigger than the sum of its individual parts: it affords some of the best views in the country and is the gateway to one of Ireland's most scenic drives.

3

⬊ SLEA HEAD

One of Europe's great scenic circular routes is Slea Head (p219), at the western tip of the Dingle Peninsula. It is one of the country's most dynamic Gaeltacht (Irish-language) areas and is peppered with ancient sites: spread about the 50km route are beehive huts, forts, church sites and inscribed stones from Ireland's ancient past.

4

◤ SKELLIG MICHAEL

This desolate, storm-lashed rocky outcrop off the Kerry coast was the ideal spot for a group of foolhardy monks to set up shop in ancient times. Today the Unesco World Heritage site of Skellig Michael (p212) reminds us not just of the extraordinary efforts they went to for a little solitude but of how magnificent untrammelled nature can truly be.

5

◤ THE ENGLISH MARKET

County Cork, renowned as the gourmet food basket of Ireland, has no better example of its commitment to good, locally sourced produce than Cork city's English Market (p194), where vendors sell all kinds of meats, cheeses, veg and other goodies. It's also home to the excellent Farmgate Café, one of the region's best eateries.

6

◤ KINSALE

History, scenery and great food conspire to make Kinsale (p196) one of Ireland's top destinations, a picture-postcard idyll at the head of a sheltered bay. After walking around the bay to explore the vast Charles Fort (p196), recharge your batteries with a memorable seafood platter at the Fishy Fishy Cafe (p197).

2, 3 & 6 RICHARD CUMMINS; 4 GARETH MCCORMACK; 5 OLIVER STREWE

2 Ross Castle, Killarney National Park (p205), County Kerry; 3 Slea Head (p219), County Kerry; 4 Skellig Michael (p212), County Kerry; 5 Coolea cheese, English Market, Cork city (p194); 6 Charles Fort, Kinsale (p196), County Cork

SOUTHWEST IRELAND

SOUTHWEST IRELAND'S BEST...

SOUTHWEST IRELAND'S BEST...

◥ BEAUTY SPOTS

- Kinsale (p196) The perfect southern town.
- Ladies' View (p208) Queen Victoria and her ladies loved the scenery.
- Gap of Dunloe (p207) An awe-inspiring mountain pass.
- Connor Pass (p218) Ireland's highest pass has stunning views.
- Bantry Bay (p200) Watery perfection.

◥ LOCAL ACTIVITIES

- Taking in a game of Gaelic football (p202) in Killarney.
- Trout or salmon fishing (p203) in the rivers around .
- Birdwatching (p211) on the Skellig islands.
- Improving your cooking (p196) at Ballymaloe House.

◥ HISTORIC NOTABLES

- Skellig Michael (p212) One of the most impressive monastic sites in the world.
- Lisnagun (p198) A perfectly rebuilt ring fort on its original site.
- Kerry Bog Village Museum (p210) A typical 19th-century bog village.
- Slea Head (p219) Packed with Stone Age monuments.
- Skibbereen Heritage Centre (p199) Harrowing Famine exhibits.

◥ MEMORABLE DRIVES

- The Ring of Kerry (p209), especially the stretch between Kenmare and Killarney.
- The R575 coastal road between Allihies and Lauragh, on the north side of the Beara Peninsula (p201).
- The Healy Pass (p202) between Cork and Kerry.
- The 5km drive to Brandon's Point (p218) on the Dingle Peninsula.

LEFT: RICHARD CUMMINS; RIGHT: RICHARD MILLS

Left: Jaunting car, Gap of Dunloe (p207), County Kerry; Right: Bantry House gardens (p200), County Cork

THINGS YOU NEED TO KNOW

⬈ VITAL STATISTICS

- **Area** 14,889 sq km
- **Population** 804,388
- **Best time to go** Autumn

⬈ AREAS IN A NUTSHELL

- **County Cork** (p190) Ireland's largest county is home to its second-largest city.
- **County Kerry** (p202) Is there any county that epitomises the classic Irish experience more than Kerry? Kerry folk don't think so.
- **County Limerick** (p221) A reputation for being a trouble spot is entirely undeserved.

⬈ ADVANCE PLANNING

- **Two months before** Book hotels, especially in popular areas such as Killarney, the Dingle Peninsula and West Cork.
- **One month before** Book now if you want a place in a cooking course at the likes of Ballymaloe.
- **Two weeks before** Make a list of sweater sizes for friends and family *not* travelling with you.

⬈ GETTING AROUND

- **Bus** Good bus networks cover most of the southwest, but it's a slow way of exploring.
- **Train** The main towns are linked, but not necessarily to each other.
- **Car** The region's beauty is off the beaten path; you'll need a car to get there.

⬈ RESOURCES

- **People's Republic of Cork** (www.peoplesrepublicofcork.com) Picking up on the popular nickname for this liberal-leaning city, this indie website has excellent info.
- **Discover Ireland** (www.discoverireland.ie/southwest) Official tourist website.
- **Killarney** (www.killarney.ie) The official site for the town, with lots of tourism links.
- **Adare Village** (www.adarevillage.com) Official town website.

⬈ BE FOREWARNED

- **Crowds** Summer crowds and traffic jams – especially on the Ring of Kerry – are a mainstay of the peak tourist season.
- **Weather** The southwest has a microclimate, which allows for warm summers and the growth of palm trees(!) but, like the rest of the island, the weather can be very unpredictable.
- **Gaelic football** It's a *religion* in Kerry, which makes sense as they're the best county at it by far.

SOUTHWEST IRELAND ITINERARIES

SOUTHWEST BLITZ Three Days

Having only three days to visit such an extraordinary region is a real tragedy, but here's more than a decent flavour of the southwest's delights. Start in **(1) Killarney** (p202), visiting Killarney National Park (p205) before embarking on the Ring of Kerry (p209), taking in **(2) Killorglin** (p209), **(3) Caherciveen** (p210), **(4) Waterville** (p213) and **(5) Kenmare** (p213). On day two, cross over to **(6) Bantry** (p200), before heading east to **(7) Cork City** (p190). Spend the day discovering the city, visiting the excellent Crawford Municipal Art Gallery (p190) and unmissable English Market (p194). With the taste of Cork's gourmet genius now firmly on the palate, head east to **(8) Midleton** (p195) and wrap up your lightning tour with a meal in the sublime Farmgate Restaurant (p195).

THE SOUTHERN PANTRY Five Days

County Cork has earned itself a justifiable reputation as the gourmet capital of Ireland. Start in West Cork, where gourmet cuisine is taken for granted. In **(1) Clonakilty** (p197), Edward Twomey is where you can buy the best black pudding, for which the town is famous. Cork is also known for its cheese, and in **(2) Durrus** (p199) you can visit the local cheesemakers before making a pit stop at the superb Good Things Café. Further east **(3) Kinsale** (p196) is full of top nosh, including the Fishy Fishy Cafe (p197), which is only open during the day. Over the weekend enrol in a cooking course at the world-famous **(4) Ballymaloe House** (p196), south of Cork city. All of this eating will cause a thirst, which you can quench at the Franciscan Well Brewery (p193) in **(5) Cork city**, where you can also stock up at the daily English Market (p194). Then head east to **(6) Midleton** (p195) and the Farmgate Restaurant (p195) – one of Ireland's best – and visit the classic Old Jameson Distillery (p195). Midleton's farmers market is better than the one in Cork city, but it's only a weekly affair (Saturdays).

THE MAIN PENINSULAS One Week

The southwest's three main peninsulas are unquestionably the reason this region can claim to be Ireland's most beautiful – and the millions of visitors won't disagree. Start your travels in the **(1) Beara Peninsula** (p201), which doesn't quite earn the kudos of its Kerry neighbours, but still has plenty to offer. Start the loop on the southern side, moving clockwise towards the northern end, which is the most scenic. At its western tip, the village of Allihies (p201) mightn't be at the end

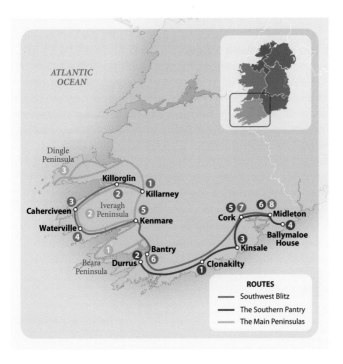

of the world, but you can see it from there. It's easy enough to cut across into County Kerry and start the second peninsula loop, around the world-famous (2) Iveragh Peninsula (p209), better known as the Ring of Kerry. Because it's so popular, visitors are strongly advised to do the route in a counter-clockwise fashion, so you'll need to pass through Killarney (p202) and move on from there. Besides the highlights outlined above in the Southwest Blitz itinerary, be sure to visit Daniel O'Connell's home (p213). We've left the best until last – once you begin exploring the simply sublime (3) Dingle Peninsula (p214), you'll know exactly what we mean. From lovely Dingle (p215) itself, with its rich Gaeltacht heritage, travel northward through Cloghane (p217) and go west through the magnificent Connor Pass (p218) to Slea Head (p219), site of one of Europe's richest collections of prehistoric artefacts.

DISCOVER SOUTHWEST IRELAND

The southwest corner of Ireland – Counties Cork, Kerry and a chunk of Limerick – epitomises romantic, rustic and rural Ireland more than anywhere else. It may creak and groan under the weight of tourist numbers, but the southwest never fails to astonish and beguile those who drive, cycle, walk and amble through the twists, turns and inlets of the eroded coasts and the endless fields of green criss-crossed by stone walls and ancient monuments.

Yet the southwest is not just about amazing views and wondrous rambles. It's about food: Cork city and the surrounding county have deservedly earned a reputation as the gourmet heart of Ireland. It's about history: from the monuments of the Beara Peninsula to the monastic ruins on unforgiving Skellig Michael and the extraordinary collection of Celtic runes and stones around Dingle. But it's really about the experience of Ireland: if you could visit only one part of the Emerald Isle, the southwest would leave you feeling like you didn't miss a thing.

COUNTY CORK

CORK CITY

pop 120,000

Cork over Dublin? That's what the locals cheerfully believe and what many travellers think as well. The city has much to recommend it: great restaurants fed by a solid foodie scene, a walkable centre surrounded by interesting waterways, and a location that is close to the tourist mecca of the Irish west coast. If it's a tad weak in the 'atmospheric old boozer' department, it makes up for it with appealing modern cafes and bars.

INFORMATION

Cork City Tourist Office (☎ 021-425 5100; www.cometocork.com; Grand Pde; ⏰ 9am-6pm Mon-Sat, 10am-5pm Sun Jul & Aug, 9.15am-5pm Mon-Fri, 9.30am-4.30pm Sat Sep-Jun) Souvenir shop and information desk with plenty of brochures and books about the city and county, as well as Ordnance Survey maps. Stena Line ferries (see p407) has a desk here.

SIGHTS

CRAWFORD MUNICIPAL ART GALLERY

Cork's public gallery (☎ 021-490 7855; www.crawfordartgallery.com; Emmet Pl; admission free; ⏰ 10am-5pm Mon-Sat) houses a small but excellent permanent collection, featuring works by Irish artists, such as Jack Yeats and Seán Keating.

ST FINBARRE'S CATHEDRAL

Spiky spires, gurning gargoyles and rich sculpture make up the exterior of Cork's Protestant cathedral (☎ 021-496 3387; www.cathedral.cork.anglican.org; Bishop St; adult/child €3/1.50; ⏰ 9.30am-5.30pm Mon-Sat, 12.30-5pm Sun Apr-Sep, 10am-12.45pm, 2-5pm Mon-Sat Oct-Mar), an attention-grabbing mixture of French Gothic and medieval whimsy. Local legend says that the golden angel on the eastern side will blow its horn

CORK

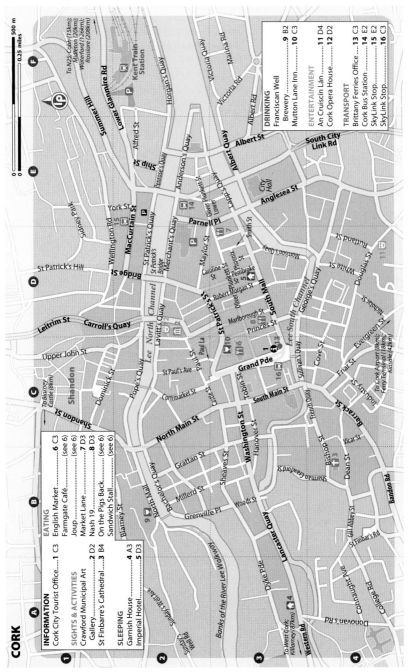

INFORMATION
Cork City Tourist Office.....**1** C3

SIGHTS & ACTIVITIES
Crawford Municipal Art
Gallery........................**2** D2
St Finbarre's Cathedral.....**3** B4

SLEEPING
Garnish House...............**4** A3
Imperial Hotel...............**5** D3

EATING
English Market...............**6** C3
Farmgate Café................(see 6)
Joup..........................(see 6)
Market Lane..................**7** D3
Nash 19.......................**8** D3
On the Pigs Back............(see 6)
Sandwich Stall...............(see 6)

DRINKING
Franciscan Well
  Brewery.....................**9** B2
Mutton Lane Inn.............**10** C3

ENTERTAINMENT
An Cruiscín Lán.............**11** D4
Cork Opera House............**12** D2

TRANSPORT
Brittany Ferries Office.....**13** C3
Cork Bus Station............**14** E2
SkyLink Stop.................**15** E2
SkyLink Stop.................**16** C3

when the Apocalypse is due to start… Yikes!

The cathedral sits at an aloof distance south of the centre, on the spot where Cork's patron saint, Finbarre, founded his monastery in the 7th century.

FESTIVALS & EVENTS

Book well in advance, particularly for the October jazz and film festivals.

Cork Film Festival (www.corkfilmfest.org) Eclectic week-long program of international films held in October/November.

Cork Pride (www.corkpride.com) Week-long gay-pride celebrations take place in May/June.

Cork World Book Fest A huge book festival with loads of authors in late April; sponsored by the Cork City Library.

Guinness Jazz Festival (www.corkjazzfestival.com) All-star line-up in venues across town, held in October.

International Choral Festival (www .corkchoral.ie) A major event held from late April to early May in the City Hall and other venues.

SLEEPING & EATING

our pick Garnish House (☎ 021-427 5111; www.garnish.ie; Western Rd; r €60-200; P 🛜) Every attention is lavished upon guests at this award-winning B&B. The legendary breakfast menu (30 choices!) includes fresh fish, French toast, omelettes and a whole lot more.

Imperial Hotel (☎ 021-427 4040; www.flynn hotels.com; South Mall; r €90-220; P 💻) Fast approaching her bicentenary, the Imperial knows how to age gracefully. Public spaces resonate with opulent period detail such as marble floors, elaborate floral bouquets and more. The 130 rooms are of four-star hotel standards: writing desk, restrained decor, and modern touches, like a digital music library. A posh Aveda spa is a recent addition – something unheard of when Charles Dickens stayed here.

our pick Nash 19 (☎ 021-427 0880; www. nash19.com; Princes St; mains €8-20; ⏱ 7.30am-5.30pm Mon-Fri) A sensational bistro with a small market; local foods are honoured from breakfast to lunch and on to tea. Fresh scones draw in the crowds early;

RICHARD CUMMINS

Waterfront houses on the River Lee, Cork city

daily fresh specials (soups, salads, desserts etc) and an incredible burger keep them coming throughout the rest of the day.

our pick **Market Lane** (☎ 021-427 4710; www.marketlane.ie; 5 Oliver Plunkett St; mains €10-26; ☻ noon-late Mon-Sat, 1-9pm Sun) It's always hopping at this bright corner bistro with an open kitchen. Service is quick and attentive, but you may want to pause at the long wooden bar anyway. The menu is broad, and changes often to reflect what's fresh. Smoked haddock perched on creamy potatoes is better here than it ever was back in the day. Steaks come with awesome aioli. At lunch, however, you might just get enraptured by the bacon sandwich. Lots of wines by the glass.

DRINKING

Mutton Lane Inn (☎ 021-427 3471; Mutton Lane) Tucked down the tiniest of laneways off St Patrick's St, this inviting pub, lit by candles and fairy lights, is one of Cork's most intimate drinking holes. It's minuscule and much admired, so try to get in early to bag the snug, or join the smokers perched on beer kegs outside.

Franciscan Well Brewery (☎ 021-421 0130; www.franciscanwellbrewery.com; 14 North Mall) The copper vats gleaming behind the bar give the game away: the Franciscan Well brews its own beer. The best place to enjoy it is in the enormous beer garden at the back. The pub holds regular beer festivals with other small (and often underappreciated) Irish breweries – check the website for details.

ENTERTAINMENT

Cork Opera House (☎ 021-427 0022; www.corkoperahouse.ie; Emmet Pl; ☻ box office 9am-8.30pm, to 5.30pm nonperformance nights) This leading venue has been entertaining the city for more than 150 years with everything from opera and ballet to stand-up and puppet shows. Performances are as varied as *Carmen,* Brian Kennedy, and the drama *Jane Eyre.*

An Cruiscín Lán (☎ 021-484 0941; www.cruiscin.com; Douglas St) Trad bands and world, blues and pop musicians all play at this acclaimed bar south of the river.

GETTING THERE & AWAY
AIR

Cork Airport (ORT; ☎ 021-431 3131; www.cork-airport.com) is 8km south of the city on the N27. Facilities include ATMs and car-hire desks. Airlines servicing the airport include Aer Lingus, BMI, Ryanair and Wizz. There are flights to Dublin, London Heathrow and a few cities in Europe.

See p195 for information on getting into town.

BOAT

Brittany Ferries (☎ 021-427 7801; www.brittanyferries.ie; 42 Grand Pde) sails to Roscoff (France) weekly from the end of March to October. The crossing takes 15 hours and fares are widely variable. The ferry terminal is at Ringaskiddy.

See p195 for information on getting into town.

BUS

Bus Éireann (☎ 021-450 8188; www.buseireann.ie) operates from the bus station on the corner of Merchant's Quay and Parnell Pl. You can get to most places in Ireland from Cork, including Dublin (€12, 4¼ hours, six daily), Killarney (€16, 1¾ hours, 14 daily), Kilkenny (€17, three hours, three daily) and Waterford (€18, 2¾ hours, 14 daily).

Citylink (☎ 1890 280 808; www.citylink.ie) operates services to Galway (3¼ hours) and Limerick. Buses are frequent and fares are as low as €10.

SOUTHWEST IRELAND

COUNTY CORK

CHRIS ROUT/ALAMY

Food stalls at the English Market

◥ ENGLISH MARKET

It could just as easily be called the Victorian Market for its ornate vaulted ceilings and columns, but the English Market is a true gem, no matter what you name it. Scores of vendors sell some of the very best local produce, meats, cheeses and takeaway food to go in the region. On decent days, take your lunch to nearby Bishop Lucey Park, a popular alfresco eating spot. A few favourites:

Joup Has a range of soups and Med-flavoured salads, plus sandwiches on a variety of homemade breads.

On the Pigs Back Boasts house-made sausages and incredible cheeses, many ready to munch.

Sandwich Stall Has a drool-worthy display of remarkable and creative sandwiches.

On a mezzanine overlooking part of the market is one of Cork's best eateries. **our pick** Farmgate Café is an unmissable experience. Like its sister restaurant in Midleton (see p195), this cafe has mastered the magic art of producing delicious meals without fuss or faddism. The food, from rock oysters to the lamb for an Irish stew, is sourced from the market below. There are tables but the best seats are at the balcony counter, where you can ponder the passing parade of shoppers. We still have memories of the seafood chowder and the raspberry crumble.

Things you need to know: English Market (🕙 9am-5.30pm Mon-Sat); Joup (☎ 021-422 6017); On the Pigs Back (☎ 021-427 0232); Farmgate Café (☎ 021-427 8134; English Market; lunch €4-13, dinner €18-30; 🕙 8.30am-10pm Mon-Sat)

TRAIN

Kent Train Station (☎ 021-450 4777) is north of the River Lee on Lower Glanmire Rd. Bus 5 runs into the centre (€1.60) and a taxi costs from €9 to €10.

The train line goes through Mallow, where you can change for the line to Tralee; Limerick Junction, for the line to Ennis (and the new extension to Galway); and then on to Dublin (€36, three hours, 16 daily).

GETTING AROUND
TO/FROM THE AIRPORT

SkyLink (☎ 021-432 1020; www.skylinkcork. com; adult/child €5/2.50; ⏱ hourly) buses pick up from around central Cork and take up to 30 minutes.

A taxi into town costs €15 to €20.

TO/FROM THE FERRY TERMINAL

The ferry terminal is at Ringaskiddy, 15 minutes by car southeast of the city centre along the N28. Taxis cost €28 to €35. Bus Éireann runs a service from the bus station to link up with sailings (bus 223; adult/child €5.50/3.50, 50 minutes). Confirm times. There's also a service to Rosslare Harbour (bus 40; adult/child €23.50/16, four to five hours).

AROUND CORK CITY
BLARNEY CASTLE

One of the most inexplicably popular tourist stops in Ireland is Blarney Castle (☎ 021-438 5252; www.blarneycastle.ie; Blarney; adult/child €10/3.50; ⏱ 9am-7pm Mon-Sat, 9am-5.30pm Sun Jun-Aug, 9am-6.30pm Mon-Sat, 9.30am-5.30pm Sun May & Sep, 9am-sundown Sun Oct-Apr, last admission 30min before closing). Crowds flock here to kiss the Blarney Stone, a cliché that has entered every lexicon and tour route.

The stone is perched at the top of the 15th-century castle, reached by a steep climb up slippery spiral staircases. On the battlements, you bend backwards over a long, long drop (with safety grill and attendant to prevent tragedy) to kiss the stone; as your shirt rides up, coach loads of onlookers stare up your nose. Once you're upright, don't forget to admire the stunning views before descending. Try not to think of the local lore about all the fluids that drench the stone *other* than saliva. Better yet, just don't do it.

MIDLETON & AROUND
pop 3900

Most visitors sweep through the Midleton area on their way east or west on the N25, but it's worth a bit more of your time. Rather ambitiously named the 'Irish Riviera' by the tourist board, the region is nonetheless full of pretty villages, craggy coastline and some heavenly rural hotels. Midleton itself is a pleasant and bustling market town, although with plenty of accommodation in the surrounding area, there's no real reason to stay here.

The tourist office (☎ 021-461 3702; www. eastcorktourism.com; ⏱ 9.30am-1pm & 2-5.15pm Mon-Sat May-Sep) is by the entrance gate to the distillery.

SIGHTS

The big attraction in town here is the Old Jameson Distillery (☎ 021-461 3594; www.jamesonwhiskey.com; tours adult/child €13.50/8; ⏱ shop 9am-6.30pm, tour times vary). Coachloads pour in to tour the restored 200-year-old building and purchase bottles from the gift shop. Exhibits and tours explain the process of taking barley and creating whiskey (Jameson is today made in a modern factory in Cork).

EATING

our pick Farmgate Restaurant (☎ 021-463 2771; The Coolbawn; ⏱ coffee & snacks 9am-5.30pm, lunch noon-3.30pm Mon-Sat, dinner 6.30-9.30pm Thu-Sat) The original and sister establishment to Cork's Farmgate Café (p194), the Midleton restaurant offers the same superb blend of traditional and modern Irish in its approach to cooking. The front shop sells amazing baked goods and local produce, including organic fruit and vegetables, cheeses and preserves. Behind is the farmhouse-style restaurant, where you'll eat as well as anywhere in Ireland.

WESTERN CORK

KINSALE

pop 4100

Kinsale (Cionn tSáile) may be the perfectly sized Irish coastal town. Narrow winding streets, tiny houses and bobbing fishing boats and yachts give it a seductive picture-postcard feel. Its sheltered bay is guarded by a huge and engrossing fort, just outside the town at Summercove.

Kinsale enjoys a food reputation beyond its size and boasts numerous good restaurants, including one excellent seafood bistro. The compact centre is good for walking and there are artsy little shops aplenty. More walks wander off along the shore in both directions.

INFORMATION

Tourist office (☎ 021-477 2234; www.kinsale.ie; cnr Pier Rd & Emmet Pl; ⏰ 9.15am-5pm Tue-Sat Nov-Mar, Mon Apr-Jun, Sep & Oct, 10am-5pm Sun Jul & Aug) Has a good map detailing walks in and around Kinsale.

SIGHTS

One of the best-preserved 17th-century star-shaped forts in Europe, **Charles Fort** (☎ 021-477 2263; adult/child €4/2; ⏰ 10am-5pm; ℗) would be worth a visit for its spectacular views alone. But there's much more here: ruins inside the vast site date from the 18th and 19th centuries and make for some fascinating wandering. Displays explain the typically tough lives led by the soldiers who served here and

---

POSH RETREAT: BALLYMALOE

Drawing up at wisteria-clad Ballymaloe House (☎ 021-465 2531; www.ballymaloe.ie; Shanagarry; s/d from €175/260; ℞ ⏛), you know you've arrived somewhere special. The Allen family has been running this superb hotel and restaurant in the old family home for more than 40 years; Myrtle is a living legend, acclaimed internationally for her near single-handed creation of fine Irish cooking. The rooms have been individually decorated in period furnishings and are a pleasing mass of different shapes and sizes. Guests enjoy beautiful grounds and amenities, which include a tennis court, a swimming pool, a shop, minigolf and public rooms. And don't forget the celebrated restaurant, whose menu is drawn up daily to reflect the availability of produce from Ballymaloe's extensive farms and other local sources. The hotel also runs wine and gardening weekends; check the website for details.

A few kilometres down the road on the R628, TV personality Darina Allen runs a famous cooking school (☎ 021-464 6785; www.cookingisfun.ie). Lessons, from half-day sessions (€55 to €105) to 12-week certificate courses (around €9800), are often booked well in advance. There are pretty cottages amid the 40 hectares of grounds for overnight students.

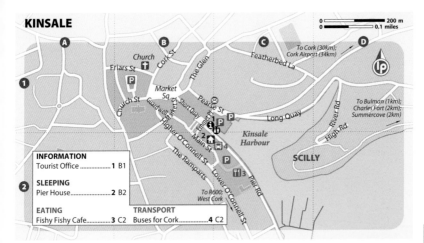

KINSALE

INFORMATION
Tourist Office 1 B1

SLEEPING
Pier House....................... 2 B2

EATING
Fishy Fishy Cafe.............. 3 C2

TRANSPORT
Buses for Cork................ 4 C2

the comparatively comfortable lives of the officers. Built in the 1670s to guard Kinsale Harbour, the fort was in use until 1921, when much of it was destroyed as the British withdrew. The best way to get here is to walk – follow the signs on the lovely walk around the bay from Scilly to Summercove, 3km east of Kinsale.

SLEEPING & EATING

Pier House (☎ 021-477 4475; www.pierhouse kinsale.com; Pier Rd; r €120-140; 🛜) This superb guesthouse, set back from the road in a sheltered garden, is a lovely place to rest your head. Pristine rooms, decorated with shell-and-driftwood sculptures, have black-granite bathrooms with power showers and underfloor heating. Four of the rooms also have balconies and views of the milling mobs outside.

ourpick **Fishy Fishy Cafe** (☎ 021-470 0415; www.fishyfishy.ie; Crowley's Quay; mains €13-33; 🕑 noon-4pm Mon-Fri, noon-4.30pm Sat & Sun) Fishy Fishy is a superb place for fish. The setting is beautifully understated, with stark white walls splashed with bright artwork and a terrific decked terrace at the front. All the fish is caught locally; order the cold seafood platter, a tasty spectacle that's a concert of what's fresh. Scallops are dollops of goodness. Front-of-house staff are charmers, but waitstaff can look as tired as week-old haddock.

Bulman (☎ 021-477 2131; www.thebulman. com; Summercove; mains €16-21; 🕑 12.30-9.30pm) This is seaside eating at its best. Escape from central Kinsale to this gastro pub in an unspoilt harbourside venue, where salty informality is a style in its own right. Seafood excels here, whether swimming in chowder or laid out seductively on a platter. Much of everything is sourced locally; herbs are right from the kitchen garden.

GETTING THERE & AWAY

Bus Éireann (☎ 021-450 8188) services connect Kinsale with Cork (€7, 50 minutes, 14 daily Monday to Friday, 11 Saturday and five Sunday) via Cork airport. The bus stops on Pier Rd, near the tourist office.

CLONAKILTY
pop 4200

Cheerful, brightly coloured Clonakilty is a bustling market town that serves as a hub for the score of beguiling little coastal towns that surround it. You'll find smart

Kinsale (p196)

MAX PAOLI & RUTH EASTHAM

B&Bs, top restaurants and cosy pubs alive with music. Little waterways coursing through add a drop of charm.

Clonakilty is famous as the birthplace of Michael Collins, a matter of extreme pride to the community. A large statue of the Big Fella stands on the corner of Emmet Sq.

SIGHTS

Of the more than 30,000 ring forts scattered across Ireland, Lisnagun (Lios na gCon; ☎ 023-883 2565; www.liosnagcon.com; adult/child €5/3; ☯ tours noon-4pm summer) is the only one that's been reconstructed on its original site. Complete with souterrain and central thatched hut, it gives a vivid impression of life in a 10th-century farmstead. To get there, take the turn signposted to Bay View House B&B at the roundabout at the end of Strand Rd. Follow the road uphill to the T-junction, turn right, then continue for about 800m before turning right again (signposted).

SLEEPING

Bay View House (☎ 023-883 3539; www.bay viewclonakilty.com; Old Timoleague Rd; r €50-90; ☜) This frothy pink house offers immaculate B&B standards, a genial welcome and great breakfasts. Rooms 5 and 6, and the cosy landing lounge, offer fantastic views over the fields that slope down to Clonakilty Bay.

EATING

Clonakilty is the source of the best black pudding in Ireland. It features on many local restaurant menus and you can buy varieties based on 19th-century recipes from Edward Twomey (☎ 023-883 3733; www.clonakiltyblackpudding.ie; 16 Pearse St; puddings from €2.50). Try to pay a visit to the twice-weekly farmers market (McCurtain Hill; ☯ 10am-2pm Thu & Sat).

Gleesons (☎ 023-882 1834; www.gleesons. ie; 3-4 Connolly St; dinner €19-29; ☯ 6.30-9.30pm Mon-Fri, 6-10pm Sat) Gleesons is a temple of fine dining that melds Irish produce with continental technique. The surrounds are nicely understated, with a wood and slate decor. The seafood, not surprisingly, is tasty. Early diners can enjoy a good-value three-course set menu (€35).

ENTERTAINMENT
our pick **De Barra's** (☎ 023-883 3381; www.debarra.ie; 55 Pearse St) A marvellous atmosphere, walls splattered with photos, press cuttings, masks and musical instruments, plus the cream of live music every night of the week (starting around 9.30pm) make this a busy pub.

GETTING THERE & AWAY
There are eight daily buses Monday to Saturday and seven Sunday to Cork (€11.50, 65 minutes) and Skibbereen (€8, 40 minutes). Buses stop across from Harte's Spar shop on the bypass going to Cork.

SKIBBEREEN
pop 2300
Skibbereen (Sciobairín) was once a typical market town: unvarnished, down to earth and warm-hearted. It's still all those things but there is now an overlay of glitz, which attests to the wealth of the weekending swells and yachties from Dublin.

It's a good West Cork pit stop, and an hour's stroll is a nice diversion.

SIGHTS
Constructed on the site of the town's old gasworks, the **Skibbereen Heritage Centre** (☎ 028-40900; www.skibbheritage.com; Old Gasworks Bldg, Upper Bridge St; adult/child €6/3; 10am-6pm Tue-Sat Oct-May, daily Jun-Sep) houses a haunting exhibition about the Famine, with actors reading heartbreaking contemporary accounts. A visit here puts Irish history into harrowing perspective. There's also a smaller exhibition about nearby Lough Hyne, the first marine nature reserve in Ireland, and a genealogical centre.

SLEEPING & EATING
our pick **Bridge House** (☎ 028-21273; monabestbridgehouse@yahoo.com; Bridge St; s/d €40/70) Mona Best has turned her entire house into a work of art, filling the rooms with fabulous Victorian tableaux and period memorabilia. The whole place bursts at the seams with cherished clutter, crazed carvings, dressed-up dummies and fragrant fresh flowers. Guests can request black satin sheets.

Over the Moon (☎ 028-22100; 46 Bridge St; lunch €8-14, dinner mains €25; noon-2pm & 6-9pm Wed-Mon, closed Sun lunch) The classic deep-blue and white exterior plus the beguiling logo make you want to walk inside; you should. Locally sourced foods (purveyors are listed) star on a creative and changing menu of fresh fare. Local ham, cheese and seafood star.

DURRUS
pop 900
Durrus is a perky little crossroads at the head of Dunmanus Bay and is a popular access point for both the Mizen Head and Sheep's Head Peninsulas.

Located on Dunmanus Bay, **Good Things Café** (☎ 027-61426; www.thegoodthingscafe.com; Ahakista Rd; lunch mains €10-20, dinner mains €21-38; 12.30-3pm & 7-9pm Thu-Mon mid-Jun–Dec) is a haven for foodies. The restaurant serves great contemporary dishes made with organic, locally sourced ingredients; think everything from a fluffy omelette with locally smoked haddock to grilled lobster. Tables on a vast terrace have views of nervous sheep. Popular cooking courses include a two-day 'miracle' program (€375) for those whose cooking skills stop after reading the microwave directions on the frozen meal.

SOUTHWEST IRELAND

COUNTY CORK

DURRUS CHEESE

If we were cows, we would be happy grazing in the rugged green fields of West Cork. Irish bovines must agree, because the area is a centre of excellence for artisan dairy production. If you want to see cheesemaking in action, call in at Durrus Cheese (☎ 027-61100; www.durruscheese.com). Founder Jeffa Gill is happy to talk visitors through the process of making her much-lauded creamy, rich rounds, which are for sale. Be sure to call ahead if you want to visit (the best times are 10.30am to noon Thursday and Friday). Follow the Ahakista road out of Durrus for 500m; turn right at the church and keep going for 3km until you see the dairy's sign.

BANTRY

pop 3300

Vast Bantry Bay, framed by the craggy Caha Mountains, draws your eye no matter where you are in Bantry. The tidy town has been on a long upswing from the 19th century, when poverty and mass emigration left entire swaths of land depopulated.

The last several decades have been more prosperous, thanks to commerce and the bay: you'll see Bantry oysters and mussels on menus throughout County Cork. Today it is a small and compact community that makes an essential break on your coastal journey.

SIGHTS

With its melancholic air of faded gentility, 18th-century Bantry House (☎ 027-50047; www.bantryhouse.com; Bantry Bay; adult/child €10/3; ⏱ 10am-6pm mid-Mar–Oct) makes for an intriguing visit. Experienced pianists are invited to tinkle the ivories of the ancient piano in the library.

The gardens of Bantry House are its great glory. Lawns sweep down from the front of the house towards the sea, and the formal Italian garden has an enormous 'stairway to the sky', offering spectacular views.

Bantry House is 1km southwest of the town centre (a 10-minute walk) on the N71.

SLEEPING & EATING

Bantry House (☎ 027-50047; www.bantry house.com; Bantry Bay; r €140-250; ⏱ Apr-Oct) Bantry House's guestrooms, decorated in pale hues and with a mixture of antiques and contemporary furnishings, are luxurious places to while away the hours. Rooms 22 and 25 are double winners, with views of both the garden and the bay. Enhance the dream by playing croquet, lawn tennis or billiards and lounging in the house's library once the doors are shut to the public. And if you see French ships offshore, go tell someone immediately!

our pick Fish Kitchen (☎ 027-56651; New St; mains €8-20; ⏱ noon-9pm Tue-Sat) Fittingly located above Bantry's fish vendors, the Fish Kitchen is a welcome addition to town. Everything is unfussy, from the decor to the food styles to the prices, but one thing is exacting: the care shown in the kitchen. The finest mussels, scallops, haddock and more are prepared perfectly.

GETTING THERE & AWAY

Bus Éireann (www.buseireann.ie) has eight buses daily Monday to Saturday (four on Sunday) between Bantry and Cork (€15.50, two hours). There are one or two daily to Glengarriff. Heading north to the Ring of Beara, Kenmare and Killarney requires backtracking through Cork.

Bantry Rural Transport (☎ 027-52727; www.ruraltransport.ie; 5 Main St) runs a useful series of circular routes to Dunmanway, Durrus, Goleen, Schull, Skibbereen and outlying villages. There's a set price of €4/6 one-way/return. Service is not frequent; check the website for details.

BEARA PENINSULA (RING OF BEARA)

The Beara Peninsula is the third major 'ring' in the west. Dingle and Kerry are comfortably in the number one and two spots respectively, leaving Beara in third place, which is just about right.

ORIENTATION & INFORMATION

A small part of the peninsula lies in Kerry, but is dealt with in this section for convenience. Castletownbere in Cork and Kenmare in Kerry make good bases for exploring the area.

You can easily drive the 137km around the coast in one day, but you would miss the spectacular **Healy Pass** road (R574), which cuts across the peninsula from Cork to Kerry. In fact, if pressed for time, skip the rest and do the pass.

NORTH SIDE OF THE BEARA

The entire north side is the scenic highlight of the Beara Peninsula.

ALLIHIES

This edge-of-the-world village has dramatic vistas and plenty of walks, where you will get lungs full of bracing air.

There are inviting pubs and B&Bs in Allihies (Na hAilichí), and a small tourist information kiosk, beside the church, opens in summer.

EYERIES TO LAURAGH

Heading north and east from Allihies, the beautiful coastal road (R575), with hedges of fuchsias and rhododendrons, twists and turns for about 12km to **Eyeries**. This cluster of brightly coloured houses overlooking Coulagh Bay is often used as a film set. The town is also home to **Milleens cheese** (☎ 027-74079; www.milleenscheese.com), from pioneering producer Veronica

Beara Peninsula
RICHARD CUMMINS

COUNTY KERRY

Steele. She welcomes visitors to her farm; phone ahead.

From Eyeries, forsake the R571 for the even smaller coast roads (lanes, really) to the north and east. This is Beara at its most spectacular – and intimate. Tiny coves are like pearls in a sea of rocks; the views of the Ring of Kerry to the north are sublime.

From Lauragh, a serpentine road travels 11km south across the other-worldly **Healy Pass** and down to Adrigole, offering spectacular views of the rocky inland scenery. About 1km west of Lauragh, along the R571, is a road to **Glanmore Lake**, with the remains of an old hermitage on a tiny island in the middle. There are walking opportunities in the area, but gaining access can be problematic: ask locally for advice.

COUNTY KERRY

KILLARNEY

pop 16,900

Killarney is a well-lubed tourism machine in the middle of the sublime scenery of its namesake national park. Its studied tweeness is renowned. However, it has many charms beyond the obvious proximity to lakes, waterfalls, woodland and moors dwarfed by 1000m-plus peaks. In a town that's been practising the tourism game for over 250 years, competition keeps standards high, and visitors on all budgets can expect to find good restaurants, fine pubs and plenty of accommodation.

Mobbed in summer, Killarney is perhaps at its best in the late spring and early autumn when the weather allows enjoyment of its outdoor charms and the crowds have thinned.

INFORMATION

Guide Killarney (☎ 064-663 1108; www. guidekillarney.com) is a good annual local guide filled with artful maps (form over function) and mountains of excellent info and background. It's marked '€5' but can be found for free all over town.

The **tourist office** (☎ 064-663 1633; www. corkkerry.ie; Beech Rd; ⏱ 9am-8pm Jun-Aug,

FOOTBALL CRAZY

Gaelic football clubs are as common in Ireland as green fields and pub signs bearing the 'G' word. However, among Kerrymen, the obsession with the sport reaches fever pitch. Forget about soccer or even hurling; this obsession is akin to rugby in New Zealand and soccer in Brazil.

Run by the GAA (Gaelic Athletic Association), the 15-a-side game is played with a heavy leather ball on a rectangular grass pitch with H-shaped, net-backed goals. Teams score through a confusing combination of kicking, carrying, hand-passing and *soloing* (dropping and toe-kicking the ball into the hands). The game, which closely resembles Australian Rules football, dates back to the 16th century, but took its current form in the 19th century.

If you would like to watch some Gaelic football and you're in town during the season (February to September), head to the Fossa GAA Ground on the N72, 1.6km west of Killarney's centre. To learn about the game from some lifelong pub commentators, have a drink at the bar-cum-Gaelic football shrine **Jimmy O'Brien's** (College St) in Fair Hill. Nearby Tatler Jack's (p205) is also a big GAA bar.

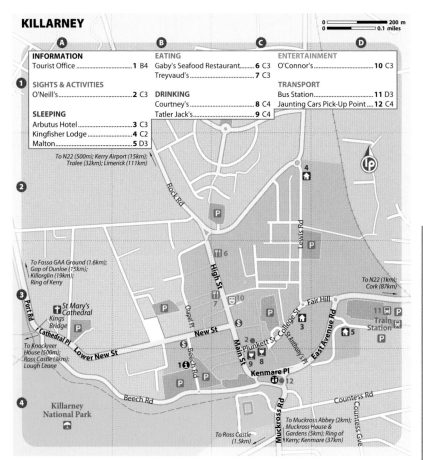

KILLARNEY

INFORMATION
Tourist Office **1** B4

SIGHTS & ACTIVITIES
O'Neill's **2** C3

SLEEPING
Arbutus Hotel **3** C3
Kingfisher Lodge **4** C2
Malton **5** D3

EATING
Gaby's Seafood Restaurant **6** C3
Treyvaud's **7** C3

DRINKING
Courtney's **8** C4
Tatler Jack's **9** C4

ENTERTAINMENT
O'Connor's **10** C3

TRANSPORT
Bus Station **11** D3
Jaunting Cars Pick-Up Point **12** C4

9.15am-5pm Sep-May) is busy, but efficient. It can handle almost any query, especially dealing with transport intricacies.

ACTIVITIES

You can fish for trout and salmon in the Rivers Flesk (per day €10) and Laune (per day €25); a state salmon licence is needed. Or you can fish for brown trout for free in Killarney National Park's lakes. Information, permits, licences and hire equipment can be obtained at **O'Neill's** (☎ 064-663 1970; 6 Plunkett St), which looks like a gift shop, but is a long-established fishing centre.

SLEEPING

Kingfisher Lodge (☎ 064-663 7131; www. kingfisherlodgekillarney.com; Lewis Rd; r €50-100; P ⊚) Lovely back gardens are a highlight at this immaculate B&B on a strip with others close to the centre. The 11 rooms are slightly posh. Walkers will be especially happy here as the owner, Donal Carroll, is a certified guide with years of experience walking and hiking in the region. Much local knowledge is on offer.

Arbutus Hotel (☎ 064-663 1037; www. arbutuskillarney.com; College St; s/d from €80/150; ⌇ Feb-Nov; ◻) The 34 bedrooms range

Plunkett St, Killarney

RICHARD CUMMINS

from those with 1920s Celtic deco furniture to more modern rooms with black-and-white bathrooms and the bath in a sweeping alcove. Trad sessions fire up in Buckley's Bar on many nights and Sunday lunchtimes.

Malton (☎ 064-663 8000; www.themalton. com; r €120-300; P 🖳 📶) So commanding it doesn't need an address, the Malton is pillared, ivy-covered and a throwback to Victorian elegance – at least from the outside. The inside has been thoroughly refurbished, much to the disdain of Colonel Blimp types, though most others find the stylish surrounds a breath of fresh air. Of the 172 rooms, those in the 1852 wing are best, retaining their period opulence.

EATING

ourpick Treyvaud's (☎ 064-663 3062; 62 High St; lunch mains €8-15, dinner mains €15-30; 🕙 noon-10pm) Michael Treyvaud's modish restaurant has a strong reputation for subtle dishes that merge trad Irish with seductive European influences. The seafood chowder at lunch is an enticing repast; dinner mains include the best of local lamb and a winsome bacon and cabbage plate.

Gaby's Seafood Restaurant (☎ 064-663 2519; 27 High St; mains €18-50; 🕙 6-10pm Mon-Sat) Gaby's is a refined dining experience for those who want superb seafood served in a traditional manner. Peruse the menu by the fire before drifting past the wine cellar to the low-lit dining room, where you'll savour exquisite Gallic dishes such as lobster in a sauce that includes cognac and cream. Specials are legion depending on what's fresh. The wine list is long and the advice unerring.

DRINKING & ENTERTAINMENT

O'Connor's (☎ 064-663 0977; High St) Typically, this tiny pub with leaded glass doors is one of Killarney's most popular haunts. There's entertainment every night, from trad sessions to stand-up comedy, storytelling and pub theatre.

Courtney's (Yer Man's; ☎ 064-663 2689; Plunkett St) Timeless pub with trad sessions many nights year-round. This is where locals come to see their old mates perform.

Tatler Jack's (☎ 064-663 2361; Plunkett St) Sports photos of proud local teams line the walls at this surprisingly large pub, which features pool tables, the comfiest stools in town and merciless craic (conversation).

GETTING THERE & AWAY

Bus Éireann (☎ 064-663 0011; www.buseireann.ie) operates from the east end of the Killarney Outlet Centre, offering regular links to Cork (€16, two hours, 15 daily); Dublin (€23, six hours, six daily); Galway (€22, seven hours, seven daily) via Limerick (€16.50, 2¼ hours); Tralee (€8, 40 minutes, hourly); and Waterford (€21.50, 4½ hours, hourly).

Killarney's train station is behind the Malton hotel, just east of the centre. **Irish Rail** (☎ 064-663 1067; www.irishrail.ie) has up to three direct trains a day to Cork (€20, 1½ hours) and nine to Tralee (€9.50, 45 minutes). There are direct trains to Dublin (€36, 3½ hours), but you usually have to change at Mallow.

KILLARNEY NATIONAL PARK

You can escape Killarney for the surrounding wilderness surprisingly quickly. Buses rumble up to Ross Castle and Muckross House, but it's possible to find your own refuge in the 10,236 hectares, among Ireland's only wild herd of native red deer, the country's largest area of ancient oak woods and views of most of its major mountains.

The glacial Lough Leane (the Lower Lake or 'Lake of Learning'), Muckross Lake and the Upper Lake make up about a quarter of the park. Their peaty waters are as rich in wildlife as the surrounding soil: cormorants skim across the surface, deer swim out to graze on the islands, and salmon, trout and perch prosper in a pike-free environment. The Lower Lake has vistas of reeds and swans.

Designated a Unesco Biosphere Reserve in 1982, the park extends to the southwest of town. There are pedestrian entrances opposite St Mary's Cathedral, with other entrances (for drivers) off the N71.

KNOCKREER HOUSE & GARDENS

Near the St Mary's Cathedral entrance to the park stands Knockreer House, with gardens featuring a terraced lawn and a summerhouse. The original 1870s structure burned; the present incarnation dates from 1958. The house isn't open to the public, but its gardens have views across the lakes to the mountains. From the St Mary's Cathedral entrance, follow the path immediately to your right uphill for about 500m.

ROSS CASTLE

Restored by Dúchas, **Ross Castle** (☎ 064-663 5851; www.heritageireland.ie; Ross Rd; adult/child €6/2; ⏰ 9am-6.30pm Jun-Aug, 9.30am-5.30pm Sep–mid-Oct & mid-Mar–May) dates back to the 15th century, when it was a residence of the O'Donoghues. It was the last place in Munster to succumb to Cromwell's forces, thanks partly to its cunning spiral staircase, in which every step is a different height, in order to break an attacker's stride.

The castle is a lovely 3km walk from the St Mary's Cathedral pedestrian park entrance, and you may well see red deer. If you're driving from Killarney, turn right opposite the Texaco petrol station at the start of Muckross Rd. Access is by guided tour only.

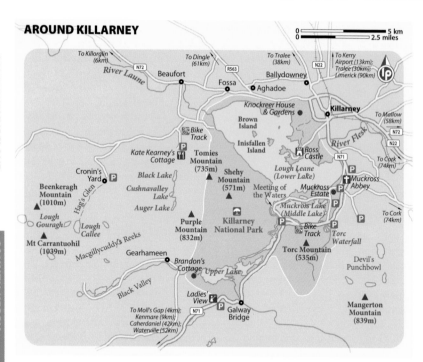

INISFALLEN ISLAND

The first monastery on Inisfallen Island (at 9 hectares, the largest of the national park's 26 islands) is said to have been founded by St Finian the Leper in the 7th century. The island's fame dates from the early 13th century when the Annals of Inisfallen were written here. Now in the Bodleian Library at Oxford, they remain a vital source of information on early Munster history. On Inisfallen ('island') are the ruins of a 12th-century oratory with a carved Romanesque doorway and a monastery on the site of St Finian's original.

You can hire boats from Ross Castle to row to the island. Alternatively, boaters charge passengers around €7.50 each for the crossing. Some Gap of Dunloe boats and bus tours also stop here.

MUCKROSS ESTATE

The core of Killarney National Park is the Muckross Estate, donated to the state by Arthur Bourn Vincent in 1932. **Muckross House** (☎ 064-667 0144; www.muckross-house.ie; adult/child €7/3, combined ticket with farms €12/6; 9am-7pm Jul & Aug, to 6pm Sep-Jun) is a 19th-century mansion, restored to its former glory and packed with contemporaneous fittings. Entrance is by guided tour.

The beautiful gardens slope down, and a block behind the house contains a restaurant, craft shop and studios where you can see potters, weavers and bookbinders at work. Jaunting cars wait to run you through deer parks and woodland to Torc Waterfall and Muckross Abbey (about €10 each return).

our pick **Garden Restaurant** (☎ 064-663 1440; meals €4-10; 9am-5pm), in the visitor centre (which also has excellent maps and books), is one of the region's best places for lunch. It serves an array of fresh and interesting dishes from snacky to full-on. It's all cafeteria style so you can wander around choosing from the array of organic and locally sourced foods.

Muckross House is 5km south of town, signposted from the N71. The house is included in some half-day tours of Killarney, and it would be possible to work it into a circuit of the park and the Gap of Dunloe.

If you're walking or cycling to Muckross, there's a cycle track alongside the Kenmare road for most of the first 2km. A path then turns right into Killarney National Park. Following this path, after 1km you'll come to **Muckross Abbey**, which was founded in 1448 and burned by Cromwell's troops in 1652. William Thackeray called it 'the prettiest little bijou of a ruined abbey ever seen'. Muckross House is another 1.5km from the abbey ruins.

Cycling around Muckross Lake (Middle Lake) is easier and more scenic when done in an anticlockwise direction.

GAP OF DUNLOE

Geographically, the Gap of Dunloe is outside Killarney National Park, but most people include it in their park visit. The land is ruggedly beautiful and fast-changing weather conditions add drama.

In winter, the Gap is an awe-inspiring mountain pass, overshadowed by Purple Mountain and Macgillycuddy's Reeks. In high summer though, it's a bottleneck for the tourist trade, with buses depositing countless visitors at Kate Kearney's Cottage for the one-hour jaunting car (horse-and-buggy) ride through the Gap.

In the south, **Brandon's Cottage** (snacks €3-6; ◷ 9am-4pm Apr-Oct) is a simple old 19th-century hunting lodge with a fine open-air cafe and a dock for boats crossing the Upper Lake. It is surrounded by lush, green pastures. From here a narrow road weaves up the hill to the Gap. Heading down towards the north the scenery is a fantasy of rocky bridges over clear mountain streams and lakes.

Eventually you'll reach the 19th-century pub **Kate Kearney's Cottage**

RICHARD CUMMINS

Cycling through the Gap of Dunloe

(☎ 064-664 4146; lunch €10.50-13), where many drivers park in order to walk up to the Gap.

GETTING THERE & AROUND

The best way to see the Gap is to hire a bike in Killarney and cycle to Ross Castle. Get there before 11am to catch a boat up the lakes to Brandon's Cottage, then cycle through the Gap and back to town via the N72 and a path through the golf course (for bike hire and boat trip, it's about €30).

The 1½-hour boat ride alone justifies the trip. It crosses all the lakes, passing islands and bridges and winding between the second two lakes via Meeting of the Waters and the Long Range.

On land, walking, pony or a four-person trap can be substituted for cycling. The Gap pony men charge €50 per hour or €80 for the two-hour trip between Brandon's Cottage and Kate Kearney's Cottage.

Note that it is hard to do the Gap as part of a walking loop. You can get as far as Kate Kearney's, but from there back to Killarney it is a long slog on busy roads – no fun at all. Your best bet would be to call a cab from there.

You can also drive this route, but really only outside of summer and even then walkers and cyclists have the right of way. On the plus side, to reach Brandon's Cottage by car you have to drive a long, scenic detour on the N71 to the R568 and then come back down a gorgeous rugged valley. It takes about 45 minutes.

KILLARNEY TO KENMARE

The vista-crazy N71 to Kenmare (32km) winds between rock and lake, with plenty of lay-bys to stop and admire the views. Watch out for the buses squeezing along the road. About 2km south of the entrance to Muckross House, a path leads 200m to the pretty Torc Waterfall. After another 8km on the N71 you come to Ladies' View, where the fine views along Upper Lake were much enjoyed by Queen Victoria's ladies-in-waiting. There are cafes here and 5km further on, at Moll's Gap, another good viewpoint.

EOIN CLARKE

Torc Waterfall

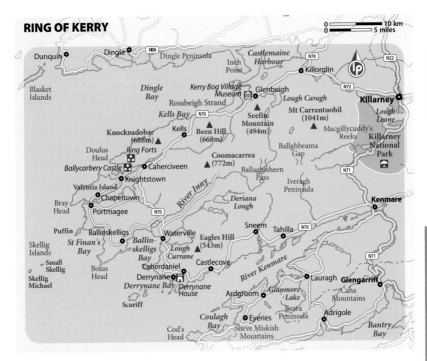

RING OF KERRY

The second of Ireland's big circle drives (number one Dingle, number three Beara), the Ring of Kerry is the longest and the most diverse. It combines jaw-dropping coastal scenery with more mundane stretches of land that's simply emerald green and sorta blissful.

This 179km circuit of the Iveragh Peninsula pops up on tourist itineraries for a good reason. The road winds past pristine beaches, the island-dotted Atlantic, medieval ruins, mountains and loughs (lakes). Even locals stop their cars to gawk at the rugged coastline – particularly between Waterville and Caherdaniel in the southwest of the peninsula. And even in summer the remote Skellig Ring can be uncrowded and serene (starkly beautiful too).

And for many, the Ring is simply music to their ears as traditional pubs with music sessions dot the villages.

KILLORGLIN

pop 3900

Travelling anticlockwise from Killarney, the first town on the Ring is Killorglin (Cill Orglan). The town is quieter than the waters of the River Laune that lap against the eight-arched bridge, built in 1885. In August, there's an explosion of time-honoured ceremonies and libations at the famous pagan festival, the Puck Fair.

The **tourist office** (☎ 066-976 1451; Library Pl; 9am-5pm Mon-Sat) has maps, walking guides, fishing licences and souvenirs for sale, and free internet access at the **library** (☎ 066-976 1272; Library Pl; 10am-5pm Tue-Sat). The name of **Books & Gifts** (☎ 066-979 6006; Upper Bridge St) says it all.

FESTIVALS

The lively **Puck Fair Festival** (Aonach an Phuic; ☎ 066-976 2366; www.puckfair.ie) takes place 10–12 August. First recorded in 1603, its origins are hazy. It is based around the custom of installing a billy goat (a poc, or puck), the symbol of mountainous Kerry, on a pedestal in the town, its horns festooned with ribbons. Other entertainment ranges from the horse fair and bonny baby competition to street theatre and the pubs staying open until 3am. Accommodation is as hard to find as a goat in a tin-can factory.

SLEEPING & EATING

our pick **Bianconi** (☎ 066-976 1146; www.bianconi.ie; Annadale; r €65-100; ☻ restaurant 5-9pm Mon-Sat) The rooms are as good as the food at this classic 15-room guesthouse right in the centre. Everything is gracious here, including the restaurant, where you'll find lively takes on local seafood (mains €12 to €25) like the killer prawns in a creamy garlic and green onion sauce, mussels in garlic sauce and much more.

KERRY BOG VILLAGE MUSEUM

Located on the N70 between Killorglin and Glenbeigh, the **Kerry Bog Village Museum** (☎ 066-976 9184; www.kerrybogvillage.ie; adult/child €6/4; ☻ 9am-7pm Easter-Oct, to 6pm rest of year) re-creates a 19th-century bog village, typical of the small communities that carved out a precarious living in the harsh environment of Ireland's ubiquitous peat bogs. You'll see the homes of the turfcutter, blacksmith, thatcher and labourer, and a dairy. Commune with the Kerry Bog ponies.

CAHERCIVEEN

pop 1300

Caherciveen's population, over 30,000 in 1841, was decimated by the Great Famine and emigration to the New World. A sleepy outpost remains, overshadowed by the 688m peak of Knocknadobar. It looks rather dour compared with the peninsula's other settlements, but it's close to a cool castle and some good accommodation. In many ways this village does more to recall the tough 1930s in Ireland than any other you'll see in Kerry. The town makes a good staging area for the ferry to Valentia Island.

The best attraction locally is the ruins of **Ballycarbery Castle**, 2.4km along the road to White Strand Beach from the barracks. The 16th-century castle was inhabited by the McCarthy More chieftains and, later, Sir Valentine Brown, surveyor general of Ireland under Elizabeth I. Today the atmospheric remains are surrounded by green pastures inhabited by cows who like to get in the pictures.

SKELLIG ISLANDS

gannet pop 45,000

The Skellig Islands (Oileáin na Scealaga) are impervious to the ever-pounding waves of the Atlantic. George Bernard Shaw said Skellig Michael was 'the most fantastic and impossible rock in the world'. A visit is a test of endurance for your stomach, bladder and brain – the latter because the sheer magnificence of the natural beauty and ancient ruins is mind-blowing.

You'll need to do your best grisly seadog impression ('argh!') on the 12km crossing, which can be rough. There are no toilets or shelter on Skellig Michael, the only island visitors are permitted to land on. Bring something to eat and drink and wear stout shoes and weatherproof clothing. (Boat operators can often lend passengers old waterproof duds for the crossing.)

RICHARD CUMMINS

Recreated traditional house, Kerry Bog Village Museum

ACTIVITIES

The Skelligs are a **birdwatching** paradise. Keep a sharp lookout during the boat trip and you may spot diminutive storm petrels (also known as Mother Carey's chickens) darting above the water like swallows. Gannets are unmistakable with their savage beaks, imperious eyes, yellow caps and 100cm-plus wing spans. They dive like tridents into the sea, from up to 30m at well over 100km per hour, to snatch fish below the surface. Kittiwakes – small, dainty seabirds with black-tipped wings – are easy to see and hear around Skellig Michael's covered walkway as you step off the boat. They winter at sea then land in their thousands to breed between March and August.

Further up the rock you'll see stubby-winged fulmars, with distinctive bony 'nostrils' from which they eject an evil-smelling green liquid if you get too close. Look also for razorbills, black-and-white guillemots, and the delightful puffins with their multicoloured beaks and waddling gait. In May, puffins come ashore to lay a solitary egg at the far end of a burrow, and parent birds can be seen guarding their nests. Puffins stay only until the first weeks of August.

SMALL SKELLIG

While Skellig Michael looks like two triangles linked by a spur, Small Skellig is longer, lower and much craggier. From a distance it looks as if someone battered it with a feather pillow that burst. Close up you realise you're looking at a colony of over 20,000 pairs of breeding gannets, the second-largest breeding colony in the world. Most boats circle the island so you can see the gannets, and you may see basking seals as well. Small Skellig is a bird sanctuary; no landing is permitted.

GETTING THERE & AWAY

Skellig Michael's fragility places limits on the number of daily visitors. The 15 boats are licensed to carry no more than 12 passengers each, for a maximum of 180 people there at any one time. So it's

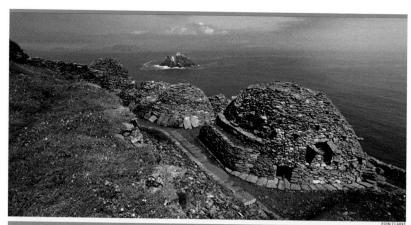

Beehive cells, Skellig Michael   EOIN CLARKE

⬎ SKELLIG MICHAEL

The jagged, 217m-high rock of Skellig Michael (Archangel Michael's Rock; like St Michael's Mount in Cornwall and Mont Saint Michel in Normandy) is the larger of the two islands and a Unesco World Heritage site. It looks like the last place on earth that anyone would try to land, let alone establish a community, yet early Christian monks survived here from the 6th until the 12th or 13th century. Influenced by the Coptic Church (founded by St Anthony in the deserts of Egypt and Libya), their determined quest for ultimate solitude led them to this remote, windblown edge of Europe.

The monastic buildings are perched on a saddle in the rock, some 150m above sea level, reached by 600 steep steps cut into the rock face. The astounding 6th-century oratories and beehive cells vary in size; the largest cell has a floor space of 4.5m by 3.6m. You can see the monks' south-facing vegetable garden and their cistern for collecting rainwater. The most impressive structural achievements are the settlement's foundations – platforms built on the steep slope using nothing more than earth and drystone walls.

The guides on the island ask you to do your picnicking on the way up to the monastery, or at Christ's Saddle just before the last flight of steps, rather than among the ruins. This is to keep sandwich-loving birds and their droppings away from the monument.

wise to book ahead in July and August, bearing in mind that if the weather's bad the boats may not sail (about two days out of seven). Trips usually start running around Easter, depending, again, on weather.

Boats leave around 10am and return at 3pm, and cost about €45 per person. You can depart from Portmagee, Knightstown, Caherciveen, Ballinskelligs or Derrynane. The boat owners try to restrict you to two hours on the island, which is the bare minimum, on a good day, to see the monastery, look at the birds and have a picnic. The crossing takes about 1½ hours from Portmagee, one hour from Ballinskelligs and 1¾ hours from Derrynane.

Local pubs and B&Bs will point you in the direction of operators, including:

Casey's (☎ 066-947 2437; www.skelligislands. com; Portmagee)

Dan & Donal McCrohan (☎ 066-947 6142; Valentia Island)

John O'Shea (☎ 087 689 8431; johnoshea33@ hotmail.com; Caherdaniel)

Sea Quest (☎ 066-947 6214; www.skelligs rock.com; Valentia Island, Reenard Point)

WATERVILLE

pop 550

Waterville, a line of colourful houses strung on the N72 between Lough Currane and Ballinskelligs Bay, is charm-challenged in the way of many such mass-consumption beach resorts. A vast golf resort hopes to give the town an élan it once had when Charlie Chaplin visited – a statue of him in costume leers along the seafront.

CAHERDANIEL

pop 350

Hiding between Derrynane Bay and the foothills of Eagles Hill, Caherdaniel barely qualifies as a tiny hamlet. Businesses are scattered about the undergrowth like smugglers, fitting since this was once a haven for same.

This is the ancestral home of Daniel O'Connell, 'The Liberator' (see p357), whose family made money smuggling from their base by the dunes. The area boasts a Blue Flag beach, plenty of activities, good hikes and some pubs where you may be tempted to break into pirate talk and boast about your love for Arrrgh-gentina. Lines of wind-gnarled trees add to the wild air.

SIGHTS

Derrynane House (☎ 066-947 5113; Derrynane; adult/child €3/1; ☾ 9am-6pm Mon-Sat, 11am-6pm Sun May-Sep, 1-5pm Tue-Sun Apr & Oct, 1-5pm Sat & Sun Nov-Mar, last admission 45min before closing) is the family home of Daniel O'Connell, the campaigner for Catholic emancipation. His ancestors bought the house and surrounding parkland having grown rich on smuggling with France and Spain. It's largely furnished with O'Connell memorabilia, including the restored triumphal chariot in which he lapped Dublin after his release from prison in 1844.

The gardens, warmed by the Gulf Stream, hold palms, 4m tree ferns, gunnera (giant rhubarb) and other South American species. A walking track through them leads to wetlands, beaches and cliff-tops. You can spot wild pheasants and other birds, whose musical calls add a note of contrast to the dull roar of the surf. The chapel, which O'Connell added to Derrynane House in 1844, is a copy of the ruined one on Abbey Island, which can usually be reached on foot across the sand.

Look out for the Ogham stone on the left of the road to the house. With its carved notches representing the simple Ogham alphabet of the ancient Irish, the stone has several missing letters, but may represent the name of a local chieftain.

KENMARE

pop 2500

The copper-covered limestone spire of Holy Cross Church, drawing the eye to the wooded hills above town, may make you forget for a split second that Kenmare is a seaside town. But with rivers named Finnihy, Roughty and Sheen emptying into Kenmare Bay, you couldn't be anywhere other than southwest Ireland.

Kenmare is an ideal stop, whether your itinerary includes the Ring of Beara, the Ring of Kerry or both. Elegant streets with beguiling restaurants and shops fan out from Fair Green in a handy triangular loop. It gets busy in summer, but is less hectic than Killarney.

SLEEPING & EATING

ourpick **Virginia's Guesthouse** (☎ 064-664 1021; www.virginias-kenmare.com; Henry St; s/d from €50/80; 🛜) You can't get more central than this award-winning B&B, whose creative breakfasts celebrate organic local produce (rhubarb and blueberries in season, for example). Its eight excellent rooms are perfectly comfortable but not posh. Excellent value.

Sheen Falls Lodge (☎ 064-664 1600; www.sheenfallslodge.ie; r from €350; 🕑 Feb-Dec; 🗙 🖳 🛜) The Marquis of Landsdowne's former summer residence still feels like an aristocrats' playground. The lodge is an elegant and luxurious retreat with a spa and 66 rooms with DVD players and Italian marble bathrooms. With views of the falls and across Kenmare Bay to Carrantuohil, it's a beautiful escape. Amenities are many (clay-pigeon shooting, anyone?).

ourpick **Prego** (☎ 064-664 2350; Henry St; mains €8-25; 🕑 8.30am-9pm, to 10.30pm summer) A restaurant for all seasons – and times. Local and organic produce is the basis of this all-day restaurant. The breakfast menu is long and varied and the antidote to every bit of dodgy black pudding you've avoided on your B&B plate; lunches feature many specials and are known for their soups and salads. At dinner, the Italian zest here shines with a lot of Med flavours on pastas and seafood.

DINGLE PENINSULA

The northernmost promontory in Kerry and Cork's proud collection, the Dingle Peninsula is first among stiff competition. Its ever-varied and multihued landscape is one of green hills and golden sands, and culminates in Europe's most westerly point, gazing across the sound at the ghost town on Great Blasket Island. Mt Brandon, the Connor Pass and other

Mt Brandon

RICHARD CUMMINS

DINGLE PENINSULA

high areas add drama but it's where the land meets the ocean – either in conflict at whitewater-pounded rocks or in little coves where it just dissolves away – that Dingle's beauty is unforgettable.

Centred on charming Dingle town, the peninsula has a high concentration of ring forts and other ancient ruins. Activities on offer range from diving to playing the bodhrán (hand-held goatskin drum). There's an alternative way of life here, lived by the artisans and idiosyncratic characters and found at trad sessions and folkloric festivals across Dingle's tiny settlements.

The classic loop drive around the peninsula from Dingle town is 50km. Base yourself in Dingle for two nights (at least) and take a day to do the drive.

DINGLE

pop 1800

Wandering the hilly streets in this naturally quaint town, you quickly realise that the peninsula's capital is a very special place indeed. It's one of Ireland's largest Gaeltacht towns; many pubs double as shops, so you can enjoy Guinness and a singalong among screws and nails, wellies and horseshoes. These charms have long

drawn runaways from across the world, making the port town a surprisingly cosmopolitan, creative place. In summer it can be mobbed, there's no way around it; in the other seasons its authentic charms are yours for the savouring. Excellent seafood restaurants can be enjoyed year-round.

Note that although this is Gaeltacht country, the locals have voted to retain the name Dingle rather than go by the officially sanctioned – and dictated – An Daingean.

INFORMATION

Tourist office (☎ 066-915 1188; www.dingle -peninsula.ie; the Pier; ☉ 9am-7pm Jul & Aug, 9am-1pm & 2-6pm May-Jun & Sep, to 5pm Oct-Apr) Busy but helpful, this place has maps, guides and plenty of information on the entire peninsula. It books accommodation for a €4 fee.

SIGHTS

Dingle is one of those towns whose very fabric is the sight. Wander up and down hills, poke around back alleys, head off across the docks, and amble into shops and pubs at random and see what you find.

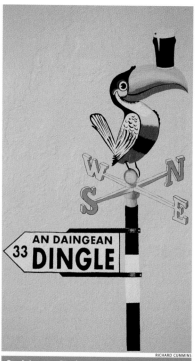

RICHARD CUMMINS

Road sign near Dingle

Boats leave the pier daily for one-hour dolphin-spotting trips of Dingle's famous tourism patron, **Fungie the dolphin**; the **Dingle Boatmen's Association** (☎ 066-915 2626; the Pier; adult/child €16/8) is the co-operative running things. It's free if Fungie doesn't show, but he usually does. The association also runs a daily two-hour boat trip for enthusiasts who want to **swim with Fungie** (per person €25, plus wetsuit hire adult €25, child €15-20; ☺ 8am Jun-Aug, 9am rest of the year). Organise it in advance through **Brosnan's** (☎ 066-915 1967; Cooleen), where you can hire wetsuits and snorkelling gear.

SLEEPING

Russells (☎ 066-915 1747; maryr@iol.ie; the Mall; s/d from €50/90; Ⓟ) Who can resist this location set back from a tiny babbling brook coursing through town? The modern rooms are tastefully decorated and an extensive breakfast menu includes kippers, salmon and French toast.

55 John St (Stella Doyle's; ☎ 066-915 2378; www.stelladoyle.com; 55 John St; s/d €55/75; ☺ May-Sep) A surprise awaits as you enter the plain-fronted, plum-coloured facade here: a vision of colour and light from the back garden which, while small, is alive with blooms. The two rooms are plainly comfortable; breakfast is a challenge as Stella, a chef, will cook whatever you want. Go on, order.

Captain's House (☎ 066-915 1531; captigh @eircom.net; the Mall; s/d €60/100; ☺ mid-Mar–mid-Nov; Ⓟ) A streamside garden and beautiful interior furnishings make this handsome house a great choice. Snuggle in one of the eight rooms or by the peat fire.

EATING

Goat Street Café (☎ 066-915 2770; Goat St; snacks & mains €4-12; ☺ 10.30am-5pm Mon-Sat, to 9pm Thu-Sat) A budget mecca, the perennially popular Goat Street Café gets mobbed in summer with folks seeking out its tasty salads, tarts and tagines. Dinner brings fresh seafood. It's at the top of Main St.

Half Door (☎ 066-915 1600; John St; mains €22-50, set menu €25; ☺ 12.30-2.30pm Mon-Sat, plus 5.30-10pm daily) Fish and shellfish are superbly presented at this outstanding seafood restaurant, which exudes a dignified, genteel air. The menu reflects what's fresh down on the docks; the local shrimp and larger crustaceans are especially good here.

ourpick Out of the Blue (☎ 066-915 0811; the Wood; lunch €10-20, dinner mains €15-30; ☺ 12.30-3pm & 6-9.30pm Thu-Tue mid-Mar–mid-Nov) The funky blue-and-yellow exterior might make you think 'chipper'. Wrong!

Dingle's best restaurant has an intense devotion to local seafood; if they don't like the catch, they don't open. Dishes are creative and change nightly. The surrounds are slightly shambolic – have a glass of wine from the tiny, overwhelmed bar and chill. Booking for dinner is essential. Lunchtime choices are simple and can be enjoyed outside.

DRINKING

ourpick Dick Mack's (☎ 066-915 1960; Green St) Announced by stars in the pavement bearing the names of its celebrity customers, Dick Mack's has an irrepressible sense of self. Ancient wood and ancient snugs dominate the interior, which is lit like the inside of a whiskey bottle. Out back there's a warren of tables, chairs and characters.

Hannie Agnes (☎ 087 949 0832; Green St) Local haunt that's known for its smooth Guinness and, during the summer, trad sessions and Irish coffee. The windows are frosted and the interior is spare – like a good pint.

GETTING THERE & AWAY

Bus Éireann (www.buseireann.ie) buses stop outside the car park behind the supermarket. To Tralee, where you can connect across Ireland or hop on the train, there are four buses Monday to Saturday and three on Sunday (€11, 80 minutes). Check for additional summer services.

There are eight buses a week to Dunquin and Ballydavid, on Monday, Tuesday, Thursday and Friday.

NORTH OF DINGLE
CLOGHANE & AROUND
pop 280

Cloghane (An Clochán) is another little piece of beauty tucked away on the Dingle Peninsula. The village's friendly pubs and accommodation nestle between Mt Brandon and Brandon Bay, with views across the water to the Stradbally Mountains. If you don't fancy scaling Mt Brandon, there are plenty of coastal strolls.

On the last weekend in July, Cloghane celebrates the ancient Celtic harvest

HOLGER LEUE

Lower Main St, Dingle

Waterfall, Connor Pass

RICHARD CUMMINS

festival **Lughnasa** with events – especially bonfires – both in the village and atop Mt Brandon. In late August, the **Brandon Regatta** is a race in traditional *currach* canoes.

The 5km drive out to **Brandon's Point** from Cloghane follows ever-narrower single-track roads, culminating in cliffs with fantastic views north and east. Sheep wander the constantly eroding rocks oblivious to their tenuous positions.

You can get tourist information in Cloghane from the shop and post office near the hostel and pub. Pick up copies of the local walking and hiking guides from the shop or your accommodation.

The vacuum-silent **St Brendan's Church** has a stained-glass window with depictions of the Gallarus Oratory and Ardfert Cathedral.

CONNOR PASS

At 456m, the Connor (or Conor) Pass is the highest in Ireland and offers spectacular views of Dingle Harbour to the south and Mt Brandon to the north. On a foggy day you'll see nothing but the road just in front of you. The road is in very good shape, excepting that it is very narrow and very steep (large signs portend doom for buses and trucks).

The summit car park yields **views** down to two lakes in the rock-strewn valley below plus the remains of walls and huts where people once lived impossibly hard lives. When visibility is good, the 10-minute climb to the summit is well worthwhile for the kind of views that inspire mountain-climbers.

WEST OF DINGLE

At the tip of the peninsula is the Slea Head drive along the R559. It has the greatest concentration of ancient sites in Kerry, if not the whole of Ireland. Specialist guides on sale in the tourist office (p215) in Dingle list the most interesting and accessible sites.

This part of the peninsula is a Gaeltacht area. The landscape is dramatic, especially in shifting mist, although full-on sea fog obliterates everything. For the best views, follow the Slea Head drive in a clockwise direction. Cross the bridge west of Dingle and keep straight on to Ventry. Beyond Ventry the road hugs the coast past Dunbeg Fort (below), then round the rocky outposts of Slea Head and Dunmore Head (below). Continuing along the coast to Dunquin (right), then turning east to Ballyferriter, the views of the Blasket Islands (p220) give way to views of 951m-high Mt Brandon and its neighbours. Beyond Ballyferriter is the Gallarus Oratory (p221) and numerous other historic sites, not to mention a confusing clutter of lanes. From Gallarus, the R599 circles back to Dingle.

Although a mere 50km in length, doing this drive justice will require a full day, at least.

SLEA HEAD & DUNMORE HEAD

Overlooking the mouth of Dingle Bay, Slea Head has fine beaches, good walks, and views of Mt Eagle and the Blasket Islands. It's understandably popular with coach parties, and cake vendors stand at the ready. But it's also an excellent area to see some well-preserved structures from Dingle's ancient past.

Dunmore Head is the westernmost point on the Irish mainland and the site of the wreckage in 1588 of two Spanish Armada ships.

About 7km southwest of Ventry on the road to Slea Head is the Iron Age **Dunbeg Fort**, a dramatic example of a promontory fortification, perched atop a sheer sea cliff. The fort has four outer walls of stone. Inside are the remains of a house and a beehive hut, as well as an underground passage.

The Slea Head area is dotted with **beehive huts**, **forts**, **inscribed stones** and **church sites**. The **Fahan huts**, including two fully intact huts, are 500m west

of Dunbeg Fort on the inland side of the road.

When the kiosks are open in summer, you'll be charged about €2 to €3 for entrance to the sights.

DUNQUIN

Yet another pause on a road of scenic pauses, Dunquin is a scattered village beneath Mt Eagle and Croaghmarhin. It's a hub for all things Blasket. The local website (www.dunchaoin.com) notes that it is the next parish to America.

The **Blasket Centre** (Ionad an Bhlascaoid Mhóir; ☎ 066-915 6444; www.heritageireland.ie; adult/child €4/2; ☒ 10am-7pm Jul & Aug, to 6pm mid-Mar–Jun, Sep & Oct, last admission 45min before closing) is a wonderful interpretive

Slea Head
JOHN ELK III

Gallarus Oratory

RICHARD CUMMINS

centre in a long, white hall ending in a wall-to-ceiling window overlooking the islands. Great Blasket's rich community of storytellers and musicians is profiled along with its literary visitors like John Millington Synge, writer of *Playboy of the Western World*. The more prosaic practicalities of island life are covered by exhibits on shipbuilding and fishing. There's a cafe with Blasket views, and a useful bookshop.

Dunquin Hostel (☎ 066-915 6121; www. anoige.ie; dm €15-19, tw €42; ☼ Feb-Nov) has a terrific location, near the Blasket Centre and not too far from Dunquin Pier. There are stunning views. This An Óige member closes between 10am and 5pm.

Mustard-coloured **De Mórdha B&B** (☎ 066-915 6276; www.demordha.com; s/d from €45/70; ☼ Easter-Oct) is a pleasant little B&B with all mod cons and great views. The pub is under a 1km walk away.

An Portán (☎ 066-915 6212; www.anportan. com; meals €12-25; ☼ Easter-Sep) serves traditional Irish meals with an international flavour. It has a separate guesthouse with

14 modern, large and fairly unadorned rooms.

BLASKET ISLANDS

The Blasket Islands (Na Blascaodaí), 5km out into the Atlantic, are the most westerly in Ireland. At 6km by 1.2km, Great Blasket (An Blascaod Mór) is the largest and most visited, and mountainous enough for strenuous walks, including a good one detailed in Kevin Corcoran's *Kerry Walks*. All of the Blaskets were inhabited at one time or another; there is evidence of Great Blasket being inhabited during the Iron Age and early Christian times. The last islanders left for the mainland in 1953 after they and the government agreed that it was no longer feasible to live in such isolated and harsh conditions (although a few people still make their home out here for part of the year).

You can camp on the islands, but there are no facilities. There's accommodation in Dunquin.

Weather can cause ferry cancellations, but otherwise the options for getting there and away are similar:

Blasket Island Ferries (☎ 066-915 1344, 066-915 6422; www.blasketisland.com; adult/child €20/10; ☒ 10.30am-3.30pm Easter-Sep) Boats depart hourly and take 20 minutes; add €15 for an ecotour of the island.

Blasket Islands Ferry (☎ 066-915 4864, 087 231 6131; www.blasketislands.ie; adult/child €20/10; ☒ 9.55am-4.55pm Easter-Oct) Boats depart hourly and take 15 minutes; add €15 for an ecotour of the island.

RIASC MONASTIC SETTLEMENT

The remains of this 5th- or 6th-century monastic settlement are one of the peninsula's more impressive and haunting sites, particularly the pillar with beautiful Celtic designs. Excavations have also revealed the foundations of an oratory first built with wood and later stone, a kiln for drying corn and a cemetery. The ruins are signposted as 'Mainistir Riaisc' along a narrow lane off the R559, about 2km east of Ballyferriter.

GALLARUS ORATORY

This dry-stone oratory is quite a sight, standing in its lonely spot beneath the brown hills as it has done for some 1200 years. It has withstood the elements perfectly, apart from a slight sagging in the roof. Traces of mortar suggest that the interior and exterior walls may have been plastered. Shaped like an upturned boat, it has a doorway on the western side and a round-headed window on the eastern side. Inside the doorway are two projecting stones with holes that once supported the door.

The **oratory** (☎ 066-915 6444; www.heritageireland.ie; admission free) is signposted off the R559, about 2km further on from the Riasc Monastic Settlement turn-off. Parking by the site is extremely limited and tends to become a mess in summer. There is a nearby private parking area with a **visitor centre** (☎ 066-915 5333; adult/child €3/free; ☒ 9am-9pm Jun-Aug, 10am-6pm Feb-May & Sep-10 Nov) that shows a 15-minute audiovisual display and offers clean toilets.

COUNTY LIMERICK
LIMERICK CITY
pop 56,000

Hardscrabble and Limerick city will always be linked. And why shouldn't they? Efforts at glitz and gloss only try to obscure an unflinchingly honest town that doesn't shy away from a tough past, as portrayed in Frank McCourt's *Angela's Ashes*.

INFORMATION

Limerick Tourist Office (☎ 061-317 522; www.shannonregiontourism.ie; Arthur's Quay; ☒ 9.30am-1pm & 2-5.30pm Mon-Fri, 9.30am-1pm Sat) A large, impressive facility with amazingly helpful staff; open longer hours in summer. Ask here about *Angela's Ashes* tours. Also look around town for red-clad 'street ambassadors' offering advice and information.

SIGHTS
KING JOHN'S CASTLE

The massive curtain walls and towers of Limerick's showpiece **castle** (☎ 061-360 788; www.shannonheritage.com; Nicholas St; adult/child €9.50/5.50; ☒ 10am-5pm Mon-Fri, to 5.30pm Sat & Sun, last admission 1hr before closing) are best viewed from the west bank of the River Shannon. The castle was built by King John of England between 1200 and 1212 on the site of an earlier fortification. It served as the military and administrative centre of the rich Shannon region.

MARTIN MOOS

King John's Castle (p221) overlooking the River Shannon

Inside there are recreations of brutal medieval weapons like the trebuchet, as well as excavated Viking sites, reconstructed Norman features and other artefacts. Walk the walls and pretend you're carrying a bucket of boiling oil.

HUNT MUSEUM

Although named for its benefactors, this **museum** (☎ **061-312 833; www.huntmuseum.com; Palladian Custom House, Rutland St; adult/child €8/4.25, free Sun; 10am-5pm Mon-Sat, 2-5pm Sun**) might well be named for the kind of hunt you do for treasure. Visitors are encouraged to open drawers and otherwise poke around the finest collection of Bronze Age, Iron Age and medieval treasures outside Dublin. The 2000-plus items are from the private collection of the late John and Gertrude Hunt, antique dealers and consultants, who championed historic preservation throughout the region. Look out for a tiny but exquisite bronze horse by da Vinci, and a Syracusan coin thought to have been one of the 30 pieces of silver paid to Judas for his betrayal of Christ. Cycladic sculptures, a Giacometti drawing and paintings by Renoir, Picasso and Jack B Yeats add to the feast. Guided tours from the dedicated and colourful volunteers are available.

SLEEPING & EATING

George (☎ **061-460 400; www.thegeorgeboutiquehotel.com; O'Connell St; s/d from €80/90; P**) This sleek place has a popular atrium lobby and small terrace above the busy streets of the city centre. The design looks like something out of a Sunday supplement – all warm colours with luxurious touches. The 127 rooms have wi-fi, iPod docks, evening cordials and more.

our pick **Sage Cafe** (☎ **061-409 458; 67-68 Catherine St; meals €7-15; 9am-6pm Mon-Sat**) Hardscrabble my arse. After you've followed the crowds to this amazing lunch spot, you'll enjoy some of the best food in Ireland. The decor says it all: superb taste that doesn't call attention to itself. Breakfast treats and baked goods give

⬊ GALWAY & THE WEST

GALWAY & THE WEST

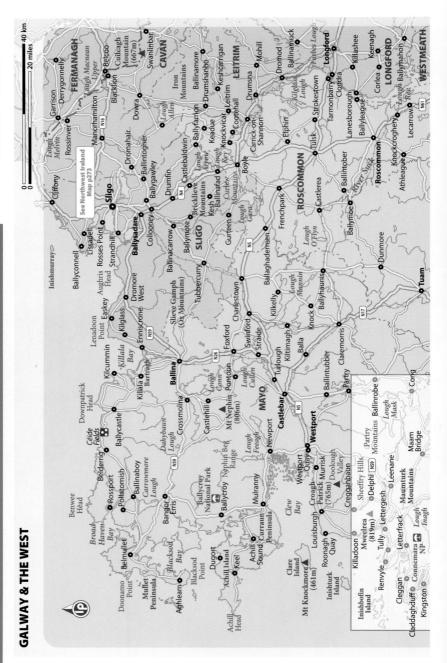

See Northwest Ireland Map p273

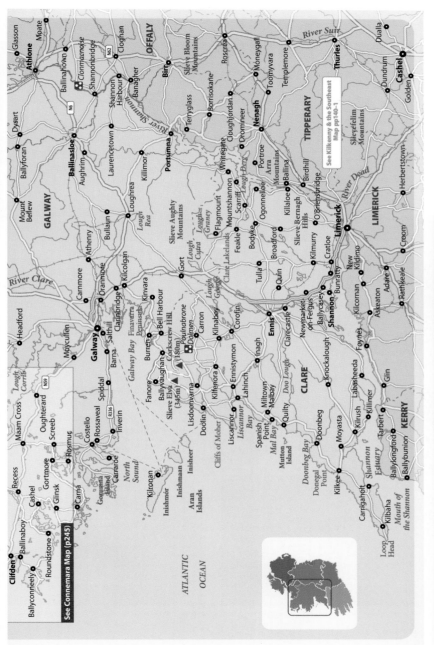

Glasson
Moate
Athlone
Ballinahown
Clonmacnoise
Shannonbridge
Cloghan
OFFALY
Dysart
Ballyforan
Birr
Slieve Bloom Mountains
Roscrea
Moneygall
Dunalla
River Suir
Thurles
Dundrum
Cashel
Golden
N6
N62
Ballinasloe
Aughrim
Shannon Harbour
Banagher
Terryglass
Borrisokane
Cloughjordan
Toomyvara
Templemore
TIPPERARY
Herbertstown
Mount Bellew
GALWAY
Laurencetown
Killimor
Portumna
Whitegate
Scarriff
Dromineer
Nenagh
Portroe
Arra Mountains
Birdhill
Ballina
Slievefelim Mountains
See Kilkenny & the Southeast Map pp140–1
Athenry
Bullaun
Loughrea
Lough Rea
Slieve Aughty Mountains
Flagmount
Mountshannon
Feakle
Bodyke
Broadford
Ogonnelloe
Slieve Bernagh Hills
Killaloe
Kilmurry
Cratloe
O'Briensbridge
LIMERICK
River Dead
Croom
LIMERICK
Carnmore
Oranmore
Kilcolgan
Kinvara
Gort
Lough Cutra
Lough Graney
Clare Lakelands
Lough George
Tulla
Quin
Limerick
New Kildimo
Adare
Rathkeale
River Clare
Headford
Moycullen
Claregalway
Bell Harbour
Burren
Poulnabrone Dolmen (180m)
Corkscrew Hill
Carron
Kilnaboy
Corofin
Kilfenora
Ennistymon
Inagh
Ennis
Clarecastle
Newmarket-on-Fergus
Bunratty
Shannon
Kilcornan
Askeaton
Maam Cross
Oughterard
Screebe
Spiddal
Galway
Salthill
Barna
Finavarra Peninsula
Ballyvaughan
Slieve Elva (345m)
Lisdoonvarna
Doolin
Lahinch
Miltown Malbay
Quilty
Doonbeg
Ballycasey
Foynes
Glin
KERRY
N59
Recess
Cashel
Gortmore
Glinsk
Costello
Rossaveal
Inverin
Carraroe
Carná
Fanore
Cliffs of Moher
Liscannor
Spanish Point
Mal Bay
Liscannor Bay
Mutton Island
Doonbeg Bay
Donegal Point
Kilkee
Doo Lough
CLARE
Knockalough
Labasheeda
Kilrush
Killimer
Tarbert
Ballylongford
Ballybunion
R336
See Connemara Map (p245)
Clifden
Ballyconneely
Roundstone
Ballinaboy
Gorumna Island
Kilronan
Inishmaan
Inisheer
Aran Islands
Inishmor
North Sound
Moyasta
Kilbaha
Carrigaholt
Shannon Estuary
Mouth of the Shannon
Loop Head
ATLANTIC OCEAN
River Shannon
Lough Corrib
Lough Derg

GALWAY & THE WEST HIGHLIGHTS

1 CONNEMARA

BY STEVE WHITFIELD, OUTDOOR INSTRUCTOR, KILLARY ADVENTURE CENTRE

Connemara is the 'real Ireland' and one of the few places where you'll still hear Irish spoken in the local pubs. Peat bogs are still being cut and dried by farmers and local fishermen can still be seen using *currachs* (rowboats) on the Killary Fjord.

⬊ STEVE WHITFIELD'S DON'T MISS LIST

❶ KAYAKING THE KILLARY FJORD

As you paddle your way through this **fjord** (p249), often with seals, dolphins and sea otters for company, you can follow the old famine track – used during the Great Famine – along the shoreline all the way to the Atlantic.

❷ HIKING THE TWELVE BENS

Although dedicated fell runners have been known to summit all 12 peaks in a single day, just climbing one is an unforgettable experience – the views from the top are spectacular, whether you're looking out to the coastline or inland to the brooding expanse of **Connemara National Park** (p248).

❸ KYLEMORE ABBEY

Kylemore Abbey (p248) looks like a fairy-tale castle shimmering in the lake. In 1920 it was handed over to the Benedictines; today it's a girls' school. Spend a couple of hours wandering about the castle or the gorgeous gardens.

Clockwise from top: Kylemore Abbey (p248), County Galway; Ruins amid wildflowers, Connemara (p245), County Galway; Roundstone (p246), County Galway; Benbaun, Connemara National Park (p248), County Galway

CLOCKWISE FROM TOP: RICHARD CUMMINS; RICHARD CUMMINS; JOHN ELK III; RICHARD CUMMINS

❹ ROUNDSTONE

The road into **Roundstone** (p246) is one of the most spectacular coastal drives in the country, but the village itself is just as beautiful. It's home to some great seafood restaurants and craft shops, the beach is always busy with lobster trawlers and *currachs* and there are fine beaches nearby.

❺ KILLARY ADVENTURE CENTRE

For an action-packed adventure while enjoying the surrounds of Connemara, this **adventure centre** (p249) is the place for you. There's such a huge range of activities – from rock climbing, gorge walking and kayaking to bungee jumps, speed boating, sailing and lots more.

❶ Killary Fjord
❷ Twelve Bens
❸ Kylemore Abbey
❹ Roundstone
❺ Killary Adventure Centre

⬎ THINGS YOU NEED TO KNOW

Best time to visit May to July **Getting around** Sleepzone (p249) runs a summer Connemara Loop bus; otherwise public transport is patchy and you're better off with your own wheels **Fitness levels** Activities abound for all, from couch potatoes to adrenaline junkies **For more on Connemara, see p245.**

GALWAY & THE WEST HIGHLIGHTS

2 | TRADITIONAL MUSIC IN CLARE

BY DICK O'CONNELL, SET DANCE INSTRUCTOR AT THE LIBRARY BAR, ENNIS

If you want to get to the heart of Irish traditional music, you have to come to County Clare. Other counties have their various styles, but nowhere else will you find such a concentration of talent – musicians, singers and dancers.

⬊ DICK O'CONNELL'S DON'T MISS LIST

❶ SET DANCING

I may be a little biased, but there's nowhere better to see the finest set dancing in the country – and to learn the basic steps – than at **Cois na hAbhna** (p254), where some of the finest talents in Ireland gather on a regular basis to show off their best moves.

❷ DOOLIN

Of all of Clare's musical towns and villages, none is more justifiably famous than **Doolin** (p262), which is known throughout the world. Many of the country's top musicians have gone to live there to perfect their craft and enjoy the blas, or flavour, of the place, which is all about music and a bit of craic (fun).

❸ FESTIVALS

It seems that not a week goes by without there being some kind of traditional music festival. Most are small and relatively informal, but there are a few showstoppers not to miss. Ennis

Clockwise from top: Traditional *seisiún* at O'Connor's (p263); Pub sign in Doolin (p262), County Clare; Irish musician playing accordian; Music shop sign in Doolin (p262); Irish musicians playing at O'Connor's (p263)

CLOCKWISE FROM TOP: DOUG MCKINLAY; JULIET COOMBE; ANN CECIL; JULIET COOMBE; DOUG MCKINLAY

has the **Fleadh Nua** (p254) and the **Ennis Trad Festival** (p254), but don't forget the **Willie Clancy Irish Music Festival** (p259) and the **Fleadh na gCuach** (p249), just over the border in Galway.

❹ SEISIÚNS

From Kinvara to Ennis, the beating heart of traditional music is the informal *seisiún* – literally a 'session' – where musicians gather for an organised or impromptu gig in a 'music house' (more often than not, a pub). Besides the festivals, this is where you'll hear the best music in Ireland. There are also regular ones held in Corofin, Ennistymon, Kilrush and Killaloe.

❺ KILFENORA CÉILI BAND

In 2009, this **band** (p265) celebrated its 100th anniversary, and they've come a long way since they were founded to raise money for local charities. They're Ireland's most recognized *céili* band, and you can see many of them playing regularly in **Linnane's** (p265).

⚓ THINGS YOU NEED TO KNOW

Best time to visit Busy summers have music festivals; off-season *seisiúns* are atmospheric **Getting around** There's a local bus network, or explore best with your own car **Enjoying *seisiúns*** Tap your feet, clap your hands, but don't start singing (it's not a back-up band!) **For more on traditional music, see p385.**

GALWAY & THE WEST HIGHLIGHTS

3

⌄ GALWAY

The 'City of the Tribes' is one of Ireland's loveliest burgs, a thriving centre that has retained much of its easygoing charm. The real treat is enjoying its wonderful pubs, not least Séhán Ua Neáchtain (p241), a contender for finest watering hole in Ireland, and Tig Cóilí (p241), where Galway's famed traditional musicians take a break from playing for everyone else.

4

⌄ ARAN ISLANDS

These islands are the embodiment of a traditional, almost mystical Ireland. From the breathtaking stone fort of Dún Aengus on Inishmór (p243) to the jagged, rocky coastlines and sparse population of Inishmaan (p244), they're a powerful reminder of a world that has long since disappeared almost everywhere else – but where you can still get an internet connection and a decent coffee.

◥ CLIFFS OF MOHER

Rising to a height of 203m from the churning Atlantic, the Cliffs of Moher (p261) are one of Ireland's most visited natural attractions. Yet unlike so many oversubscribed wonders, the hype is spot on, especially if you wend your way past the open-mouthed crowds and venture south beyond the viewing areas to observe the entirely vertical cliffs as nature intended them.

◥ CLONMACNOISE

Ireland's most important ecclesiastical site, Clonmacnoise (p250) is one of the main reasons Ireland was known as the 'land of saints and scholars'. Scholars and monks from all over Europe came to study in what was then a thriving city, and while it's quieter these days, the ruined temples and cathedral – as well as the superb collection of high crosses – are still impressive.

◥ CROAGH PATRICK

Rising 765m over County Mayo's Clew Bay, Croagh Patrick (p267) is where St Patrick is said to have banished venomous snakes from the country during a 40-day fast. Ascending the summit is a popular pilgrimage for the faithful (especially on the last Sunday in July), but you don't have to be a Catholic to enjoy the magnificent views from the summit.

3 OLIVER STREWE; 4 & 7 EOIN CLARKE; 5 STEPHEN SAKS; 6 RICHARD CUMMINS

3 Galway city (p238); 4 Stone fort, Inishmaan (p244), Aran Islands, County Galway; 5 Sea stack at Cliffs of Moher (p261), County Clare; 6 Clonmacnoise (p250), County Offaly; 7 Pilgrimage to Croagh Patrick (p267), County Mayo

GALWAY & THE WEST'S BEST...

MUSIC HOUSES

- **Tig Cóilí** (p241) Where Galway's musicians go to hear music.
- **Cíaran's Bar** (p254) Nightly trad.
- **Matt Molloy's** (p269) Owner Matt Molloy plays fife for The Chieftains.
- **O'Friel's Bar** (p258) In the traditional heartland.
- **MacDiarmada's** (p263) The definition of great craic.

BEAUTY SPOTS

- **Oughterard** (p246) William Thackeray's idea of heaven.
- **Roundstone** (p246) Lovely village.
- **Croagh Patrick** (p267) The perfect summit.
- **Inishmaan** (p244) Traditional living.
- **Cliffs of Moher** (p261) Hardly a surprise, but always capable of springing one.

SCENIC DRIVES

- **Sky Road** (p247) A spectacular loop from Clifden to Kingston.

- **Lough Inagh Valley** (p246) Cut through Connemara in the shadow of the brooding Twelve Bens.
- **Killary Harbour** (p249) A drive along Ireland's only fjord.
- **The Burren** (p260) Cut through this bizarre landscape from Ballyvaughan to Ennistymon.
- **Clare Coast** (p261) Scenic coastal route from the Cliffs of Moher to Ballyvaughan.

UNLIKELY ACTIVITIES

- **Patrician Pilgrimage** (p267) Even nonbelievers will be struck by the spirituality of the climb.
- **Get Adventurous** (p249) Try kayaking, rock climbing or even spelunking…
- **Go Medieval** (p250) A medieval banquet in a 16th-century castle.
- **Clonmacnoise Cruise** (p253) Via the Shannon to the monastic site.
- **Dive With Dolphins** (p258) OK, not quite 'swim with', but watch these creatures frolic.

Sunset over Clifden Bay as seen from the Sky Road (p247)

THINGS YOU NEED TO KNOW

⬊ VITAL STATISTICS

- **Area** 17,239 sq km
- **Population** 439,800
- **Best time to go** Summer or autumn

⬊ AREAS IN A NUTSHELL

- **County Galway** (p238) Has the west's hippest city, a filigreed coastline and a stunning interior.
- **County Offaly** (p250) Straddling the Shannon and home to the 6th century's buzziest city.
- **County Clare** (p253) Beautiful trad music to match the unique landscape.
- **County Mayo** (p265) In the shadow of Ireland's most sacred mountain.

⬊ ADVANCE PLANNING

- **Two months before** Book hotels, especially in popular areas such as Galway city, Connemara and the music towns of County Clare if there's a festival on.
- **One month before** Book your flight to the Aran Islands if you don't fancy a stormy crossing.
- **Two weeks before** Check out the weather forecast for an Aran Island crossing, then ignore it – weather changes every 20 minutes.

⬊ RESOURCES

- **Discover Ireland** (www.discover ireland.ie/west) Official tourist site.
- **Galway.Net** (www.galway.net) Unofficial tourist site.
- **Visit Mayo** (www.mayo.ie) Attractions, restaurants, pubs, clubs.
- **Surf Mayo** (www.surfmayo.com) Beaches, breaks and other surf info.
- **Visit Clare** (www.visitclare.net) Official East Clare Tourism Authority.

⬊ GETTING AROUND

- **Bus** Good bus networks cover most of the region, but it's a slow way of exploring.
- **Train** Only the major towns – Galway, Ennis and Westport – are served by train.
- **Car** You'll need your own car to really explore the Burren and Connemara.
- **Boat** The most straightforward way of getting to the Aran Islands.

⬊ BE FOREWARNED

- **Crowds** Summer festival season sees throngs flooding into Clare.
- **Weather** The Aran Islands can be weather-bound, making crossings impossible.
- **Reek Sunday** 20,000-plus people will climb Croagh Patrick on the third Sunday in July. You've been warned!

GALWAY & THE WEST ITINERARIES

GALWAY & AROUND Three Days

You could spend a week in (1) Galway city (p238) and not get bored, such is the variety of things to enjoy in the west's largest city. Explore the old section, including the Spanish Arch (p238) and medieval walls (p238), and if you're in town between May and June, make your way up to the salmon weir (p239) to see the fish pass down on their final descent to the sea. Visit the house (p239) where James Joyce courted the love of his life, Nora Barnacle. Then indulge in local culture with a pint (or more) in one of Ireland's great bars, Séhán Ua Neáchtain (p241) – there's a good chance you'll have musical accompaniment of the traditional kind as you quench your thirst. If you can tear yourself away, get out of town and visit the small fishing village of (2) Claddagh (p242) – perhaps buying the classic ring of love and fidelity at its source – before heading to pretty (3) Kinvara (p249), which is the doorway to the Burren and County Clare.

A MUSICAL LANDSCAPE Five Days

This five-day route takes in the traditional charms of the region, both musical and otherwise. Begin in central Clare in (1) Ennis (p253), from which you can reach any part of the county in under two hours. Head west to (2) Miltown Malbay (p258) and begin your exploration of the area's rich musical heritage by attending a formal (or informal) pub 'session'. Continue your explorations in (3) Ennistymon (p259) and (4) Kilfenora (p265) before crossing the heart of the Burren – with a pit stop in (5) Doolin (p262) before making your way to (6) Galway city (p238). From here, take the boat (or plane from Minna, about 35km west of the city) and make the short hop across the choppy waters to (7) Inishmór (p243) and get to grips with a traditional life that hasn't changed much for centuries. You could easily spend a couple of days here, or use the time to visit the other two islands, (8) Inishmaan (p244) and Inisheer (p245), where life really is untroubled by the demands of the modern age.

BEST OF THE WEST One Week

Begin at the excavated (1) Céide Fields (p270) in County Mayo. Wind your way round the coast, stopping at some of Ireland's wildest beaches, to the pretty village of (2) Pollatomish (p269). Head to the pub-packed heritage town of (3) Westport (p268), continue past (4) Croagh Patrick (p267) – although on a beautiful day climbing the peak of Ireland's holiest mountain is one of the top activity highlights of any trip here – and through (5) Leenane (p249), situated on Ireland's

only fjord, to (6) Connemara National Park (p248). Take the beautiful coastal route, passing (7) Kylemore Abbey (p248) and Clifden's scenic (8) Sky Road (p247) through pretty (9) Roundstone (p246), and then through the stunning wilderness of the inland route through Maam Cross to (10) Galway city (p238). Move on to the fishing villages of (11) Kinvara (p249) and (12) Ballyvaughan (p264), in the heart of the karst landscape of the Burren (p260), and visit the ancient (13) Aillwee Caves (p264).

DISCOVER GALWAY & THE WEST

In the heart of the west, Galway city is a swirl of enticing old pubs that hum with trad music sessions throughout the year. To the north, the Connemara Peninsula matches the beauty of the other Atlantic outcrops: tiny roads wander along a coastline studded with islands, surprisingly white beaches and intriguing old villages with views over it all. This is the place to don the hiking boots and take to the well-marked network of trails that wander through lonely valleys and past hidden lakes before ending at sprays of surf from the Atlantic. Beyond Connemara, the rugged beauty stretches through County Mayo, home to Ireland's most sacred pilgrimage site, Croagh Patrick, which rewards the penitent with stunning views of the surrounding countryside.

West of Galway, County Offaly has Clonmacnoise, one of Ireland's most important monastic sites; to the south, County Clare combines the stunning natural beauty of its long and meandering coastline with unique, windswept landscapes and a year's worth of dollops of Irish culture.

COUNTY GALWAY
GALWAY CITY
pop 72,400

Arty, bohemian Galway (Gaillimh) is renowned for its entertainment scene. Brightly painted pubs heave with live music, while cafes offer front-row seats from which to observe all manner of street performers.

Steeped in history, the city nonetheless has a contemporary vibe. Students make up a quarter of its population, and remnants of the medieval town walls lie between shops selling Aran sweaters, handcrafted Claddagh rings, and stacks of secondhand and new books. Bridges arc over the salmon-filled River Corrib, and a long promenade leads to the seaside suburb of Salthill, on Galway Bay, the source of the area's famous oysters.

INFORMATION
Ireland West Tourism (☎ 091-537 700; www.discoverireland.ie/west; Forster St; ⏰ 9am-

5.45pm daily Easter-Sep, 9am-5.45pm Mon-Sat Oct-Easter) Large, efficient information centre that can help arrange local accommodation, and regional bus tours and ferry trips.

Tourist Information Booth (Eyre Sq; ⏰ 1.30-5.30pm Sun Oct-Easter, 9am-5.30pm daily Easter-Sep) Operated by the main tourist office, it dispenses free city maps and local info.

SIGHTS & ACTIVITIES
SPANISH ARCH & MEDIEVAL WALLS
Framing the river east of Wolfe Tone Bridge, the Spanish Arch (1584) is thought to be an extension of Galway's medieval walls. The arch appears to have been designed as a passageway through which ships entered the city to unload goods, such as wine and brandy from Spain.

Today it reverberates to the beat of bongo drums, and the lawns and riverside form a gathering place for locals and visitors on any sunny day. Many watch kayak-

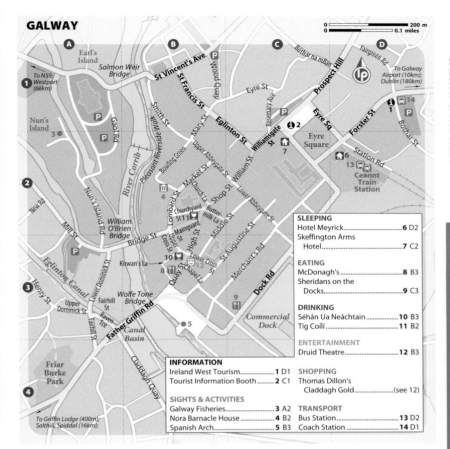

GALWAY

SLEEPING
Hotel Meyrick....................................**6** D2
Skeffington Arms
   Hotel...**7** C2

EATING
McDonagh's.......................................**8** B3
Sheridans on the
   Docks...**9** C3

DRINKING
Séhán Ua Neáchtain....................**10** B3
Tig Coílí..**11** B2

ENTERTAINMENT
Druid Theatre..................................**12** B3

INFORMATION
Ireland West Tourism.......................**1** D1
Tourist Information Booth.............**2** C1

SIGHTS & ACTIVITIES
Galway Fisheries................................**3** A2
Nora Barnacle House **4** B2
Spanish Arch......................................**5** B3

SHOPPING
Thomas Dillon's
   Claddagh Gold.......................(see 12)

TRANSPORT
Bus Station.......................................**13** D2
Coach Station **14** D1

ers manoeuvre over the minor rapids of River Corrib.

SALMON WEIR

Upstream from Salmon Weir Bridge, which crosses the River Corrib just east of the cathedral, the river cascades down the great weir, one of its final descents before reaching Galway Bay.

The salmon and sea-trout seasons usually span February to September, but most fish pass through the weir during May and June. To obtain fishing permits and book a time, contact the manager at

Galway Fisheries (☎ 091-562 388; www.wrfb. ie; Nun's Island). A half-day's fishing costs as little as €18.

NORA BARNACLE HOUSE

James Joyce courted his future wife Nora Barnacle (1884–1951) at this little **house** (☎ 091-564 743; www.norabarnacle.com; 8 Bowling Green), beginning in 1909. It's now a privately owned museum displaying the couple's letters and photographs among evocatively arranged furniture. Hours are erratic; call ahead or check with the

AND THE FUN NEVER ENDS

Galway's packed calendar of festivals turns the city and surrounding communities into what feels like one nonstop party – streets overflow with revellers, and pubs and restaurants often extend their opening hours.

Highlights include the following:

Cúirt International Festival of Literature (☎ 091-565 886; www.galwayartscentre.ie/cuirt) Top-name authors converge on Galway in April for Ireland's premier literary festival, featuring poetry slams, theatrical performances and readings.

Galway Arts Festival (☎ 091-566 700; www.galwayartsfestival.ie) A two-week extravaganza of theatre, music, art and comedy in mid-July.

Galway Film Fleadh (☎ 091-751 655; www.galwayfilmfleadh.com) One of Ireland's biggest film festivals, held in July around the same time as the arts festival.

Galway International Oyster Festival (☎ 091-522 066; www.galwayoysterfest.com) Oysters are washed down with plenty of pints in the last week in September.

Galway Race Week (☎ 091-753 870; www.galwayraces.com) Horse races in Ballybrit, 3km east of the city, are the centrepiece of Galway's biggest, most boisterous festival of all. Thursday is a real knees-up: by night the swells have muddy knees on their tuxes and are missing random high heels. The week occurs in late July or early August.

tourist office. Expect to pay around €3 admission.

SLEEPING

Griffin Lodge (☎ 091-589 440; www.irishholidays.com/griffin.shtml; 3 Father Griffin Pl; s €45-60, d €55-80; P 💻) You'll be welcomed like a long-lost friend at this completely renovated B&B, which has eight immaculate rooms in soothing shades of spearmint and moss green. Frills are kept to a minimum, with just a few elegant framed prints and crocheted cotton bedspreads.

our pick **Skeffington Arms Hotel** (☎ 091-563 173; www.skeffington.ie; Eyre Sq; r €75-190; 🔀 💻 🛜) Rooms at the Skeff, overlooking Eyre Sq, eschew the frilly cliché. In fact the only lace you may find in any of the 24 rooms is on your underwear. Pass through the arched traditional entrance into a minimalist haven. Air-con allows early risers to cut out noise from the frolic-

some masses roaming the streets on long summer nights.

Hotel Meyrick (☎ 091-564 041; www.hotelmeyrick.ie; Eyre Sq; r €165-250; P 💻) Known as the Railway Hotel when it opened in 1852, and later as the Great Southern Hotel, this stately showpiece looms large over Eyre Sq. A massive renovation artfully combines traditional decor with savvy modern touches. Note the zebra prints on the lobby chairs. Definitely not original equipment: the rooftop hot tub. All 97 guestrooms include bath-tubs and high-speed internet.

EATING

McDonagh's (☎ 091-565 001; 22 Quay St; fish & chips from €8, restaurant mains €15-25; 🕐 cafe & takeaway counter noon-midnight Mon-Sat, 5-11pm Sun, restaurant 5-10pm Mon-Sat) Divided into two parts, with a takeaway counter and a cafe with long communal wooden tables on one side, and a more upmarket restaurant on the other, Galway's best chippy churns out battered cod, plaice, haddock, whiting and salmon nonstop, all accompanied by homemade tartar sauce.

our pick **Sheridans on the Docks** (☎ 091-566 905; 3 Dock Rd; mains €17-26; 🕑 6.30-10.30pm Tue-Sat) This excellent restaurant is located in a vintage stone building overlooking the harbour. The menu changes regularly, but the dishes, such as cockle beignets, wild sea bass with purple sprouted broccoli and baked rhubarb, celebrate the best of locally produced foods.

DRINKING

Séhán Ua Neáchtain (☎ 091-568 820; 17 Upper Cross St) Painted a bright cornflower blue, this 19th-century pub, known simply as Neáchtain's (*nock*-tans), has a wraparound string of tables outside, many shaded by a large tree. It's a place where locals plop down and let the world pass them by – why not stop and join them for a pint?

our pick **Tig Cóilí** (Mainguard St) Two live *céilidhs* a day draw the crowds to this authentic fire-engine-red pub, just off High St. It's where musicians go to get drunk or drunks go to become musicians…or something like that. A gem.

ENTERTAINMENT

Druid Theatre (☎ 091-568 617; www.druid theatre.com; Chapel Lane) This theatre, established in 1975, is famed for showing experimental works by young Irish playwrights, as well as new adaptations of classics. Its home is an old tea warehouse, which was renovated in 2009.

GETTING THERE & AWAY
BUS

Bus Éireann (www.buseireann.ie) has services to all major cities in the Republic and the North from the **bus station** (☎ 091-562 000) just off Eyre Sq, near the train station. The one-way fare to Dublin (3¾ hours) is €14.

Several private bus companies are based at the glossy new **coach station**

Quay St, Galway city

CHRIS MELLOR

Claddagh ring store sign

RICHARD CUMMINS

CLADDAGH RINGS

The fishing village of Claddagh once had its own king as well as its own customs and traditions. Now subsumed into the Galway city centre, virtually all remnants of the original village are gone, but Claddagh rings survive as both a timeless reminder and a timeless source of profits.

Popular with people of real or imagined Irish descent everywhere, the rings depict a heart (symbolising love) between two outstretched hands (friendship), topped by a crown (loyalty). Rings are handcrafted at jewellers around Galway, and start from about €20 for a silver band to well over €1000 for a diamond-set blinged-up version worthy of Tony O'Soprano.

Jewellers include Ireland's oldest jewellery shop, **Thomas Dillon's Claddagh Gold**, which was established in 1750. It has some vintage examples in its small back-room 'museum'.

Things you need to know: ☎ 091-566 365; www.claddaghring.ie; 1 Quay St

---

(**Bothar St**) near the tourist office. They include the following:

Citylink (☎ 1890-280 808; www.citylink.ie) Services to Dublin (3¼ hours), Dublin

Airport, Cork, Limerick and Connemara. Service is frequent and fares are as low as €10.

gobus.ie (☎ 091-564 600; www.gobus.ie) Frequent services to Dublin and Dublin Airport. Buses have wi-fi.

TRAIN

From the **train station** (☎ 091-564 222), just off Eyre Sq, there are up to five trains daily to/from Dublin's Heuston Station (one-way from €35, three hours). Connections with other train routes can be made at Athlone (one hour). In late 2009, it was expected that the line between Galway, Ennis and Limerick would be reopened after a massive rebuilding program.

GETTING AROUND

Bus Éireann (www.buseireann.ie) operates numerous daily services from Shannon airport to Galway (€13.50, two hours). **Citylink** (www.citylink.ie) also runs services between Galway and Shannon airport (€15). Citylink and gobus.ie serve Dublin Airport.

ARAN ISLANDS

Easily visible from large swaths of coastal Galway and Clare, the Aran Islands sing their own siren song to thousands of travellers each year who find their desolate beauty beguiling. Day trippers shuttle through in a daze of rocky magnificence, while those who stay longer find places that, in many ways, seem further removed from the Irish mainland than a 40-minute ferry ride or 10-minute flight.

GETTING THERE & AWAY
AIR

All three islands have landing strips. The mainland departure point is Connemara regional airport at Minna, near Inverin (Indreabhán), about 35km west of Galway.

GALWAY & THE WEST

COUNTY GALWAY

Stone walls, Inisheer (p245)
DENIS O'BYRNE

Aer Arann Islands (☎ 091-593 034; www.aerarannislands.ie) offers return flights to each of the islands several times daily (hourly in summer) for adult/child/student €45/25/37; the flights take about 10 minutes, and groups of four or more can get group rates.

BOAT

Operating year-round, **Island Ferries** (☎ 091-568 903, 091-572 273; www.aranislandferries.com; 4 Forster St, Galway; adult/child/student €25/13/20) serves all three islands and also links Inishmaan and Inisheer.

Aran Direct (☎ 091-566 535; www.arandirect.com; return adult/child/concession €25/15/20; ☼ April-late Sep) serves Inishmór.

INISHMÓR

pop 1300

Most visitors who venture out to the islands don't make it beyond Inishmór (Árainn) and its main attraction, Dún Aengus, the stunning stone fort perched perilously on the island's towering cliffs. The arid landscape west of Kilronan (Cill

Rónáin), Inishmór's main settlement, is dominated by stone walls, boulders, scattered buildings and the odd patch of deep-green grass and potato plants.

INFORMATION

The useful **tourist office** (☎ 099-61263; Kilronan; ☼ 11am-7pm Jun-Sep, 11am-2pm & 3-5pm Oct-May), on the waterfront west of the ferry pier in Kilronan, changes money, as does the **post office**.

DÚN AENGUS

Three spectacular forts stand guard over Inishmór, each believed to be around 2000 years old. Chief among them is **Dún Aengus** (Dún Aonghasa; ☎ 099-61008; www.heritageireland.ie; adult/child €3/1; ☼ 10am-6pm), which has three nonconcentric walls that run right up to sheer drops to the ocean below. It is protected by remarkable *chevaux de frise*, fearsome and densely packed defensive stone spikes that surely helped deter ancient armies from invading the site.

EOIN CLARKE

Old cottage, Inishmaan

Powerful swells pound the 60m-high cliff face. A complete lack of rails or other modern additions that would spoil this amazing ancient site means that you can not only go right up to the cliff's edge but also potentially fall to your doom below quite easily. When it's uncrowded, you can't help but feel the extraordinary energy that must have been harnessed to build this vast site.

A small visitor centre has displays that put everything in context. A slightly strenuous 900m walkway wanders uphill through a rocky landscape lined with hardy plants to the fort.

SLEEPING

Man of Aran Cottage (☎ 099-61301; www.manofarancottage.com; Kilmurvey; s/d from €60/90; ⌚ Mar-Oct) Built for the 1930s film of the same name, this thatched B&B doesn't trade on past glories – its authentic stone-and-wood interiors define charming. The owners are avid organic gardeners and their bounty (the tomatoes are famous) can become your meal.

DRINKING

Tigh Fitz (☎ 099-61213; Killeany) Near the airport, this jovial pub has traditional sessions and set dancing every weekend and does excellent bar food (noon to 5pm) from June to August. It's 1.6km from Kilronan (about a 25-minute walk).

American Bar (☎ 099-61130; Kilronan) Two large rooms fill with happy pint quaffers throughout the year. In low season sloshed locals anticipate the next year of tourists (especially the bar's namesakes). The room on the right as you enter, with its windows and access to the terrace, is the best bet.

GETTING AROUND

To see the island at a gentler pace, **pony traps** (⌚ Mar-Nov) with a driver are available for trips between Kilronan and Dún Aengus; the return journey costs between €60 and €100 for up to four people.

INISHMAAN

pop 200

The least-visited of the islands, with the smallest population (a little over 100 in winter, 200 during the summer population boom), Inishmaan (Inis Meáin) is a rocky respite. Inishmaan's scenery is breathtaking, with a jagged coastline of startling cliffs, empty beaches, and fields where the main crop seems to be stone.

INISHEER
pop 300

Inisheer (Inis Oírr), the smallest of the Aran Islands, has a palpable sense of enchantment, enhanced by the island's deep-rooted mythology and ethereal landscapes.

CONNEMARA

Think of the best crumble you've ever had, one with a craggy crust that accumulates hollows of perfect flavour. Similarly, the filigreed coast of the Connemara Peninsula is endlessly pleasing, with pockets of sheer delight awaiting discovery. A succession of seaside hamlets entice, including the jewel-like fishing harbour at Roundstone, and sleepy Leenane on Killary Harbour, the country's only fjord. Clifden, Connemara's largest town, is

spectacularly sited on a hill, while offshore lies the idyllic island of Inishbofin.

Connemara's interior is a kaleidoscope of rusty bogs, lonely valleys and shimmering black lakes. At its heart are the Maumturk Mountains and the pewter-tinged quartzite peaks of the Twelve Bens mountain range, with a network of scenic hiking and biking trails.

Galway's tourist office (p238) has a wealth of information on the area. Online, **Connemara Tourism** (www.connemara.ie) and **Go Connemara** (www.goconnemara.com) have regionwide info and links.

GETTING THERE & AROUND
BUS
Bus Éireann (☎ 091-562 000; www.buseireann. ie) serves most of Connemara. Services can be sporadic, and many buses operate May to September only, or July and August only. Some drivers will stop in between towns if arrangements are made at the beginning of the trip.

Citylink (☎ 1890-280 808; www.citylink.ie) has several buses a day linking Galway city with Clifden, with stops in Moycullen, Oughterard, Maam Cross and Recess, and

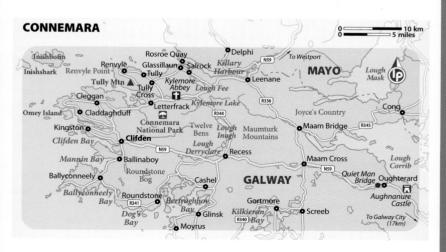

CONNEMARA

on to Cleggan and Letterfrack. If you're going somewhere between towns (a hostel in the countryside, for example), you might be able to arrange a drop-off with the driver.

CAR

Your own wheels are the best way to get off this scenic region's beaten track – though watch out for the narrow roads' stone walls, just waiting to scrape the sides of your car.

Heading west from Galway, you can either take the coast road (R336) through Salthill, Barna and Spiddal, or the direct inland route (N59) through Oughterard. The journey from Maam Cross northwest to Leenane (R336) or northeast to Cong (R345) in County Mayo takes you through the stunning mountainous region of Joyce's Country.

Many road signs in this area are in Irish only, so take note of the Irish place names (in parentheses) that are listed in this section.

OUGHTERARD & AROUND

pop 2400

The writer William Makepeace Thackeray sang the praises of the small town of Oughterard (Uachtar Árd), saying, 'A more beautiful village can scarcely be seen'. Fortunately, little has changed in the intervening years. Just 27km along the main road from Galway city to Clifden, near Lough Corrib, this pretty gateway to Connemara is one of Ireland's principal angling centres.

Immediately west of Oughterard, the countryside opens up to sweeping panoramas of lakes, mountains and bogs, which get more spectacular the further west you travel. Nearby attractions include Aughnanure Castle, a spiritual Celtic garden, and the *Quiet Man* Bridge.

LOUGH INAGH VALLEY

Magnificent desolation. This stark brown landscape beguiles by its very simplicity. Cloud shadows throw patterns on the jutting peaks; pause and let the ceaseless winds tousle your hair.

The R344 enters the valley from the south, just west of playfully named Recess. The moody waters of Loughs Derryclare and Inagh reflect the colours of the moment. On the western side is the brooding **Twelve Bens** mountain range. At the north end of the valley, the R344 meets the N59, which loops around Connemara to Leenane (p249).

Towards the northern end of the valley, a track leads west off the road up a blind valley, which is well worth exploring.

ROUNDSTONE

pop 400

Clustered around a boat-filled harbour, Roundstone (Cloch na Rón) is one of Connemara's gems. Colourful terrace houses and inviting pubs overlook the dark recess of Bertraghboy Bay, which is home to lobster trawlers and traditional *currachs* with tarred canvas bottoms stretched over wicker frames.

SLEEPING & EATING

Roundstone House (☎ 091-35864; www.roundstonehousehotel.com; Main St; r €65-120; ☼ Apr-Oct) A dignified presence lining Main St, this sprawling inn has 13 restful rooms with tea kettles and other creature comforts, plus views across the bay. The pub has trad sessions some nights in summer and you can enjoy pints and local seafood out on the terrace.

O'Dowd's (☎ 091-35809; Main St; mains €15-22; ☼ restaurant noon-10pm Apr-Sep, noon-3pm & 6-9.30pm Oct-Mar) This well-worn, comfortable old pub hasn't lost any of its authenticity since it starred in the Hollywood flick

Clifden

RICHARD CUMMINS

The Matchmaker. Specialities at its adjoining restaurant include seafood sourced off the old stone dock right across the street.

CLIFDEN

pop 1900

Known as Connemara's 'capital', Clifden (An Clochán), is an appealing Victorian-era country town with an imperfect oval of streets offering evocative strolls. It presides over the head of the narrow bay where the River Owenglin tumbles into the sea. The surrounding countryside beckons you to walk through woods and above the shoreline.

Heading directly west from Clifden's Market Sq, **Sky Road** traces a spectacular loop out to the township of Kingston and back to Clifden, taking in some rugged, stunningly beautiful coastal scenery en route. The round trip of about 12km can be easily walked or cycled, but, if you're short on time, you can also drive.

Connemara's ponies are a docile bunch. If you'd like to strike up a friendship, try going for a ride with **Errislannan Manor** (☎ 095-21134; www.connemaraponyriding.com; **Ballyconneely Rd**). Guides provide lessons and lead treks along the beach and up into the hills. Rates start at €35 per hour and depend on the type and length of ride you want to take. The centre is 3.5km south of Clifden on the R341.

SLEEPING

our pick **Dun Ri Guesthouse** (☎ 095-21625; www.dunri.ie; Hulk St; r €50-100; 🛜) Just down the hill from the centre, in a quiet spot near the pony track, this appealing modern inn has 13 spacious rooms. The included breakfast offers many choices; the cheese plate was one of the finest we've been served.

EATING & DRINKING

Lowry's Bar (☎ 095-21347; Market St; meals €4-9; 🕙 10.30am-midnight Sun-Thu, 10.30am-1am Fri & Sat) A time-worn local, Lowry's has traditional pleasures, ranging from the age-old, unadorned look of the place to its *céilidh* sessions, which take place at

RICHARD CUMMINS

Dunguaire Castle (p250)

least a couple of nights a week. The food is 'unpretentious Irish' (eg bangers and mash).

LETTERFRACK & AROUND
pop 200

Founded by Quakers in the mid-19th century, Letterfrack (Leitir Fraic) is ideally situated for exploring Connemara National Park, Renvyle Point and Kylemore Abbey. The village is barely more than a crossroads with a few pubs and B&Bs, but the forested setting and nearby coast are a magnet for outdoors adventure seekers. A 4km walk to the peak of Tully Mountain takes 40 minutes and affords wonderful ocean views.

SIGHTS
KYLEMORE ABBEY

A few kilometres east of Letterfrack stands **Kylemore Abbey** (☎ 095-41146; www.kyle moreabbey.com; adult/under 12yr/student €12/ free/7; ☻ visitor centre, abbey & church 9am-5pm, gardens 10am-4.30pm mid-Mar–Oct). Magnificently situated on the shores of

a lake, this crenellated 19th-century neo-Gothic fantasy was built for a wealthy English businessman, Mitchell Henry, who spent his honeymoon in Connemara. His wife died tragically young.

Kylemore's tranquillity is shattered in high summer with the arrival of dozens of tour coaches per day, each one followed through the gates by an average of 50 cars (yes, about 2750 cars every day).

CONNEMARA NATIONAL PARK

Immediately southeast of Letterfrack, **Connemara National Park** (☎ 095-41054; www.npws.ie, www.heritageireland.ie; Letterfrack; admission free; ☻ visitor centre & facilities 10am-5.30pm Mar-May & Sep-early Oct, 9.30am-6.30pm Jun-Aug, grounds open year-round) spans 2000 dramatic hectares of bog, mountain and heath. The visitor centre is in a beautiful setting off a parking area 300m south of the Letterfrack crossroads.

The park encloses a number of the **Twelve Bens**, including Bencullagh, Benbrack and Benbaun. The heart of the park is **Gleann Mór** (Big Glen), through which the River Polladirk flows. There's fine walking up the glen and over the surrounding mountains. There are also short, self-guided walks and, if the Bens look too daunting, you can hike up **Diamond Hill** nearby.

The visitor centre offers an introduction to the park's flora, fauna and geology, and visitors can scrutinise maps and various trails here before heading out into the park. Various types of flora and fauna native to the area are explained, including the Mothra-sized elephant hawkmoth.

Guided nature walks (Jul & Aug) depart from the visitor centre. They last two to three hours and cover rough, boggy terrain.

GETTING THERE & AWAY
Bus Éireann (www.buseireann.ie) and **Citylink** (www.citylink.ie) buses continue to Letterfrack several times daily from Clifden, 15km southwest on the N59.

LEENANE & KILLARY HARBOUR
The small village of Leenane (also spelled Leenaun) drowses on the shore of dramatic Killary Harbour. Dotted with mussel rafts, the harbour is widely believed to be Ireland's only fjord. Slicing 16km inland and more than 45m deep in the centre, it certainly looks like a fjord, although some scientific studies suggest it may not actually have been glaciated. **Mt Mweelrea** (819m) towers to its north.

Leenane boasts both stage and screen connections. It was the location for *The Field* (1989), a movie with Richard Harris based on John B Keane's poignant play about a tenant farmer's ill-fated plans to pass on a rented piece of land to his son. The village's name made it onto the theatrical map with the success in London and New York of Martin McDonagh's play *The Beauty Queen of Leenane.*

The local website (www.leenanevillage.com) is a good source of information.

ACTIVITIES
Canoeing, sea kayaking, sailing, rock climbing, windsurfing and day hikes are but a few of the activities on offer at **Killary Adventure Centre** (095-43411; www.killaryadventure.com; 10am-5pm), approximately 3km west of Leenane on the N59. Rates begin at adult/child €50/32.

SLEEPING
Sleepzone Connemara (095-42929; www.sleepzone.ie; campsites from €12, dm €20-26, s €50, d €70; Mar-Oct;) This renovated 19th-century property has over 100 beds in spotless dorms and private rooms. Popular with walkers, its amenities include a bar, barbecue terrace, tennis court and bike hire. Ask about the transport scheme with a Galway-based tour company.

SOUTH OF GALWAY CITY
KINVARA
pop 400
The small stone harbour of Kinvara (sometimes spelt Kinvarra) sits snugly at the southeastern corner of Galway Bay, which accounts for its Irish name, Cinn Mhara (Head of the Sea). Traditional Galway hooker sailing boats race here each year on the second weekend in August in the **Cruiniú na mBáid** (Gathering of the Boats).

Kinvara's other big date on its annual calendar is **Fleadh na gCuach** (Cuckoo Festival), a traditional music festival in late May that features over 100 musicians performing at upwards of 50 organised sessions. Spin-off events include a parade.

Details of both festivals are available on Kinvara's **website** (www.kinvara.com).

GALWAY & THE WEST

COUNTY OFFALY

SIGHTS & ACTIVITIES

The chess-piece-style **Dunguaire Castle** (☎ 091-637 108; adult/child €6/3; ☯ 9.30am-5pm May-Oct) was erected around 1520 by the O'Hynes clan and is in excellent condition following extensive restoration. It is widely believed that the castle occupies the former site of the 6th-century royal palace of Guaire Aidhne, the king of Connaught. Dunguaire's owners have included Oliver St John Gogarty (1878–1957), the famed poet, writer, surgeon and Irish Free State senator.

The least authentic way to visit the castle is to attend a **medieval banquet** (☎ 061-360 788; www.shannonheritage.com; banquet adult/child €56/28; ☯ 5.30pm & 8.45pm May-Oct). Yuck-filled stage shows and shtick provide diversions while you plow through a big group meal.

GETTING THERE & AWAY

Bus Éireann (www.buseireann.ie) services 50 and 423 link Kinvara with Galway city (30 minutes) and towns in County Clare, such as Doolin, several times daily.

COUNTY OFFALY
CLONMACNOISE

Gloriously placed overlooking the River Shannon, **Clonmacnoise** (☎ 090-967 4195; www.heritageireland.ie; adult/child €6/2; ☯ 9am-7pm mid-May–mid-Sep, 10am-6pm mid-Sep–Oct & mid-Mar–mid-May, 10am-5.30pm Nov–mid-Mar, last admission 45min before closing; Ⓟ) is one of Ireland's most important ancient monastic cities.

HISTORY

Roughly translated, Clonmacnoise (Cluain Mhic Nóis) means 'Meadow of the Sons of Nós'. The marshy land in the area would have been impassable for early traders, who instead chose to travel by water or on eskers (raised ridges formed by glaciers). When St Ciarán founded a monastery here in AD 548, it was the most important crossroads in the country, the intersection of the north-south River Shannon, and the east-west Esker Riada (Highway of the Kings).

The giant ecclesiastical city had a humble beginning and Ciarán died just seven

High crosses and ruins, Clonmacnoise

HOLGER LEUE

CLONMACNOISE

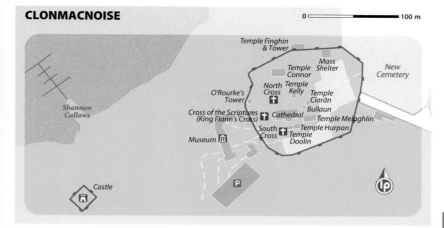

months after building his first church. Over the years, however, Clonmacnoise grew to become an unrivalled bastion of Irish religion, literature and art and attracted a large lay population. Between the 7th and 12th centuries, monks from all over Europe came to study and pray here, helping to earn Ireland the title of the 'land of saints and scholars'. Even the high kings of Connaught and Tara were brought here for burial.

SIGHTS
MUSEUM
Three connected conical huts near the entrance house the museum and echo the design of early monastic dwellings. The centre's 20-minute audiovisual show is an excellent introduction to the site.

The exhibition area contains the original high crosses (replicas have been put in their former locations outside), and various artefacts uncovered during excavation, including silver pins, beaded glass and an Ogham stone. It also contains the largest collection of early Christian grave slabs in Europe. Many are in remarkable condition, with inscriptions clearly vis-

ible, often starting with *oroit do* or *ar* (a prayer for).

HIGH CROSSES
There's a real sense of drama as you descend to the foot of the imposing sandstone **Cross of the Scriptures**, one of Ireland's finest. It's very distinctive, with unique upward-tilting arms and richly decorated panels depicting the Crucifixion, the Last Judgement, the arrest of Jesus, and Christ in the tomb.

Only the shaft of the **North Cross**, which dates from around AD 800, remains. It is adorned by lions, convoluted spirals and a single figure, thought to be the Celtic god Cernunnos (or Cernenus), who sits in a Buddha-like position. The richly decorated **South Cross** has mostly abstract carvings – swirls, spirals and fretwork - and, on the western face, the Crucifixion plus a few odd cavorting creatures.

CATHEDRAL
The biggest building at Clonmacnoise, the cathedral was originally built in AD 909, but was significantly altered and remodelled over the centuries. Its most

O'Connell St, Ennis

RICHARD CUMMINS

interesting feature is the intricate 15th-century Gothic doorway with carvings of Sts Francis, Patrick and Dominic. A whisper carries from one side of the door to the other, and this feature was supposedly used by lepers to confess their sins without infecting the priests.

The last high kings of Tara – Turlough Mór O'Connor (died 1156) and his son Ruairí (Rory; died 1198) – are said to be buried near the altar.

TEMPLES

The small churches are called temples, a derivation of the Irish word *teampall* (church). The little, roofed church is **Temple Connor**, still used by Church of Ireland parishioners on the last Sunday of the summer months. Walking towards the cathedral, you pass the scant foundations of **Temple Kelly** (1167) before reaching tiny **Temple Ciarán**, reputed to be the burial place of St Ciarán, the site's founder.

The floor level in Temple Ciarán is lower than outside because local farmers have

been taking clay from the church for centuries to protect their crops and cattle. The floor has been covered in slabs, but handfuls of clay are still removed from outside the church in the early spring.

Near the temple's southwestern corner is a **bullaun** (ancient grinding stone), supposedly used for making medicines for the monastery's hospital. Today the rainwater that collects in it is said to cure warts.

Continuing round the compound you come to 12th-century **Temple Melaghlin**, with its attractive windows, and the twin structures of **Temple Hurpan** and **Temple Doolin**.

ROUND TOWERS

Overlooking the River Shannon is the 20m-high **O'Rourke's Tower**. Lightning blasted the top off the tower in 1135, but the remaining structure was used for another 400 years.

Temple Finghin and its round tower are on the northern boundary of the site, also overlooking the Shannon. The building dates from around 1160 and has some fine Romanesque carvings. The herringbone-patterned tower roof is the only one in Ireland that has never been altered. Most round towers became shelters when the monasteries were attacked, but this one was probably just used as a bell tower since the doorway is at ground level.

GETTING THERE & AWAY

Clonmacnoise is 7km northeast of Shannonbridge on the R444 and about 24km south of Athlone in County Westmeath. By car you can explore this interesting and evocative area at leisure.

Silver Line (☎ 057-915 1112; www.silver linecruisers.com; adult/child one-way €7/4) runs three boat trips on Saturday and Sunday from June to September from Shannonbridge to Clonmacnoise.

There are also river cruises to Clonmacnoise from Athlone in County Westmeath.

A **taxi** (☎ 090-647 4400) from Athlone will cost roughly €50 to €70 round-trip, including an hour's wait.

COUNTY CLARE
ENNIS
pop 19,000

Ennis (Inis) is the busy commercial centre of Clare. It lies on the banks of the smallish River Fergus, which runs east, then south into the Shannon Estuary.

It's the place to stay if you want a bit of urban flair; from Ennis, you can reach any part of Clare in under two hours. Short on sights, the town's strengths are its food, lodging and traditional entertainment. The town centre, with its narrow,

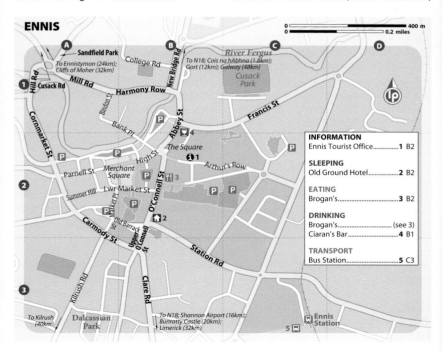

Musician playing bodhrán

IAN CONNELLAN

➥ IF YOU LIKE...

If you like the **Willie Clancy Irish Music Festival** (p259), you'll like these other great trad festivals:

- **Fleadh Nua** (☎ 065-682 4276; www. fleadhnua.com) A lively traditional music festival held in Ennis in late May, with singing, dancing and workshops.
- **Ennis Trad Festival** (www.ennis tradfestival.com) Traditional music in venues across town for one week in early November.
- **Fleadh na gCuach** (www.kinvara. com) Over 100 trad musicians descend on Kinvara in late May for the 'Cuckoo Festival' that involves over 50 organised sessions.
- **Craiceann Inis Oírr International Bodhrán Summer School** (☎ 099-75067; www.craiceann.com) Week-long festival in late June on Inisheer that keeps the focus strictly on the bodhrán (handheld goatskin drum), includes masterclasses and workshops as well as great music.

pedestrian-friendly streets, is home to large stores.

SLEEPING

`ourpick` **Old Ground Hotel** (☎ 065-682 8127; www.flynnhotels.com; O'Connell St; s/d from €90/150; **P ☐ ☎**) The lobby at this local institution is always a scene: old friends sprawl on the sofas, deals are cut at the tables and ladies from the neighbouring church's altar society exchange gossip over tea. Parts of this rambling landmark date back to the 1800s. The 83 rooms vary greatly in size and decor – don't hesitate to inspect a few.

EATING

`ourpick` **Brogan's** (☎ 065-682 9859; 24 O'Connell St; meals €8-20; ☾ 10am-10pm) The peas at this popular old pub are always well cooked, and the supply of spuds never-ending. Standards like roasts get top billing although you can ferret out more modern fare. Three-course specials cost €12.

DRINKING & ENTERTAINMENT

`ourpick` **Cíaran's Bar** (☎ 065-684 0180; Francis St) Slip into this small place by day and you can be just another geezer pondering a pint. At night there's usually trad music. We bet you wish you had a copy of the Guinness mural out front!

Brogan's (☎ 065-682 9859; 24 O'Connell St) On the corner of Cooke's Lane, Brogan's sees a fine bunch of musicians rattling even the stone floors from about 9pm Monday to Thursday, plus even more nights in summer. It's a big pub that stretches a long way back from the street.

Cois na hAbhna (☎ 065-682 0996; www. coisnahabhna.ie; Gort Rd) This pilgrimage point for traditional music and culture is housed in a custom-built pentagonal hall 1.5km north of town along the N18. It has frequent performances and a full range of classes in dance and music. The archive is a resource centre and a library of Irish traditional music, song, dance and folklore relating mainly to County Clare; books and recordings are on sale.

GETTING THERE & AWAY
BUS

The bus station has **Bus Éireann** (☎ 065-682 4177; www.buseireann.ie) services. Buses run from Ennis to Cork (€14, three hours, nine daily); Doolin (€11, 1½ hours, three daily) via Corofin, Ennistymon, Lahinch and Liscannor; Galway (€9, 1½ hours, hourly) via Gort; Limerick (€8.50, 40 minutes, hourly) via Bunratty; and Shannon Airport (€6.50, 50 minutes, hourly). For Dublin, connect through Limerick.

TRAIN

Irish Rail (www.irishrail.ie) trains from **Ennis station** (☎ 065-684 0444) comprise nine daily to Limerick (€9, 40 minutes), where you can connect to trains to places further afield like Dublin. At time of research it was expected that the line between Ennis and Galway would be reopened in late 2009 after a massive rebuilding program.

BUNRATTY

Conveniently located beside the N18 motorway and with plenty of bus-sized parking, Bunratty – home to government schemes for hawking tourism hard – draws more tourists than any other place in the region. The namesake castle has stood over the area for centuries. In recent decades it's been spiffed up and surrounded by attractions. A theme park recreates a clichéd Irish village of old (where's the horseshit, lash and disease, we ask?) and each year more and more shops crowd the access roads – many selling authentic Irish goods just out of the container from China. There are some rather pricey group-dining options that are big with the bus crowd.

There's a small **visitor information office** (☎ 364 321; ◷ 9am-5.30pm Mon-Fri Oct–Mid-May, daily mid-May–Sep) in Bunratty Village Mills, a strip mall near the castle. There are also ATMs and exchange services.

BUNRATTY CASTLE & FOLK PARK
BUNRATTY CASTLE

Square and hulking, **Bunratty Castle** (◷ 9am-4pm) is only the latest of several

RICHARD CUMMINS

Bunratty Castle

Bunratty Folk Park

constructions to occupy its location beside the River Ratty. Vikings founded a settlement here in the 10th century, and other occupants included the Norman Thomas de Clare in the 1270s. The present structure was put up in the early 1400s by the energetic MacNamara family, falling shortly thereafter to the O'Briens, kings of Thomond, in whose possession it remained until the 17th century. Admiral Penn, father of William Penn, who was the Quaker founder of the US state of Pennsylvania and the city of Philadelphia, lived here for a short time.

BUNRATTY FOLK PARK
The **folk park** (9am-6pm Jun-Aug, 9am-5.30pm Sep-May, last admission 45min before closing) adjoins the castle. It is a reconstructed traditional Irish village with cottages, a forge and working blacksmith, weavers and pie-makers. There's a complete village street with a post office, pub and small cafe.

The entire place is attractive in the way that Disneyland has its own charm. But you'll find far more surviving authentic-

ity of rural village Ireland in a place like Ennistymon than you will here.

The **Traditional Irish Night** (061-360 788; adult/child €50/25; 7-9.30pm Apr-Oct) is held in a corn barn in the folk park. Lots of red-haired (real or fake, it's clearly a big help in securing employment) servers dish up trad music, dancing, Irish stew, apple pie and soda bread. There's non-traditional wine as well, which may put you in the mood for the singalong.

MEDIEVAL BANQUETS
If you skip the high-jinks in the corn barn, you may opt for a **medieval banquet** (061-360 788; adult/child €57.50/28.75; 5.30pm & 8.45pm), replete with harp-playing maidens, court jesters and food with a medieval motif (lots of meaty items, but somehow we think the real stuff would empty the place right out). It's all washed down with mead – a kind of honey wine – and you eat with your fingers. The banquets are very popular with coach parties, so it's advisable for independent travellers

to book well ahead. Various actors interact with choral singers.

KILLALOE & BALLINA
pop 1750

Facing each other across a narrow channel, Killaloe and Ballina are really one destination, even if they have very different personalities (and counties). A fine old 13-arch one-lane bridge spans the river, linking the pair. You can walk it in five minutes or drive it in about 20 (a Byzantine system of lights controls traffic).

Killaloe (Cill Da Lúa) is picturesque Clare at its finest. It lies on the western banks of lower Loch Deirgeirt, the southern extension of Lough Derg, where the lough narrows at one of the principal crossings of the River Shannon. The village lies snugly against the Slieve Bernagh Hills that rise abruptly to the west. The Arra Mountains create a fine balance to the east and all of Lough Derg is at hand. The village is also on the 180km East Clare Way.

Not as quaint as Killaloe, Ballina is in County Tipperary and actually manages to have some of the better pubs and restaurants. It lies at the end of a scenic drive from Nenagh along Lough Derg on the R494.

From Killaloe and Ballina, the Shannon is navigable all the way north to Lough Key in County Sligo; in summer the towns are jammed with weekend sailors.

EATING & DRINKING

our pick **Crotty's** (☎ 061-376 965; Bridge St, Killaloe; meals €8-18) The most atmospheric spot on the Clare side of the water, Crotty's has picnic tables outside that you won't want to leave, especially on long summer nights. Inside it could be the model for the perfect old pub anywhere (and it's the real deal). Fish and chips and burgers rise above the norm, and the purveyors of the foods are listed.

KILRUSH
pop 2700

Kilrush (Cill Rois) is a small, interesting town that overlooks the Shannon Estuary and the hills of Kerry to the south. The main street, Frances St, runs directly to the harbour. It is more than 30m wide, reflecting Kilrush's origins as a port and market town in the 19th century when there was much coming and going between land and sea. It has the western coast's biggest **marina** (www.kilrushcreekmarina.ie) at Kilrush Creek, and a centre for the research and viewing of dolphins living in the Shannon.

Tourist information (☎ 065-905 1577; Francis St; ☑ varies) can be found at Katie O'Connor's Holiday Hostel (p258).

In Market Sq there's an ACC bank with an ATM and on Frances St you'll find the post office and an AIB ATM. **KK Computing** (☎ 065-905 1806; Frances St; per hr €5; ☑ 10am-10pm, shorter hours in winter) has internet access.

SIGHTS & ACTIVITIES

St Senan's Catholic church (Toler St) contains eight detailed examples of stained glass by well-known early-20th-century artist Harry Clarke. East of town is **Kilrush Wood**, which has some fine old trees and a picnic area.

Vandeleur Walled Garden (☎ 065-905 1760; adult/child €5/2; ☑ 10am-6pm Apr-Oct, to 5pm Nov-Mar) is a remarkable 'lost' garden. It was the private domain of the wealthy Vandeleur family – merchants and landowners who engaged in harsh evictions and forced emigration of local people in the 19th century. The gardens lie within a large walled area and have been redesigned and planted with colourful tropical and rare plants. Woodland trails wind around the area, and there's also a cafe.

Near the marina, **Shannon Dolphin and Wildlife Centre** (☎ 065-905 2326; www.shannondolphins.ie; Merchants Quay; ☺ 10am-4pm May-Sep) is a research facility that monitors the 100 or so dolphins swimming out in the Shannon. Look for the mural of the dolphin on the front of the building, which houses exhibits on the playful cetaceans. It's also a stop on the well-marked **Kilrush Shannon Dolphin Trail**, which ends 3km out of town at **Aylevarro Point**, where signs have more information and where you can often see dolphins frolicking offshore. Follow the road south of the harbour to get here.

The local flora and fauna are the inspiration at **Naturequest Gallery** (☎ 065-905 1309; Burton St; ☺ 1-4pm Thu-Sat), an artist-run gallery just off the Butter Market.

SLEEPING & EATING

B&Bs are about as common here as driftwood on a beach.

Katie O'Connor's Holiday Hostel (☎ 065-905 1133; katieoconnors@eircom.net; Frances St; dm/d from €19/40; ☺ mid-Apr–Oct) This fine old main-street house dates from the 18th century, and was one of the town houses of the Vandeleur family. There are 16 beds in two rooms at this delightfully funky IHH-affiliated hostel.

ourpick Crotty's (☎ 065-905 2470; www.crottyspubkilrush.com; Market Sq; s/d from €45/70) Brimming with character, Crotty's has an old-fashioned high bar, intricately tiled floors and a series of snugs decked out with traditional furnishings. You can enjoy music many nights in summer. Food is served daily (meals €6 to €16) and offers high-end versions of pub fare. Upstairs are seven small, traditionally decorated rooms.

Hillcrest View (☎ 065-905 1986; www.hillcrestview.com; Doonbeg Rd; s/d from €60/80; ☺) This large house, at the top of the hill where

the Doonbeg road climbs out of Kilrush, is about 1km from the centre. Its six rooms have vaguely posh furnishings. Breakfast is served in a bright conservatory.

The local **farmers market** (☺ 9am-2pm Thu) is held on the Butter Market square.

GETTING THERE & AROUND

Bus Éireann has one or two buses daily to Limerick (1¾ hours), Ennis (one hour) and Kilkee (15 minutes). Fares average €7.

MILTOWN MALBAY

pop 1600

Miltown Malbay was a resort favoured by well-to-do Victorians, though the town isn't actually on the sea: the beach is 2km south at Spanish Point. A classically friendly place in the chatty Irish way, Miltown Malbay has a thriving music scene. Every year it hosts the Willie Clancy Irish Music Festival (p259), one of Ireland's great trad music events.

For local information, drop by **An Ghiolla Finn Gift Shop** (☎ 065-688 9239; Main St; ☺ 10.30am-6pm Mon-Sat). The wonderful Maureen Kilduff knows everything and everybody.

Possibly the friendliest welcome in town is at **An Gleann B&B** (☎ 065-708 4281; angleann@oceanfree.net; Ennis Rd; s/d €45/80). Off the R474 about 1km from the centre, the rooms here are basic and comfy and owner Mary Hughes is a delight. Cyclists are catered for.

Across the road from the gift shop, **Baker's Cafe** (☎ 065-708 4411; Main St; meals €4; ☺ 7am-7pm Mon-Sat) has excellent baked goods and creates enormous sandwiches – perfect for seaside picnics. Nearby, the **Old Bake House** (☎ 065-708 4350; Main St; meals €6-15; ☺ noon-9pm) serves a more ambitious menu and does so well.

O'Friel's Bar (Lynch's; ☎ 065-708 4275; The Square) is one of a couple of genuine old-style places with occasional trad sessions. The other is the dapper Hillery's (Main St).

Bus Éireann service is paltry. Expect one or two buses daily north and south along the coast and inland to Ennis.

LAHINCH

pop 650

Surf's up, dude! This scruffy old holiday town is now one of the centres of Ireland's hot surfing scene. Schools and stores dedicated to riding the waves cluster here, like surfers waiting for the perfect set.

Lahinch (Leacht Uí Chonchubhair) has always owed its living to beach-seeking tourists. The town sits on protected Liscannor Bay and has a fine beach. Free-spending mobs descend in summer, many wielding golf clubs for play at the famous, traditional-style Lahinch Golf Club (☎ 065-708 1003; www.lahinchgolf.com; green fees from €100).

The tourist office, Lahinch Fáilte (☎ 065-708 2082; www.lahinchfailte.com; The Dell; ⏰ 9am-8pm Jun-Aug, 10am-5pm Sep-May), is off the northern end of Main St and is part of a well-stocked gift shop.

SLEEPING & EATING

Atlantic Hotel (☎ 065-708 1049; www.atlantic hotel.ie; s/d from €95/140; 🖥) There's still a pleasant air of times gone by in the reception rooms and bars at this town-centre classic with 14 well-appointed rooms. The restaurant offers fine seafood choices (mains from €15) and the pub is the perfect spot for nursing a pint on a blustery day.

Barrtra Seafood Restaurant (☎ 065-708 1280; Miltown Malbay Rd; mains €16-28) The 'Seafood Symphony' menu item says it all at this rural repose 3.5km south of Lahinch. Enjoy views over pastures to the sea from the homey dining rooms. The

RICHARD CUMMINS

Musician playing Irish bagpipes

⌦ A FESTIVAL FOR EVERYONE

Half the population of Miltown Malbay seems to be part of the annual Willie Clancy Irish Music Festival, a tribute to a native son and one of Ireland's greatest pipers. The eight-day festival usually begins in the first or second week in July, when impromptu sessions occur day and night, the pubs are packed, and Guinness is consumed by the barrel. Workshops and classes underpin the event; don't be surprised to attend a recital with 40 noted fiddlers. Asked how such a huge affair has happened for almost four decades, a local who teaches fiddle said: 'No one knows, it just does.'

Things you need to know: ☎ 065-708 4148

cooking eschews flash and lets the inherent tastiness of the food shine.

ENNISTYMON

pop 880

Ennistymon (Inis Díomáin) is a timeless country village just 4km inland from Lahinch, but worlds away in terms of atmosphere. People go about their business (which involves a lot of cheerful chatting) barely noticing the characterful buildings lining Main St. And behind this facade there's a surprise: the roaring Cascades, the stepped falls of the River Inagh. After heavy rain they surge, beer-brown and foaming, and you risk getting drenched on windy days in the flying drizzle. You'll find them through an arch by Byrne's Hotel.

SLEEPING & EATING

Byrne's (☎ 065-707 1080; Main St; r €80-120) The Cascades are just out back at this historic guesthouse and restaurant. When the air is not heavy with mist, you can enjoy a drink at a back-deck table. The menu is substantial, with plenty of seafood specials (mains €15 to €25). Six comfortable rooms await up the creaky heritage stairs.

ENTERTAINMENT

Eugene's (☎ 065-707 1777; Main St) Not to be missed, Eugene's is a classic pub that defines craic. It's intimate, cosy and has a trademark collection of visiting cards covering its walls, alongside photographs of famous writers and musicians. The inspiring collection of whiskey (Irish) and whisky (Scottish) will have you smoothly debating their relative merits.

THE BURREN

The Burren region is rocky and windswept, an apt metaphor for the hardscrabble lives of those who've eked out an existence here. Stretching across northern Clare, from the Atlantic coast to Kinvara in County Galway, it's a unique limestone landscape that was shaped beneath ancient seas, then forced high and dry by a great geological cataclysm. The sea is not muted here by offshore islands or muffled promontories, as it sometimes is on the coasts of Kerry and Galway. In the Burren,

land and sea seem to merge into one vast, exhilarating space beneath huge skies.

Boireann is the Irish term for 'rocky country', a plain but graphic description of the Burren's acres of silvery limestone karst pavements. Known as 'clints', these lie like huge, scattered bones across the swooping hills. Between the seams of rock lie narrow fissures, known as 'grikes'. Their humid, sheltered conditions support exquisite wildflowers in spring, lending the Burren its other great charm: brilliant, if ephemeral, colour amid so much arid beauty. There are also intriguing villages to enjoy, especially along the coast and in the south Burren. These include Doolin on the west coast, Kilfenora inland and Ballyvaughan in the north, on the shores of Galway Bay. The Burren's coastline is made up of rocky foreshores, occasional beaches and bare limestone cliffs, while inland lies a haunting landscape of rocky hills peppered with ancient burial chambers and medieval ruins. If driving, take any road – the smaller the better – and see what you discover: you'll never be lost for long.

Large areas of the Burren, about 40,000 hectares in all, have been designated as Special Areas of Conservation. Apart from being against the law, it makes ecological sense not to remove plants or to damage walls, ancient monuments or the landscape itself. Visitors are also asked to resist the temptation to erect 'sham' replicas of dolmens and other monuments, however small, including *Spinal Tap* Stonehenge size.

INFORMATION

The **Burrenbeo Trust** (www.burrenbeo.com) is a nonprofit dedicated to promoting the natural beauty of the Burren and increasing awareness. Its website is a tremendous resource.

GALWAY & THE WEST

COUNTY CLARE

Cliffs of Moher

GARETH MCCORMACK

↘ CLIFFS OF MOHER

Star of a million tourist brochures, the Cliffs of Moher (Aillte an Mothair, or Ailltreacha Mothair) are one of the most popular sights in Ireland. But like many an ageing star, you have to look beyond the famous facade to appreciate the inherent attributes behind the postcard image.

The entirely vertical cliffs rise to a height of 203m, their edge falling away abruptly into the constantly churning sea. A series of heads, the dark limestone seems to march in a rigid formation that amazes, no matter how many times you look.

Such appeal comes at a price, however: mobs. This is check-off tourism big time and busloads come and go constantly in summer. A vast visitor centre handles the hordes. However, like so many oversubscribed natural wonders, there's relief and joy if you're willing to walk for 10 minutes. Past the end of the 'Moher Wall' south, there's still a trail along the cliffs to Hag's Head – few venture this far. There's also a path heading north, but you're discouraged from it, so use your common sense. With binoculars you can spot the more than 30 species of birds – including darling little puffins – that make their homes among the fissure-filled cliff faces. On a clear day you can see the Aran Islands etched on the waters of Galway Bay, and beyond, the hills of Connemara in western Galway.

For uncommon views of the cliffs and wildlife you might consider a cruise. The boat operators in Doolin (p262), 6km away, offer popular tours of the cliffs.

Bus Éireann runs one to three buses daily past the cliffs on the Doolin–Ennis/Limerick routes.

Things you need to know: ☎ 065-708 6141; www.cliffsofmoher.ie; ⏱ 8.30am-9pm Jun-Aug, 8.30am-7pm May & Sep, 9am-6pm Mar, Apr & Oct, 9.30am-5pm Nov-Feb

Poulnabrone Dolmen (p265)

RICHARD CUMMINS

FLORA & FAUNA

Soil may be scarce on the Burren, but the small amount that gathers in the cracks is well drained and rich in nutrients. This, together with the mild Atlantic climate, supports an extraordinary mix of Mediterranean, Arctic and Alpine plants. Of Ireland's native wildflowers, 75% are found here, including a number of beautiful orchids, the creamy-white burnet rose, the little starry flowers of mossy saxifrage and the magenta-coloured bloody cranesbill.

The Burren is a stronghold of Ireland's most elusive mammal, the weasel-like pine marten. It's rarely seen, although there are certainly some living in the Caher Valley. Badgers, foxes and even stoats are common throughout the region. Otters and seals haunt the shores around Bell Harbour, New Quay and Finavarra Point.

The estuaries along this northern coast are rich in birdlife and frequently attract brent geese during the winter. More than 28 of Ireland's 33 butterfly and moth spe-cies are found here, including one endemic species, the Burren green.

As they have elsewhere, modern farming and 'land improvement' grants have had their effect on the Burren. Weedkillers, insecticides and fertilisers favour grass and little else, often fatally undermining fragile ecological systems.

GETTING THERE & AWAY

Various **Bus Éireann** (www.buseireann.ie) buses pass through the Burren. The main routes include one from Limerick and Ennis to Corofin, Ennistymon, Lahinch, Liscannor, the Cliffs of Moher, Doolin and Lisdoonvarna; another connects Galway with Ballyvaughan, Lisdoonvarna and Doolin. Usually there are one to three buses daily, with the most in summer.

DOOLIN

pop 250

Doolin gets plenty of press and chatter as a centre of Irish traditional music, owing to a couple of pubs that have sessions through the year. It's also known for its setting - 6km north of the Cliffs of Moher and down near the ever-unsettled sea, the land is windblown, with huge rocks exposed by the long-vanished top soil.

Given all its attributes, you might be surprised when you realise that Doolin as it's known barely exists. Rather, when you arrive you might be forgiven for exclaiming, 'There's no there here!' For what's called Doolin is really three infinitesimally small neighbouring villages. **Fisherstreet** is right on the water, **Doolin** itself is about 1km east on the little Aille River and **Roadford** is another 1km east. None has more than a handful of buildings, which results in a scattered appearance, without a centre.

SLEEPING

Aille River Hostel (☎ 065-707 4260; ailleriver@ esatclear.ie; Roadford; dm €18-25, d €50; ☷ mid-Mar–Dec; ▯ ☎) In a picturesque spot by the river in the upper village, this converted 17th-century farmhouse is a great choice. There are turf fires, hot showers and a free laundry. This award-winning IHH hostel has 30 beds, along with campsites costing from €16.

Cullinan's Guest House (☎ 065-707 4183; www.cullinansdoolin.com; Doolin; s €50-80, d €80-100; ☎) The eight B&B rooms here are all of a high standard, with power showers and commodious fittings. Right on the Aille (two rooms have balconies), it has a lovely back terrace for enjoying the views. The restaurant is one of the village's best. The owner is a well-known local musician.

Sea View House (☎ 065-707 4826; www. ireland-doolin.com; Fisherstreet; r €60-100; ☎) On high ground right above Fisherstreet village, this big house and its terrace have sweeping ocean views. The common lounge has a telescope for enjoying the

vantage point. The four rooms have solid mahogany furnishings.

DRINKING & ENTERTAINMENT

Doolin's rep is largely based on music. A lot of musicians live in the area, and they have a symbiotic relationship with the tourists: each desires the other and each year things grow a little larger.

O'Connor's (☎ 065-707 4168; Fisherstreet) Right on the water, this sprawling favourite packs them in and has a rollicking atmosphere when the music and drinking are in full swing. The food's good, too.

McGann's (☎ 065-707 4133; Roadford) McGann's has all the classic touches of a full-on Irish music pub; the action often spills out onto the street. Food is also served here and there's a small outside covered area.

MacDiarmada's (☎ 065-707 4700; Roadford) Also known as McDermott's, this simple red-and-white old pub can be the rowdy favourite of locals. Music sessions are up to the best Doolin standards.

GETTING THERE & AWAY
BOAT

Doolin is one of two ferry departure points to the Aran Islands (p242) from April to October. Three ferry companies offer numerous departures in season. It takes around 20 to 30 minutes to cover the 8km to Inisheer (€30 return), the closest of the three islands. A boat to Inishmór takes one to 1½ hours with an Inisheer stop (€40 return). Ferries to Inishmaan are infrequent. Sailings are often cancelled due to high seas. Call and confirm times and book in advance.

BUS

Bus Éireann runs one to three buses daily to Doolin from Ennis (€11, 1½ hours) and Limerick (€15, 2½ hours) via Corofin,

Irish musician at O'Connor's (p263)

DOUG MCKINLAY

Lahinch and the Cliffs of Moher. Buses also go to Galway (€14, 1½ hours, one or two daily) via Ballyvaughan.

BALLYVAUGHAN & AROUND

pop 200

Something of a hub for the otherwise dispersed charms of the Burren, Ballyvaughan (Baile Uí Bheacháin) sits between the hard land of the hills and a quiet leafy corner of Galway Bay. It makes an excellent base for visiting the northern reaches of the Burren.

SIGHTS & ACTIVITIES

About 6km south of Ballyvaughan on the Lisdoonvarna road (N67) is a series of severe bends up **Corkscrew Hill**

(180m). The road was built as part of a Great Famine relief scheme in the 1840s. From the top there are spectacular views of the northern Burren and Galway Bay, with Aillwee Mountain and the caves on the right, Cappanawalla Hill on the left, and the partially restored 16th-century Newtown Castle, erstwhile residence of the O'Lochlains, directly below.

SLEEPING & EATING

Rusheen Lodge (☎ 065-707 7092; www.rusheenlodge.com; Lisdoonvarna Rd; s/d from €70/100; ☼ Feb-Nov; ☐ ☎) Stylish, imaginative furnishings make this nine-room guesthouse a winner. Enjoy a romp in the colourful gardens. It's about 750m south of the village on the N67.

Monk's Bar & Restaurant (☎ 065-707 7059; Old Pier; mains €10-20; ☼ kitchen noon-8pm) Famed for its excellent seafood, Monk's is a cheerful, spacious and comfortable place. Peat fires warm in winter, while sea breezes cool you at the outdoor tables in summer. The pub is open late and there are trad sessions some nights in high season.

CENTRAL BURREN
AILLWEE CAVES

Popular with kids, the **Aillwee Caves** (☎ 065-707 7036; www.aillweecave.ie; Ballyvaughan; adult/child €17/10; ☼ 10am-5.30pm) are a large tourist attraction. The main cave penetrates 600m into the mountain, widening into larger caverns, one with its own waterfall. The caves were carved out by water some two million years ago. Near the entrance are the remains of a brown bear, extinct in Ireland for more than 10,000 years. Often crowded in summer, there's a cafe and other time killers like a cheese factory on-site. A large raptor exhibit has captive hawks, owls and more.

POULNABRONE DOLMEN

What would a Burren brochure designer do without it? Also known as the Portal Tomb, Poulnabrone Dolmen is one of Ireland's most photographed ancient monuments. The dolmen (a large slab perched on stone uprights) stands amid a swath of rocky pavements, surprising even the most jaded traveller with its otherworldly appearance; the capstone weighs five tonnes. The site is about 8km south of Aillwee and is visible from the R480. A large free parking area and excellent displays make it visitor friendly.

KILFENORA

pop 360

Underappreciated Kilfenora (Cill Fhionnúrach) lies on the southern fringes of the Burren, 8km (a five-minute drive) southeast of Lisdoonvarna. It's a small place, with a diminutive 12th-century cathedral. Several high crosses adorn the churchyard, and low polychromatic buildings surround the compact centre.

The town has a strong music tradition that rivals that of Doolin, but without the crowds. The **Kilfenora Céili Band** (☎ 065-684 2228; www.kilfenoraceiliband.com) is a celebrated community that's been playing for 100 years. Its traditional music features fiddles, banjos, squeezeboxes and more. It often plays Wednesday nights at Linnane's (below).

EATING & ENTERTAINMENT

Linnane's (☎ 065-708 8157; Main St; meals €5-12; ☺ kitchen noon-8pm) Irish standards like smoked salmon and more are fully honoured here. Peat fires warm the almost bare interior; nary a frill in sight. There's trad music many nights in summer.

ourpick Vaughan's Pub (☎ 065-708 8004; Main St; meals €9-15; ☺ kitchen 10am-9pm) Seafood, traditional foods and local pro-duce feature on the Vaughan's appealing menu. The pub has a big reputation in Irish music circles. There's music in the bar every night during the summer and on many nights the rest of the year. The adjacent barn is the scene of terrific set-dancing sessions on Thursday and Sunday nights. Have a pint under the big tree out front.

COUNTY MAYO
CONG

pop 150

Sitting on a sliver-thin isthmus between Lough Corrib and Lough Mask, Cong complies with romantic notions of a traditional Irish village. Time appears to have stood still ever since the evergreen classic *The Quiet Man* was filmed here in 1951. As such, the arrival of the morning's first tour bus instantly doubles the number of people strolling the town's tiny streets, but the wooded trails between the lovely old abbey and stately Ashford Castle offer genuine quietude.

INFORMATION

The **tourist office** (☎ 094-954 6542; Abbey St; ☺ 10am-6pm Mar-Nov) is in the old courthouse building opposite Cong Abbey.

There are no banks or ATMs, but you can change money at the post office on Main St, or at the museum (p266).

SIGHTS
CONG ABBEY

An evocative reminder of ecclesiastical times past, the weathered shell of Cong's 12th-century **Augustinian abbey** (admission free; ☺ dawn-dusk) is scored by wizened lines from centuries of exposure to the elements. Nevertheless, several finely sculpted features have survived, including a carved doorway, windows and lovely medieval arches (touched up in the 19th century).

Founded in 1120 by Turlough Mór O'Connor, high king of Ireland and king of Connaught, the abbey occupies the site of an earlier 6th-century church. The community once gathered in the Chapter House to confess their sins publicly.

From the abbey, moss-encrusted trees guard a path to the river and the diminutive 16th-century monk's fishing house, built midway over the river so that the monks could haul their catch straight up through a hole in the floor.

QUIET MAN MUSEUM

Modelled on Sean Thornton's White O' Mornin' Cottage from the film, the Quiet Man Museum (☎ 094-954 6089; Circular Rd; adult/student/family €5/4.50/15; ☼ 10am-5pm Mar-Oct) also squeezes in a fascinating regional archaeological and historical exhibition of items from 7000 BC to the 19th century. Film fanatics (or those with a postmodern fascination for the way reality and fiction blur) can take a 75-minute location tour (€10), which includes museum entry.

ASHFORD CASTLE

Just beyond Cong Abbey, the village abruptly ends and the woodlands surrounding Ashford Castle (☎ 094-954 6003; www.ashford.ie; admission to grounds €5; ☼ 9am-dusk) begin. First built in 1228 as the seat of the de Burgo family, owners over the years included the Guinness family (of stout fame). Arthur Guinness turned the castle into a regal hunting and fishing lodge, which it remains today.

The only way to peek into its immaculately restored interior is to stay or dine here (right). But the surrounding estate – 140 hectares of parkland, covered with forests, streams, bridle paths and a golf course – is open to the public. Heading through the Kinlough Woods gets you away from the golfers and out to the shores of Lough Corrib. You can also walk along the riverbanks to the monk's fishing house (left).

SLEEPING

Danagher's Hotel (☎ 094-954 6028; Abbey St; s/d €40/80; mains €12.50-24.50; ☜) Upstairs from a comfy old pub in the village centre, some of Danagher's 11 rooms, all with bathroom, have countryside views. It's named for Victor McLaglen's character in the movie (we'll assume you know *which* movie), while its restaurant, Mary Kate's Kitchen, is named for Maureen O'Hara's character. Traditional music takes place on Thursdays year-round and nightly during summer.

ourpick Lisloughrey Lodge (☎ 094-954 5400; www.lisloughrey.ie; The Quay; s €135-165, d €170-230; P ▣ ☜) The lodge, built in the 1820s by Ashford Castle's owners, has been stunningly renovated in bold, contemporary cranberry and blueberry tones, with 50 guestrooms named for wine regions and champagne houses. Kick back in the bar, billiards room, or beanbag-strewn Wii room.

Ashford Castle (☎ 094-954 6003; www.ashford.ie; r €295-750; P ▣ ☜) Break the bank to stay here and feel like a film star yourself. Rooms and service are exquisite. Nonguests can book a table d'hôte dinner (from €75) in the castle's George V restaurant, but you'll need to dress the part (guys: jacket and tie). Nonguests can also reserve in advance to dine at the less formal Cullen's at the Cottage (mains €15 to €25, 12.30pm to 9.30pm April to October) on the grounds.

EATING & DRINKING

Fennel Seed (☎ 094-954 6004; Ryan's Hotel, Main St; bar food €8-12, mains €15-25; ☼ dinner

Mon-Sat, 1-7pm Sun) Michael Crowe and Denis Lenihan used to cook at Ashford Castle and have brought their culinary skills to the village, with great success (don't miss their signature 'smoky bake' pie, filled with trout, salmon, mackerel and haddock). Bar food's served in the adjoining Crowe's Nest Pub until 7pm.

GETTING THERE & AWAY

Bus Éireann (☎ 096-71800; www.buseireann. ie) has regular services from Galway (one way/return €10.30/14) and Westport (€11.40/15.20). The bus stops in front of the Quiet Man Coffee Shop on Main St.

If you're driving or cycling further into County Mayo, skip the main N84 to Castlebar and head west to Leenane (also spelt Leenaun) then north to Westport via Delphi through the extraordinary Doolough Valley.

CROAGH PATRICK

Just 8km southwest of Westport, St Patrick couldn't have picked a better spot for a pilgrimage than this conical mountain (also known as 'the Reek'). On a clear day the tough two-hour climb rewards with stunning views over Clew Bay and its sandy islets.

It was on Croagh Patrick that Ireland's patron saint fasted for 40 days and nights, and where he reputedly banished venomous snakes. Climbing the 765m holy mountain is an act of penance for thousands of pilgrims on the last Sunday of July (Reek Sunday). The truly contrite take the original 40km route from Ballintubber Abbey, Tóchar Phádraig (Patrick's Causeway), and ascend the mountain barefoot.

The trail taken by less contrite folk begins in the village of Murrisk (Muraisc) beside a **visitor centre** (☎ 098-64114; www. croagh-patrick.com; ☺ 11am-5pm mid-Mar–Oct). Opposite the car park is the **National Famine Memorial**, a spine-chilling sculpture of a three-masted ghost ship wreathed in swirling skeletons, commemorating the lives lost on so-called 'coffin ships' employed to help people escape the Famine (1845–51). The path down past the memorial leads to the scant remains

EOIN CLARKE

Ashford Castle

Pilgrims climbing Croagh Patrick (p267)

ANDREW MARSHALL & LEANNE WALKER

of **Murrisk Abbey**, founded by the O'Malleys in 1547.

Ruth and Myles O'Brien, the proprietors of the raspberry-pink-painted pub **ourpick** The Tavern (☎ 098-64060; Murrisk; bar food €8.95-21.95, restaurant mains €15-30, set menu €27.50; ☯ bar food noon-9pm daily year-round, restaurant lunch Fri & Sat, dinner nightly May-Sep), reckon 'the locals really own the place; we just pay the mortgage', which explains the convivial atmosphere around its turf fires. The restaurant's lobsters, cockles, prawns, mussels, scallops and oysters are delivered fresh from their fishermen next-door-neighbours.

WESTPORT
pop 5163

Westport (Cathair na Mairt) is exceedingly proud of its Tidy Town status, having won the nation's top honours three times in the past decade alone. To be sure, the town's Georgian streets, lime-tree-shaded riverside mall and colourful pubs are about as photogenic as Ireland gets. A couple of kilometres west on Clew Bay, the town's

harbour, Westport Quay, is a picturesque spot for a sundowner.

Westport is Mayo's nightlife hub (though it has clamped down on hen-and-stag revellers), and its central location makes it a convenient and enjoyable base for exploring the county.

INFORMATION
Tourist office (☎ 098-25711; www.discover ireland.ie/west; James St; ☯ 9am-6pm Mon-Sat, 10am-6pm Sun Jul & Aug, 9am-5.45pm Mon-Sat Apr-Jun & Sep, 9am-12.45pm & 2-5pm Mon-Fri rest of year) Mayo's only official tourist office to open year-round.

SIGHTS
WESTPORT HOUSE
The charms of this 1730-built country **mansion** (☎ 098-25430; www.westporthouse. ie; Quay Rd; house & gardens adult/child €12/6.50, house, gardens & Pirate Adventure Park adult/child €21/16.50; ☯ house & gardens 10am-4pm Sat & Sun Mar, 10am-4pm daily Apr, Jun, Sep & Oct, 10am-5pm daily May, 10am-5.30pm daily Jul & Aug) set in glorious gardens on the ruins

of the 16th-century castle built for Grace O'Malley (Gráinne Ní Mháille or Granuaile), Ireland's pirate queen, outshines its commercial overhaul of recent years. It's now a kind of stately home theme-park hybrid, incorporating a kid-friendly **Pirate Adventure Park** (10am-4pm mid-Apr & Jun, 10am-5pm bank holiday weekend & Sun thereafter May, 10am-5.30pm Jul & Aug, 10am-4pm Sat & Sun Sep) complete with a swinging pirate ship, a 'pirate's playground' and a roller-coaster-style flume ride through a water channel.

To reach Westport House, head out of Westport on Quay Rd towards Croagh Patrick and Louisburgh. Just before Westport Quay, take a small road to the right and through the grand gateway.

SLEEPING

Westport Woods Hotel (098-25811; www.westportwoodshotel.com; Quay Rd; s €75-120, d €100-190; P) Behind part of Westport House's 1840s-built stone wall, this large mid-20th-century hotel is green and then some. Eco-initiatives include solar power, wood-pellet boilers, reused timber and stone, playground matting made from recycled tyres and running shoes, and even recycled cooking oil fuelling the hotel's vehicles. Skylights fill the neutral-toned interiors with natural light. Service is professional but impressively personalised, too, for a hotel its size.

EATING

our pick **Sheebeen** (098-26528; Rosbeg; mains €15-25; noon-9pm daily mid-Mar–Oct, Sat & Sun only Nov–mid-Mar) Father and son Colm and Simon Cronin have turned this thatched treasure on the shores of Clew Bay into one of the best seafood restaurants in the west. Starters such as steamed mussels in cream and white wine from the bay out front are followed by mains like pan-fried king halibut with crab butter, but there are also inventive meat and vegetarian choices. Save room for the warm ginger and banana cake.

DRINKING & ENTERTAINMENT

Matt Molloy's (098-26655; Bridge St) Matt Molloy, the fife player from the Chieftains, opened this old-school pub years ago and the good times haven't let up. Head to the back room around 9pm and you'll

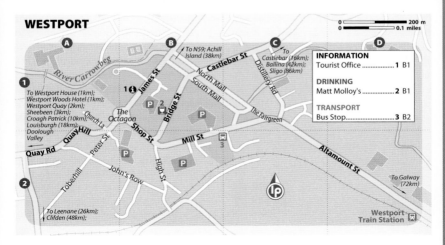

WESTPORT

catch live *céilidh*. Or perhaps an old man will simply slide into a chair and croon a few classics.

GETTING THERE & AWAY

Bus Éireann (☎ 096-71800) travels to Achill Island (€12.50, 30 minutes, two daily), Dublin (€18.50, five hours, three daily), Galway (€14.40, two hours, eight daily) and Sligo (€16.70, two hours, two daily). Buses depart from and arrive at the Mill St stop. There are limited services on Sunday.

The **train station** (☎ 098-25253) is 800m from the town centre. There are three daily connections to Dublin (€35 to €48.50, 3½ hours).

POLLATOMISH

pop 150

Irresistibly remote and pretty, Pollatomish (Poll an Tómais), also spelled Pullathomas, drowses in a serene bay some 16km east of Belmullet, signposted on the road to Ballycastle (R314). Those who find their way here often extend their stay to stroll on its sandy beach and walk up to **Benwee Head** to take in sensational views.

our pick **Kilcommon Lodge Hostel** (☎ 097-84621; www.kilcommonlodge.net; Pollatomish; dm/d €16/40; breakfast €6, dinner €16; P ⬛ 🛜) is a garden-set hostel a short stroll from the beach, now headed up by the longtime owners' son, Ciarán, an outdoors enthusiast who can organise surfing, guided walks and rock climbing, as well as Irish-language courses. Less energetic travellers can curl up with books and board games by the turf fire in the common room.

BALLYCASTLE & AROUND

pop 250

The superbly sited village of Ballycastle (Baile an Chaisil) consists of a sole sloping street. Its main draw (apart from breathtaking coastal scenery) is its megalithic tombs – one of the greatest concentrations in Europe.

SIGHTS
CÉIDE FIELDS

A famous wit once described archaeology as being all about 'a series of small walls'. But it's not often that such walls have had experts hopping up and down with such excitement than at **Céide Fields** (Achaidh Chéide), 8km northwest of Ballycastle.

During the 1930s, local man Patrick Caulfield was digging in the bog when he noticed a lot of piled-up stones buried beneath it. About 40 years later, his son Seamus, who had become an archaeologist on the basis of his father's discovery, began extensive exploration of the area. What he, and later others, uncovered was the world's most extensive Stone Age monument, consisting of stone-walled fields, houses and megalithic tombs – about half a million tonnes of stone. Astonishingly, five millennia ago a thriving farming community lived here, growing wheat and barley and grazing sheep and cattle. The award-winning **Interpretive Centre** (☎ 096-43325; www. heritageireland.ie; R314; adult/child incl tour €4/2; ⊙ 10am-6pm Jun–mid-Oct, 10am-5pm Easter-May & mid-Oct–end Oct, last tour 1hr prior to closing), in a glass pyramid overlooking the site, gives a fascinating glimpse into these times.

STEPHEN SAKS

Slieve League (p294)

NORTHWEST IRELAND

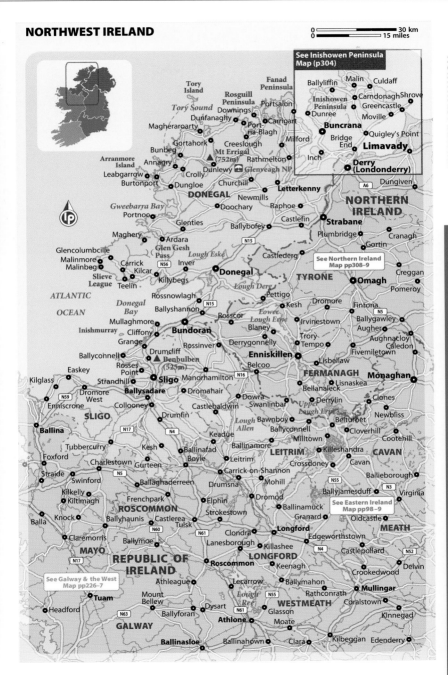

30 km
15 miles

See Inishowen Peninsula Map (p304)

Tory Island
Fanad Peninsula
Ballyliffin Malin Culdaff
Rosguill Peninsula Portsalon
Tory Sound Downings
Dunfanaghy Carrigart Inishowen Peninsula Carndonagh Shrove
Maghéraroarty Port-na-Blagh Dunree Greencastle
Milford Moville
Gortahork Creeslough Buncrana
Bunbeg Mt Errigal (752m) Rathmelton Bridge End Quigley's Point
Arranmore Island Annagry Dunlewy Glenveagh NP Inch Limavady
Leabgarrow Crolly Churchill
Burtonport Dungloe DONEGAL Newmills Letterkenny Derry (Londonderry)
Gweebarra Bay Doochary Raphoe Dungiven
Portnoo Castlefin NORTHERN IRELAND
Glenties Ballybofey Strabane
Maghery Ardara Plumbridge Cranagh
Glencolumbcille Glen Gesh Pass Inver Castlederg Gortin
Malinmore Carrick Lough Eske See Northern Ireland Map pp308–9 Creggan
Malinbeg Kilcar Donegal TYRONE Omagh
Slieve League Teelin Killybegs Lough Derg Pomeroy
ATLANTIC OCEAN Rossnowlagh Pettigo Dromore Fintona
Donegal Bay Ballyshannon Kesh Ballygawley
Mullaghmore Rosscor Lower Lough Erne Irvinestown Augher
Inishmurray Cliffony Bundoran Blaney Aughnacloy
Grange Rossinver Derrygonnelly Trory Caledon
Ballycohnell Drumcliff Enniskillen Tempo Fivemiletown
Easkey Rosses Point Benbulben (525m) Belcoo Lisbellaw
Kilglass Strandhill Sligo Manorhamilton FERMANAGH Monaghan
Dromore West Ballysadare Dromahair Lisnaskea
Enniscrone Colloney Castlebaldwin Dowra Bellanaleck
SLIGO Drumfin Swanlinbar Derrylin Clones
Lough Allen Bawnboy Upper Lough Erne Belturbet Newbliss
Ballina Keadue Ballyconnell Cloverhill Cootehill
Tubbercurry Kesh Ballinafad Ballinamore Milltown Killeshandra CAVAN
Foxford Charlestown Boyle Leitrim Crossdoney Cavan
Straide Gurteen Carrick-on-Shannon LEITRIM Bailieborough
Kilkelly Swinford Ballaghaderreen Drumsna Mohill Ballyjamesduff Virginia
Kiltimagh Frenchpark Elphin Dromod See Eastern Ireland Map pp98–9
Balla Knock Ballyhaunis Castlerea Strokestown Ballinamuck Oldcastle MEATH
Claremorris ROSCOMMON Tulsk Granard Castlepollard
MAYO Ballymoe Clondra Longford Edgeworthstown Delvin
Ballinasloe Lanesborough Killashee LONGFORD Crookedwood
REPUBLIC OF IRELAND Roscommon Keenagh Castlepollard
See Galway & the West Map pp226–7 Athleague Lecarrow Ballymahon Mullingar
Tuam Mount Bellew Lough Ree Rathconrath Coralstown
Headford Dysart Glasson WESTMEATH Kinnegad
Ballyforan Athlone Moate
GALWAY Ballinasloe Ballinahown Clara Kilbeggan Edenderry

NORTHWEST IRELAND HIGHLIGHTS

1 SURFING BEACHES

BY NEIL BRITTON, PRO TOUR SURF JUDGE & OWNER OF FIN MCCOOL SURF SCHOOL, ROSSNOWLAGH

Northwest Ireland's location and the particular geology of large stretches of coastline mean we have a surfer's paradise. There are beaches ideal for the beginner, high-performance breaks for the competent surfer or massive wave spots for the truly adventurous.

↘ NEIL BRITTON'S DON'T MISS LIST

❶ BUNDORAN, COUNTY DONEGAL
This traditional seaside town (p292) is home to four surf schools and has turned itself into an Irish Surf City. If you wait until low tide and look straight out to sea you will see The Peak, one of the best surf breaks in Europe, which has already hosted two European Surfing Championships.

❷ EASKEY, COUNTY SLIGO
For a really authentic Irish surfing experience, you don't need to go any further

than Easkey (p288), in County Sligo. There are two intermediate surf breaks right under the iconic ruins of Easkey Castle, and images of this distinctive landmark have been in surfing magazines throughout the world.

❸ MULLAGHMORE, COUNTY SLIGO
Sleepy fishing village Mullaghmore (p289) is a big-wave-surfer's mecca. The wave itself – only for experienced professionals – is about 500m past the harbour, easily accessible on a seaside

Clockwise from top: Learning to surf, County Sligo; Surfboards; Tullan Strand beach, Bundoran (p292), County Donegal; Mullaghmore beach (p289), County Sligo

walk. You'll often spot pro surfers being towed into the 40ft wave by jet ski.

❹ ROSSNOWLAGH, COUNTY DONEGAL

This 2km-long sandy **beach** (p293) is the safest and easiest spot on which to learn how to surf. The views are stunning and it's home to the Surfer's Bar, full of memorabilia stretching back to the earliest days of Irish surfing, the 1960s.

❺ MUCKROSS, COUNTY DONEGAL

Heading west out of Killybegs, look out for a road off to the left past the **Blue Haven Hotel** (p294). This lovely scenic road leads down to the sheltered beach of **Muckross**, which is a great area to get away from the crowds.

❶ Bundoran ❸ Mullaghmore
❷ Easkey ❹ Rossnowlagh
0 ——— 10 km ❺ Muckross
0 ——— 5 miles

Slievetooey ○ ○ Ardara ○ Glenties
Doonalt ○
Carrick N56 Inver ● **Donegal**
Malinbeg ○ ○ Kilcar ○ Killybegs
Teelin ○ ○
Muckross ❺
Rossnowlagh N15
Donegal Bay ❹ ○
Ballyshannon ○
ATLANTIC Mullaghmore ○ ❸ ○ **Bundoran**
OCEAN Cliffony ○ ❶
Grange ○ Rossinver ○
Ballyconnell ○ Cashelgarran ○
❷ Rosses
○ Easkey Point ○ ● **Sligo** N16
Strandhill ○
N59 ○ Dromore ○ Dromahair
West ● **Ballysadare**
○ Colloney
○ Drumfin *Lough Allen*
N17
Tubbercurry ○ ○ Keadue ○
Kesh ○ ○ Ballinafad

⟱ THINGS YOU NEED TO KNOW

Best time to visit September to Christmas **Advance planning** Best to do two to three days ahead to get the best conditions **Resources** Irish Surfing Association (www.isasurf.ie); Longboard Ireland (www.longboardireland .com); Irish Surfer (www.irishsurfer.com)

NORTHWEST IRELAND HIGHLIGHTS

↘ MT ERRIGAL

At a very manageable 752m, Donegal's highest **mountain** (p300) might not seem that impressive, but this stunning pyramid-shaped peak will leave you breathless…with the sheer beauty of its summit views, which take in most of the coastline and the offshore islands. Otherwise, it's a relatively easy climb up either of two routes, unless it's misty or raining, when the climb is far more challenging.

↘ SLIEVE LEAGUE

The Cliffs of Moher might draw greater numbers, but that's the only concession **Slieve League** (p294) makes to its southern rival. Plunging some 600 vertical metres into an often wild and raging sea, these cliffs are the tallest and most spectacular in Europe. With viewing locations like the aptly named One Man's Pass, they can be quite treacherous, too.

4

◥ ARDARA WEAVERS

Sure, you can buy Irish-made wool or tweed anywhere in the world, but how often do you get the chance to see it hand-woven at the source? Pretty Ardara (p296) is the heart of Donegal's traditional knitwear and tweed, and virtually all its manufacturers will gladly let you observe the process…before gently inviting you to purchase the fruit of their looms!

5

◥ DRUMCLIFF & BENBULBEN

Ireland's greatest poet, WB Yeats, lies buried in the graveyard of the small Protestant church in Drumcliff (p288), County Sligo. His final resting place lies in the shadow of the magnificent Benbulben (p288), as beautiful a bit of raised earth as you'll see anywhere on your Irish travels.

6

◥ GOLF LINKS

If Scotland is the home of golf, then Ireland is where golf goes on holidays – particularly to the northwest, dotted with some of the world's best links. The world-famous County Sligo Golf Course (p285), at Rosses Point, is in the shadow of Benbulben, and there are less renowned but equally beautiful links at Ballyliffin (p305) and Rosapenna (p301).

2 & 5 GARETH MCCORMACK; 3 CHERYL FORBES; 4 STEPHEN SAKS; 6 CHRISTOPHER HILL PHOTOGRAPHIC/SCENICIRELAND.COM/ALAMY

2 Mt Errigal (p300), County Donegal; 3 Slieve League (p294), County Donegal; 4 Weaver operating hand loom;
5 Benbulben (p288), County Sligo; 6 Golf course near Benbulben, County Sligo

NORTHWEST IRELAND'S BEST...

⬎ BEAUTY SPOTS

- **Glen Gesh Pass** (p295) A touch of the Alps in southwestern Donegal.
- **Poisoned Glen** (p300) A stunning ice-carved rock face overshadows.
- **Horn Head** (p297) This towering headland has superb views.
- **Benbulben** (p288) A mountain so beautiful that Yeats wanted to be buried in its shadow.
- **Rosguill Peninsula** (p300) Its rugged splendour is best seen by car.

⬎ WALKING BEACHES

- **Portsalon** (p302) Ireland's most beautiful beach.
- **Enniscrone** (p288) The beautiful Hollow stretches for 5km.
- **Mullaghmore** (p289) Sligo's only Blue Flag beach has safe shallow waters lapping up to its sweeping arc of golden sand.
- **Tramore** (p297) This stunning beach was recently voted the second-best walking beach in Ireland.

- **Trá na Rossan** (p300) A gorgeous, secluded beach near Carrigart.

⬎ HISTORICAL SITES

- **Glencolumbcille** (p294) The ruins of a 6th-century monastery.
- **Carrowkeel Passage Tomb Cemetery** (p287) Cairns, dolmens and graves from the late Stone Age.
- **Carrowmore** (p285) Home to Ireland's largest Stone Age cemetery.
- **Glenveagh National Park** (p299) Irish history still resonates here.
- **Grianán of Aileách** (p306) A pre-Celtic site with a stone fort.

⬎ LIVE MUSIC PUBS

- **Hargadons** (p284) Blues, rock and traditional music every Saturday.
- **Smugglers Creek** (p293) Live rock and folk on summer weekends.
- **Molly's Bar** (p299) Traditional, jazz and blues most nights.
- **Reel Inn** (p292) Traditional music every night.

IAN CONNELLAN

Gaelic football training at Kilcar (p294)

THINGS YOU NEED TO KNOW

VITAL STATISTICS

- Area 6426 sq km
- Population 232,156
- Best time to go Anytime but winter…but a clear, crisp January day offers its own stunning beauty!

AREAS IN A NUTSHELL

- County Sligo (p282) From the delights of Sligo town to the wild beauty of its coastline, Sligo may be small but it straddles the geography, history and outlook of the well-trodden west and the more isolated northwest.
- County Donegal (p289) Isolated from the rest of the Republic by geography and history, Donegal has retained a more traditional feel and offers a more authentic experience of the Ireland of yore.

ADVANCE PLANNING

- Two months before Learn some basic Irish words to impress in Donegal's Gaeltacht.
- One month before Book a surf lesson.
- Two weeks before Check out the weather forecast. Then ignore it.
- Upon arrival Realise that Donegal Irish sounds nothing like what you heard on those tapes.

RESOURCES

- Donegal Tourism (www.donegaldirect.ie) Donegal Tourism's official website.
- Failte Ireland (www.discoverireland.ie) The national tourism authority.
- John McGinley Bus (www.johnmcginley.com) Bus operator serving northwestern Donegal from Dublin.

GETTING AROUND

- Bus There are excellent national services to main towns. You'll have to rely on private operators for transport between smaller towns.
- Train Good for Sligo but service in Donegal is nonexistent.
- Car The best way of getting around; watch out for sheep and boy racers!

BE FOREWARNED

- Roads Torturously winding narrow roads can make travel in the northwest quite slow; it's a good thing there's plenty of scenery to keep you occupied!
- Seasonal tourism Many hotels and restaurants shut down between December and Easter.
- Weather Warm, sunny summers and ferocious winters make the northwest a place of extremes.

NORTHWEST IRELAND ITINERARIES

SLIGO SURROUNDS Three Days

The northwest's most dynamic town is unquestionably **(1) Sligo town** (p280), a pleasant spot on the River Garavogue that has its own distractions but is also a fine base from which to explore the surrounding area. The Yeats connection is everywhere around here, from the room devoted to the two brothers, poet and dramatist William Butler and painter Jack Butler, in the Sligo County Museum (p282), to WB Yeats' final resting place in **(2) Drumcliff** (p288), under the shadow of the memorable Benbulben. You can appreciate the majesty of the mountain and spoil a good walk by playing the stunning **(3) County Sligo Golf Course** (p285), designed in such a way that almost every hole is in view of the peak. Then unwind by immersing yourself in a traditional **(4) seaweed bath** (p287) in Strandhill before returning to Sligo town.

DELIGHTS OF DONEGAL Five Days

Five days is barely enough time to make a dent in what Donegal has to offer, but the following itinerary should whet your appetite for a longer visit. Start in the southwest, perhaps basing yourself in **(1) Donegal town** (p289) for visits to the beach at **(2) Rossnowlagh** (p293) and the sea cliffs at **(3) Slieve League** (p294). On day three, move in a northwesterly arc around the county, checking out the monastic ruins at **(4) Glencolumbcille** (p294) before heading towards **(5) Dunfanaghy** (p296), which is a fine base from which to explore the county's northern coasts. Your remaining two days could include **(6) Glenveagh National Park** (p299) and the **(7) Rosguill Peninsula's** (p300) superbly scenic Atlantic Drive. Finally, the remote beauty of the Inishowen Peninsula will leave you at Ireland's northernmost point – the seaside resort of **(8) Buncrana** (p305) is very popular with summer visitors from Derry, but in the off-season it is a quiet resort.

NORTHWEST ON ADRENALIN One Week

The single biggest rush you'll get in the northwest is trying to stay on a surfboard, and you can do that pretty much anywhere. We recommend the beaches at **(1) Easkey** (p289), **(2) Mullaghmore** (p289) and **(3) Bundoran** (p293), but the northwest is about a lot more than breaks and riptides. You can learn how to weave tweed or knitwear (or watch it being done) in **(4) Ardara** (p296) or do some **(5) sea angling** (p294) in the shadow of Slieve League. If there's a golfer in you, welcome to paradise: between the two counties you can play four courses that will challenge your skills but reward you with some of

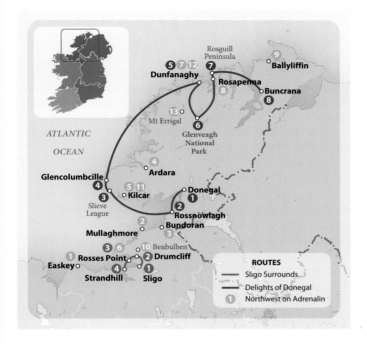

the best scenery in the world. Start at (6) County Sligo Golf Course
(p285) and move around the coast, playing (7) Dunfanaghy (p297),
(8) Rosapenna (p301) and (9) Ballyliffin (p305) on successive days,
giving yourself a well-deserved break on day five. If you're of a mind
that golf is a good walk spoiled, enjoy the latter on (10) Benbulben
(p288), around (11) Kilcar (p294), in southern Donegal, and along the
sublime (12) Tramore Beach (p297), just outside Dunfanaghy. Finally,
if you've got a good climb in you, take on (13) Mt Errigal (p300).

DISCOVER NORTHWEST IRELAND

Packing as much poetry, myth and folklore into its broody, dramatic landscapes as any shamrock lover could ever hope for, Ireland's northwest matches any other part of the country for sheer beauty but has no equal when it comes to wildness. To the south is County Sligo, inevitably associated with Nobel laureate, poet and dramatist William Butler Yeats (1865–1939), who helped cement its pastoral reputation through verse, and his brother Jack B Yeats (1871–1957), who did the same with a paintbrush, while the coast's surf is internationally renowned.

To the north is County Donegal, the wild child of the Irish family. Its rugged landscapes, relative isolation and impetuous weather have all served to forge the county's distinct character, which remains stubbornly independent and reluctant to concede to the niceties of a tamer existence. Yet it too has plenty to offer the visitor, from the magnificent coastlines that boast some of the best surfing spots in Europe, to the equally memorable interiors, as worthy of a postcard photo as any in Ireland.

COUNTY SLIGO

SLIGO TOWN

pop 19,402

Sligo town is in no hurry to shed its cultural traditions but it doesn't sell them out, either. Pedestrian streets lined with inviting shop fronts, stone bridges spanning the River Garavogue, and *céilidh* (traditional music and dance) sessions spilling from pubs contrast with genre-bending contemporary art and glass towers rising from prominent corners of the compact town (which is currently vying for city status).

Sligo's population almost triples each day with workers and shoppers converging on it, and on warm days busy restaurant tables along the quay have the atmosphere of a giant street party.

INFORMATION

Tourist office (☎ 071-916 1201; www.discov erireland.ie/northwest; Temple St; ⏰ 9am-6pm Mon-Fri, 9am-5pm Sat, 10am-4pm Sun Jun-Aug, 9am-5pm Mon-Fri, 10am-4pm Sat Mar-May & Sep, 9am-5pm Mon-Fri Oct-Feb) Info on the whole northwest region.

SIGHTS

The major draw of the **Sligo county museum** (☎ 071-914 1623; Stephen St; admission free; ⏰ 10.30am-12.30pm & 2.30-4.30pm Mon-Sat Jun-Sep, 2-5pm Tue-Sat Apr, May & Oct) is the Yeats room. There are photographs, letters and newspaper cuttings connected with the poet WB Yeats, and drawings by his brother Jack B Yeats, one of Ireland's most important modern artists (who said he never painted anything without putting a thought of Sligo into it).

FESTIVALS & EVENTS

Yeats International Festival (www. yeats-sligo.com; ⏰ late Jul–mid-Aug) Irish poetry, music and culture are celebrated with three weeks of performances and events around town.

SLEEPING

Tree Tops B&B (☎ 071-916 0160; www. sligobandb.com; Cleveragh Rd; s €48-52, d €74; Ⓟ ⓢ) When we visited, some wag had pointed the road sign reading 'Tree Tops Guests' into a nearby graveyard. Fear not: this cosy family home is highly recommended, with attractive, comfortable rooms. Coming from Pearse Rd, turn *left* at the graveyard; it's just before the superette on your left.

Riverside Suites Hotel (☎ 071-914 8080; www.riversidesuiteshotelsligo.com; Millbrook; 1-bedroom apt €101-119, 2-bedroom apt €129-159;

Ⓟ ⓢ) Riverside's state-of-the-art apartments are fantastic value. All come with kitchens equipped with cookers, microwaves and dishwashers, and many have fabulous river views. One-bedroom apartments can sleep four adults comfortably, while two-bedroom apartments sleep six adults, with kids' cots and roll-out beds also available. There's a stylish Thai restaurant and bar in the same building.

Glass House (☎ 071-919 4300; www.the glasshouse.ie; Swan Point; r €109-130; Ⓟ Ⓟ) Sligo's boldest architectural statement is this svelte study in glass and geometry

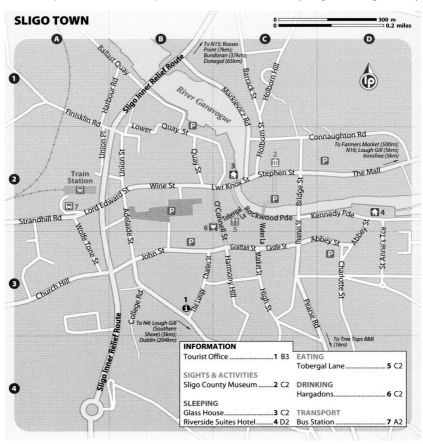

SLIGO TOWN

INFORMATION	EATING
Tourist Office **1** B3	Tobergal Lane **5** C2
SIGHTS & ACTIVITIES	**DRINKING**
Sligo County Museum **2** C2	Hargadons **6** C2
SLEEPING	**TRANSPORT**
Glass House **3** C2	Bus Station **7** A2
Riverside Suites Hotel **4** D2	

Irish horse racing

EOIN CLARKE

➘ IF YOU LIKE…

If you like the Yeats International Festival, you might enjoy these other festivals in town:

- **Sligo Races** (www.countysligoraces. com; early May-early Oct) The town's racetrack pulls in punters during its colourful racing season.
- **Sligo Jazz Festival** (www.sligojazz project.com; mid-Jul) Sligo swings during this three-day festival.
- **Sligo Live** (www.sligolive.ie; ☽ Oct) Sligo's biggest cultural event is this live-music festival.
- **Sligo International Choral Festival** (www.sligochoralfest.org; Nov) Gospel, folk and barbershop quartets are among the categories of this high-level competition.

overlooking the river. In the public areas, things get wilder, with '70s-style circular staircases and swirled carpets. Even that doesn't prepare you for the bedrooms, which come in either lurid lime green or psychedelic orange (fortunately there are no minibars, since neither would be good to wake up to with a hangover).

EATING & DRINKING

our pick **Tobergal Lane** (☎ 071-914 6599; Tobergal Lane; lunch dishes €7.50-12.95, dinner mains €19.95-20.95; ☽ 10am-10pm, closed Mon

Nov-Easter) Suppliers have top billing on Tobergal Lane's menu, which includes specialities like freshwater arctic charr fish served pan-fried with hollandaise sauce, or baked on creamed potatoes with almond and lemon-butter sauce. All baking is done in-house. Sligo's creative community head here for the weekly jazz 'brunch' (3pm to 5pm Sunday), and 'Café Beats': lounge-y DJ sets that take place every second Saturday evening. Alternate Saturday evenings feature 'Penthouse' DJ sets upstairs, with a cover charge of €5.

our pick **Hargadons** (☎ 071-915 3709; O'Connell St; lunch mains €10.50-12.95, tapas dishes €6.50-9; ☽ from 10am Mon-Sat, from 6pm Sun, lunch Mon-Sat, tapas 4-8pm Thu-Sat) Hargadons has polished up its original 1864 fittings – including its bowed former grocery shelves, snug, uneven stone floors, turf fire, and swivelling 'confession box' frosted glass panels above the marble bar – without compromising the pub's character. There's no TV or DJs, but you can catch live music on Saturday nights. Tapas dishes range from mussels in white wine to warm crab cake.

GETTING THERE & AWAY

Bus Éireann (☎ 071-916 0066) leaves from the bus station, situated below the train station on Lord Edward St. Destinations include Ballina (€12.90, 1½ hours, five daily), Westport (€16.70, two hours, twice daily) and Dublin (€17.10, four hours, four daily), as well as Galway and Donegal town. Services are less frequent on Sunday.

Feda O'Donnell (☎ 074-9548114; www.feda odonnell.com) operates a service between Crolly (County Donegal) and Galway twice daily (four times Friday). Call to confirm departure points.

Trains leave the **station** (☎ 071-916 9888) for Dublin (€32, 3½ hours, four or five daily) via Boyle, Carrick-on-Shannon and Mullingar.

AROUND SLIGO TOWN
ROSSES POINT

pop 872

Rosses Point (An Ros) is a picturesque seaside resort with grassy dunes rolling down to the strand, birdlife and Benbulben, Sligo's most recognisable landmark, arching skywards in the distance. It holds special appeal for the golf-minded traveller as much of the prime real estate here is dominated by trimmed greens. Accommodation is limited, but Rosses Point is Sligo town's backyard, so you can easily pop by for the day.

Offshore, the 1821-installed **Metal Man** beacon is an exact replica of the one in Tramore, County Waterford.

Established in 1894, **County Sligo Golf Course** (☎ 071-917 7134; www.countysligogolf club.ie; green fees €75 Mon-Thu, €90 Fri-Sun Apr-Oct, €40 Mon-Thu, €50 Fri-Sun Nov-Mar) is one of Ireland's most challenging and renowned links courses, attracting golfers from all over Europe. Its position on the peninsula is breathtaking.

SLEEPING & EATING

Yeats Country Hotel (☎ 071-917 7211; www.yeatscountryhotel.com; s/d from €65/130; P ☒) There isn't a town centre as such, so this huge three-star hotel more or less stands in for the heart of Rosses Point. It has a commanding presence overlooking the beach and the golf course, and attracts golfers and families. Rooms are large and many afford sea views. There's a popular restaurant; food is also served at its two bars.

CARROWMORE MEGALITHIC CEMETERY

Welcome to the largest Stone Age cemetery in Ireland and the second-biggest in Europe: **Carrowmore** (☎ 071-916 1534; adult/child/concession €3/1/2; ☼ 10am-6pm Easter-Sep, final admission 5pm; P) impresses for its variety and sheer scale. Everywhere you look you'll see rolling hills beaded with stone circles, passage tombs and dolmens – there are about 60, all told.

RICHARD CUMMINS

Rosses Point

GARETH MCCORMACK

Carrowmore Megalithic Cemetery (p285)

The conventional wisdom is that the site pre-dates Newgrange in County Meath by some 700 years. Over the centuries, many of the stones have been destroyed, and several remaining stones are on private land.

The delicately balanced dolmens were originally covered with stones and earth, so it requires some effort to picture what this 2.5km-wide area might once have looked like. To help (or some would say hinder) the imagination, Dúchas (which operates the site) has launched a decapitated reconstruction of one cairn, caged by wire and sliced open by a gaping entrance. An exhibit in the roadside visitor centre gives the full low-down on this fascinating site.

To get here, leave town by Church Hill and follow the signposts south for 5km.

STRANDHILL
pop 1413

The great Atlantic rollers that sweep the shorefront of Strandhill (An Leathras) make this long, red-gold beach unsafe for swimming. They have, however, made it a surfing mecca. Its handy 24-hour surfcam (www.strandhillsurfcam.com) brings surfers scurrying whenever the surf's up.

Gear hire and lessons can be arranged through Perfect Day Surf Shop (☎ 087 202 9399; www.perfectdaysurfing.com; Shore Rd) and Strandhill Surf School (☎ 071-916 8483; www.strandhillsurfschool.com; Beach Front), as well as Strandhill Hostel (below).

Alternatively, take a gentler, warmer dip in the Voya Seaweed Baths (see boxed text, right).

A few kilometres towards Sligo, you can walk – at low tide only! – to Coney Island (no relation to its New York namesake). The island's wishing well is reputed to have been dug by St Patrick (who, if all these tales are to be trusted, led a *very* busy life). Check tide times to avoid getting stranded.

SLEEPING & EATING

Strandhill Hostel & Knocknarea House (☎ 071-916 8313; www.strandhillaccommodation. com; Shore Rd; hostel dm/s/d €16/20/30, Knocknarea

House d €60-70; (P) (💻) (📶)) Surfer dudes and dudettes thaw out by the open fire in the common room of this well-run, 34-bed hostel a few paces from the strand. Next door, Knocknarea House is a former B&B that retains its frilly decor, but offers privacy by way of single, double and triple rooms (some with their own bathroom). Breakfast's not included at the hostel or the house, but Knocknarea guests can use the hostel kitchen. The owners operate a surf school, with lessons starting from €30 for two hours, including gear rental.

Bella Vista Bar & Bistro (☎ 071-912 2222; Shore Rd; lunch dishes €3.50-11.95, dinner mains €11.95-24.95; 🕑 food served 10am-10pm; 📶) The best place to eat in town (amid admittedly limited options) is lively Bella Vista, which prepares a fine rack of Irish lamb, crispy beer-battered cod, and vegetarian dishes including gourmet pizzas, pasta with homemade pesto sauce, and peppers stuffed with aromatic rice.

GETTING THERE & AWAY
Rosses Point is 8km northwest of Sligo along the R291, while Strandhill is situated 8km due west of Sligo off the R292 airport road. **Bus Éireann** (☎ 071-916 0066) buses run from Sligo to both towns (each €3.50, five to seven Monday to Saturday), but there's no public transport to other places of interest in the area. It's possible to walk to Carrowmore and Knocknarea from town, but it's a *long* day's return trek.

SOUTH OF SLIGO TOWN
CARROWKEEL PASSAGE TOMB CEMETERY
With a God's-eye view of the county from high in the Bricklieve Mountains, it's little wonder this hilltop site was sacred in prehistoric times. The windswept location is simultaneously eerie and uplifting, dotted with around 14 cairns, dolmens and the scattered remnants of other graves. It's possible to squeeze into at least one

---

MERMAID DREAMS
Ireland's only native spa therapy is the stuff of mermaid (or merman) fantasies. Part of Irish homeopathy for centuries, steaming your pores open then submerging yourself in a seaweed bath is said to help rheumatism and arthritis, thyroid imbalances, even hangovers. Certainly it leaves your skin feeling babysoft: seaweed's silky oils contain a massive concentration of iodine, a key presence in most moisturising creams.

Seaweed baths are prevalent along the west coast but two places stand out. **Kilcullen's Seaweed Baths** (☎ 091-36238; www.kilcullenseaweedbaths.com; Enniscrone; s/tw bath €24/32; 🕑 10am-9pm May-Oct, noon-8pm Mon-Fri, 10am-8pm Sat & Sun Nov-Apr) is the most traditional. Set within a grand Edwardian structure, Kilcullen's has loads of character, with original gigantean porcelain baths and stout brass taps still operating. For an altogether more modern setting, try **Voya Seaweed Baths** (☎ 071-916 8686; www.celticseaweedbaths.com; Shore Rd, Strandhill; s/tw €25/35; 🕑 10am-8pm), which has a beachfront location.

If too much relaxation is barely enough, both establishments also offer the chance to indulge in various other seaweed treatments, including body wraps and massages.

limestone chamber, although bigger folk are liable to get stuck. The place has been dated to the late Stone Age (3000 to 2000 BC).

West off the N4 road, Carrowkeel is closer to Boyle than Sligo town. From the latter, turn right in Castlebaldwin, then left at the fork; it's 2km uphill from the gateway. You can take an Athlone bus from Sligo and ask to be dropped off at Castlebaldwin.

EASKEY & ENNISCRONE

The town of Easkey (Eascaigh; sometimes spelt Easky) seems blissfully unaware that it's one of Europe's best year-round surfing destinations. Pub conversations revolve around hurling and Gaelic football, and the road to the beach isn't even signposted (turn off next to the childcare centre). Facilities are few; most surfers camp (free) around the castle ruins by the sea. If you're planning on hitting the waves, information and advice are available from **Easkey Surfing & Information Centre** (Irish Surfing Association; ☎ 096-49428; www.isasurf.ie).

Some 14km south at Enniscrone (Innis Crabhann), a stunning beach known as the Hollow stretches for 5km. The town is also famous for its seaweed baths (see boxed text, p287). Surf lessons and board hire are available from Enniscrone-based **Seventh Wave Surf School** (☎ 087 971 6389; www.seventhwavesurfschool.com).

GETTING THERE & AWAY

Bus Éireann (☎ 071-916 0066) express service 23 to Sligo from Dublin (€19, 3¾ hours) and service 64 between Galway (€16, 2½ hours) and Derry (€19, 2½ hours) stop outside Quigley's in Collooney. From Easkey, buses run four times daily (once on Sunday) to Sligo (€10.30, 50 minutes) and Ballina (€7.60, 30 minutes). From Enniscrone, buses also run four times daily (once on Sunday) to Sligo (€12.70, 65 minutes) and Ballina (€4.20, 15 minutes).

NORTH OF SLIGO TOWN
DRUMCLIFF & BENBULBEN

Visible right along Sligo's northern coast, Benbulben (525m), often written Ben Bulben, resembles a table covered by a pleated cloth: its limestone plateau is uncommonly flat, and its near-vertical sides are scored by earthen ribs. Walking here can be dangerous for the uninitiated – the **Sligo Mountaineering Club** (☎ 071-914 1267) has advice.

Benbulben's beauty was not lost on WB Yeats. Before the poet died in Menton, France in 1939, he had requested: 'If I die here, bury me up there on the mountain, and then after a year or so, dig me up and bring me privately to Sligo'. His wishes weren't honoured until 1948, when his body was interred in the churchyard at Drumcliff (sometimes spelt Drumcliffe), where his great-grandfather had been rector.

Yeats' grave is next to the doorway of the Protestant church, and his youthful bride Georgie Hyde-Lee is buried alongside. Almost three decades her senior, Yeats was 52 when they married. The poet's epitaph is from his poem *Under Ben Bulben*:

> Cast a cold eye
> On life, on death.
> Horseman, pass by!

Visiting the grave is somewhat disturbed by traffic noise along the N15 that no doubt has Yeats rolling over.

In an incomparable location 10km west of the N15 on the Drumcliff-to-Raghly road, the fifth-generation family-run property **Ardtarmon House** (☎ 071-916 3156; www.ardtarmon.com; Ballinfull; s €64-69, d €88-110, dinner by arrangement €30; ☺ closed late Dec-early Jan; Ⓟ 📶) has four spacious rooms in the manor house, and five self-contained cottages in converted farm buildings (from €155 for a two-night stay). A 460m stroll through wildflower-strewn gardens brings you to the beach. Its ecoventures include home-grown produce and woodchip-boiler-powered energy.

MULLAGHMORE

Sligo's only Blue Flag **beach**, Mullaghmore (An Mullach Mór), is a sweeping arc of dark-golden sand and safe shallow waters. (It wasn't so safe for Lord Mountbatten when the IRA rigged his boat with explosives and assassinated him in 1979.)

Take time to cycle or drive the scenic road looping around Mullaghmore Head, where wide shafts of rock slice into the Atlantic surf. En route you'll pass **Classiebawn Castle** (closed to the public), a neo-Gothic turreted pile built for Lord Palmerston in 1856 and later home to the ill-fated Lord Mountbatten.

Mullaghmore's clear waters, rocky outcrops and coves are ideal for diving. **Offshore Watersports** (☎ 071-919 4769, 087 610 0111; www.offshore.ie; The Pier) runs dive trips and rents gear.

GETTING THERE & AWAY

Bus Éireann (☎ 071-916 0066) buses run from Sligo to Drumcliff (€3.40, 15 minutes), Grange (€5.40, 20 minutes) and Cliffony (€6.40, 25 minutes). In Drumcliff the bus stop is near the church; in Grange it's outside Rooney's newsagency; and in Cliffony it's O'Donnell's Bar.

COUNTY DONEGAL
DONEGAL TOWN
pop 2339

Pretty Donegal town occupies a strategic spot at the mouth of Donegal Bay, on the River Eske in the shadow of the Bluestack Mountains. It was once a stamping ground of the O'Donnells, the great chieftains who ruled the northwest from the 15th to 17th

Classiebawn Castle, Mullaghmore

GARETH MCCORMACK

centuries, who left behind an atmospheric old castle. Today, despite being the county's namesake, it's neither its largest (Letterkenny), nor the county town (the even smaller town of Lifford), but its compact town centre makes a lively base for exploring the wild coastline nearby.

INFORMATION

Tourist office (☎ 074-972 1148; donegal@ failteireland.ie; Quay St; ⏰ 9am-6pm Mon-Sat, noon-4pm Sun Jul & Aug, 9.30am-5.30pm Mon-Sat Sep-Jun) In the new 'Discover Ireland' building.

SIGHTS

Guarding a picturesque bend of the River Eske, **Donegal Castle** (☎ 074-972 2405; Castle St; adult/child €4/2; ⏰ 10am-6pm mid-Mar–Oct, 9.30am-4.30pm Thu-Mon Nov-Dec) remains an imperious monument to both Irish and English might. Built by the O'Donnells in 1474, it served as the seat of their formidable power until 1607, when the English decided to be rid of pesky Irish chieftains once and for all. Rory O'Donnell was no pushover, though, torching his own castle before fleeing to France in the infamous Flight of the Earls. Their defeat paved the

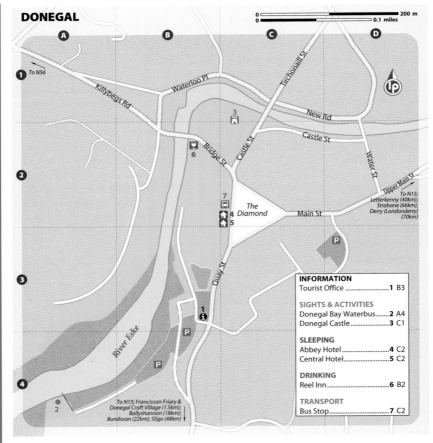

DONEGAL

GARETH MCCORMACK

Bluestack Mountains and Lough Eske

way for the Plantation of Ulster by thousands of newly arrived Scots and English
Protestants, creating the divisions that still
afflict the island to this day.

The castle was rebuilt in 1623 by Sir Basil
Brooke, along with the adjacent three-
storey Jacobean house. Much of the castle is gutted today, but enough has been
preserved that it's worth a look-see.

The most enjoyable way to explore
the highlights of Donegal Bay is to take
one of the boat tours run by **Donegal
Bay Waterbus** (☎ 074-972 3666; www.don
egalbaywaterbus.com; Donegal Pier; adult/child
€15/7). Aboard a 20m tour boat, the 1¼-
hour tour covers everything from historic
sites to seal-inhabited coves, admiring an
island manor and a ruined castle along
the way. The tour runs up to three times
daily from Easter to October, and may be
possible at other times depending on the
weather.

SLEEPING
Abbey Hotel (☎ 074-972 1014; www.abbeyho
teldonegal.com; The Diamond; s €80-90, d €130-150;

P ⓢ) Housing 118 rooms, this enormous
stone building surprises with its contemporary interior. Rooms out the back overlook the river. The hotel offers access to
a gym and has a stylish restaurant and
bar.

Central Hotel (☎ 074-972 1027; www.central
hoteldonegal.com; The Diamond; s €80-90, d €130-
150; P ⓢ) Next door to the Abbey, and
run by the same owners, the aptly named
Central has 112 rooms of its own behind a
tomato-red facade, and also offers all mod
cons and river views from rear rooms.
There is regular live music in the bar. If
you're in town for a while, ask about its
new self-catering apartments.

EATING & DRINKING
Aroma (☎ 074-972 3222; Donegal Craft Village;
dishes €4.50-12; ☷ 9.30am-5.30pm Mon-Sat)
Hidden in the far corner of Donegal's
craft village, the name aptly describes
the home baking and Donegal's best
coffee wafting through its tiny interior.
Blackboard specials utilise seasonal local

GARETH MCCORMACK

Surfing at Bundoran

⤴ SURFING

Bundoran has two main surf spots: The Peak, an imposing reef break directly in front of the town – which should only be attempted by highly experienced surfers – and the less formidable beach break at Tullan Strand, just north of the town centre.

Bundoran hosts the annual **Irish National Surfing Championships**, which are usually held in April.

The town has three **surf schools**, each of which rents gear and has its own lodge accommodation:

Bundoran Surf Co Offers deals on surf and accommodation packages.

Donegal Adventure Centre Youth-oriented place that also offers kayaking and gorge walking.

Turf n Surf Also runs hill walking tours (from €15).

Things you need to know: Irish National Surfing Championships (www.isasurf.ie); Bundoran Surf Co (☎ 071-984 1968; www.bundoransurfco.com; surf lessons per 3hr €35, gear rental per day €20, dm/s/d €20/40/50); Donegal Adventure Centre (☎ 071-984 2418; www.donegal-holidays.com; Bay View Ave; surf lessons per 3hr €25, gear rental per 2hr €10, dm €20-25); Turf n Surf (☎ 071-984 1091; www.turfnsurf.ie; Main St; surf lessons per 3hr €35, gear rental per day €20, dm/d €20/50)

produce such as white wine risotto with steamed asparagus.

Reel Inn (Bridge St) The best craic in town is invariably found at this old-school pub. Its owner plays the button-box accordion, and his pals join him in traditional music sessions most nights.

GETTING THERE & AWAY

Bus Éireann (☎ 074-913 1008; www.bus eireann.ie) services connect Donegal with Sligo (€12.50, 1¼ hours, six daily), Galway (€18.90, 3½ hours, two to three daily) and Killybegs (€6.90, 35 minutes, three daily); Derry (€14.30, 1½ hours, seven Monday to Saturday, three Sunday) and Belfast

(€19.50, 3½ hours, frequent); and Dublin (€17.60, four hours, six daily). The bus stop is on the western side of the diamond.

Feda O'Donnell (☎ 074-954 8114; www. fedaodonnell.com) runs to Galway (single/return €20/30, 3½ hours, twice daily, three on Friday and Sunday) via Ballyshannon, Bundoran and Sligo. Call to confirm departure point. Fares within Donegal range from €7 to €20.

AROUND DONEGAL TOWN
ROSSNOWLAGH
pop 50

The gentle rollers at the 5km-long Blue Flag **beach** at Rossnowlagh (Ross Neamblach), 17km southwest of Donegal town, are great for learning to surf or honing your skills. Tuition and gear rental is available from **Fin McCool Surf School** (☎ 071-985 9020; www.finmccoolsurfschool.com; gear rental per 3hr €25, 2hr lesson incl gear rental €35; ☼ 10am-7pm Easter-Oct, 10am-7pm Sat & Sun mid-Mar–Easter & Nov-Christmas). The school is headed up by Pro Tour surf judge Neil Britton, cousin of two-time Irish women's champion Easkey Britton (who's named after County Sligo's surfing hotspot). In the school's surf shop, flip through four decades of iconic posters drawn by Neil's uncle, Barry Britton, for the **Rossnowlagh Intercounty Surf Contest** (☼ late Oct), Ireland's largest and most social surf event.

Deep in the adjacent forest is a **Franciscan friary** (☎ 071-985 1342; admission free; ☼ 10am-8pm Mon-Sat) with tranquil gardens; the way of the cross takes you through a hillside smothered with rhododendron to spectacular hilltop views.

The combined pub/restaurant/guesthouse **Smugglers Creek** (☎ 071-985 2367; smugcreek@eircom.net; s/d €60/100; ☼ Easter-Oct; Ⓟ) perches on the hillside above the bay. It's justifiably popular for its excellent food

(mains €15 to €20) and sweeping views (room 4 has the best vantage point and a balcony into the bargain). There's live music on summer weekends.

Smugglers Creek's owners also operate the nearby B&B **Ardeelan Lodge** (☎ 071-985 2367; smugcreek@eircom.net; s/d €50/70; ☼ Easter-Oct) in a cosy salmon-coloured building by the Franciscan friary.

Once an extravagant 19th-century fishing lodge, the beachside **Sandhouse Hotel** (☎ 071-985 1777; www.sandhouse-hotel. ie; d €180-250; ☼ Easter-Dec; Ⓟ) has a festive atmosphere in its restaurant and bars, and a soothing marine spa. There are good deals on multiday stays.

Rossnowlagh isn't served by public transport.

BUNDORAN
pop 1964

If you're after ends-of-the-earth wilderness, you'll probably want to skip the blinking amusement arcades, hurdy-gurdy fairground rides and fast-food diners of Bundoran (Bun Dobhráin). But if you're looking for a cheery seaside atmosphere – as well as scenic walks and superb surf – Donegal's best-known seaside resort fits the bill. Outside summer, the carnival atmosphere abates and the town can be very quiet.

SOUTHWESTERN DONEGAL
KILLYBEGS
pop 1280

The salty scent of fish hauled from the ocean and the sound of cawing seagulls welcome you to Ireland's largest fishing port, Killybegs (Ceala Beaga). A charming working town, Killybegs' oddly angled streets collide at its diamond, a block from the pier. The community-run **tourist office** (☎ 074-973 2346; Quay St; ☼ vary seasonally) is in a cabin near the harbour. The **Bank of Ireland** (Main St) has an ATM and bureau de change.

KILCAR, CARRICK & AROUND
pop 260

Kilcar (Cill Chártha) and its more attractive neighbour Carrick (An Charraig) make good bases for exploring the breathtaking coastline of southwestern Donegal, especially the stunning sea cliffs at Slieve League.

This is fantastic walking country, particularly if you don't mind hoofing up and down a few hills. Kilcar Tourism has some pointers for walking the Kilcar Way; ask at the **Aísleann Cill Cartha** (☎ 074-973 8376; Main St, Kilcar; ☼ 9am-10pm Mon-Fri, 2-6pm Sat), a community centre that provides information for tourists. Just outside Kilcar is a small, sandy beach.

Local information is available at the excellent cultural centre, the **Tí Linn Centre** (☎ 074-973 9077; www.sliabhleague.com; Teelin, Carrick; ☼ 10.30am-5.30pm daily Easter-Sep, Fri-Tue Feb-Easter & Oct-Nov), in Teelin (Tí Linn), which also has an artisan cafe, and art and craft gallery.

SIGHTS & ACTIVITIES

The Cliffs of Moher get more publicity, but the sea cliffs at **Slieve League** (Sliabh Liag) are higher. In fact, these spectacular polychrome cliffs are thought to be the highest in Europe, plunging some 600m to the sea. Looking down, you'll see two rocks nicknamed the school desk and chair by locals for reasons that are immediately obvious. From the lower car park, there's a path skirting up around the near-vertical rock face to the aptly named **One Man's Pass**. You can now also drive all the way to the top, where there's a new car park. Be aware that mist and rain can

roll in unexpectedly and rapidly, making conditions treacherous.

Take the turn-off signposted Bunglass from the R263 at Carrick, 5km northwest of Kilcar, and continue beyond the narrow track signposted Slieve League to the one that's signposted Bunglass.

The cliffs are, if possible, even more impressive when viewed from the ocean below. Sightseeing boat trips along the Slieve League cliffs can be arranged by contacting **Nuala Star Teelin** (☎ 074-973 9365; www.nualastarteelin.com; ☼ Mar-Oct, weather permitting). Prices are €20 to €50 per person, depending on numbers, with reductions for children. The 12-seater boat departs from the Teelin pier approximately every two hours. Sea angling and diving trips can also be arranged.

SLEEPING & EATING

Blue Haven (☎ 074-973 8090; www.bluehaven. ie; Kilcar-Killybegs Rd; mains €14.50-26; ☼ dinner Mon-Fri, noon-9.30pm Sat & Sun late Apr-Oct, noon-9.30pm Sat & Sun Nov-late Apr) Blue Haven's modern restaurant nevertheless focuses on time-honoured 'home cooking'. The place can be quite festive, and its sunset views are stunning. Views also extend from its 15 guestrooms (single/double €55/100), all of which have access to a communal balcony.

GETTING THERE & AWAY

Bus Éireann (☎ 074-912 1309) service 490 connects Kilcar (€2.60) and Carrick (€5.40) with Killybegs and Glencolumbcille (€7.60) once daily Monday to Friday and Sunday (twice daily Saturday). In July and August an extra bus runs Monday to Saturday.

GLENCOLUMBCILLE & AROUND
pop 255

'There's nothing feckin' here!', endearingly blunt locals forewarn visitors to

Glencolumbcille (Gleann Cholm Cille). But, with some stunning walks fanning out from the three-pub village, scalloped beaches, an excellent Irish language and culture centre, and a fine little folk museum, chances are you'll disagree.

Approaching Glencolumbcille via the Glen Gesh Pass does, however, reinforce just how cut off this starkly beautiful coastal haven is from the rest of the world. You drive past miles and miles of hills and bogs before the ocean appears, followed by a narrow, green valley and the small Gaeltacht village within it.

This spot has been inhabited since 3000 BC and you'll find plenty of Stone Age remains throughout the collection of tiny settlements. It's believed that the 6th-century St Colmcille (Columba) founded a monastery here (hence the name, meaning 'Glen of Columba's Church'), and incorporated Stone Age standing stones called *turas* (after the Irish word for a pilgrimage, or journey) into Christian usage by inscribing them with a cross. At midnight on Colmcille's Feast Day (9 June) penitents begin a walkabout of the *turas* and the remains of Colmcille's church before attending Mass at 3am in the local church.

MAGHERY & THE GLEN GESH PASS
pop 640

On the northern edge of the peninsula, tiny Maghery has a picturesque waterfront. If you follow the strand westward, you'll get to a rocky promontory full of caves. During Cromwell's 17th-century destruction, 100 villagers sought refuge here but all except one were discovered and massacred.

About 1.5km east of Maghery is the enchanting **Assarancagh Waterfall**, beyond which is the beginning of a 10km marked trail to the **Glen Gesh Pass** (Glean Géis, meaning 'Glen of the Swans'). It's almost alpine in appearance; cascading mountains and lush valleys are dotted with isolated farmhouses and small lakes. If you're driving or cycling, you can get to the pass directly from Glencolumbcille by following the road signs for Ardara.

STEPHEN SAKS

Glen Gesh Pass

Horn Head

GARETH MCCORMACK

ARDARA
pop 564

The heart of Donegal's traditional knit-wear and hand-woven tweed, Ardara (Árd an Rátha) is a pretty gateway to the switchbacks of Glen Gesh Pass just south-west of the town. Tourist information is available from the **Triona Design visitor centre** (☎ 074-914 1422; www.trionadesign.com; Main St; ☺ 9am-7pm). On the diamond the Ulster Bank has an ATM; the post office is nearby on Main St.

SHOPPING
Signs in the town centre point you to the town's knitwear producers.

Eddie Doherty (☎ 074-954 1304; www.hand woventweed.com; Front St) Behind Doher-ty's bar, you can usually catch Eddie Doherty hand-weaving here on a tra-ditional loom.

John Molloy's (☎ 074-954 1133; www.john molloy.com; Ardara) Handmade and ma-chine-knitted woollies are available here at its flagship establishment and at its factory outlet in Glencolumbcille.

Kennedy's (☎ 074-954 1106; Front St) In business for over a century, Kennedy's helped establish Ardara's reputation as a sweater mecca.

Triona Design (☎ 074-914 1422; www.triona design.com; Main St) Weavers keep tradi-tional skills alive while demonstrating their techniques for visitors.

GETTING THERE & AROUND
Bus Éireann (☎ 074-912 1309) service 492 from Killybegs (€3.40, 25 minutes, three daily) stops outside O'Donnell's in Ardara.

Don Byrne's of Ardara (☎ 074-954 1658; Main St; ☺ 9.30am-6pm Jun-Sep, 5.30-8.30pm Mon-Fri, 9.30am-6pm Sat Oct-May), at the east-ern edge of the town centre, rents bikes for €15/70 per day/week.

NORTHWESTERN DONEGAL
DUNFANAGHY & AROUND
pop 316

Clustered around the waterfront, Dun-fanaghy's small, attractive town centre has a surprisingly wide range of accommodation and some of the finest dining options in the county's northwest. Glistening beaches, dramatic coastal cliffs, mountain trails and forests are all within a few kilometres.

There are no ATMs in town but the **post office** (Main St) has a bureau de change.

SIGHTS

The towering headland of **Horn Head** (Corrán Binne) has some of Donegal's most spectacular coastal scenery and plenty of birdlife. Its dramatic quartzite cliffs, covered with bog and heather, rear over 180m high, and the view from their tops is heart-pounding.

The road circles the headland and the best approach by bike or car is in a clockwise direction from the Falcarragh end of Dunfanaghy. On a fine day, you'll encounter tremendous views of Tory, Inishbofin, Inishdooey and tiny Inishbeg islands to the west; Sheep Haven Bay and the Rosguill Peninsula to the east; Malin Head to the northeast; and the coast of Scotland beyond. Take care in bad weather as the route can be perilous.

ACTIVITIES

WALKING

For an exhilarating hike, take the road from Dunfanaghy towards Horn Head until the bridge. After crossing, go through the gate on your left and stroll along the track until you reach the dunes. A well-beaten path will lead you to the magnificent **Tramore Beach**. Turn left and follow it to the end, where you can find a way up onto a path leading north to **Pollaguill Bay**. Continue to the cairn at the end of the bay and follow the coastline for a stupendous view of the 20m **Marble Arch**, carved out by the sea.

A shorter walk begins at Marble Hill Beach in Port-na-Blagh. Take the path on the left side of the beach past the cottage and work your way about 500m through the brush and along the top of the cliff until you reach **Harry's Hole**, a small crevice in the cliff that is popular with daredevil kids, who dive 10m into the water below.

GOLF

Dunfanaghy Golf Club (☎ 074-913 6335; www.dunfanaghygolfclub.com; green fees weekdays/weekends €30/40) is a stunning waterside 18-hole links course just outside the village on the Port-na-Blagh road.

HORSE RIDING

Exploring the expansive beaches and surrounding countryside on horseback can be arranged through **Dunfanaghy Stables** (☎ 074-910 0980; www.dunfanaghystables.com; Main St; adult/child per hr €30/25; ☺ vary seasonally).

SEA ANGLING

Richard Bowyer (☎ 074-913 6640; Port-na-Blagh) organises sea-angling trips from the small pier in Port-na-Blagh between Easter and September.

SURFING, WINDSURFING & KAYAKING

Windsurfing lessons and gear hire are available through **Marble Hill Windsurfing** (☎ 074-913 6231; richardharshaw@eircom.net; the Cottage, Marble Hill, Port-na-Blagh; ☺ daily Jul & Aug, by appointment May, Jun & Sep).

Jaws Watersports (☎ 086 173 5109; www.jawswatersports.com; Main St) rents surfboards (€20 per half day) and offers lessons (€30), and also has kayak rental (from €25 per half day) and runs kayaking trips (€35).

SLEEPING

Arnold's Hotel (☎ 074-913 6208; www.arnoldshotel.com; Main St; s €55-85, d €130; ☺ Apr-Oct;

Derryveagh Mountains, Glenveagh National Park
GARETH MCCORMACK

(P) (□)) Open since 1922, this 30-room hotel is run with tangible pride by the third generation of the Arnold family. Public areas with tartan carpeting are strewn with deep-red velour armchairs. Some front guestrooms have window seats where you can curl up with a book or simply gaze out over Sheep Haven Bay. Fine Irish food is served in the elegant bar (mains €16 to €30).

Shandon Hotel Spa & Wellness (☎ 074-913 6137; www.shandonhotel.com; Sheep Haven Bay, Dunfanaghy; d €184-244; ☺ Easter-Oct; (P) (☎)) Harried parents will love this 1950s hotel. You can drop off the kids at the free supervised playroom, and indulge at its award-winning spa or work out in the gym. Family-friendly facilities also include kids' and adults' swimming pools, a tennis court, pitch and putt, and laundry facilities. Most of the 70 spacious rooms have a spectacular vantage of Marble Hill Beach and all have in-room fridges. Dinner is available in the hotel restaurant (three-course menu €39). Backpackers can enquire about cheaper annexe rooms

available on a room-only basis. Follow the signposts off the N56 along 3km of winding country lanes.

EATING

Cove (☎ 074-913 6300; Rockhill, Port-na-Blagh; lunch menu €21, dinner mains €17.50-24; ☺ lunch Sun, dinner Tue-Sun, closed Jan–mid-Mar) Owners Siobhan Sweeney and Peter Byrne are perfectionists who tend to every detail in Cove's art-filled dining room and on your plate. The seafood-skewed cuisine is inventive and deceptively simple with subtle Asian influences. After dinner, retire to the elegant lounge upstairs. It's on the main road in Port-na-Blagh.

Mill Restaurant & Guesthouse (☎ 074-913 6985; www.themillrestaurant.com; Figart, Dunfanaghy; 3-course menu €43.50; ☺ dinner Tue-Sun mid-Mar–mid-Dec; (P)) An exquisite country setting and perfectly composed meals make dining here a treat. It occupies an old flax mill that was for many years the home of renowned watercolour artist Frank Eggington. It also has six high-class guestrooms (single/double

€70/100). It's just south of the town on the Falcarragh road.

DRINKING
Molly's Bar (☎ 074-910 0739; Main St) Be sure to at least peek inside the cherry-red Molly's Bar, a wonderfully old-fashioned pub with proper snugs. It also hosts regular live music (traditional, jazz, blues and more) and events including quiz nights.

GETTING THERE & AWAY
Feda O'Donnell (☎ 074-954 8114) buses from Crolly (€7, 40 minutes) to Galway (€20, five hours) stop in Dunfanaghy square twice daily Monday to Saturday and three times on Friday and Sunday.

John McGinley (☎ 074-913 5201) buses to Dublin stop in Dunfanaghy (€20, 4¾ hours).

The **Lough Swilly** (☎ 074-912 2863) bus from Dungloe stops in Dunfanaghy once daily Monday to Friday (€11.40, two hours) en route to Letterkenny and Derry.

GLENVEAGH NATIONAL PARK
Lakes shimmer like dew in the mountainous valley of **Glenveagh National Park** (Páirc Náisiúnta Ghleann Bheatha; www.glenveagh nationalpark.ie; admission free; ☼ 10am-6pm mid-Mar–Oct, 9am-5pm Nov–mid-Mar). Alternating between great knuckles of rock, green-gold swaths of bog and scatterings of oak and birch forest, the 6500-hectare protected area is magnificent walking country. Its wealth of wildlife includes the golden eagle, which was hunted to extinction here in the 19th century but was reintroduced in 2000.

Such serenity came at a heavy price. The land was once farmed by 244 tenants, who were forcibly evicted by landowner John George Adair in the winter of 1861 following what he called a 'conspiracy', but really because their presence ob-

structed his vision for the valley. Adair put the final touches on his paradise (1870-73) by building the spectacular lakeside Glenveagh Castle, while his wife, Adelia, introduced the park's definitive red deer and rhododendrons.

If anything, things got even more surreal after the Adairs' deaths. The castle was briefly occupied by the IRA in 1922. Then in 1929 the property was acquired by Kingsley Porter, professor of art at Harvard University, who mysteriously disappeared in 1933 (presumed drowned, but rumoured to have been spotted in Paris afterwards). Six years later the estate was bought by his former student, Henry McIlhenny, once described by Andy Warhol as 'the only person in Philadelphia with glamour'. In 1975, McIlhenny sold the whole kit and caboodle to the Irish government.

The park features nature trails along lakes, through woods and blanket bog, as well as a viewing point that's a short walk behind the castle.

The **Glenveagh Visitor Centre** (☎ 074-913 7090; Churchill) has a 20-minute audiovisual display on the ecology of the park and the infamous Adair. The restaurant serves hot food and snacks, and the reception sells the necessary midge repellent, as vital in summer as walking boots and waterproofs are in winter. Camping is not allowed.

GLENVEAGH CASTLE
This delightfully showy **castle** (adult/child €3/1.50) was modelled in miniature on Scotland's Balmoral Castle. Henry McIlhenny made it a characterful home with liberal reminders of his passion for hunting deer. In fact you'll be hard pressed to find a single room without a representation – or taxidermied remains – of a stag.

An entertaining 30-minute guided tour takes in a series of flamboyantly decorated rooms that remain as if McIlhenny has just stepped out. The most eye-catching, including the tartan-and-antler-covered music room and the pink candy-striped room demanded by Greta Garbo whenever she stayed here, are in the round tower.

The exotic gardens are similarly spectacular, boasting a host of terraces, an Italian garden, a walled kitchen garden, and the Belgian Walk, built by Belgian soldiers who stayed here during WWI. Their cultured charm is in marked contrast to the wildly beautiful landscape that enfolds the area.

The last guided tours of the castle leave about 45 minutes before closing time. **Minibuses** (adult/child return €2/1) shuttle between the visitor centre and the castle roughly every 15 minutes; the journey takes a mere five or so minutes; alternatively it's a scenic 3.6km walk.

DUNLEWEY & AROUND
pop 700

Blink and chances are you've missed the tiny hamlet of Dunlewy (Dún Lúiche) beside Lough Dunlewy. You won't miss Mt Errigal, however, whose bare face towers over the surrounding area.

MT ERRIGAL

The looming presence of Mt Errigal (752m) seemingly dares walkers to attempt the tough but beautiful climb to its pyramid-shaped peak. If you're keen to take on the challenge, pay close attention to the weather. It's a dangerous climb on misty or wet days, when the mountain is shrouded in cloud and visibility is minimal.

There are two paths to the summit: the easier route, which covers 5km and takes

around two hours; and the more difficult 3.3km walk along the northwestern ridge, which involves scrambling over scree for about 2½ hours. Details of both routes are available at the Dunlewey Lakeside Centre.

POISONED GLEN

Legend has it that the stunning ice-carved rock face of the Poisoned Glen got its sinister name when the ancient one-eyed giant king of Tory, Balor, was killed here by his exiled grandson, Lughaidh, whereupon the poison from his eye split the rock and poisoned the glen. The less interesting truth, however, lies in a cartographic gaffe. Locals were inspired to name it An Gleann Neamhe (the Heavenly Glen), but when an English cartographer mapped the area, he carelessly marked it An Gleann Neimhe – the Poisoned Glen.

The R251 has several viewpoints overlooking the glen. It's possible to walk through it, although the ground is rough and boggy. From the lakeside centre a return walk along the glen is 12km and takes two to three hours. Watch out for the green lady – the resident ghost!

NORTHEASTERN DONEGAL
ROSGUILL PENINSULA

The best way to appreciate Rosguill's rugged splendour is by driving, cycling or even walking the 15km **Atlantic Drive**. It's signposted to your left as you come into the sprawling village of **Carrigart** (Carraig Airt) from the south. There are plenty of thirst-quenching pubs in the village, and a pretty, secluded beach at **Trá na Rossan**. On no account should you swim in Mulroy Bay or the surrounding areas, as it's unsafe. Perhaps this is why the summer crowds don't linger here. Most prefer to travel 4km northward to

Historic bridge, Poisoned Glen

GARETH MCCORMACK

Downings (often written as Downies), where the beach is spectacular, though it's much more built-up.

Designed by St Andrew's Old Tom Morris in 1891 and remodelled by Harry Vardon in 1906, the scenery at the **Rosapenna Golf Club** (☎ 074-915 5301; www.rosapennagolflinks.ie; Downings; green fees €50-85) is as spectacular as the layout, which can challenge even the lowest handicapper.

SLEEPING & EATING

Downings Bay Hotel (☎ 074-915 5586; www.downingsbayhotel.com; Downings; s/d from €70/120; P ⊚) Just footsteps from the strand, rooms at this spacious, if slightly austere, hotel have subtle checked and striped fabrics. There's an adjacent night-club, a couple of bars (bar food €12.50 to €23.50) and an excellent restaurant, the Haven (Sunday lunch €18.50, dinner €60 to €70 for two including wine).

ourpick **Olde Glen Bar and Restaurant** (☎ 074-915 5130; Glen, Carrigart; mains €18-24; ⏰ dinner Tue-Sat late May–mid-Sep, Fri-Sun Easter–late May, Sat & Sun mid-Sep–Easter) Authentic down to its original 1700s uneven stone floor, this treasure of a traditional pub in the tiny hamlet of Glen serves a sensational pint. Out the back, its small farmhouse-style restaurant serves outstanding blackboard specials. It doesn't take reservations and is popular with locals – turn up by 5.30pm to get a table for the 6pm seating, or by 6.30pm for a table at the 7.30pm seating. By the time you leave, you'll feel like a local yourself.

GETTING THERE & AROUND

A local bus connects Carrigart and Downings (contact Patrick Gallagher, ☎ 074-913 7037), but you really need your own transport for this area.

FANAD PENINSULA

The second-most northerly point in Donegal, Fanad Head thrusts out into the Atlantic to the east of Rosguill. The peninsula curls around the watery expanses of Mulroy Bay to the west, and Lough Swilly to the east, the latter trimmed by high

RICHARD CUMMINS

Lighthouse at Fanad Head

cliffs and sandy beaches. Most travellers stick to the peninsula's eastern flank, visiting the beautiful beach and excellent golf course at Portsalon, and the quiet heritage towns of Rathmelton and Rathmullan. Accommodation is relatively limited, so book ahead in summer.

PORTSALON & FANAD HEAD

Once named the second-most beautiful beach in the world by British newspaper the *Observer,* the tawny-coloured Blue Flag beach in Ballymastocker Bay, which is safe for swimming, is the principal draw of tiny Portsalon (Port an tSalainn). For golfers, however, the main attraction is the marvellously scenic **Portsalon Golf Club** (☎ 074-915 9459; www.portsalongolfclub. ie; Portsalon; green fees weekdays/weekends €40/50).

It's another 8km to the lighthouse on the rocky tip of Fanad Head, the best part of which is the scenic drive there. Following the roller-coaster road that hugs the cliffs back to Rathmullan, you'll pass the early-19th-century **Knockalla**

Fort, built to warn off any approaching French ships.

The peninsula has some crankin' surf – for lessons contact **Adventure One Surf School** (☎ 074-915 0262; www.adventureone. net; Ballyheirnan Bay, Fanad). Two-hour lessons including gear rental cost €30.

The **Lough Swilly** (☎ 074-912 2863) bus leaves Letterkenny three times daily Monday to Friday, twice Saturday for Milford (€4.60, one hour).

INISHOWEN PENINSULA

The Inishowen (Inis Eoghain) Peninsula reaches just far enough into the Atlantic to qualify as the northernmost point on the island of Ireland: Malin Head. It is remote, rugged, desolate and sparsely populated, making it a special and quiet sort of place. Ancient sites and ruined castles abound, as do traditional thatched cottages that aren't yet demoted to storage sheds.

Surrounded by vast estuarine areas and open seas, the Inishowen Peninsula naturally attracts a lot of birdlife. The variety is tremendous, with well over 200 species passing through or residing permanently on the peninsula. Inishowen regularly receives well-travelled visitors from Iceland, Greenland and North America. Irregular Atlantic winds mean rare and exotic species also blow in from time to time. Twitchers should check out *Ireland's Birds,* by Eric Dempsey and Michael O'Clery, or visit www.birdsireland.com.

MALIN HEAD

If you've already seen Ireland's southernmost point and its westernmost point, you'll still be impressed when you clap your eyes on Malin Head (Cionn Mhálanna), the island's northern extent. The head's rocky, weather-battered slopes feel like they're being dragged unwillingly into the sea. It's great for wandering on foot, absorbing the stark natural setting and pondering deep subjects as the wind tries to blow the clothes off your back. Bring cash with you, as there are no ATMs here.

On the northernmost tip, called **Banba's Crown** (Fíorcheann Éireann), stands a cumbersome cliff-top **tower** that was built in 1805 by the British admiralty and later used as a Lloyds signal station. Around it are unattractive concrete huts that were used by the Irish army in WWII as lookout posts. To the west from the fort-side car park, a path leads to **Hell's Hole**, a chasm where the incoming waters crash against the rocky formations. To the east a longer headland walk leads to the **Wee House of Malin**, a hermit's cave in the cliff face.

Several endangered bird species thrive here. This is one of the few places in Ireland where you can still hear the call of the endangered corncrake in summer. Other birds to look out for are choughs, snow buntings and puffins.

The Plantation village of **Malin** (Málainn), on Trawbreaga Bay, 14km southeast of

Malin Head, has a pretty movie-set quality. Walkers can head out from the tidy village green on a circular route that takes in **Knockamany Bens**, a local hill with terrific views, as well as **Lagg Presbyterian Church** (3km northwest from Malin), the oldest church still in use on the peninsula. The massive sand dunes at Five Fingers Strand, another 1km beyond the church, are a dog's dream.

SLEEPING & EATING

Malin Hotel (☎ 074-937 0606; www.malin hotel.ie; Malin; lunch mains €12-19, dinner menu €32.50; ☽ lunch & dinner; Ⓟ ⊚) From the village green you'll first spot the old pub, but look beyond it and you'll also see a modern, boxlike hotel behind. Designer

Cottage near Malin Head

GARETH MCCORMACK

INISHOWEN PENINSULA

0 _____ 10 km
0 _____ 5 miles

Banba's Crown
Malin Head
Ballyhillin
Knockamany Bens
Lagg Presbyterian Church
Ballyhillin Beach
Inishtrahull Sound
Crockalough (280m)
Glengad Head
ATLANTIC OCEAN
Carrickabraghey Castle
Tullagh Point
Tullagh Strand
Dunaff
Malin
Doagh Famine Village
Culdaff
Dunmore Head
Ballyliffin
Clonmany
Bocan Stone Circle
Kinnagoe Bay
Donagh Cross
Clonca Church & Cross
Carrowmore High Crosses
Inishowen Head
Shrove
Raghtin More (502m)
Mamore Hill (421m)
Glenevin Waterfall
Carndonagh
Gleneely
R238
Lough Swilly
R238
Gap of Mamore
R244
Slieve Snaght (615m)
Glentogher
Cooley Cross
Greencastle
Green Castle
Urris Hills
Dunree
River Crana
R240
Slieve Main
Moville
Redcastle
Magilligan Point
Ned's Point Fort
Buncrana
DONEGAL
Scalp Mountain (477m)
Quigley's Point
Lough Foyle
A2
Fanad Peninsula
Rathmullan
St Mura Cross
Fahan
Inch Island
Inch
Burnfoot
R238
Muff
River Eagle
City of Derry Airport
Limavady
A2
A37
Burt
Bridge End
Grianán of Aileách
River Roe
N13
Derry (Londonderry)
A2
DERRY

wallpapers adorn the lavish rooms (single/double from €90/150), and the pub-restaurant serves up good Irish standards. There's weekend entertainment.

McClean's (Malin) Easily spotted by the petrol pumps out front, this treasure of an old-time pub has the best craic in Malin and often has live music.

GETTING THERE & AROUND
The best way to approach Malin Head is by the R238/242 from Carndonagh, rather than up the eastern side from Culdaff.

Lough Swilly (☎ 074-912 2863) operates two buses Monday to Friday, three on Saturday, between Derry and Carndonagh (€7.40, 50 minutes).

Northwest Busways (☎ 074-938 2619) runs connecting services from Carndonagh to Malin Head from Tuesday to Saturday.

BALLYLIFFIN & CLONMANY
pop 700

These two quaint villages and their surrounds have plenty to occupy visitors for a day or two. Both have post offices but no banks.

With two championship courses, **Ballyliffin Golf Club** (☎ 074-937 6119; www.ballyliffingolfclub.com; Ballyliffin; green fees weekday/weekend Old Links €75/80, Glashedy €80/90; ⚇ restaurant lunch & dinner) is among the best places to golf in Donegal. The scenery is so beautiful that it can distract even the most focused golfer. Its above-average restaurant, Linx, overlooks the fairways (mains €9.50 to €20).

SLEEPING & EATING

`our pick` **Glen House** (☎ 074-937 6745; www.glenhouse.ie; Straid, Clonmany; s €40-80, d €70-90, menus from €17; ⚇ tearoom 10am-6pm daily Jun-Aug, Sat & Sun Sep-May, restaurant lunch Sun, dinner Tue-Sun Jun-Aug, lunch Sun, dinner Thu-Sun Sep-May) In a sparkling white manor house, the welcome couldn't be friendlier or more professional at this gem of a guesthouse. Its eight airy rooms look like they've been decorated for an interior-design magazine spread, and two have stunning sea views. The walking trail to Glenevin Waterfall starts next door to the tearoom, which opens to a timber deck.

From September to May there's a minimum two-night stay.

Ballyliffin Lodge (☎ 074-937 8200; www.ballyliffinlodge.com; s/d €120/250; ⓟ ⚇ ⚇) This elegant 40-room hotel has ultraspacious autumn-hued rooms. An extra €35 gets you a sublime view over the ocean. You can treat yourself at the state-of-the-art spa, golf course, sophisticated Holly Tree Restaurant (mains €16 to €26.50), or in the laid-back Mamie Pat's (bar food €11.50 to €22.50).

GETTING THERE & AWAY

Lough Swilly (☎ 074-912 2863) buses run twice Monday to Friday, once Saturday, between Clonmany and Carndonagh (€2.50, 20 minutes).

BUNCRANA

pop 3411

On the tame side of the peninsula, Buncrana (Bun Cranncha) is a busy but appealing town with its fair share of pubs and a 5km sandy beach on the shores of Lough Swilly.

GARETH McCORMACK

Inishowen Peninsula (p302)

Sunset over Malin Head (p303)

RICHARD CUMMINS

With plate-glass windows facing the lough, the aptly named **Beach House** (☎ 074-936 1050; The Pier, Swilly Rd; lunch mains €6.50-17.50, dinner mains €16-26; ☾ 5pm-late Tue-Fri, noon-late Sat & Sun) cafe/restaurant projects an elegant simplicity. Although the menu is also intrinsically simple, the quality and preparation are a cut above: 'surf and turf', for example, comes with fillet steak, crab claws, langoustines and creamy bisque.

GRIANÁN OF AILEÁCH

This amphitheatre-like stone **fort** (admission free; ☾ 10am-6pm; (P)) encircles the top of Grianán Hill like a halo, 18km south of Buncrana near Burt, signposted off the N13. Locals open the gate each day, giving visitors the chance to take in eye-popping views of the surrounding loughs and all the way to Derry. Its mini-arena can resemble a circus whenever a tour bus rolls up and spills its load inside the 4m-thick walls.

The fort may have existed at least 2000 years ago, but it's thought that the site itself goes back to pre-Celtic times as a temple to the god Dagda. Between the 5th and 12th centuries it was the seat of the O'Neills, before being demolished by Murtogh O'Brien, king of Munster. Most of what you see now is a reconstruction built between 1874 and 1878.

↘ NORTHERN IRELAND

NORTHERN IRELAND

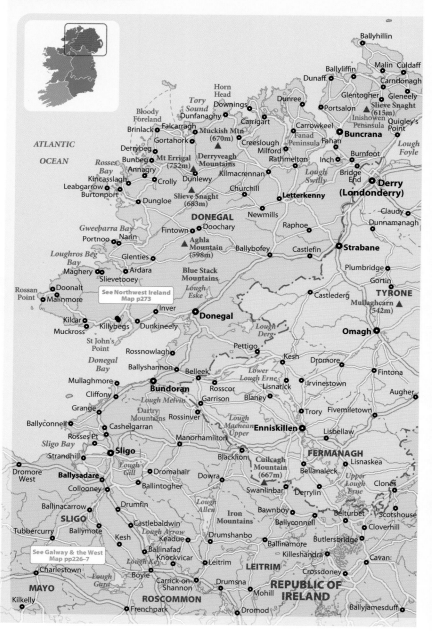

ATLANTIC
OCEAN

Ballyhillin
Malin Culdaff
Ballyliffin
Dunaff Carndonagh
Glentogher Gleneely
Slieve Snaght
Portsalon (615m)
Inishowen Quigley's
Carrowkeel Peninsula Point
Buncrana
Horn
Head
Dunree
Downings
Tory
Sound
Dunfanaghy
Carrigart
Bloody
Foreland
Brinlack Falcarragh
Muckish Mtn Creeslough Fanad Fahan
Gortahork (670m) Peninsula
Milford Burnfoot
Derrybeg Rathmelton Lough
Inch Foyle
Bunbeg Mt Errigal Derryveagh Rosses Kilmacrennan Bridge
Annagry (752m) Mountains End
Kincasslagh Crolly Churchill Lough Derry
Leabgarrow Dunlewy Swilly (Londonderry)
Burtonport Slieve Snaght Letterkenny
Dungloe (683m) Claudy
Newmills Dunnamanagh
DONEGAL
Gweebarra Bay Fintown Doochary Raphoe
Portnoo Narin Aghla Castlefin Strabane
Glenties Mountain Ballybofey
Loughros Beg (598m) Plumbridge
Bay Ardara
Maghery Blue Stack Gortin
Slievetooey Mountains Castlederg TYRONE
Rossan Doonalt Lough Mullaghcarn
Point Malinmore Eske (542m)
Kilcar Inver Donegal Omagh
Muckross Killybegs Dunkineely
St John's Lough
Point Pettigo Derg
Donegal Rossnowlagh Kesh
Bay Ballyshannon Belleek Dromore Fintona
Mullaghmore Lower
Cliffony Lough Erne Irvinestown Augher
Bundoran Lisnarick
Grange Rosscor Trory Fivemiletown
Ballyconnell Dartry Garrison Blaney
Rosses Pt Mountains Rossinver Lough Enniskillen Lisbellaw
Sligo Bay Cashelgarran Macnean
Strandhill Manorhamilton Upper FERMANAGH
Sligo Lisnaskea
Dromore Ballysadare Lough Blacklion Cuilcagh Bellanaleck Upper
West Gill Dromahair Dowra Mountain Derrylin Lough Clones
Collooney Ballintogher (667m) Erne Scotshouse
Ballinacarrow Swanlinbar Belturbet Cloverhill
Drumfin Lough Bawnboy
SLIGO Allen Iron Ballyconnell Butlersbridge
Tubbercurry Castlebaldwin Mountains Ballinamore Cavan
Ballymote Kesh Drumshanbo Killeshandra
Keadue Ballinamore
Ballinafad Crossdoney
Charlestown Knockvicar Leitrim LEITRIM Ballyjamesduff
Lough Key Boyle Drumsna
MAYO Lough Carrick-on- Mohill REPUBLIC OF
Kilkelly Gara Shannon Dromod IRELAND
ROSCOMMON
Frenchpark

See Northwest Ireland
Map p273

See Galway & the West
Map pp226–7

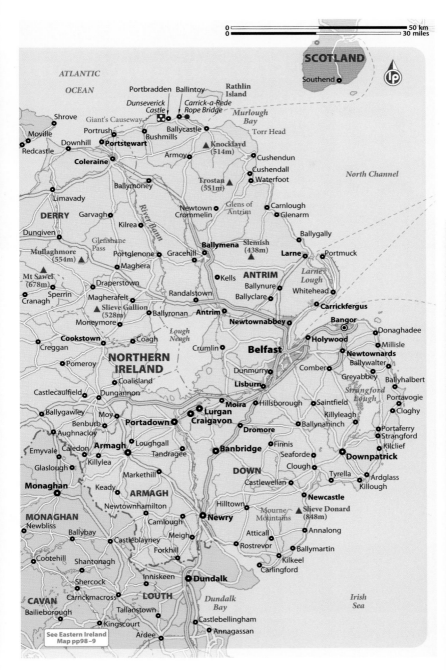

0   50 km
0   30 miles

SCOTLAND

Southend

ATLANTIC
OCEAN

Shrove
Moville
Redcastle
Downhill
Portstewart
Portrush
Bushmills
Giant's Causeway
Dunseverick
Castle
Portbradden
Ballintoy
Carrick-a-Rede
Rope Bridge
Rathlin
Island
Ballycastle
Murlough
Bay
Torr Head
Armoy
Knocklayd
(514m)
Cushendun
Cushendall
Waterfoot
Coleraine
Ballymoney
Limavady
Trostan
(551m)
North Channel

DERRY
Garvagh
Kilrea
Newtown
Crommelin
Glens of
Antrim
Carnlough
Glenarm
Dungiven
Glenshane
Pass
Portglenone
Gracehill
Ballymena
Slemish
(438m)
Larne
Ballygally
Portmuck
Mullaghmore
(554m)
Maghera
Mt Sawel
(678m)
Draperstown
Magherafelt
Randalstown
Kells
ANTRIM
Ballynure
Ballyclare
Larne
Lough
Whitehead
Sperrin
Cranagh
Slieve Gallion
(528m)
Moneymore
Ballyronan
Antrim
Newtownabbey
Carrickfergus
Bangor
Donaghadee
Cookstown
Creggan
Coagh
Lough
Neagh
Crumlin
Belfast
Holywood
Millisle
Pomeroy
NORTHERN
IRELAND
Coalisland
Dungannon
Dunmurry
Lisburn
Comber
Newtownards
Ballywalter
Greyabbey
Ballyhalbert
Castlecaulfield
Ballygawley
Moy
Benburb
Aughnacloy
Portadown
Lurgan
Craigavon
Loughgall
Moira
Hillsborough
Dromore
Saintfield
Killyleagh
Ballynahinch
Strangford
Lough
Portavogie
Cloghy
Portaferry
Strangford
Armagh
Emyvale
Caledon
Killylea
Glaslough
Tandragee
Markethill
Banbridge
Finnis
Seaforde
Clough
Kilclief
Downpatrick
Monaghan
Keady
ARMAGH
Castlewellan
Tyrella
Ardglass
Killough
DOWN
MONAGHAN
Newbliss
Newtownhamilton
Camlough
Newry
Hilltown
Mourne
Mountains
Slieve Donard
(848m)
Newcastle
Annalong
Ballybay
Castleblayney
Meigh
Forkhill
Atticall
Rostrevor
Ballymartin
Cootehill
Shantonagh
Kilkeel
Carlingford
Shercock
Inniskeen
Dundalk
Carrickmacross
LOUTH
Dundalk
Bay
Irish
Sea
CAVAN
Bailieborough
Tallanstown
Kingscourt
Ardee
Castlebellingham
Annagassan

See Eastern Ireland
Map pp98–9

NORTHERN IRELAND HIGHLIGHTS

1 | THE COASTAL CAUSEWAY ROUTE

BY JASON POWELL, CAUSEWAY COASTS & GLENS TOURISM

There is nothing better than driving along on a sunny day with the green Glens of Antrim on your left and the Irish Sea with views over to Scotland on your right, and as you turn each bend you get another spectacular view.

↘ JASON POWELL'S DON'T MISS LIST

❶ GIANT'S CAUSEWAY

The **Giant's Causeway** (p332) is Northern Ireland's most popular attraction and my favourite place. The 40,000 basalt columns, the 400ft cliffs and the views all show the magnificence of Mother Nature. Best time to visit? When the weather is a bit stormy and the Atlantic waves crash in on the rocks!

❷ RATHLIN ISLAND

There is no better place to get away from it all than **Rathlin Island** (p334). Just 5 miles from Ballycastle, it is a world away from the mainland. There are only a few cars on the island so it is ideal for walking or cycling, and it is a great place to see seabirds – it is home to the largest seabird colony in Northern Ireland.

❸ MORTON'S FISH & CHIPS

Morton's (☎ 028-2076 1100; 22 Bayview Rd, Ballycastle) is tiny but serves the best fish and chips around. You have to wait about 10 minutes as they make it all fresh, but once you have your order you can just sit out on the harbour and watch the fishing boats sailing around.

Clockwise from top: The Giant's Causeway (p332) at dusk; Ess-na-Larach Waterfall, Glenariff Forest Park (p335); Rock formations at the Giant's Causeway (p332); Rathlin Island (p334) as seen from Fair Head

❹ GLENARIFF FOREST PARK

Glenariff Forest Park (p335) is a great place to get back to nature, with great walks that take you past three wonderful waterfalls. As you get to the higher ground you will reach some magnificent mountain viewpoints.

❺ NORTH WEST 200

When I first stood at the grid of the **North West 200** (see p47), with the bikes revving ready to go, I could feel the tension and adrenalin of the country's biggest sporting event. The noise was unbelievable; I could feel the vibrations going right through my body. At that moment I was converted.

❶ Giant's Causeway
❷ Rathlin Island
❸ Morton's Fish & Chips
❹ Glenariff Forest Park
❺ North West 200

0 ——————— 20 km
0 ——————— 10 miles

➘ THINGS YOU NEED TO KNOW

Best time to visit April to September **Advance planning** Book your accommodation early, especially around the time of the North West 200 (www.northwest200.org)

NORTHERN IRELAND HIGHLIGHTS

2 THE BOGSIDE, DERRY

BY TOM KELLY, KEVIN HASSON & WILLIAM KELLY, BOGSIDE ARTISTS

The Bogside is our home, and always had a medieval character about it, with the Church at the centre of the community and St Columb's College in the heart of it. Yet after 30 years of conflict, the Bogside is returning to the type of community that we all thought had disappeared for good.

↘ THE BOGSIDE ARTISTS' DON'T MISS LIST

❶ THE PEOPLE'S GALLERY
Our murals are the result of a vision from the start to tell our story in the form of a simple but edifying panorama, not just for locals but for anyone. The People's Gallery is without doubt the number one attraction in the Bogside.

❷ FREE DERRY CORNER GABLE-END
The gable-end is a significant feature of the Bogside. Its slogan was derived from Berkeley's famous 'You Are Now

Entering Free Berkeley' and for years many people came forward to claim the inspired idea to be originally theirs! Still, it is a site of great importance for Bogsiders as a moment in their history captured forever.

❸ BLOODY SUNDAY MEMORIAL
This memorial lists the names of the 14 victims killed on 30 January 1972 by British soldiers and is situated close to where most of the victims were killed. It is visited by countless tourists each

Clockwise from top: Houses in the Bogside (p338) ; *Petrol Bomber* mural, People's Gallery (p339); City walls, Derry (p337); Political mural, Bogside; *Operation Motorman* mural, People's Gallery (p339)

year and wreaths are often laid there on commemorative occasions.

❹ LONG TOWER CHAPEL

The Long Tower is a true Bogside landmark: so many local people were baptised and married there. The pews and very bricks of the building have been sanctified by the sufferings and anguish of Bogside Catholics during the Troubles. If the walls could speak, they would moan.

❺ THE PETROL BOMBER MURAL

Originally titled 'The Battle of the Bogside', our first mural was created to commemorate the events of August 1969, one of the first major confrontations of the Troubles. The mural shows

a young boy in a gas mask – which he used to try to protect himself from the CS gas (tear gas) used by the Royal Ulster Constabulary – holding a petrol bomb.

⬦ THINGS YOU NEED TO KNOW

Best time to visit Any time! **Security concerns** None at all – despite its troubled past, the Bogside is safe and well explored by visitors curious about the place **Resources** Bogside Artists' own website (www.bogsideartists. com) **For full details on the Bogside, see p338.**

NORTHERN IRELAND HIGHLIGHTS

☄ THE ANTRIM COAST

It's a no-brainer, but the number one tourist destination in Northern Ireland deserves all of the kudos it gets. The **Antrim coast** (p330), though, is about more than just coastline: from the intoxicating charms of the **Bushmills Distillery** (p331) to the more sedate pleasures of **Rathlin Island** (p334), there's something for everyone. Oh, and let's not forget the **Giant's Causeway** (p332).

☄ WEST BELFAST

For more than three decades **West Belfast** (p323) was synonymous with violence, sectarianism and the politics of hatred. Though divisions remain entrenched, the violence has long since abated and the Shankill and Falls communities are openly welcoming of visitors, who can witness firsthand the extraordinary regeneration of communities that not so long ago were literally dying on their feet.

5

⬆ HISTORIC DERRY

Northern Ireland's second city, Derry (p335) is second to none in terms of history and character. Highlights are a walk around the historic walls of Ireland's only surviving walled city and an exploration of the storied Bogside district, which, like West Belfast, was at the heart of the Troubles but is in the midst of restoring itself and its battered community.

6

⬆ MOURNE MOUNTAINS

One of Northern Ireland's most magnificent corners is the hump-backed granite hills of the Mourne Mountains (p329), flecked with yellow gorse and dotted with whitewashed cottages and dry-stone walls. Some of the province's best walking is in these gentle hills, especially around the magnificent Silent Valley Reservoir.

7

⬆ CARRICK-A-REDE ROPE BRIDGE

There are many superb activities to be done in Northern Ireland, but none is quite as breathtaking or as frightening (depending on your acrophobia) as walking across the 20 swaying metres of the Carrick-a-Rede Rope Bridge (p333) to the eponymous island. It's a short, stunning clamber that will linger long in your memory.

3 & 4 RICHARD CUMMINS; 5 KEVIN O'HARA/PHOTOLIBRARY; 6 & 7 GARETH MCCORMACK

3 Giant's Causeway rock formations (p332); 4 Political mural, West Belfast (p323); 5 City walls, Derry (p337); 6 Hiker in the Mourne Mountains (p329); 7 Carrick-a-Rede rope bridge (p333), County Antrim;

NORTHERN IRELAND

NORTHERN IRELAND'S BEST...

NORTHERN IRELAND'S BEST...

⬏ SPOTS TO LAY YOUR HEAD

- **Malmaison Hotel** (p305) Belfast's snazziest digs.
- **Briers Country House** (p328) Farmhouse B&B with fab views.
- **Merchant's House** (p339) Derry's best historic Georgian townhouse.
- **Whitepark House B&B** (p333) Eighteenth-century town house filled with Asian gewgaws.

⬏ CULTURAL STOPS

- **Ulster Folk Museum** (p328) Brings to life the stories of 18th- and 19th-century local folk.
- **Ulster Transport Museum** (p328) See the ill-fated DeLorean car.
- **Bushmills Distillery** (p331) A fine Irish whiskey.
- **Ormeau Baths Gallery** (p322) The North's top modern art gallery.
- **Museum of Free Derry** (p339) One of the best political museums in Europe.

⬏ BITES

- **Deane's Restaurant** (p325) Michael Deane has Northern Ireland's only Michelin star.
- **Cellar Restaurant** (p334) Top spot for local produce.
- **Mourne Seafood Bar** (p325) Enormously popular restaurant looks like a ramshackle pub.
- **55 Degrees North** (p331) Great food and great views have made this place famous.
- **Bushmills Inn Restaurant** (p331) Excellent restaurant attached to the renowned distillery.

⬏ SCENIC WALKS

- **Mourne Mountains** (p329) The best walks in the province.
- **Cushendun** (p335) Bracing coastal walks.
- **Glenariff Forest Park** (p335) Beautiful forest trails.
- **Derry City Walls** (p337) Walk the length of the 16th-century walls.

LEFT: GARETH MCCORMACK; RIGHT: GARETH MCCORMACK

Left: Hiker in the Mourne Mountains (p329); Right: Belfast (p320)

THINGS YOU NEED TO KNOW

➤ VITAL STATISTICS

- **Area** 13,843 sq km
- **Population** 1,775,000
- **Best time to go** Summer is best, except the days leading up to and including 12 July, when sectarian tensions are inflamed and the possibility of community clashes increase during the infamous 'marching season'.

➤ AREAS IN A NUTSHELL

- **Belfast** (p320) A metropolis growing in confidence and distractions after years of living under a violent shadow.
- **County Antrim** (p330) Scenic coastline stretching virtually the entire length of the north of the province, from just north of Belfast to just east of Derry.
- **Derry/Londonderry** (p335) The province's second city has a more intimate character and plenty of history.

➤ ADVANCE PLANNING

- **Two months before** Book your accommodation, especially along the Antrim Coast.
- **One month before** Read a book on Northern Ireland's turbulent history.
- **Two weeks before** Make reservations for the province's top restaurants.

➤ RESOURCES

- **Discover Northern Ireland** (www. discovernorthernireland.com) The official website of the Northern Ireland Tourism Bureau.
- **Antrim** (www.countyantrim.com) Attractions, accommodation and restaurants in Antrim.
- **Belfast Tourism** (www.gotobelfast. com) The Belfast Welcome Centre.
- **Derry Tourism** (www.derryvisitor.com) The city's official website.

➤ GETTING AROUND

- **Bus** Excellent regional service on all main routes linking all towns and cities.
- **Train** Good between Belfast and Derry, and serving the Antrim Coast.
- **Car** Probably the easiest way of getting around.

➤ BE FOREWARNED

- **Sectarianism** Broad divisions still exist, especially in so-called 'interface' areas in parts of Belfast; these are best avoided, as is most of the province, around the days of 11–12 July, when Loyalists march throughout the province.
- **Seasonal tourism** Many hotels and restaurants shut down between December and Easter, especially in rural areas and along parts of the coast. Everything remains open in the cities.

NORTHERN IRELAND

THINGS YOU NEED TO KNOW

NORTHERN IRELAND ITINERARIES

BEST OF BELFAST Three Days

This itinerary is all about the province's capital and biggest city, (1) Belfast (p320). Start your visit with a free, guided tour of City Hall (p322). Take a black taxi tour of the West Belfast murals (p325), then ask the taxi driver to drop you off at the John Hewitt Bar & Restaurant (p326) for lunch. Catch a Titanic Tour (p324) boat trip around the harbour, then walk across to cover the Titanic Trail (p322). Round off the day with dinner at Deane's Restaurant (p325). On your second day get outside the city centre, visiting the (2) Ulster Folk and Transport Museums (p3280), which includes the original design drawings for the world's most famous doomed ocean liner. On your return take in a meal at the superb Mourne Seafood Bar (p325). On your final day, head to where the Mourne Seafood Bar gets all its fresh catch by visiting the seaside resort town of (3) Newcastle (p328) and, if you fancy something a little more energetic, you can go for a nice walk in the (4) Mourne Mountains (p329).

THE ANTRIM COAST Five Days

Most visitors naturally make their way to the Antrim coast, the province's number one tourist destination and favourite of many locals. You could drive it in a couple of hours but this five-day itinerary is all about taking a bit of time to enjoy it. Start north of Belfast at the (1) Glens of Antrim (p335), taking time to walk in (2) Glenariff Forest Park (p335), before driving north to the seaside village of (3) Cushendun (p335), famous for its National Trust Cornish-style cottages. Take the (4) Torr Head Scenic Road (p335) to Ballycastle, from which you can explore the bird sanctuary of (5) Rathlin Island (p334) and, if you're up for it, make the short but devilishly challenging crossing to (6) Carrick-a-Rede Island (p333), for which you'll need real sea legs! Your next stop is the historic town of (7) Bushmills (p331), home of the famous distillery that should be a highlight of a visit here. And, finally, you'll get to clamber across the most famous site in all of Northern Ireland, the (8) Giant's Causeway (p332).

NORTHERN IRELAND NUTSHELL One Week

Northern Ireland is not especially big, so you can see pretty much everything worth seeing in a week. The historic city of (1) Derry (p335) could keep you occupied for that amount of time and more, but three days is plenty to explore its historic walls (p337), thriving city centre and the world-famous Bogside (p338), which has finally re-emerged from the shadow of violence to become one of Europe's most inter-

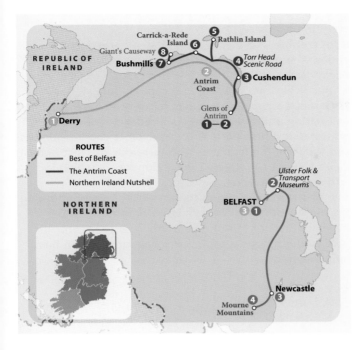

esting examples of how a community restores itself after decades of war. Although it's only a two-hour drive to Belfast, take your time on the (2) Antrim coast (p330), taking in all or some of the attractions in the previous itinerary. Finally, when you get to (3) Belfast (p320) be sure to contrast your experiences of the exclusively Catholic and Nationalist Bogside with the two communities of West Belfast (p323) – the Loyalist and Protestant Shankill and the Nationalist Falls.

DISCOVER NORTHERN IRELAND

Once a byword for trouble, Northern Ireland has emerged from nearly four decades of sectarian conflict to finally take its place as one of the loveliest corners of the island, with as much to offer as any of Ireland's tourist havens. The regional capital, Belfast, has shrugged off its bomb-scarred past and has reinvented itself as one of the most exciting and dynamic cities in Britain – of which Northern Ireland remains a firm part. You can explore the tensions as they're expressed today in the iconic neighbourhoods of West Belfast or in the province's second city, Derry (or Londonderry), which is leading the North's cultural revival.

And it wouldn't be Ireland if it didn't have its fair share of stunning landscapes: from the Antrim coast and its world-famous Giant's Causeway to the mountains of Mourne in south County Down, Northern Ireland's credentials as a top-class scenic destination have once again been cemented.

BELFAST

Once lumped with Beirut, Baghdad and Bosnia as one the four 'B's for travellers to avoid, Belfast has pulled off a remarkable transformation from bombs-and-bullets pariah to hip-hotels-and-hedonism party town.

INFORMATION

Belfast Welcome Centre (☎ 028-9024 6609; www.gotobelfast.com; 47 Donegall Pl; ☺ 9am-7pm Mon-Sat, 11am-4pm Sun Jun-Sep, 9am-5.30pm Mon-Sat, 11am-4pm Sun Oct-May) Provides information about the whole of Northern Ireland, and books accommodation anywhere in Ireland and Britain. Services include left luggage (not overnight), currency exchange and internet access.

Cultúrlann McAdam Ó Fiaich (☎ 028-9096 4188; 216 Falls Rd; ☺ 9.30am-5.30pm Mon-Fri) This cultural centre (p324) in West Belfast has a tourist information desk.

Fáilte Ireland (Irish Tourist Board; ☎ 028-9026 5500; www.ireland.ie; 53 Castle St; ☺ 9am-5pm Mon-Fri year-round, 9am-12.30pm Sat

Jun-Aug) Can book accommodation in the Republic of Ireland.

Tourist information desks George Best Belfast City Airport (☎ 028-9093 5372; ☺ 8am-7pm Mon-Sat, 8am-5pm Sun); Belfast International Airport (☎ 028-9448 4677; ☺ 7.30am-7pm Mon-Sat, 8am-5pm Sun)

DANGERS & ANNOYANCES

Even at the height of the Troubles, Belfast wasn't a particularly dangerous city for tourists, and today you're less at risk from crime here than you are in London. It's best, however, to avoid the so-called 'interface areas' – near the peace lines in West Belfast, Crumlin Rd and the Short Strand (just east of Queen's Bridge) – after dark; if in doubt about any area, ask at your hotel or hostel.

One irritating legacy of the Troubles is the absence of left-luggage facilities at bus and train stations. You will also notice a more obvious security presence than elsewhere in the UK and Ireland, in the form of armoured police Land

BELFAST

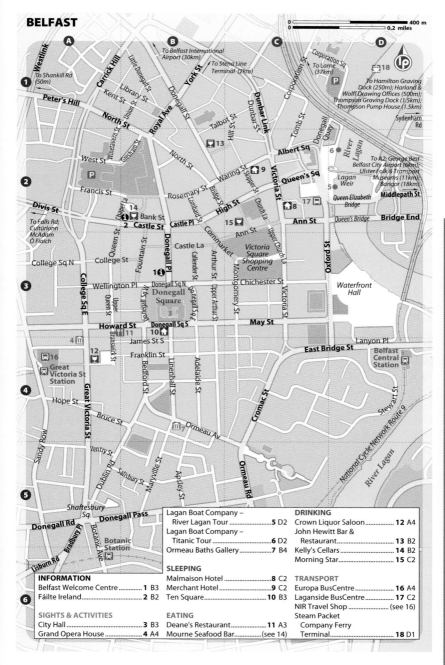

Lagan Boat Company – River Lagan Tour	**5** D2
Lagan Boat Company – Titanic Tour	**6** D2
Ormeau Baths Gallery	**7** B4

SLEEPING

Malmaison Hotel	**8** C2
Merchant Hotel	**9** C2
Ten Square	**10** B3

INFORMATION

Belfast Welcome Centre	**1** B3
Fáilte Ireland	**2** B2

SIGHTS & ACTIVITIES

City Hall	**3** B3
Grand Opera House	**4** A4

EATING

Deane's Restaurant	**11** A3
Mourne Seafood Bar	(see 14)

DRINKING

Crown Liquor Saloon	**12** A4
John Hewitt Bar & Restaurant	**13** B2
Kelly's Cellars	**14** B2
Morning Star	**15** C2

TRANSPORT

Europa BusCentre	**16** A4
Laganside BusCentre	**17** C2
NIR Travel Shop	(see 16)
Steam Packet Company Ferry Terminal	**18** D1

Rovers, fortified police stations, and security doors on some shops (mostly outside the city centre) where you have to press the buzzer to be allowed in. There are doormen on many city-centre shops and pubs.

If you want to take photos of fortified police stations, army posts or other military or quasi-military paraphernalia, get permission first, just to be on the safe side. In the Protestant and Catholic strongholds of West Belfast it's best not to photograph people without permission; always ask first and be prepared to accept a refusal. Taking pictures of the murals is not a problem.

SIGHTS
CITY HALL

The Industrial Revolution transformed Belfast in the 19th century, and its rapid rise to muck-and-brass prosperity is manifested in the extravagance of City Hall (☎ 028-9027 0456; www.belfastcity.gov. uk; Donegall Sq; admission free; ☺ guided tours 11am, 2pm & 3pm Mon-Fri, 2pm & 3pm Sat). Built in classical Renaissance style in fine, white Portland stone, it was completed in 1906 and paid for from the profits of the gas supply company. It is equipped with facilities for the disabled.

GRAND OPERA HOUSE

One of Belfast's great Victorian landmarks is the Grand Opera House (☎ 028-9024 1919; www.goh.co.uk; Great Victoria St; guided tours adult/child £5/3; ☺ tours by arrangement), across the road from the Crown Liquor Saloon. Opened in 1895, and completely refurbished in the 1970s, it suffered grievously at the hands of the IRA, having sustained severe bomb damage in 1991 and 1993. It was said that as the Europa Hotel next door was the home of the media during the Troubles, the IRA brought the bombs

to them so they wouldn't have to leave the bar.

ORMEAU BATHS GALLERY

Housed in a converted 19th-century public bathhouse, the Ormeau Baths Gallery (☎ 028-9032 1402; www.ormeaubaths.co.uk; 18a Ormeau Ave; admission free; ☺ 10am-5.30pm Tue-Sat) is Northern Ireland's principal exhibition space for contemporary visual art. The gallery stages changing exhibitions of work by Irish and international artists, and has hosted controversial showings of works by Gilbert and George, and Jake and Dinos Chapman. The gallery is a few blocks south of Donegall Sq.

TITANIC TRAIL

Queen's Rd strikes northeast from the Odyssey Complex into the heart of the Titanic Quarter, a massive redevelopment area that is part industrial wasteland, part building site and part high-tech business park. Not much remains of the time when the RMS *Titanic* was built, but a series of information boards along Queen's Rd point out items of interest.

You can hire a hand-held multimedia device from the Belfast Welcome Centre, which leads you on a self-guided walking tour of the Titanic Trail (☎ 028-9024 6609; per device for up to 3hr £8), complete with GPS technology, audio commentary and video presentations.

First up is the Hamilton Graving Dock, which is slated to be the permanent mooring for the SS Nomadic (☎ 028-9027 7652; www.nomadicbelfast.com) – the only surviving vessel of the White Star Line, the shipping company that owned the *Titanic*. In 2006 she was rescued from the breaker's yard and brought to Belfast. The little steamship, which once served as a tender ferrying 1st- and 2nd-class passengers between Cherbourg Harbour and the giant

Grand Opera House facade, Belfast

DOUG MCKINLAY

Olympic Class ocean liners (which were too big to dock at the French port), was undergoing restoration work in Barnett Dock at the time of research, but should have moved to Hamilton Dock and be open to the public by summer 2010.

Just along the road are the original **Harland and Wolff Drawing Offices**, where the designs for the *Titanic* were first drawn up (not open to the public); behind them, and best seen from a boat tour on the river, are the two massive **slipways** where the *Titanic* and her sister ship, the *Olympic*, were built and launched.

A few hundred metres further on you'll reach the most impressive monument to the days of the great liners – the huge **Thompson Graving Dock** where the *Titanic* was fitted out. Its vast size gives you some idea of the scale of the ship, which could only just fit into it. Beside the dock is the **Thompson Pump House** (☎ 028-9073 7813; www.titanicsdock.com; admission free, guided tour £5; ☽ visitor centre 10.30am-4pm, tours 11am & 2pm), which houses an exhibition on Belfast shipbuilding, and a

cafe. The guided tour includes a video of original film footage from the shipyards, and a visit to the inner workings of the pump house and dock.

In the dock on the far side of the pump house, naval history buffs can ogle **HMS Caroline**, a WWI Royal Navy cruiser built in 1914, and now serving as a Royal Naval Reserve training ship (not open to the public).

WEST BELFAST (GAELTACHT QUARTER)

Though scarred by three decades of civil unrest, the former battleground of West Belfast is one of the most compelling places to visit in Northern Ireland. Recent history hangs heavy in the air, but there is a noticeable air of optimism and hope for the future.

The main attractions are the powerful murals that chart the history of the conflict as well as the political passions of the moment, and for visitors from mainland Britain there is a grim fascination to be found in wandering through the former 'war zone' in their own backyard.

Despite its past reputation, the area is safe to visit. The best way to see West Belfast is on a black taxi tour (see p325). The cabs visit the more spectacular murals as well as the Peace Line (where you can write a message on the wall) and other significant sites, while the drivers provide a colourful commentary on the history of the area.

There's nothing to stop you visiting under your own steam, either walking or using the shared black taxis along Falls or Shankill Rds. Alternatively, buses 10A to 10F from Queen St will take you along Falls Rd; buses 11A to 11D from Wellington Pl go along Shankill Rd.

You can also pick up a range of free leaflets at the Belfast Welcome Centre that describe walking tours around the Falls and Shankill districts.

FALLS ROAD
Although the signs of past conflict are in-escapable, the Falls today is an unexpect-edly lively, colourful and optimistic place. Local people are friendly and welcoming, and community ventures such as Conway Mill, the Cultúrlann centre and black taxi tours have seen tourist numbers increase dramatically.

SHANKILL ROAD
Although the Protestant Shankill district (from the Irish *sean chill,* meaning 'old church') has received less media and tour-ist attention than the Falls, it also contains many interesting murals. The people here are just as friendly, but the Shankill has far fewer tourists than the Falls. Loyalist communities seem to have more difficulty in presenting their side of the story than the Republicans, who have a far more pol-ished approach to public relations.

TOURS
Lagan Boat Company (☎ 028-9033 0844; www.laganboatcompany.com; adult/child/family £10/8/28) offers two 1¼-hour boat tours: the **River Lagan Tour** (☻ 2pm & 3.30pm Mon, 12.30pm, 2pm & 3.30pm Sat & Sun Jun-Sep,

Taxi drivers, Belfast

MARTIN MOOS

12.30pm & 2pm Sat & Sun Oct) heads upstream to Stranmillis, departing from the Lagan Lookout, while the excellent **Titanic Tour** (12.30pm, 2pm & 3.30pm daily Apr-Sep, 12.30pm & 2pm Oct, Sat & Sun only Nov, Feb & Mar) explores the derelict docklands downstream of the weir, taking in the slipways where the liners *Titanic* and *Olympic* were launched and the huge dry dock where they could fit with just nine inches to spare. The Titanic Tour departs from Donegall Quay near the *Bigfish* sculpture.

Black taxi tours of the murals of West Belfast – known as the 'bombs and bullets' or 'doom and gloom' tours – are offered by a large number of taxi companies and local cabbies. They can vary in quality and content, but in general are an intimate and entertaining way to see the sights and can be customised to suit your own interests. There are also historical taxi tours of the city centre. For a one-hour tour expect to pay from £25 total for one or two people, and £10 per person for three to six people. Call and they will pick you up from anywhere in the city centre.

The following are recommended:
Harpers Taxi Tours (07711 757178; www.harperstaxitours.co.nr)
Official Black Taxi Tours (028-9064 2264, toll-free 0800 052 3914; www.belfasttours.com)
Original Belfast Black Taxi Tours (07751 565359)

SLEEPING

our pick **Malmaison Hotel** (028-9022 0200; www.malmaison-belfast.com; 34-38 Victoria St; r from £95, ste from £315;) Housed in a pair of beautifully restored Italianate warehouses (originally built for rival firms in the 1850s), the Malmaison is a luxurious haven of king-size beds, deep leather sofas and roll-top baths big enough for two, all done up in a decadent decor of black, red, dark chocolate and cream. The massive, rock-star Samson suite has a giant bed (almost 3m long), a bathtub big enough for two and, wait for it…a billiard table. With purple baize.

Merchant Hotel (028-9023 4888; www.themerchanthotel.com; 35-39 Waring St; r/ste from £160/240;) Belfast's most flamboyant Victorian building, the old Ulster Bank head office, has been converted into the city's most flamboyant boutique hotel, a fabulous fusion of old-fashioned elegance and contemporary styling.

Ten Square (028-9024 1001; www.tensquare.co.uk; 10 Donegall Sq S; r from £170;) This former bank building to the south of City Hall has been given a designer feng-shui makeover: Ten Square is an opulent, Shanghai-inspired boutique hotel with friendly and attentive service. Magazines such as *Cosmopolitan* and *Condé Nast Traveller* drool over the dark lacquered wood, cream carpets, low-slung futon-style beds and sumptuous linen, and the list of former guests includes Bono, Moby and Brad Pitt.

EATING

Mourne Seafood Bar (028-9024 8544; 34-36 Bank St; mains £10-17; noon-6pm Mon, noon-9.30pm Tue & Wed, noon-10.30pm Thu-Sat, 1-6pm Sun) This informal, publike place, all red brick and dark wood with old oil lamps dangling from the ceiling, is tucked behind a fishmonger's shop, so the seafood is as fresh as it gets. On the menu are oysters served au naturel or Rockefeller, meltingly sweet scallops, lobster, langoustines, gurnard and John Dory. Hugely popular, so best book ahead, especially on Sunday.

Deane's Restaurant (028-9033 1134; 34-40 Howard St; mains £15-23, 2-/3-course lunch £18/22; noon-2.30pm & 6-9.30pm Tue-Sat) Chef Michael Deane heads the kitchen in Northern Ireland's only Michelin-starred

RICHARD CUMMINS

Interior, Crown Liquor Saloon

restaurant, where he takes the best of Irish and British produce – beef, game, lamb, seafood – and gives it the gourmet treatment. Typical dishes include pan-fried scallops with apple black pudding, glazed pork belly and butternut squash purée, and saddle of rabbit wrapped in bacon with macaroni gratin, roast cep mushrooms and caramelised salsify. The ultra-cool dining room is open plan and minimalist.

DRINKING

Crown Liquor Saloon (☎ 028-9024 9476; 46 Great Victoria St) Belfast's most famous bar has a wonderfully ornate Victorian interior. Despite being a tourist attraction, it still fills up with crowds of locals at lunchtime and in the early evening.

Morning Star (☎ 028-9023 5986; 17 Pottinger's Entry) One of several traditional pubs hidden away in the pedestrian alleys off High St, the Morning Star dates back to at least 1810 when it was mentioned in the *Belfast News Letter* as a terminal for the Dublin to Belfast stagecoach. It has

a big sweeping horseshoe bar, and cosy snugs for privacy.

our pick **John Hewitt Bar & Restaurant** (☎ 028-9023 3768; 51 Donegall St) Named for the Belfast poet and socialist, the John Hewitt is one of those treasured bars that has no TV and no gaming machines; the only noise here is the murmur of conversation. As well as Guinness, the bar serves Hilden real ales from nearby Lisburn, plus Hoegaarden and Erdinger wheat beers. There are regular sessions of folk, jazz and bluegrass from 9pm most nights.

GETTING THERE & AWAY
AIR

Flights from North America, continental Europe and several major UK airports land at **Belfast International Airport** (☎ 028-9448 4848; www.belfastairport.com; Aldergrove), 30km northwest of the city. For further information, see p405.

There are direct flights from Cork and most British cities to the convenient **George Best Belfast City Airport** (☎ 028-

9093 9093; www.belfastcityairport.com; Airport Rd), just 6km northeast of the city centre.

BOAT

The terminal for **Stena Line** (☎ 08705 707070; www.stenaline.co.uk) car ferries from Belfast to Stranraer in Scotland is 2km north of the city centre; head north along York St, and turn right into Dock St (just past the Yorkgate Centre). Other car ferries to and from Scotland dock at Larne, 37km north of Belfast.

Norfolkline (☎ 0844 499 0007; www.norfolkline-ferries.co.uk) ferries between Belfast and Liverpool dock at the Victoria Ferry Terminal, 5km north of town. Take the M2 motorway north and turn right at junction No 1.

The **Steam Packet Company** (☎ 0871 222 1333; www.steam-packet.com) operates car ferries between Belfast and the Isle of Man (two or three a week, April to September only). They dock at Donegall Quay, a short distance from the city centre.

For more information on ferry routes and prices, see p407.

BUS

Belfast has two bus stations. The main **Europa BusCentre** (☎ 028-9066 6630) is behind the Europa Hotel and next door to Great Victoria St train station, reached via the Great Northern Mall beside the hotel. It's the main terminus for buses to Derry, Dublin and destinations in the west and south of Northern Ireland. The smaller **Laganside BusCentre** (☎ 028-9066 6630; Oxford St), near the river, is mainly for buses to County Antrim, eastern County Down and the Cookstown area.

There are **information desks** (⏱ 7.45am-6.30pm Mon-Fri, 8am-6pm Sat) at both bus stations, where you can pick up regional bus timetables, and you can contact **Translink**

(☎ 028-9066 6630; www.translink.co.uk) for timetable and fares information.

TRAIN

Trains to Dublin and all destinations in Northern Ireland depart from **Belfast Central Station** (East Bridge St), east of the city centre. **Great Victoria St Station** (Great Northern Mall), next to the Europa BusCentre, has trains for Portadown, Lisburn, Bangor, Larne Harbour and Derry.

For information on train fares and timetables, contact **Translink** (☎ 028-9066 6630; www.translink.co.uk). The **NIR Travel Shop** (☎ 028-9023 0671; Great Victoria St Station; ⏱ 9am-5pm Mon-Fri, to 12.30pm Sat) books train tickets, ferries and holiday packages.

If you arrive by train at Central Station, your rail ticket entitles you to a free bus ride into the city centre.

GETTING AROUND
TO/FROM THE AIRPORTS

The Airport Express 300 bus runs from Belfast International Airport to the Europa BusCentre (one way/return £7/10, 30 minutes) every 10 or 15 minutes between 7am and 8pm, every 30 minutes from 8pm to 11pm, and hourly through the night; a return ticket is valid for one month. A taxi costs about £25.

The Airport Express 600 bus links George Best Belfast City Airport with the Europa BusCentre (one way/return £1.50/2.60, 15 minutes) every 15 or 20 minutes between 6am and 10pm. The taxi fare to the city centre is about £7.

TO/FROM THE FERRY TERMINALS

You can walk from Donegall Quay to City Hall in about 15 minutes. Alternatively, Laganside BusCentre is only a five-minute walk away. There is no public transport to the Stena Line and Norfolk Line ferry terminals.

Trains to the ferry terminal at Larne Harbour depart from Great Victoria St Station.

AROUND BELFAST
ULSTER FOLK & TRANSPORT MUSEUMS

Two of Northern Ireland's finest **museums** (☎ 028-9042 8428; www.uftm.org.uk; Cultra, Holywood; per museum adult/child £5.40/3.40, combined ticket £6.80/3.90; ☉ 10am-6pm Mon-Sat, 11am-6pm Sun Jul-Sep, 10am-4pm Mon-Fri, 10am-5pm Sat, 11am-5pm Sun Oct-Feb, 10am-5pm Mon-Fri, 10am-6pm Sat, 11am-6pm Sun Mar-Jun) lie close to each other on either side of the A2.

On the south side is the Folk Museum, where farmhouses, forges, churches and mills, and a complete village have been reconstructed, with human and animal extras combining to give a strong impression of Irish life over the past few hundred years. From industrial times, there are red-brick terraces from 19th-century Belfast and Dromore. In summer, thatching and ploughing are demonstrated and there are characters dressed in period costume.

On the other side of the road is the Transport Museum, a sort of automotive zoo with displays of captive steam locomotives, rolling stock, motorcycles, trams, buses and cars.

The highlight of the car collection is the stainless steel-clad prototype of the ill-fated DeLorean DMC, made in Belfast in 1981. The car was a commercial disaster but achieved fame in the *Back to the Future* films.

Most popular is the RMS *Titanic* **display** (www.titanicinbelfast.com), which includes the original design drawings for the *Olympic* and *Titanic,* photographs of the *Titanic's*

construction and reports of its sinking. Most poignant are the items of pre-sailing publicity, including an ad for the return trip that never was.

Buses to Bangor stop nearby. Cultra Station on the Belfast to Bangor train line is within a 10-minute walk.

SOUTH DOWN & THE MOURNE MOUNTAINS
NEWCASTLE

pop 7500

In recent years the Victorian seaside resort of Newcastle (An Caisleán Nua) has undergone a multimillion-pound makeover, and now sports a snazzy new promenade, stretching for more than 1km along the seafront, complete with modern sculptures and an elegant footbridge over the Shimna River. The facelift makes the most of Newcastle's superb setting on a 5km strand of golden sand at the foot of the Mourne Mountains, and there are hopes that it will transform the town's fortunes from fading bucket-and-spade resort to outdoor activities capital and gateway to the proposed Mourne National Park.

The **tourist information centre** (☎ 028-4372 2222; newcastle.tic@downdc.gov.uk; 10-14 Central Promenade; ☉ 9.30am-7pm Mon-Sat, 1-7pm Sun Jul & Aug, 10am-5pm Mon-Sat, 2-6pm Sun Sep-Jun) sells local-interest books and maps, and a range of traditional and contemporary crafts.

Newcastle's main attraction is the **beach**, which stretches 5km northeast to **Murlough National Nature Reserve** (admission free, car park May-Sep £3; ☉ 24hr), where footpaths and boardwalks meander among the grassy dunes, with great views back towards the Mournes.

Briers Country House (☎ 028-4372 4347; www.thebriers.co.uk; 39 Middle Tollymore Rd; s/d from £40/60; ℗) A peaceful farmhouse B&B with a country setting and views of the

RICHARD CUMMINS

Exhibit at the Ulster Transport Museum

Mournes, Briers is just 1.5km northwest of the town centre (signposted off the road between Newcastle and Bryansford). Huge breakfasts – vegetarian if you like – are served with a view over the garden, and evening meals are available by prior arrangement.

The bus station is on Railway St. Ulsterbus 20 runs to Newcastle from Belfast's Europa BusCentre (£7, 1¼ hours, at least hourly Monday to Saturday, eight Sunday) via Dundrum. Bus 37 continues along the coast road from Newcastle to Annalong and Kilkeel (£4, 35 minutes, hourly Monday to Saturday, eight Sunday).

Goldline Express bus 240 takes the inland route from Newry to Newcastle (£5, 50 minutes, six daily Monday to Saturday, two Sunday) via Hilltown and continues on to Downpatrick. You can also get to Newry along the coast road, changing buses at Kilkeel.

MOURNE MOUNTAINS

The humpbacked granite hills of the Mourne Mountains dominate the horizon as you head south from Belfast towards Newcastle. This is one of the most beautiful corners of Northern Ireland, with a distinctive landscape of yellow gorse, grey granite and whitewashed cottages, the lower slopes of the hills latticed with a neat patchwork of drystone walls cobbled together from huge, rounded granite boulders.

The Mournes offer some of the best hill walking and rock climbing in the North. Specialist guidebooks include *The Mournes: Walks* by Paddy Dillon and *A Rock-Climbing Guide to the Mourne Mountains* by Robert Bankhead. You'll also need an Ordnance Survey map, either the 1:50,000 Discoverer Series (Sheet No 29: *The Mournes*), or the 1:25,000 Activity Series *(The Mournes)*. You can buy maps at the tourist information centre in Newcastle.

SIGHTS

At the heart of the Mournes is the beautiful **Silent Valley Reservoir** (☎ 08457 440088; car/motorcycle £4.50/2, plus per adult/ child £1.60/0.60; ⏱ 10am-6.30pm Apr-Oct,

Portrush Harbour

STEPHEN SAKS

10am-4pm Nov-Mar), where the Kilkeel River was dammed in 1933. There are scenic, waymarked walks around the grounds, a **coffee shop** (⊙ 11am-5.30pm Sat & Sun Apr-Sep) and an interesting exhibition on the building of the dam. From the car park a shuttle bus (adult/child return £1.40/1) will take you another 4km up the valley to the Crom Dam. It runs daily in July and August, weekends only in May, June and September.

GETTING THERE & AWAY
In July and August only, the Ulsterbus 405 Mourne Rambler service runs a circular route from Newcastle, calling at a dozen stops around the Mournes, including Bryansford (eight minutes), Meelmore (17 minutes), Silent Valley (40 minutes), Carrick Little (45 minutes) and Bloody Bridge (one hour). There are six buses daily – the first leaves at 9.30am, the last at 5pm; a £5 all-day ticket allows you to get on and off as many times as you like.

Bus 34A (July and August only) runs from Newcastle to the Silent Valley car park (45 minutes, two daily), calling at Donard Park (five minutes) and Bloody Bridge (10 minutes).

COUNTY ANTRIM
PORTRUSH
pop 6300

The bustling seaside resort of Portrush (Port Rois) is bursting at the seams with holidaymakers in high season and, not surprisingly, many of its attractions are focused unashamedly on good, old-fashioned family fun. However, it is also one of Ireland's top surfing centres, and is home to the North's hottest nightclub.

The **tourist information centre** (☎ 028-7082 3333; portrushtic@btconnect.com; Dunluce Centre, 10 Sandhill Dr; ⊙ 9am-7pm Jul & Aug, 9am-5pm Mon-Fri, noon-5pm Sat & Sun Apr-Jun & Sep, noon-5pm Sat & Sun Mar & Oct) books accommodation and has a bureau de change.

Portrush's main attraction is the beautiful sandy beach of **Curran Strand** that stretches for 3km to the east of the town, ending at the scenic chalk cliffs of White Rocks.

The town is also famous for **Barry's** (☎ 028-7082 2340; www.barrysamusements. com; 16 Eglinton St; admission free, per ride £0.50-2; ☼ 12.30-10.30pm Jul & Aug, 10am-6pm Mon-Fri, 12.30-10.30pm Sat, 12.30-9.30pm Sun Jun, 12.30-10.30pm Sat, 12.30-9.30pm Sun Apr & May), Ireland's biggest amusement park, filled with classic, family-friendly rides, including a carousel, ghost train and dodgems.

One of the north coast's most stylish restaurants, **55 Degrees North** (☎ 028-7082 2811; 1 Causeway St; mains £11-16; ☼ 5-9pm Mon-Sat, 12.30-2.30pm & 5-7.30pm Sun) boasts a wall of floor-to-ceiling windows allowing diners to soak up a spectacular panorama of sand and sea. The food is excellent, concentrating on clean, simple flavours and unfussy presentation, with dishes such as grilled sea bass with new potatoes and leek and chorizo cream. There's an early-bird menu (mains £7 to £9) available before 7pm.

BUSHMILLS

pop 1350

The small town of Bushmills has long been a place of pilgrimage for connoisseurs of Irish whiskey. A good youth hostel and a restored rail link with the Giant's Causeway have also made it an attractive stop for hikers exploring the Causeway Coast.

Bushmills Distillery (☎ 028-2073 3218; www.bushmills.com; Distillery Rd; adult/child £6/3; ☼ 9.15am-5pm Mon-Sat, noon-5pm Sun Apr-Oct, 9.15am-5pm Mon-Sat, noon-4pm Sun Mar, 9.30am-3.30pm Mon-Fri, 12.30-3.30pm Sat & Sun Nov-Feb) is the world's oldest legal distillery, having been granted a licence by King James I in 1608. Bushmills whiskey is made with Irish barley and water from St Columb's Rill, a tributary of the River Bush, and ma-

tured in oak barrels. During ageing, the alcohol content drops from around 60% to 40%; the spirit lost through evaporation is known, rather sweetly, as 'the angels' share'. After a tour of the distillery you're rewarded with a free sample (or a soft drink), and four lucky volunteers get a whiskey-tasting session to compare Bushmills with other brands. Tours begin every 30 minutes, and there's late opening (last tour 6pm) on Wednesday and Thursday in August.

The **Giant's Causeway & Bushmills Railway** (☎ 028-2073 2844; www.freewebs. com/giantscausewayrailway; adult/child return £6.75/4.75) follows the route of a 19th-century tourist tramway for 3km from Bushmills to below the Giant's Causeway visitor centre. The narrow-gauge line and locomotives (two steam and one diesel) were brought from a private line on the shores of Lough Neagh. Trains run hourly between 11am and 5.30pm, departing on the hour from the Causeway, on the half-hour from Bushmills, daily in July and August, weekends only from Easter to June, September and October.

The Bushmills Inn's excellent **restaurant** (lunch mains £7-12, dinner mains £15-20; ☼ noon-9.30pm Mon-Sat, 12.30-9pm Sun) features intimate wooden booths set in the old 17th-century stables. It specialises in fresh Ulster produce and serves everything from sandwiches to full à-la-carte dinners.

GIANT'S CAUSEWAY TO BALLYCASTLE

Between the Giant's Causeway and Ballycastle lies the most scenic stretch of the Causeway Coast, with sea cliffs of contrasting black basalt and white chalk, rocky islands, picturesque little harbours and broad sweeps of sandy beach. It's best enjoyed on foot, following the

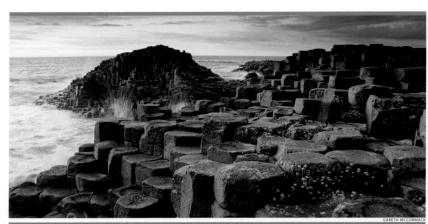

GARETH MCCORMACK

Rock formations at the Giant's Causeway

↘ GIANT'S CAUSEWAY

When you first see it you'll understand why the ancients thought the causeway was not a natural feature. The vast expanse of regular, closely packed, hexagonal stone columns dipping gently beneath the waves looks for all the world like the handiwork of giants.

This spectacular rock formation – a national nature reserve and Northern Ireland's only Unesco World Heritage site – is one of Ireland's most impressive and atmospheric landscape features, but it is often swamped by visitors. Try to visit midweek or out of season to experience it at its most evocative. Sunset in spring and autumn is the best time for photographs.

From the car park it's an easy 10- to 15-minute walk downhill on a tarmac road (wheelchair accessible) to the Causeway itself. A much more interesting approach is to follow the cliff-top path northeast for 2km to the Chimney Tops headland, which has an excellent view of the Causeway and the coastline to the west. This promontory was bombarded by the Spanish Armada in 1588, who thought it was Dunluce Castle. The wreck of the Spanish galleon *Girona* lies just off the tip of the headland. Return towards the car park and descend the Shepherd's Steps to a footpath that leads down to the Causeway. Allow 1½ hours for the round trip.

Alternatively, visit the Causeway first, then follow the lower coastal path as far as the Amphitheatre viewpoint at Port Reostan, passing impressive rock formations such as the Organ (a stack of vertical basalt columns resembling organ pipes), and return by climbing the Shepherd's Steps.

Things you need to know: Causeway (admission free, guided tour adult/child £3.50/2.25 Jun-Aug, parking per car £6 year-round); minibus from car park to Causeway (adult/child return £2/1; every 15 minutes); visitor centre (☎ 028-2073 1855; www.giantscausewaycentre. com; admission free, audiovisual show £1; ⏰ 10am-6pm Jul & Aug, to 5pm Sep-Jun)

16.5km of waymarked **Causeway Coast Way** between the Carrick-a-Rede car park and the Giant's Causeway (see the boxed text, left), although the main attractions can also be reached by car or bus.

About 8km east of the Giant's Causeway is the meagre ruin of 16th-century **Dunseverick Castle**, spectacularly sited on a grassy bluff. Another 1.5km on is the tiny seaside hamlet of **Portbradden**, with half a dozen harbourside houses and the tiny, blue-and-white **St Gobban's Church**, said to be the smallest in Ireland. Visible from Portbradden and accessible via the next junction off the A2 is the spectacular **White Park Bay** with its wide, sweeping sandy beach.

A few kilometres further on is **Ballintoy** (Baile an Tuaighe), another pretty village tumbling down the hillside to a picture-postcard harbour. The restored limekiln on the quayside once made quicklime using stone from the chalk cliffs and coal from Ballymoney.

The main attraction on this stretch of coast is the famous (or notorious, depending on your head for heights) **Carrick-a-Rede Rope Bridge** (☎ **028-2076 9839; Ballintoy; adult/child £4/2;** 🕑 **10am-7pm Jun-Aug, to 6pm Mar-May, Sep & Oct**). The 20m-long, 1m-wide bridge of wire rope spans the chasm between the sea cliffs and the little island of Carrick-a-Rede, swaying gently 30m above the rock-strewn water.

The island has sustained a salmon fishery for centuries; fishermen stretch their nets out from the tip of the island to intercept the passage of salmon migrating along the coast to their home rivers. The fishermen put the bridge up every spring as they have done for the last 200 years – though it's not, of course, the original bridge.

Crossing the bridge is perfectly safe, but it can be frightening if you have a fear of heights, especially if it's breezy (in high winds the bridge is closed). Once on the island there are good views of Rathlin Island and Fair Head to the east. There's a small National Trust information centre and cafe at the car park.

SLEEPING & EATING

Whitepark House B&B (☎ **028-2073 1482; www.whiteparkhouse.com; 150 Whitepark Rd, Ballintoy; s/d £75/100;** P 💻 📶) A beautifully restored 18th-century house overlooking White Park Bay, this B&B has traditional features such as antique furniture and a peat fire complemented by Asian artefacts gathered during the welcoming owners' oriental travels. There are three rooms – ask for one with a sea view.

MARTIN MOOS

Carrick-a-Rede Rope Bridge

Outside drinks at a pub in Derry

Cellar Restaurant (☎ 028-2076 3037; 11 The Diamond, Ballycastle; mains £9-16; ☺ noon-10pm Mon-Sat, from 5pm Sun Jun-Aug, 5-10pm Sep-May) This cosy little basement restaurant with intimate wooden booths and a big fireplace is the place to sample Ulster produce – locally caught crab claws grilled with garlic butter, and Carrick-a-Rede salmon are both on the menu, along with Irish beef and lamb, and lobster from Rathlin Island. There are also good vegetarian dishes such as baked peppers stuffed with mushrooms and shallots.

GETTING THERE & AWAY

Bus 172 between Ballycastle, Bushmills and Coleraine (eight daily Monday to Friday, two on Saturday, three Sunday) is the main, year-round service along this coast, stopping at the Giant's Causeway, Ballintoy and Carrick-a-Rede.

RATHLIN ISLAND

pop 110

In spring and summer, rugged Rathlin Island (Reachlainn), 6km offshore from Ballycastle, is home to hundreds of seals and thousands of nesting seabirds. An L-shaped island just 6.5km long and 4km wide, Rathlin is famous for the coastal scenery and birdlife at Kebble National Nature Reserve at its western end. **RSPB West Light Viewpoint** (☎ 028-2076 0062; admission free; ☺ 11am-3pm Apr–mid-Sep) provides stunning views of the neighbouring sea stacks, thick with guillemots, kittiwakes, razorbills and puffins from mid-April to August. During the summer a minibus service runs there from the harbour; public toilets and binocular hire are available.

A **ferry** (☎ 028-2076 9299; www.rathlinballycastleferry.com) operates daily (adult/child/bicycle return £11/5/3) from Ballycastle; advance booking is recommended in spring and summer. From April to September there are eight or nine crossings a day, half of which are fast catamaran services (20 minutes), the rest via a slower car ferry (45 minutes); in winter the service is reduced.

GLENS OF ANTRIM

The northeastern corner of Antrim is a high plateau of black basalt lava overlying beds of white chalk. Along the coast, between Cushendun and Glenarm, the plateau has been dissected by a series of scenic, glacier-gouged valleys known as the Glens of Antrim.

TORR HEAD SCENIC ROAD

A few kilometres east of Ballycastle, a minor road signposted Scenic Route branches north off the A2. This alternative route to Cushendun is not for the faint-hearted driver (nor for caravans), as it clings, precarious and narrow, to steep slopes high above the sea. Side roads lead off to the main points of interest – Fair Head, Murlough Bay and Torr Head. On a clear day, there are superb views across the sea to Scotland, from the Mull of Kintyre to the peaks of Arran.

CUSHENDUN

pop 350

The pretty seaside village of Cushendun is famous for its distinctive, Cornish-style cottages, now owned by the National Trust. Built between 1912 and 1925 at the behest of the local landowner, Lord Cushendun, they were designed by Clough Williams-Ellis, the architect of Portmeirion in north Wales. There's a nice sandy beach, various short coastal walks (outlined on an information board beside the car park), and some impressive **caves** cut into the overhanging conglomerate sea cliffs south of the village (follow the trail around the far end of the holiday apartments south of the river mouth).

GLENARIFF

About 2km south of Cushendall is the village of **Waterfoot**, with a 2km-long sandy beach, the best on Antrim's east

coast. From here the A43 Ballymena road runs inland along Glenariff, the loveliest of Antrim's glens. Views of the valley led the writer Thackeray to exclaim that it was a 'Switzerland in miniature', a claim that makes you wonder if he'd ever been to Switzerland!

At the head of the valley is **Glenariff Forest Park** (☎ 028-2175 8232; car/motorcycle/pedestrian £4/2/1.50; ☽ 10am-dusk) where the main attraction is **Ess-na-Larach Waterfall**, an 800m walk from the visitor centre. You can also walk to the waterfall from Laragh Lodge, 600m downstream. There are various good walks in the park; the longest is a 10km circular trail.

DERRY/ LONDONDERRY

Northern Ireland's second city comes as a pleasant surprise to many visitors. Derry (or Londonderry) may not be the prettiest of cities, and it certainly lags behind Belfast in terms of investment and redevelopment, but it has a great riverside setting, several fascinating historical sights and a determined air of can-do optimism that has made it the powerhouse of the North's cultural revival.

There's lots of history to absorb, from the Siege of Derry to the Battle of the Bogside – a stroll around the 17th-century city walls is a must, as is a tour of the Bogside murals – and the city's lively pubs are home to a burgeoning live-music scene. But perhaps the biggest attraction is the people themselves: warm, witty and welcoming.

INFORMATION

Derry Tourist Information Centre (☎ 028-7137 7577; www.derryvisitor.com; 44 Foyle St; ☽ 9am-7pm Mon-Fri, 10am-6pm Sat, 10am-5pm Sun Jul-Sep, 9am-5pm Mon-Fri,

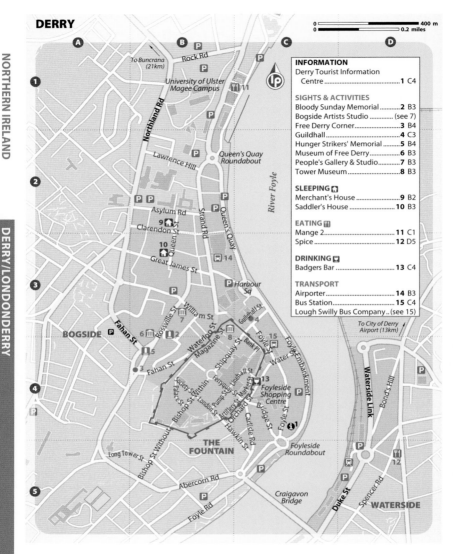

DERRY

INFORMATION	
Derry Tourist Information	
Centre **1** C4	

SIGHTS & ACTIVITIES	
Bloody Sunday Memorial **2** B3	
Bogside Artists Studio .... (see 7)	
Free Derry Corner.........................**3** B4	
Guildhall..**4** C3	
Hunger Strikers' Memorial **5** B4	
Museum of Free Derry.................**6** B3	
People's Gallery & Studio............**7** B3	
Tower Museum **8** B3	

SLEEPING	
Merchant's House **9** B2	
Saddler's House **10** B3	

EATING	
Mange 2..**11** C1	
Spice **12** D5	

DRINKING	
Badgers Bar **13** C4	

TRANSPORT	
Airporter...**14** B3	
Bus Station....................................**15** C4	
Lough Swilly Bus Company .. (see 15)	

10am-5pm Sat Mar-Jun & Oct, 9am-5pm Mon-Fri Nov-Feb) Covers all of Northern Ireland and the Republic as well as Derry. Sells books and maps, can book accommodation throughout Ireland and has a bureau de change.

SIGHTS

Derry's walled city is Ireland's earliest example of town planning. It's thought to have been modelled on the French Renaissance town of Vitry-le-François, designed in 1545 by Italian engineer

STEPHEN SAKS

Tower Museum

Hieronimo Marino; both are based on the grid plan of a Roman military camp, with two main streets at right angles to each other, and four city gates, one at either end of each street.

CITY WALLS

Completed in 1619, Derry's **city walls** (www.derryswalls.com) are 8m high and 9m thick, with a circumference of about 1.5km, and are the only city walls in Ireland to have survived almost intact. The four original gates (Shipquay, Ferryquay, Bishop's and Butcher's) were rebuilt in the 18th and 19th centuries, when three new gates (New, Magazine and Castle) were added. Derry's nickname, the Maiden City, comes from the fact that the walls have never been breached by an invader.

The walls were built under the supervision of the Honourable The Irish Society, an organisation created in 1613 by King James and the London livery companies to fund and oversee the fortification of Derry and the plantation of the surrounding county with Protestant settlers. The

society still exists today (though now its activities are mainly charitable) and it still owns Derry's city walls.

TOWER MUSEUM

Inside the Magazine Gate is the award-winning **Tower Museum** (☎ 028-7137 2411; Union Hall Pl; adult/child £4/2; 🕑 10am-5pm Mon-Sat, 11am-3pm Sun Jul & Aug, 10am-5pm Tue-Sat & bank holidays Mon Sep-Jun), housed in a replica 16th-century tower house. Head straight to the 5th floor for a view from the top of the tower, then work your way down through the excellent **Armada Shipwreck** exhibition, which tells the story of *La Trinidad Valenciera,* a ship of the Spanish Armada that was wrecked at Kinnagoe Bay in Donegal in 1588. It was discovered by the City of Derry Sub-Aqua Club in 1971 and excavated by marine archaeologists. On display are bronze guns, pewter tableware and personal items, such as a wooden comb, an olive jar and a shoe sole, recovered from the site, including a 2.5-tonne siege gun bearing the

Town centre, Derry

JOHN SONES

arms of Phillip II of Spain showing him as king of England.

OUTSIDE THE WALLS

Standing just outside the city walls opposite the Tower Museum, the neo-Gothic **Guildhall** (☎ 028-7137 7335; Guildhall Sq; admission free; ⊙ 9am-5pm Mon-Fri) was originally built in 1890, then rebuilt after a fire in 1908. As the seat of the old Londonderry Corporation, which institutionalised the policy of discriminating against Catholics over housing and jobs, it incurred the wrath of Nationalists and was bombed twice by the Irish Republican Army (IRA) in 1972. From 2000 to 2005 it was the seat of the Bloody Sunday Inquiry. The Guildhall is noted for its fine stained-glass windows, presented by the London Livery companies. Guided tours are available in July and August.

BOGSIDE

The Bogside district, to the west of the walled city, developed in the 19th and early 20th centuries as a working-class,

predominantly Catholic, residential area. By the 1960s, its serried ranks of small, terrace houses had become an overcrowded ghetto of poverty and unemployment, a focus for the emerging civil rights movement and a hotbed of Nationalist discontent.

In August 1969 the three-day 'Battle of the Bogside' – a running street battle between local youths and the Royal Ulster Constabulary (RUC) – prompted the UK government to send British troops into Northern Ireland. The residents of the Bogside and neighbouring Brandywell districts – 33,000 of them – declared themselves independent of the civil authorities, and barricaded the streets to keep the security forces out. 'Free Derry', as it was known, was a no-go area for the police and army, its streets patrolled by IRA volunteers. In January 1972 the area around Rossville St witnessed the horrific events of Bloody Sunday. 'Free Derry' ended with Operation Motorman on 31 July 1972, when thousands of British troops and armoured cars moved in to occupy the Bogside.

Since then the area has been extensively redeveloped, the old houses and flats demolished and replaced with modern housing, and the population is now down to 8000. All that remains of the old Bogside is **Free Derry Corner** at the intersection of Fahan and Rossville Sts, where the gable end of a house painted with the famous slogan 'You Are Now Entering Free Derry' still stands. Nearby is the H-shaped **Hunger Strikers' Memorial** and, a little further north along Rossville St, the **Bloody Sunday Memorial**, a simple granite obelisk that commemorates the 14 civilians who were shot dead by the British Army on 30 January 1972.

The **Museum of Free Derry** (☎ 7136 0880; www.museumoffreederry.org; 55-61 Glenfada Park; adult/child £3/2; ☼ 9.30am-4.30pm Mon-Fri year-round, 1-4pm Sat Apr-Sep, 1-4pm Sun Jul-Sep), just off Rossville St, chronicles the history of the Bogside, the civil rights movement and the events of Bloody Sunday through photographs, newspaper reports, film clips and the accounts of firsthand witnesses, including some of the original photographs that inspired the murals of the People's Gallery.

PEOPLE'S GALLERY

The 12 murals that decorate the gable ends of houses along Rossville St, near Free Derry Corner, are popularly referred to as the People's Gallery. They are the work of Tom Kelly, Will Kelly and Kevin Hasson, known as 'The Bogside Artists'. The three men have spent most of their lives in the Bogside, and lived through the worst of the Troubles.

Their murals, mostly painted between 1997 and 2001, commemorate key events in the Troubles, including the Battle of the Bogside, Bloody Sunday, Operation

Motorman (the British Army's operation to retake IRA-controlled no-go areas in Derry and Belfast in July 1972) and the 1981 hunger strike. The most powerful images are those painted largely in monochrome, consciously evoking journalistic imagery – *Operation Motorman*, showing a British soldier breaking down a door with a sledgehammer; *Bloody Sunday*, with a group of men led by local priest Father Daly carrying the body of Jackie Duddy (the first fatality on that day); and *Petrol Bomber*, a young boy wearing a gas mask and holding a petrol bomb.

The most moving image is *The Death of Innocence*, which shows the radiant figure of 14-year-old schoolgirl Annette McGavigan, killed in crossfire between the IRA and the British Army on 6 September 1971, the 100th victim of the Troubles. Representing all the children who died in the conflict, she stands against the brooding chaos of a bombed-out building, the roof beams forming a crucifix in the top right-hand corner. At the left, a downward-pointing rifle, broken in the middle, stands for the failure of violence, while the butterfly symbolises resurrection and the hope embodied in the peace process.

The final mural in the sequence, completed in 2004, is the *Peace Mural*, a swirling image of a dove (symbol of peace, and also of Derry's patron saint, Columba), rising out of the blood and sadness of the past towards the sunny yellow hope of a peaceful future.

SLEEPING

ourpick **Merchant's House** (☎ 028-7126 9691; www.thesaddlershouse.com; 16 Queen St; s/d £45/60; 🖳 🛜) Run by the same couple as the Saddler's House, this historic, Georgian-style town house is a gem of a

MARTIN MOOS

Mural protesting against oppression in East Timor, Derry

B&B. It has an elegant lounge and dining room with marble fireplaces and antique furniture, TV, coffee-making facilities and even bathrobes in the bedrooms (though only one has its own en-suite bathroom), and homemade marmalade at breakfast. Call at the Saddler's House first to pick up a key.

Saddler's House (☎ 028-7126 9691; www.thesaddlershouse.com; 36 Great James St; s/d from £50/60; 🖳 🛜) Centrally located within a five-minute walk of the walled city, this friendly B&B is set in a lovely Victorian town house. All seven rooms have private bathrooms, and you get to enjoy a huge breakfast in the family kitchen.

Da Vinci's Hotel (☎ 028-7127 9111; www.davincishotel.com; 15 Culmore Rd; r from £75, ste from £100; 🅿 🖳 🛜) This sleek boutique hotel on the west bank of the Foyle is the accommodation of choice for visiting celebrities, business people and politicians, offering spacious, stylish rooms and a hip cocktail bar and restaurant. It's 1.5km north of the city centre.

EATING & DRINKING

Spice (☎ 028-7134 4875; 162-164 Spencer Rd, Waterside; mains £9-19; 🕑 12.30-2.30pm Tue-Fri & Sun, 5.30-10pm Tue-Sat, 5-9pm Sun) If you can't decide what cuisine you fancy, this pleasantly chilled-out eatery offers a range of culinary influences, from warm duck salad with hoisin dressing, to tarragon chicken with wild mushrooms, to Madras-spiced bean stew with coriander rice. There's a separate vegetarian menu, and a three-course dinner deal for £14.

Mange 2 (☎ 028-7136 1222; 110-115 Strand Rd; mains £13-19; 🕑 noon-2.30pm Tue-Fri, noon-3.30pm Sun, 5-10pm Tue-Sun) Mange 2 may have moved from its old Georgian home to a shiny, new, glass-fronted venue on the riverfront, but the menu is still faithful to top-quality Irish produce served plain or with an Asian- or French-fusion twist – try Finnebrogue venison with sweet potato purée, pan-seared spinach and redcurrant jus; or Donegal smoked cod with champ, buttered cabbage and chive sauce.

Badgers Bar (☎ 028-7136 0763; 16-18 Orchard St) A fine polished-brass and stained-glass Victorian pub that's crammed with wood-panelled nooks and crannies, Badgers overflows at lunchtime with shoppers enjoying quality pub grub, and offers a quiet haven in the evenings when it attracts a crowd of more mature drinkers.

GETTING THERE & AWAY
AIR
City of Derry Airport (☎ 028-7181 0784; www.cityofderryairport.com) is about 13km east of Derry along the A2 towards Limavady. There are direct flights daily to Dublin (Aer Arann), London Stansted, London Luton, Liverpool, Birmingham and Glasgow Prestwick (Ryanair).

BUS
The **bus station** (☎ 028-7126 2261) is on Foyle St, just northeast of the walled city.

Bus 212, the Maiden City Flyer, is a fast and frequent service between Derry and Belfast (£10, 1¾ hours, every 30 minutes Monday to Saturday, 11 on Sunday), calling at Dungiven. Goldline Express 274 goes from Derry to Dublin (£16, four hours, every two hours daily).

Other useful Ulsterbus services include the 273 to Omagh (£8, 1¼ hours, hourly Monday to Saturday, six Sunday) and the 234 to Limavady and Coleraine (£6, one hour, five daily Monday to Saturday, two Sunday), continuing to Portstewart and Portrush on weekday evenings.

Lough Swilly Bus Company (☎ 028-7126 2017; Foyle St) has an office upstairs at the bus station, and runs buses to Buncrana, Carndonagh, Dungloe, Letterkenny (£5, 30 to 45 minutes, eight daily Monday to Friday, five on Saturday) and Greencastle (one hour, two daily Monday to Friday, one on Saturday) in County Donegal. There's also a bus from Derry to Malin Head (£6, 1¼ hours) via Carndonagh on Saturdays only – a very scenic trip.

Bus Éireann (☎ in Donegal 353-742 1309) service 64 runs from Derry to Galway (£18, 5¼ hours, three daily, two on Sundays) via Letterkenny, Donegal and Sligo; another four a day terminate at Sligo.

The **Airporter** (☎ 028-7126 9996; www.airporter.co.uk; Quayside Shopping Centre, Strand Rd) bus service runs direct from Derry to Belfast International (one-way/return £18/28, 1½ hours) and George Best Belfast City (same fare, two hours) airports. Buses depart every 90 minutes Monday to Friday, every two hours on Saturday and Sunday.

TRAIN
Derry's train station (always referred to as Londonderry in Northern Ireland timetables) is on the eastern side of the River Foyle; a free Rail Link bus connects it with the bus station on Foyle St. Trains to Belfast (£10, 2¼ hours, seven or eight daily Monday to Saturday, four on Sunday) are slower but more comfortable than the bus, and the section of line between Derry and Coleraine is very scenic. There are also frequent trains to Coleraine (£7.50, 45 minutes, seven daily), with connections to Portrush (£9, 1¼ hours).

↘ IRELAND IN FOCUS

FAMILY TRAVEL

RICHARD CUMMINS

Family cycling at Ross Castle (p205)

Ireland is generally a pretty good place to bring kids. On the whole you'll find that restaurants and hotels, especially in the countryside, will go out of their way to cater for you and your children. Bear in mind that under-16s are banned from pubs after 7pm – even if they're accompanied by their parents – but the plus side is that under-fives travel free on all public transport and most admission prices have an under-16s reduced fee. Try asking fellow travellers with (happy) children and locals on the road for tips on where to go.

Most hotels will provide cots at no extra charge and restaurants will have high chairs. Car seats (around €50/£25 per week) are mandatory in hire cars for children between the ages of nine months and four years. Bring your own seat for infants under about nine months, as only larger, forward-facing child seats are generally available. Remember not to place baby seats in the front if the car has an airbag.

Although breast-feeding is not a common sight (Ireland has one of the lowest rates of it in the world), you can do so with impunity pretty much everywhere without getting so much as a stare. Changing facilities are generally only found in the newer, larger shopping centres – otherwise you'll have to make do with a public toilet.

Two great websites are www.eumom.ie, for pregnant women and parents with young children, and www.babygoes2.com, which is an excellent travel site about family-friendly accommodation worldwide.

⬎ THE NITTY GRITTY

- **Changing facilities** Practically nonexistent, even in big cities.
- **Cots** Usually available at all accommodation except the most basic B&Bs.
- **Health** Generally, do as you would do at home.
- **High chairs** Ask and most restaurants will usually provide.
- **Nappies (Diapers)** Sold in every supermarket and convenience store.
- **Transport** Look for family passes and kids' discounts on trains and buses.

FOOD & DRINK

IRELAND IN FOCUS

FOOD & DRINK

Colcannon (mashed potatoes with cabbage)

MONKEY BUSINESS IMAGES/DREAMSTIME.COM

Generations of travellers who visited these shores during bleaker times typically mused that Irish food is great until it's cooked. They advised getting drunk before eating, or complained that a meal was more a flavourless penance rather than a pleasurable repast. Those days are long gone, and that small-but-growing creation known as Irish cuisine is actually drawing visitors to these shores.

The culinary renaissance has taken place, and the Irish are now enjoying the fine cuisine that they have long deserved. The island has always been blessed with a wealth of staples and specialities, with meat, seafood and dairy produce that are the envy of the world. At the twilight of the 20th century, a new wave of cooks began producing what is sometimes promoted as 'New Irish Cuisine'.

In truth, the new cuisine is more a confident return to the traditional practice of combining simple cooking techniques with the finest local ingredients. Many of the new chefs merely strive to offer their patrons the sort of meals that have always been taken for granted on well-run Irish farms. Whatever you want to call it, it has aroused the nation's taste buds, and you'll find local produce on menus across the country, from Dublin Bay prawns and Connemara salmon to Skeaghanore duck and Kilbrittain lamb.

STAPLES & SPECIALITIES
POTATOES

It's a wonder the Irish retain their good humour amid the perpetual potato-baiting they endure. But despite the stereotype, and however much we'd like to disprove it, potatoes are still paramount here and you'll see lots on your travels. The mashed potato dishes colcannon and champ (made with cabbage and spring onion, respectively) are two of the tastiest recipes in the country.

MEAT & SEAFOOD

Irish meals are usually meat based, with beef, lamb and pork common options. Seafood, long neglected, is finding a place on the table in Irish homes. It's widely available in restaurants and is often excellent, especially in the west. Oysters, trout and salmon are delicious, particularly if they're direct from the sea or a river rather than a fish farm. At its best, the famous Dublin Bay prawn (which is actually a lobster) is superlative, but it's priced accordingly. If you're going to splurge, do so here – but make sure you choose live Dublin Bay prawns because once these fellas die, they quickly lose their flavour.

BREAD

The most famous Irish bread, and one of the signature tastes of Ireland, is soda bread. Irish flour is soft and doesn't take well to yeast as a raising agent, so Irish bakers of the 19th century leavened their bread with bicarbonate of soda. Combined with buttermilk, it makes a superbly light-textured and tasty bread, and is often on the breakfast menus at B&Bs.

THE FRY

Perhaps the most feared Irish speciality is the fry – the heart attack on a plate that is the second part of so many B&B deals. In spite of the hysterical health fears, the fry is still one of the most common traditional meals in the country. Who can say no to a plate of fried bacon, sausages, black pudding, white pudding, eggs and tomatoes? For the famous Ulster fry, common throughout the North, simply add fadge (potato bread).

DRINKS
NONALCOHOLIC DRINKS
TEA

The Irish drink more tea, per capita, than any other nation in the world, and you'll be offered a cup as soon as you cross the threshold of any Irish home. It's a leveller and

↘ FINDING THE BEST IRISH FOOD & DRINK

- **Good Food in Cork** Excellent annual booklet detailing artisan producers in Cork, established by Myrtle Allen; pick it up from the Farmgate Café (p194) in Cork city; also available online at www.corkfreechoice.com.
- **www.bestofbridgestone.com** Extensive coverage of artisan producers, plus the best restaurants serving their produce.
- **www.bordbia.ie** Irish food board website, with a few local producers listed, as well as a comprehensive list of farmers markets.
- **www.irishcheese.ie** The farmhouse cheesemakers' association, with every small dairy covered.
- **www.slowfoodireland.com** Organisation supporting small producers, with social events across Ireland.

Guinness stout
JULIET COOMBE

an ice-breaker, and an appreciation for 'at least a cup in your hand' is your passport to conviviality here. Preferred blends are very strong, and nothing like the namby-pamby versions that pass for 'Irish breakfast tea' elsewhere.

RED LEMONADE

This product, basically a regular glass of lemonade with colouring, has been produced in Ireland since the end of the 19th century and is still made to virtually the same recipe today. Always more popular in the Republic than the North, it's a favourite for adults and children alike. It's commonly used as a mixer with brandy and whiskey.

ALCOHOLIC DRINKS

Drinking in Ireland is no mere social activity: it's the foundation on which Irish culture is built. Along with its wonderful drinks, this fact helps to explain why, through centuries of poverty and oppression, the Irish have always retained their reputation for unrivalled hospitality and good humour.

STOUT

Of all Irish drinks, the 'black stuff' is the most celebrated. While Guinness has become synonymous with stout the world over, few outside Ireland realise that there are two other major producers competing for favour: Murphy's and Beamish & Crawford, both based in Cork city. More exciting still is the recent reemergence of independent Irish brewers (the three major labels are no longer Irish-owned) to whet your appetite.

WHISKEY

While whiskey shares equal billing with stout as the national drink of Ireland, in the home it is paramount. At last count, there were almost 100 different types of Irish whiskey, brewed by only three distilleries: Jameson's, Bushmills and Cooley's. A visit to Ireland reveals a depth of excellence that will make the connoisseur's palate spin, while winning over many new friends to what the Irish call *uisce beatha* (water of life).

IRISH COFFEE

Stories about the origin of Irish coffee abound but the most common one credits Joe Sheridan, a barman at Shannon airport, with its creation in the 1940s. Travellers arriving in Ireland from the USA would stop over in Shannon for an hour or two before heading on to their final destination. Landing in the bracing cold, shivering passengers used to approach Sheridan looking for an alcoholic drink and something that might heat them up. He hit upon a blend of Irish whiskey and piping-hot coffee, topped with cream. It was just the ticket then, and still is today.

IRELAND IN FOCUS

FOOD & DRINK

> ## ⬃ A SNIFTER OF WHISKEY HISTORY
>
> Nobody really knows for sure whether whiskey was first made in Scotland or Ireland, but whiskey has been made in Ireland since the 10th century, when monks brought the art of distillation back from their ecclesiastical jaunts to the Middle East, then fiercely protected their secret for several centuries.
>
> By the way, Scotch whisky is not only spelled without the 'e', it is distilled twice rather than the three times preferred by the Irish. American bourbon is distilled but once.

POITÍN

The manufacture of *poitín* (illicit whiskey) has a folkloric respect in Ireland. Those responsible came to be regarded as heroes of the people rather than outlaws of the land, as the authorities tried to brand them. In tourist and duty-free shops, you'll see a commercial brand of *poitín,* which is strictly a gimmick for tourists. Don't bother: it's just an inferior spirit with little to credit it.

There are still *poitín* makers plying their trade in the quieter corners of Ireland. It is not uncommon in Donegal, the *poitín* capital, for deals to be sealed or favours repaid with a drop of the 'cratur'. In the quiet, desolate, peaty bogs of Connemara, a plume of smoke rising into the sky may not just be a warming fire. Or in West Cork, one of the most fiercely patriotic and traditional pockets of Ireland, a friend of a friend may know something about it.

WHERE TO EAT & DRINK

It's easy to eat well in the cities and you'll be able to find any kind of cuisine your taste buds desire, from Irish seafood to foreign fusion. Along the west coast, you'll be spoiled for choice when it comes to seafood and local produce.

If you ask a local for 'somewhere to eat', you'll probably be directed to his or her favourite pub because, outside the cities, the best place for a feed, particularly lunch, often *is* the pub. Virtually every drinking house will offer the simple fare of soup, potatoes, vegetables, steaks and chicken. Some extend themselves and have separate dining rooms, where you can get fresh soda bread and hearty meals such as shepherd's pie, casseroles and seafood dishes.

OLIVER STREWE

Lobster, Irish bread and Guinness at McDonagh's (p240), Galway

For breakfast, you're most likely to be eating at your accommodation, as most lodgings in Ireland offer B&B.

Standard restaurant hours in Ireland are from noon to around 10.30pm, with many places closed one day of the week (usually Monday, or sometimes Sunday).

VEGETARIANS & VEGANS

Veggies can take a deep breath. And then exhale. Calmly. For Ireland has come a long, long way since the days when vegetarians were looked upon as odd creatures; nowadays, even the most militant vegan will barely cause a ruffle in all but the most basic of rustic kitchens. Which isn't to say that travellers with plant-based diets are going to find the most imaginative range of options on menus outside the bigger towns and cities – or in the plethora of modern restaurants that have opened in the last few years – but you can rest assured that the overall quality of the homegrown vegetable is top-notch and most places will have at least one dish that you can tuck into comfortably.

HABITS & CUSTOMS

HOW THE IRISH EAT

The Irish have hefty appetites and eat almost 150% of the daily calorie intake recommended by the EU. This probably has as much to do with their penchant for snacks as the size of their meals (which *are* big).

When Ireland was predominantly agricultural, breakfast was a leisurely and communal meal shared with family and workers around midmorning, a few hours after rising. As with most of the developed world, it's now a fairly rushed and bleary-eyed affair involving toast and cereals. The traditional fry is a weekend indulgence, while the contracted version of bacon and eggs is still popular whenever time allows. The day's first cup of tea comes with breakfast and most people will admit to not being themselves until they've had it.

Elevenses is the next pit stop and involves tea and snacks to tide over appetites until the next main meal. Afternoon tea takes the same form and serves the same function, also breaking up the afternoon.

Lunch is traditionally the biggest meal of the day, which is probably a throwback to farming Ireland, when the workers would return home ravenous after a morning's work. However, the timing of the main meal today is one of the most visible rural/urban divides. Outside the cities, lunch is still usually the most substantial meal every day of the week, while the workers in urban areas have succumbed to nine-to-five drudgery and usually eat lunch on the run. However, on weekends, everybody has dinner mid-afternoon, usually around 4pm on Saturday and before 2pm on Sunday. They might call it 'lunch' but don't be deceived – it's the most substantial meal of the week.

'Supper' is increasingly becoming the main meal for urbanites, and takes place as soon as the last working parent gets home.

OLIVER STREWE

Irish cheeses

◥THE BEST

IRISH CHEESES

- **Ardrahan** Flavoursome farmhouse creation with a rich, nutty taste.
- **Cashel Blue** Creamy blue cheese from Tipperary.
- **Cooleeney** Award-winning Camembert-style cheese.
- **Corleggy** Subtle, pasteurised goats cheese from County Cavan.
- **Durrus** Fine-food fans will fall for this creamy, fruity cheese (p200).

IRELAND IN FOCUS

FOOD & DRINK

HISTORY

National Famine Memorial (p267), Murrisk, County Mayo

Ireland's turbulent tale begins about 10,000 years ago, as the last ice caps melted and rising sea levels cut it off from Britain.

WHO THE HELL ARE THE IRISH?

Hunters and gatherers may first have traversed the narrowing land bridge, but many more crossed the Irish Sea in small hide-covered boats. In the 8th century BC, Ireland came to the attention of the fearsome Celts, who, having fought their way across Central Europe, established permanent settlements on the island in the 3rd century BC. Despite the constantly shifting political situation, the Celts created the basis of what we now term 'Irish' culture: they devised a sophisticated code of law called the Brehon Law (which remained in use until the early 17th century), and their swirling, mazelike design style, evident on artefacts nearly 2000 years old, is considered the epitome of Irish design.

GETTING INTO THE HABIT

Arguably the most significant import into Ireland came between the 3rd and 5th centuries AD, when Christian missionaries first brought the new religion of Rome. Everyone has heard of St Patrick (see the boxed text, right), but he was merely the most famous of

10,000–8000 BC	4500 BC	700–300 BC
After the last ice age ends, the first humans arrive in Ireland.	The first neolithic farmers arrive, bringing cattle, sheep and crops.	The Celtic culture and language arrive, ushering in 1000 years of cultural and political dominance.

⬎ ST PATRICK

Ireland's patron saint (AD 389–461), remembered all around the world on 17 March, wasn't even Irish. This symbol of Irish pride hailed from what is now Wales, which at the time of his birth was under Roman occupation. Kidnapped by Irish raiders when he was 16 and made a slave, he found religion, escaped from captivity and returned to Britain. He returned to Ireland vowing to make Christians out of the Irish, and within 30 years of his return his dream had come true.

So next St Paddy's Day, as you're swilling Guinness, think of who the man really was.

many who converted the local pagan tribes by cleverly fusing traditional pagan rituals with the new Christian teaching, creating an exciting hybrid known as Celtic (Insular) Christianity. The artistic and intellectual credentials of Ireland's Christians were the envy of Europe, and led to the moniker 'the land of saints and scholars'.

RAPE, PILLAGE & PLUNDER: A VIKING'S DAY OUT

The Celts' lack of political unity made the island easy pickings for the next wave of invaders, Danish Vikings. Over the course of the 9th and 10th centuries, they established a small Viking kingdom called Dubh Linn (Black Pool) – which would later become the city of Dublin – and they founded the towns of Wicklow, Waterford and Wexford.

The biggest challenge to Viking rule in Ireland came in 1014, when Brian Ború, king of Munster, defeated the Vikings (and their Irish allies) at Clontarf. As a result, like the Celts before them, the Vikings eventually settled, giving up the rape-rob-and-run policy in favour of integration and assimilation; by intermarrying with the Celtic tribes, they introduced red hair and freckles to the Irish gene pool.

THE ENGLISH ARE COMING!

The '800 years' of English rule in Ireland nominally began in 1169, when an army of English barons landed in Wexford at the

⬎ WHO WERE THE CELTS?

Did you know that the Celts had 'rippling muscles under clear white skin' and bleached their hair by washing it in quicklime? For a concise, 10-minute read on who the Celts were – and how they were feared by virtually everyone, including the mighty Romans – see www.ibiblio.org/gaelic/celts.html.

300 BC–AD 800	AD 431–2	550–800
Ireland is divided into four provinces: Leinster, Connaught, Ulster and Munster.	Arrival of the first Christian missionaries with Bishop Palladius and, a year later, St Patrick.	The great monastic teachers begin exporting their knowledge across Europe, ushering in Ireland's 'Golden Age'.

BEYOND THE PALE

The expression 'beyond the Pale' came into use when the Pale – defined as a jurisdiction marked by a clear boundary – was the English-controlled part of Ireland, which stretched roughly from Dalkey, a southern suburb of Dublin, to Dundalk, north of Drogheda. Inland, the boundary extended west to Trim and Kells. To the British elite, the rest of Ireland was considered uncivilised.

bequest of the king of Leinster, Dermot MacMurrough, who had recently been ousted by an alliance of Irish chieftains. Who could have guessed that they and their descendants would stick around for as long as they did? Certainly not MacMurrough, who married his daughter Aoife to the barons' leader, Richard de Clare, aka Strongbow, and cemented his place at the top of the Irish traitors' list.

Two years after Strongbow's landing, the English king Henry II sent a huge invasion force, at the urging of the pope, to curb Strongbow's growing power and to bring the increasingly independent Christian missionaries to heel. It was a tale that would play itself out with ever-increasing hostility over the next 800 years.

In the meantime, the Anglo-Norman lords (as they were now known) settled quite nicely into Irish life, becoming – as the old saying went – *Hiberniores Hibernis ipsis* (more Irish than the Irish themselves). By the 16th century, they had divided the country into their own fiefdoms and the English Crown's direct control didn't extend any further than a cordon surrounding Dublin, known as 'the Pale'.

DIVORCE, DISSOLUTION & DESTRUCTION

When Henry VIII didn't get the pope's blessing for his divorce, the Anglo-Irish, desperately uncomfortable with Henry's go-it-alone action (and convinced that their Irish power base would be enough protection from retribution), opposed the English king. It was an unfortunately poor decision. Henry, eager to smash the Irish once and for all, ordered the confiscation of the lands of the rebellious lords, eliminated the power of the Irish church by ordering the dissolution of all monasteries, and had himself declared King of Ireland. His daughter Elizabeth I went even further, establishing jurisdiction in Connaught and Munster before crushing the last of the rebels, who were, ironically, the lords of Ulster, led by the crafty and courageous Hugh O'Neill, Earl of Tyrone.

The Battle of Kinsale, in 1601, spelled the end for O'Neill and for Ulster. Although O'Neill survived the battle, his power was broken and he surrendered to the English Crown. In 1607, O'Neill and 90 other Ulster chiefs sailed to Europe, leaving Ireland forever. This was known as the Flight of the Earls, and it left Ulster open to English rule.

795–841	1014	1169
Vikings plunder Irish monasteries before establishing settlements throughout the country.	Battle of Clontarf between High King Brian Ború and Viking allies of the King of Leinster.	Urged by the King of Leinster, Anglo-Norman barons, led by Strongbow, land in Ireland, taking Waterford and Wexford.

MARTIN MOOS

Ruins of Selskar Abbey, Wexford town (p157)

With the native chiefs gone, Elizabeth and her successor, James I, could pursue their policy of Plantation with impunity. Though confiscations took place all over the country, Ulster was most affected both because of its wealthy farmlands and as punishment for being home to the primary fomenters of rebellion.

BLOODY RELIGION

At the outset of the English Civil War in 1641, the native Irish and Anglo-Norman Catholics, allied under the Confederation of Kilkenny, plumped for Charles I against the Protestant Parliamentarians in the hope that this would lead to the restoration of Catholic power in Ireland. It was a major misjudgement, especially when English royalists regrouped in Ireland following their defeat and Charles' execution in 1649. Faced by a major threat to their newly established authority, the Parliamentarians, led by Oliver Cromwell, launched a massive invasion in August 1649.

Cromwell's legendary hostility to the Irish was both political and religious, and his passionate opposition to the Catholic Church and the primacy of the pope determined that his campaign would be especially harsh: his armies besieged towns with little regard for the citizenry and, in the cases of Drogheda and Wexford, were guilty of wholesale massacre. Brutal and unsparing, Cromwell's nine-month campaign was nonetheless effective, even if it took three more years of fighting before Ireland was

1171	1366	1534–41
King Henry II invades Ireland and forces Anglo-Norman warlords to accept him as their overlord.	Statutes of Kilkenny outlaw intermarriage and a host of Irish customs to stop Anglo-Norman assimilation.	Henry VIII declares war on Irish church and is declared King of Ireland.

Round tower and high cross, Monasterboice (p138)
TONY WHEELER

fully subdued. The Irish paid a heavy toll for their resistance: two million hectares of land were confiscated – more than 25% of the country – and handed over to Protestants loyal to Parliament, and many of the former owners sent into exile.

In 1689, in another attempt to resist the English in the spirit of the Confederation of Kilkenny, Irish Catholic monarchists rallied behind James II after his deposition in the Glorious Revolution and his replacement as king by the Dutch Protestant William of Orange (William III), husband to James' own (Protestant) daughter Mary. James landed in Kinsale and set about raising an army to regain his throne, attracting local support with his promise to return expropriated lands to Catholic landowners. To this end, his army besieged the walled town of Derry (Londonderry) for 105 days, leading to widespread starvation for the trapped Protestant citizenry inside. The Loyalist slogan 'No Surrender!', which acquired mythical status among Irish Protestants over the following centuries, dates from the siege.

The end for James came at the banks of the River Boyne in County Louth on 12 July 1690, when his forces were roundly defeated by William's 36,000-strong army. James' ignominious defeat (he fled the battlefield and is to this day remembered by the Irish as Seamus a Chaca, meaning 'James the Shit') was a turning point for Irish Catholics: five years later the introduction of oppressive Penal Laws, known collectively as the 'Popery Code', prohibited Catholics from owning land or entering any

1585	1594	1601
Potatoes from South America are introduced to Ireland, where they become a staple.	Hugh O'Neill, Earl of Tyrone, instigates open conflict with England and starts the Nine Years' War.	O'Neill surrenders after Battle of Kinsale and Irish rebellion against the Crown is broken.

higher profession. Irish culture, music and education were banned in the hope that Catholicism would be eradicated. By the late 18th century, Catholics owned barely 5% of the land.

IF AT FIRST YOU DON'T SUCCEED...

With Roman Catholics rendered utterly powerless, the seeds of rebellion against autocracy were planted by a handful of liberal Protestants, inspired by the ideologies of the Enlightenment and the unrest provoked by the American War of Independence and then the French Revolution.

The first of these liberal leaders was a young Dublin Protestant, Theobald Wolfe Tone (1763–98), who was the most prominent leader of a Belfast organisation called the United Irishmen. Wolfe Tone looked to France for help, and Loyalist Protestants prepared for possible conflict by forming the Orange Institution, which later

> ### ⬎ MAKING SENSE OF THE 12TH
>
> The most celebrated date in the Northern Loyalist calendar might be 12 July, but calendar confusion means it celebrates the wrong battle. According to the Julian calendar, the Battle of the Boyne took place on 1 July 1690; the Battle of Aughrim occurred on 12 July 1691. For decades thereafter, Irish Protestants celebrated the anniversary of Aughrim, but when the Gregorian calendar was adopted in 1752, shifting the Battle of the Boyne to the 12th, Protestants overcame their suspicions of anything to do with Rome and from 1795 began marking the 12th as the anniversary of the Boyne, and have done so to this day!

became known as the Orange Order. The tragic failure of the French to land an army of succour in 1796 left the organisation exposed to retribution, and the men met their bloody end in the Battle of Vinegar Hill in 1798.

The Act of Union, passed in 1801, was the British government's vain attempt to put an end to any aspirations towards Irish independence, but the nationalist genie was well out of the bottle and two distinct forms of nationalist expression began to develop. The first was a breed of radical republicanism, which advocated use of force to found a secular, egalitarian Irish republic; the second was a more moderate movement, which advocated nonviolent and legal action to force the government into granting concessions.

The most important moderate was a Kerry-born Catholic named Daniel O'Connell (1775–1847). In 1823 O'Connell founded the Catholic Association with the aim of achieving political equality for Catholics, which he did (in part) by forcing the passing of the

1641	1649–53	1690
Native Irish and Anglo-Norman Catholics support Charles I during the English Civil War.	Oliver Cromwell lays waste throughout Ireland after the Irish support Charles I.	Catholic King James II defeated by William of Orange in Battle of the Boyne, 12 July.

RICHARD CUMMINS

Georgian architecture, Merrion Square (p73), Dublin

1829 Act of Catholic Emancipation, allowing some well-off Catholics voting rights and the right to be elected as MPs.

O'Connell continued to pursue his reform campaign, turning his attention towards the repeal of the Act of Union. His main weapon was the monster rally, which attracted hundreds of thousands of people eager to hear the 'Liberator' (as he was now known) speak. But O'Connell was unwilling to go outside the law, and when the government ordered the cancellation of one of his rallies at Clontarf, he meekly stood down and thereby gave up his most potent weapon of resistance.

O'Connell's failure to defy the British was seen as a terrible capitulation as the country was in the midst of the Potato Famine (see the boxed text, right). The lack of urgency on the part of the authorities in dealing with the crisis served to bolster the ambitions of the more radical wing of the Nationalist movement, led in the 1840s by the Young Irelanders, who attempted a failed rebellion in 1848, and later by the Fenians, architects of yet another uprising in 1867.

The Irish may have been bitterly angry at the treatment meted out by the British, but they weren't quite ready to take up arms en masse against them. Instead, the Nationalist cause found itself driven by arguably the most important feature of the Irish struggle against foreign rule: land ownership. Championed by the extraordinary Charles Stewart Parnell (1846–91), the Land League initiated widespread agitation for

1795	1798	1801
A group of Protestants create the Orange Institution in Dublin.	A rising by the United Irishmen and Wolfe Tone ends in defeat and Tone's suicide.	The Act of Union unites Ireland politically with Britain, ending Irish 'independence'.

❯ THE GREAT FAMINE

As a result of the Great Famine of 1845–51, a staggering three million people died or were forced to emigrate from Ireland. This great tragedy could have been avoided: there were abundant harvests of wheat and dairy produce, but they were denied to the majority of Irish peasants, who were forced to subsist on a diet of potatoes rotten as a result of blight. Mass emigration continued to reduce the population during the next hundred years, and huge numbers of Irish emigrants who found their way abroad, particularly to the USA, carried with them a lasting bitterness.

reduced rents and improved working conditions. The conflict heated up and there was violence on both sides. Parnell instigated the strategy of 'boycotting' (named after one particularly unpleasant agent named Charles Boycott) tenants, agents and landlords who didn't adhere to the Land League's aims: these people were treated like lepers by the local population. The Land War, as it became known, lasted from 1879 to 1882 and was momentous. For the first time, tenants were defying their landlords en masse. The Land Act of 1881 improved life immeasurably for tenants, creating fair rents and the possibility of tenants owning their land.

The other element of Parnell's two-pronged assault on the British was at Westminster where, as leader of the Irish Parliamentary Party (IPP), he led the fight for Home Rule, a limited form of autonomy for Ireland. Parliamentary mathematics meant that the Liberal Party, led by William Gladstone, was reliant on the members of the IPP to maintain a majority over the Conservatives and Parnell pressed home his advantage by forcing Gladstone to introduce a series of Home Rule bills – in 1886 and 1892 – which passed the Commons but were defeated in the House of Lords. Parnell's ascendency, however, came to a sudden end in 1890 when he was embroiled in a divorce scandal – not acceptable to puritanical Irish society.

❯ CHARLES BOYCOTT

Poor Charles C Boycott. A County Mayo land agent, he was the (some would say deserving) victim of Parnell's 1880 policy of completely ostracising anyone who was seen to perpetuate the unjust practices that kept the vast majority of the Irish peasantry in landless penury. Boycott was no worse than hundreds of other such agents, but it was his name given to the uncomfortable practice of boycotting!

1828–29	1845–51	1879–82
Prime minister passes the Catholic Emancipation Act, giving limited rights to Catholics.	Between 500,000 and one million die during Potato Famine; two million more emigrate.	The Land War sees tenant farmers defying their landlords en masse.

JOHN ELK III

Dublin Castle (p70)

IRELAND GETS ITS OWN SET OF KEYS

As the 20th century dawned, Ireland was overwhelmingly committed to achieving Home Rule. A new Liberal government under Prime Minister Asquith had removed the House of Lords' power to veto bills and began to put another Home Rule for Ireland bill through Parliament. The bill was passed (but not enacted) in 1912 against strident Unionist opposition, epitomised by the mass rallies organised by the recently founded Protestant vigilante group, the Ulster Volunteer Force (UVF).

The outbreak of WWI in July 1914 merely delayed Irish ambitions as a majority of the Irish Volunteers – founded by academic Eoin MacNeill as a Nationalist answer to the UVF – heeded the call to arms and enlisted in the British army. It was felt that just as England had promised Home Rule to Ireland, so the Irish owed it to England to help her in her hour of need; the Home Rule Act was suspended and for a time the question of Ulster was left unresolved.

A few, however, did not heed the call. Two small groups – a section of the Irish Volunteers under Pádraig Pearse and the Irish Citizens' Army, led by James Connolly – conspired in a rebellion that took the country by surprise. A depleted Volunteer group marched into Dublin on Easter Monday 1916 and took over a number of key positions in the city, claiming the General Post Office on O'Connell St as its headquarters. From its steps, Pearse read out to passers-by a declaration that Ireland was now a republic

1912	1916	1919–21
Ulster Volunteer Force (UVF) created to organise resistance to Home Rule.	The Easter Rising rebels surrender to superior British forces in less than a week.	The Irish War of Independence begins in January 1919.

and that his band was the provisional government. Less than a week of fighting ensued before the rebels surrendered to the superior British forces. The rebels weren't popular and had to be protected from angry Dubliners as they were marched to jail.

The Easter Rising would probably have had little impact on the Irish situation had the British not made martyrs of the rebel leaders. Of the 77 given death sentences, 15 were executed, including the injured Connolly, who was shot while strapped to a chair. This brought about a sea change in public attitudes, and support for the Republicans rose dramatically.

By the end of WWI, Home Rule was far too little, far too late. In the 1918 general election, the Republicans stood under the banner of Sinn Féin and won a large majority of the Irish seats. Ignoring London's Parliament, where technically they were supposed to sit, the newly elected Sinn Féin deputies – many of them veterans of the 1916 Easter Rising – declared Ireland independent and formed the first Dáil Éireann (Irish assembly, or lower house), which sat in Dublin's Mansion House under the leadership of Éamon de Valera (1882–1975). The Irish Volunteers became the Irish Republican Army (IRA) and the Dáil authorised it to wage war on British troops in Ireland.

⬈ WOMEN OF THE REVOLUTION

The 1916 Proclamation was a radical document for its day, and called for equal rights between men and women (Britain only gave women full suffrage in 1928). This was thanks to Countess Markievicz (1868–1927) and Maud Gonne (1865–1953), two Englishwomen who inspired a generation of revolutionaries. Countess Markievicz was a committed Republican and socialist, as well as one of the military leaders of the 1916 Rising. Maud Gonne was also a staunch Republican but is perhaps better known as WB Yeats' gorgeous muse (and desperately unrequited love).

A KIND OF FREEDOM

The War of Independence, which began in 1919, resulted in around 1200 casualties, hardly a huge number in the context of the times. Nevertheless, it was a particularly nasty affair, as the IRA fought a guerrilla-style campaign against the British, their numbers swelled by returning veterans of WWI known as 'Black and Tans' (on account of their uniforms, a mix of khaki and black), whose experiences in the trenches had traumatised them to the point of being prone to all kinds of brutality. The IRA campaign was masterminded by the charismatic and ruthless Michael Collins (1890–1922), whose use of 'flying columns' to ambush British forces eventually led to the truce of July 1921.

1921	1921–22	1922–23
War ends in a truce on 11 July; the Anglo-Irish Treaty is signed on 6 December.	Treaty grants independence to 26 counties, allowing six Ulster counties to remain part of Great Britain.	Brief and bloody civil war between pro-Treaty and anti-Treaty forces results in victory for former.

IRELAND IN FOCUS

HISTORY

After months of difficult negotiations in London, the Irish delegation signed the Anglo-Irish Treaty on 6 December 1921. It gave 26 counties of Ireland – now known as the Irish Free State – limited independence and allowed six largely Protestant Ulster counties the choice of opting out. If they did (a foregone conclusion), a Boundary Commission would decide on the final frontiers between north and south. But the thorny issue of partition, coupled with the status of the newly established state – still headed by the British monarch, with Irish MPs having to swear an oath of allegiance to the Crown – was, at best, a bad compromise. Even the signatories of the treaty knew it: as he was affixing his signature, Collins commented that he was signing his own death warrant.

The Anglo-Irish Treaty was eventually ratified after a bitter debate, and the elections of June 1922 resulted in victory for the pro-Treaty forces. But the anti-Treaty forces, united behind the leadership of de Valera, refused to recognise the new state and within two weeks of the elections the first clashes between the two sides occurred.

Almost immediately, a bitter civil war broke out between comrades who, a year previously, had fought alongside each other. The most prominent casualty was Collins himself, who was shot in an ambush in his native County Cork. De Valera was briefly imprisoned by the new Free State government, formed by the new Cumann na Gael (Society of Gaels) party under Prime Minister William Cosgrave, which went so far as to execute 77 of its former comrades. By the time the conflict ground to an exhausted halt in 1923, a legacy of bitter division had been created that would last until the end of the century.

Defeated but unbowed, de Valera boycotted the Dáil before regrouping and founding a new party in 1926 called Fianna Fáil (Warriors of Ireland), which proceeded to win nearly half the seats in the 1927 election.

Fianna Fáil went one better in 1932, winning a majority and remaining in power for the next 16 years. A new constitution in 1937 did away with the oath of allegiance to

➘ THE VICTOR'S VERSION

Neil Jordan's epic film *Michael Collins* tells the story of the 'long fellow', idolised during his life and unquestionably one of the outstanding Irishmen of the 20th century.

Yet for much of that century Collins was seen by many as a traitor to the cause of Irish freedom, partly because he was a signatory of the Anglo-Irish Treaty, but mostly because his greatest political rival was Éamon de Valera, the embodiment of the Irish state from its foundation until the end of his life – when he left public life in 1973, aged 91, as the oldest head of state in the world.

1932	1948	1949
De Valera leads his Fianna Fáil party into government for the first time.	The new Fine Gael declares the Free State to be a republic at last.	Republic of Ireland leaves British Commonwealth and cuts its final links with Britain.

the Crown, reaffirmed the special position of the Catholic Church within Irish society and once again laid claim to the six counties of the north. De Valera's decision to stop paying land annuities to the British, as per the terms of the Anglo-Irish Treaty, provoked a trade war with Britain that may have done much to assert Ireland's growing spirit of independence but severely crippled Irish agricultural exports for more than a decade.

Fianna Fáil lost the 1948 general election to Fine Gael (as Cumann na Gael was now known), who proceeded to gazump the Republican credentials of their political rivals by leaving the British Commonwealth and officially declaring the Free State a republic. After 800 years, Ireland – or at least a big chunk of it – was finally independent.

GROWING PAINS & ROARING TIGERS

Unquestionably the most significant figure since independence, Éamon de Valera's contribution to an independent Ireland was immense. However, as the 1950s stretched into the 1960s, his vision for the country was mired in a conservative and traditional orthodoxy that was patently at odds with the reality of a country in desperate economic straits, where chronic unemployment and emigration were but the more visible effects of inadequate policy. De Valera's successor as Taoiseach (Prime Minister) was Sean Lemass, whose tenure began in 1959 with the dictum 'a rising tide lifts all boats'. By the mid-1960s his economic policies had halved emigration and ushered in a new prosperity that was to be mirrored 30 years later by the Celtic Tiger.

In 1972 the Republic (along with Northern Ireland) became a member of the European Economic Community (EEC), which brought an increased measure of prosperity thanks to the benefits of the Common Agricultural Policy, which set fixed prices and guaranteed quotas for Irish farming produce. Nevertheless, the broader global depression, provoked by the oil crisis of 1973, forced the country into yet another slump and emigration figures rose again, reaching a peak in the mid-1980s.

European aid was to prove instrumental in kick-starting the Irish economy in the early 1990s. Huge sums of money were invested in education and physical infrastructure, while the renewal of Lemass' industrial policy of incentivising foreign investment through tax breaks and the provision of subsidies made Ireland very attractive to high-tech businesses looking for a door into EU markets. In less than a decade, Ireland went from being one of the poorest countries in Europe to one of the wealthiest: unemployment fell from 18% to 3.5%, the average industrial wage somersaulted to the top of the European league and the dramatic rise in GDP meant that the government had far more money than it knew what do with. Ireland became synonymous with the Celtic Tiger, an economic model of success that was the envy of the entire world.

Coupled with Ireland's economic growth was a steady social shift away from the Catholic Church's overwhelmingly conservative influence, which was felt virtually

1972	1973–74	1981
The Republic (and the UK) join the EEC; 13 civilians are killed by soldiers in Derry.	Unionists strike against Sunningdale Agreement; new Northern Ireland Assembly dies before it begins.	Ten Republican prisoners die on hunger strike after the first, Bobby Sands, is elected to Parliament.

⬈ AMERICAN CONNECTIONS

Today there are over 40 million Americans with Irish ancestry – a legacy of successive waves of emigration, spurred by events from the Potato Famine of the 1840s to the Depression of the 1930s. Many legendary figures of American history, from Davy Crockett to John Steinbeck, and 16 out of the 44 US presidents to date – including Barack Obama – are of Irish descent.

everywhere, not least in the state's schools and hospitals and over every aspect of social policy. From the 1980s onwards, steady campaigning resulted in new laws protecting gay rights, access to contraception and a successful referendum on divorce. One major issue that remains unresolved, however, is the thorny question of abortion: in theory, abortion is legal if there is risk to the life of the woman, but the cloudy legal status does nothing for the thousands of women who still go to Britain every year for a termination.

The dramatic decline in the influence of the Church over the last two decades is primarily the result of global trends and greater prosperity in Ireland, but the devastating revelations of clerical abuse of boys and girls under the care of the Church over the last half-century have defined an almost vitriolic reaction against it, particularly among the younger generation. The Church's perceived reluctance to confront its own responsibilities in these shocking scandals – including reports of a number of senior members knowing about paedophiliac priests and consequently shuffling them from parish to parish – has heightened a sense of deep betrayal among many of the faithful.

IT'S (NOT SO) GRIM UP NORTH

Making sense of Northern Ireland isn't that easy. It's not because the politics are so entrenched (they are), or that the two sides are at such odds with each other (they are): it's because the fight is so old.

It began in the 16th century, with the first Plantations of Ireland ordered by the English Crown, whereby the confiscated lands of the Gaelic and Hiberno-Norman gentry were awarded to English and Scottish settlers of good Protestant stock. The policy was most effective in Ulster, where the newly arrived Protestants were given an extra leg-up by the Penal Laws, which successfully reduced the now landless Catholic population to second-class citizens with little or no rights.

But fast-forward to 1921, when the notion of independent Ireland moved from aspiration to actuality. The new rump state of Northern Ireland was governed until 1972 by the Protestant-majority Ulster Unionist Party, backed up by the overwhelmingly Protestant Royal Ulster Constabulary (RUC) and the blatantly sectarian B-Specials militia.

1993	mid-1990s	1994
Downing Street Declaration signed by British prime minister John Major and Irish Taoiseach Albert Reynolds.	The 'Celtic Tiger' economy transforms Ireland into one of Europe's wealthiest countries.	Sinn Féin leader Gerry Adams announces a cessation of IRA violence on 31 August.

JOHN SONES

Dunluce Castle ruins on the Causeway Coast (p331), County Antrim, Northern Ireland

As a result of tilted economic subsidies, bias in housing allocation and wholesale gerrymandering, Northern Ireland was, in effect, an apartheid state, leaving the roughly 40% Catholic and Nationalist population grossly underrepresented.

Defiance of Unionist hegemony came with the Civil Rights Movement, founded in 1967 and heavily influenced by its US counterpart. In October 1968 a mainly Catholic march in Derry was violently broken up by the RUC amid rumours that the IRA had provided 'security' for the marchers. Nobody knew it at the time, but the Troubles had begun.

Conflict escalated quickly: clashes between the two communities increased and the police openly sided with the Loyalists against a Nationalist population made increasingly militant by the resurgence of the long-dormant IRA. In August 1969 British troops went to Derry and then Belfast to maintain law and order; they were initially welcomed in Catholic neighbourhoods but within a short time they too were seen as an army of occupation: the killing of 13 innocent civilians in Derry on Bloody Sunday (30 January 1972) set the grim tone for the next two decades, as violence, murder and reprisal became the order of the day in the province and, occasionally, on the British mainland.

In the 1990s external circumstances started to alter the picture. Membership of the EU, economic progress in Ireland and the declining importance of the Catholic

1998	1998	2005
The Good Friday Agreement establishes a new Northern Ireland Assembly.	The 'Real IRA' detonates a bomb in Omagh, killing 29 people and injuring 200.	The IRA orders all of its units to commit to exclusively democratic means.

IRELAND IN FOCUS

HISTORY

Church in the South started to reduce differences between the North and the Republic. Also, American interest added an international dimension to the situation.

A series of negotiated statements between the Unionists, Nationalists and the British and Irish governments eventually resulted in the historic Good Friday Agreement of 1998, which established the power-sharing Northern Ireland Assembly. The last decade has been a tough one: the two sides have struggled to overcome their entrenched distrust of each other (the assembly was suspended on four separate occasions) and a mere meeting between representatives of the two most hardline elements – Sinn Féin, the political wing of the IRA, and the Democratic Unionist Party (DUP), founded by Presbyterian firebrand Ian Paisley – was seen as a major breakthrough.

Total peace has finally come to the province. Weapons have been decommissioned, the British Army has largely stood down and one-time mortal enemies have taken their seats in the now fully functioning Assembly. The politics are still a little heated and sectarianism remains a factor, but differences are resolved through ardent debate rather than with a bomb or a bullet.

↘ SOME FURTHER READING

- **The Course of Irish History** (TW Moody and FX Martin) Classic on Irish history.
- **The Great Hunger** (Cecil Woodham-Smith) Classic study of the Great Famine of 1845–51.
- **The Irish in America** (Michael Coffey) The turbulent experiences of Irish immigrants in the USA.
- **For the Cause of Liberty: A Thousand Years of Ireland's Heroes** (Terry Golway) Vivid description of the struggles of Irish nationalism.
- **A History of Ulster** (Jonathon Bardon) Serious and far-reaching attempt to come to grips with Northern Ireland's saga.
- **Cromwell: An Honourable Enemy** (Tom Reilly) Alternative view of Cromwell's Irish campaign.

2007	2008	2009
The Northern Ireland Assembly resumes after a five-year break as Unionists and Nationalists resolve differences.	The global financial crisis sends the Irish economy into a tailspin.	After two referendums, the Republic accepts the terms of the EU's Lisbon Treaty.

IRISH SYMBOLS & ICONS

JOHN SONES

Three-leafed shamrocks

Every country has its symbols, but Ireland's collection of icons serve to exemplify the country – or at least a simplistic version of it – to an astonishing degree. The Irish refer to it as 'Oirishness', which is what happens when you take a spud, shove it in a pint of Guinness and garnish it with shamrocks; you'll see it in cities throughout the world as the hyphenated Irish join with the nation's native sons and daughters to celebrate St Patrick's Day, their eyes made bleary by more than just emotion.

But those symbols didn't define Ireland by accident or happenstance. They have a history which is often far more interesting than the icon itself.

THE SHAMROCK

Ireland's most enduring symbol is the three-leafed white clover, known diminutively in Irish as *seamróg* and later anglicised as 'shamrock'. According to legend, when St Patrick was trying to explain the mystery of the Holy Trinity to the recently converted Celtic chieftains, he plucked the modest little weed and used its three leaves to explain the metaphysically challenging concept of the Father, the Son and the Holy Spirit as being separate but still part of the one being. This is why the shamrock is a ubiquitous part of St Patrick's Day celebrations.

THE CELTIC CROSS

Everywhere you go you will see examples of the Celtic cross: basically a cross surrounded by a ring. Its origins weren't simply a question of aesthetic design but more of practical

IRELAND IN FOCUS

IRISH SYMBOLS & ICONS

↘ THE LUCK OF THE IRISH?

Nearly a millennium of occupation, a long history of oppression and exploitation, a devastating famine, mass emigration…how *exactly* are the Irish 'lucky'? Well, they're not – or at least not any more so than anybody else. The expression was born in the mid-19th-century US during the gold and silver rushes, when some of the most successful miners were Irish or of Irish extraction. It didn't really matter that the Irish – recent escapees from famine and destitution in Ireland – were over-represented among the miners; the expression stuck. Still, the expression was always a little derisive, as though the Irish stumbled across good fortune by dumb luck rather than brains or effort!

necessity. The cross was a clever fusing of new Christian teaching (the cross itself) with established pagan beliefs: in this case, sun worship (marked by the circle).

Some of the most famous crosses in Ireland are in Monasterboice, County Louth (see p138) and Clonmacnoise, County Offaly (see p250).

THE LEPRECHAUN

The country's most enduring cliché is the myth of the mischievous leprechaun and his pot of gold, which he jealously guards from the attentions of greedy humans. Despite the twee aspect of the legend, its origin predates the Celts and belongs to the mythological Tuatha dé Danann (peoples of the Goddess Danu), who lived in Ireland 4000 years ago. When they were eventually defeated, their king, Lugh (the demigod father of Cúchulainn), was forced underground, where he became known as Lugh Chromain, or 'little stooping Lugh' – the origin of the leprechaun.

The Irish can get visibly irritated if asked whether they believe in leprechauns (you might as well ask them if they're stupid), but many rural dwellers are a superstitious lot. They mightn't necessarily *believe* that malevolent sprites who dwell in faerie forts actually exist, but they're not especially keen to test the theory either, which is why there still exist trees, hills and other parts of the landscape that are deemed to have…supernatural qualities – and so will never be touched.

THE HARP

The Celtic harp, or *clársach,* is meant to represent the immortality of the soul, which is handy given that it's been a symbol of Ireland since the days of Henry VIII and the first organised opposition to English rule. The harp was the most popular instrument at the Celtic court, with the harpist (usually blind) being ranked only behind the chief and the bard in order of importance. In times of war, the harpist played a special, jewel-encrusted harp and served as the cheerleading section for soldiers heading into battle.

During the first rebellions against the English, the harp was once again an instrument of revolutionary fervour, prompting the crown to ban it altogether; this eventually led to its decline as the instrument of choice for Irish musicians but ensured its status as a symbol of Ireland.

THE CLADDAGH RING

The most famous of all Irish jewellery is the Claddagh ring (see p242), made up of two hands (friendship) clasping a heart (love) and usually surmounted by a crown (loyalty). Made in the eponymous fishing village of County Galway since the 17th century, its symbolic origins are much older and belong to a broader family of rings, popular since Roman times, known as the *fede* rings (from *mani in fede*, or 'hands in trust'), which were used to symbolise marriage. Nevertheless, their popularity is relatively recent, and almost entirely attributable to their wearing by Irish Americans who use them to demonstrate their ties to their Irish heritage.

THE TRICOLOUR

Like most tricolours, the Irish flag – three vertical stripes of green, white and orange – was designed to marry two opposing forces, those that make up the Irish body politic. The green represents the Gaelic, nationalist tradition, while the orange marks the (largely) Protestant supporters of William of Orange and the maintenance of a union with Britain. Separating them is the white that symbolises the hope of peace and unity between the two sides.

The oldest known reference to the use of the three colours in one flag was in 1830, when tricolour cockades were used to celebrate the anniversary of the French Revolution (and its use of the tricolour), but it wasn't until 7 March 1848 that Thomas Francis Meagher, the leader of the revolutionary Young Ireland movement, unveiled an Irish tricolour from a 2nd-floor balcony in Dublin. Curiously, Meagher's influences were not exclusively French: his father was from Newfoundland, whose own tricolour is the green, white and rose.

◥ THE HOUND OF ULSTER

The most famous of all mythological Irish figures was Sétanta, the son of the demigod Lugh and (among other things) the greatest hurler in all of Ireland; after he killed the fearsome guard-dog of Culann in self-defence he offered to take its place until a replacement could be found, taking the name Cúchulainn – or 'hound of Culann' – by which he was known thereafter. He is the greatest hero in the Ulster Cycle of Irish mythology, featuring in the epic Táin Bó Cúailnge (Cattle Raid of Cooley), in which he single-handedly defends Ulster against the armies of Queen Medb (or Maeve) of Connaught.

LITERATURE

Books in Marsh's Library (p71), Dublin

HANNAH LEVY

Of all their national traits, characteristics and cultural expressions it's perhaps the way the Irish speak and write that best distinguishes them. Their love of language and their great oral tradition have contributed to Ireland's legacy of world-renowned writers and storytellers – so much so that some visitors are disappointed to discover that a way with poetry is not the birthright of every Irish person!

And all this in a language imposed on them by a foreign invader; the Irish responded to this act of cultural piracy by mastering a magnificent hybrid: English in every respect, but flavoured and enriched by the rhythms, pronunciation patterns and grammatical peculiarities of Irish.

Before there was anything like modern literature there was the Ulaid (Ulster) Cycle – Ireland's version of the Homeric epic – written down from oral tradition between the 8th and 12th centuries. The chief story is the Táin Bó Cúailnge (Cattle Raid of Cooley), about a battle between Queen Maeve of Connaught and Cúchulainn (see the boxed text, p369), the principal hero of Irish mythology. Cúchulainn appears in the work of Irish writers right up to the present day, from Samuel Beckett to Frank McCourt.

Zip forward a thousand years, past the genius of Jonathan Swift (1667–1745) and his *Gulliver's Travels,* stopping to acknowledge acclaimed dramatist Oscar Wilde (1854–1900), *Dracula* creator Bram Stoker (1847–1912) – some have optimistically claimed that the name of the count may have come from the Irish *droch fhola* (bad blood) – and the literary giant that was James Joyce (1882–1941), whose name and books elicit enormous pride in Ireland (although we've yet to meet five people who have read all of *Ulysses*!).

The majority of Joyce's literary output came when he had left Ireland for the artistic hotbed that was Paris, which was also true for another great experimenter of language and style, Samuel Beckett (1906–89). Influenced by the Italian poet Dante and the French philosopher Descartes, his work centred on fundamental, existential questions about the human condition and the nature of self. Beckett is probably best known for his play *Waiting for Godot,* but his unassailable reputation is based on a series of stark novels and plays.

Of the dozens of 20th-century Irish authors to have achieved public renown, some names to look out for include playwright and novelist Brendan Behan (1923–64), who wove tragedy, wit and a turbulent life into his best works, including *Borstal Boy, The Quare Fellow* and *The Hostage.* Inevitably, Behan died young from alcoholism.

Belfast-born CS Lewis (1898–1963) died a year earlier, but he left us the *Chronicles of Narnia,* a series of allegorical children's stories, two of which have been made into films, with a third *(The Voyage of the Dawn Treader)* scheduled for release in 2010. Other Northern writers have, not surprisingly, featured the Troubles in their work: Bernard McLaverty's *Cal* (also made into a film) and his more recent *The Anatomy School* are both wonderful.

Contemporary Irish writers are plentiful, including superstar Roddy Doyle (b 1958), author of the Barrytown trilogy *The Commitments, The Snapper* and *The Van,* as well as a host of more serious books; the Booker-prize-winning John Banville (b 1945), who nabbed the prestigious award with *The Sea;* and the wonderful Colm Tóibín (b 1955), whose book *The Master* (2004), about Henry James, won the *Los Angeles Times'* Novel of the Year award.

Ireland has produced its fair share of female writers. The 'come here and I'll tell you a story' style of Maeve Binchy (b 1940) has seen her outsell many of the giants of Irish literature, including Beckett and Behan, and her long list of bestsellers includes *Light a Penny Candle* (1982) and *Circle of Friends* (1990); both have been made into successful films.

Nuala O'Faolain (1940–2008), former opinion columnist for the *Irish Times,* 'accidentally' wrote an autobiography when a small publisher asked her to write an introduction to a collection of her columns. Her irreverent, humorous and touching prose struck a chord with readers and the essay was republished as *Are You*

➘ THE GAELIC REVIVAL

While Home Rule was being debated towards the end of the 19th century, another revolution was taking place in Irish arts, literature and identity. The poet WB Yeats and his literary friends (including Lady Gregory, Douglas Hyde, JM Synge and George Russell) championed the Anglo-Irish literary revival, unearthing old Celtic tales and writing about a romantic Ireland of epic battles and warrior queens. For a country that had suffered centuries of invasion and deprivation, these presented a much more attractive version of history. Similarly, Hyde and Eoin MacNeill did much to ensure the survival of the Irish language and the more everyday Irish customs and culture, which they believed to be central to Irish identity, forming the Gaelic League (Conradh na Gaeilge) in 1893 to push for the teaching of Irish in schools.

WAYNE WALTON

Reading on Bloomsday, James Joyce Cultural Centre (boxed text, p83)

Somebody? (1996), followed by *Almost There: The Onward Journey of a Dublin Woman* (2003), which both became international bestsellers.

Ireland can boast four winners of the Nobel Prize for Literature: George Bernard Shaw in 1925, WB Yeats in 1938, Samuel Beckett in 1969 and Seamus Heaney in 1995. The prestigious annual IMPAC awards, administered by Dublin City Public Libraries, accept nominations from public libraries around the world for works of high literary merit, offering a €100,000 award to the winning novelist. Previous winners have included David Malouf (Australian) and Nicola Barker (British).

POETRY

The Irish have always had a way with verse, with none better than Nobel laureate WB Yeats (1865–1939), whose poetry far outshines his work as a playwright. His *Love Poems*, edited by Norman Jeffares, makes a suitable introduction for anyone new to his writing.

Three of the executed leaders of the Easter Rising – Pádraig Pearse (1879–1916), Joseph Plunkett (1879–1916) and Thomas McDonagh (1878–1916) – were noted poets, but while they (along with Yeats) evoked a vision of a greater Gaelic Ireland, the emerging poets of the latter half of the 20th century found their themes in the narrowness and frustrations of contemporary Irish life. This is best explored in the work of Patrick Kavanagh (1905–67), whose *Great Hunger* and *Tarry Flynn* evoke the atmosphere and often grim realities of life for poor farming communities.

Northern Ireland has, unsurprisingly, been a rich breeding ground for the poetic muse. Of a host of top-class poets that belong to the Northern School, founded by John Hewitt (1907–87), the most renowned is Seamus Heaney (b 1939), Nobel Prize winner in 1995. His most recent collection is *District and Circle* (2006).

Cork-born Irish-language poet Louis de Paor has twice won Ireland's prestigious Lawrence O'Shaughnessy Award with collections of his poetry. Tom Paulin (b 1949) writes memorable poetry about the North (try *The Strange Museum*), as does Ciarán Carson (b 1948). Many of Paula Meehan's (b 1955) magical, evocative poems speak of cherished relationships.

Contemporary poets are in a rich vein of form, with the likes of Justin Quinn (b 1968) and Caitriona O'Reilly (b 1973) offering a thoughtful and perceptive critique of modern Ireland in all its complexities. Eavan Boland (b 1944) is a prolific and much-admired writer who combines Irish politics with outspoken feminism: *In a Time of Violence* (1995) and *The Lost Land* (1998) are two of her most celebrated collections.

If you're interested in finding out more about poetry in Ireland, visit the website of the excellent **Poetry Ireland** (**www.poetryireland.ie**), which showcases the work of new and established poets. For a taste of modern Irish poetry in print, try *Contemporary Irish Poetry,* edited by Fallon and Mahon. *A Rage for Order,* edited by Frank Ormsby, is a vibrant collection of the poetry of the North.

☑THE BEST

Long Room, Trinity College (p69)

HANNAH LEVY

CONTEMPORARY IRISH NOVELS

- **The Gathering** (Anne Enright)
- **All the Names Have Been Changed** (Claire Kilroy)
- **Brooklyn** (Colm Tóibín)
- **This is the Country** (William Wall)
- **John the Revelator** (Peter Murphy)

THE NATIONAL PSYCHE

CONOR CAFFREY

Boy wearing the tricolour (p369)

The Irish are justifiably renowned for their easygoing, affable nature. They're famous for being warm and friendly, which is just another way of saying that the Irish love a bit of a chat, whether it be with friends or strangers. They will entertain you with their humour, alarm you with their willingness to get stuck into a good debate and cut you down with their razor-sharp wit.

Slagging – the Irish version of teasing – is an art form, which may seem caustic to unfamiliar ears, but is quickly revealed as an intrinsic element of how the Irish relate to one another. It is commonly assumed that the mettle of friendship is proven by how well you can take a joke rather than by the payment of a cheap compliment.

The Irish aren't big on talking themselves up, preferring their actions to speak for themselves. They also admire the peculiar art of self-deprecation, known locally as *an beál bocht a chur ort* – literally, 'putting on the poor mouth' – the mildly pejorative practice of making out that things are far worse than they really are in order to evoke sympathy or the forbearance of creditors, of vital importance in the days when the majority of the Irish were at the mercy of an unforgiving landlord system. As a result, the Irish also have the trait of begrudgery – although it's something only recognised by them and generally kept within the wider family. It's kind of amusing, though, to note that someone like Bono is subject to more intense criticism in Ireland than anywhere else in the world.

Beneath all of the garrulous sociability and self-deprecating twaddle lurks a dark secret, which is that, at heart, the Irish are low on self-esteem. They're therefore very suspicious of praise and tend not to believe anything nice that's ever said about them. The Irish wallow in false modesty like a sport.

This goes some way towards explaining the fractious relationship Ireland has with alcohol. The country regularly tops the list of the world's biggest binge drinkers, and while there is an increasing awareness of, and alarm at, the devastation caused by alcohol to Irish society (especially to young people), drinking remains the country's most popular social pastime, with no sign of letting up; spend a weekend night walking around any town in the country and you'll get a firsthand feel of the influence and effect of the booze.

Some experts put Ireland's binge-drinking antics down to the dramatic rise in the country's economic fortunes, but statistics have long revealed that Ireland has had an unhealthy fondness for 'taking the cure', although the acceptability of public drunkenness is a far more recent phenomenon: the older generation are never done reminding the youngsters that *they* would *never* have been seen staggering in public.

⬎ IF I SHOULD FALL FROM GRACE

Once the poster child for devout Catholicism, Ireland has become largely estranged from the church that used to play such a central role in its culture and lifestyle. Globalisation, increased prosperity and a general loosening of moral codes – which brought contraception and divorce to a country once vehemently opposed to them – are important factors, but overshadowing them all are the revelations of widespread clerical abuse of minors and the systematic cover-up by church authorities that protected the worst offenders. For a nation that once saw Mass attendance as an integral part of life, the sense of betrayal by a church seen to have abandoned its flock has been profound and far-reaching.

Whatever the truth of it, there is no denying that the last couple of decades have transformed Irish society in ways no one could have foreseen, with this generation of under-30s only now having to confront the realities of a previous age, when unemployment, emigration and a cap on ambition were basic facts of life – although it must be stressed that whatever the current state of the economy, the Irish have truly come to believe that they are deserving of a seat at anyone's table.

Prosperity has served the country well, and while a huge question mark still remains over the equitable distribution of the wealth accrued during the last decade, there is no doubt that the island has seen some dramatic shifts in traditional attitudes. Not so long ago, Roman Catholicism was a central pillar of everyday life in Ireland; today, the Church's grip on society has slackened to the point that a recent survey revealed that one-third of Irish youth didn't know where Jesus was born or what was celebrated at Easter.

SPORT

WADE EAKLE

Women's hurling team, Croke Park (p91), Dublin

Sport has a special place in the Irish psyche, probably because it's one of the few occasions when an overwhelming expression of emotion won't cause those around you to wince or shuffle in discomfort. Sit in a pub while a match is on and watch the punters foam at the mouth as they yell pleasantries at the players on the screen, such as 'they should pay *me* for watching *you!'*

Just as soon as you thought that the alpha and omega of all social activity in this city occurred within an arm's length of licensed premises, you might be shocked to know that the Irish treat their sport – both watched and played – like religion. For some, it's all about faith through good works, like jogging, amateur football and yoga; for most everyone else, observance is enough, especially from the living-room armchair or the pub stool.

GAELIC FOOTBALL & HURLING

Gaelic games are at the core of Irishness: they are enmeshed in the fabric of Irish life and hold a unique place in the heart of its culture. Their resurgence towards the end of the 19th century was entwined with the whole Gaelic revival and the march towards Irish independence. The beating heart of Gaelic sports is the Gaelic Athletic Association (GAA), set up in 1884 'for the preservation and cultivation of national pastimes'. The GAA is still responsible for fostering these amateur games and it warms the heart to see that after all this time – and amid the onslaught of globalisation and the general commercialisation of sport – they are still far and away the most popular sports in Ireland.

FOOTBALL (SOCCER)

There is huge support in Ireland for the 'world game', although fans are much more enthusiastic about the likes of Manchester United, Liverpool and the two Glasgow clubs (Rangers and Celtic) than the struggling pros and part-timers that make up the National League (www.fai.ie) in the Republic and the Irish League (www.irishfa.com) in Northern Ireland. It's just too difficult for domestic teams to compete with the multimillionaire glitz and glamour of the English Premiership, which has always drawn off the cream of Irish talent.

At an international level, the Republic and Northern Ireland field separate teams; in 2009 both were performing adequately, but it was all a far cry from their relative moments of glory – the 1980s for Northern Ireland and 1988 to 2002 for the Republic.

RUGBY

Although traditionally the preserve of Ireland's middle classes, Irish rugby's governing body, the Irish Rugby Football Union (www.irishrugby.ie), has done a brilliant job selling the game of rugby outside its traditional domain, so much so that the game has finally generated a genuinely national interest.

Rugby captures the mood of the whole island from February to April during the annual Six Nations Championships, because the Irish team is drawn from both sides of the border and is supported by both nationalists and unionists. In recognition of this, the Irish national anthem is no longer played at internationals, having been replaced by the slightly dodgy but thoroughly inoffensive 'Ireland's Call', a song written especially for the purpose – although nobody seemed to mind it being played in 2009 when Ireland won its first Grand Slam (a clean sweep of victories in one campaign) since 1948.

Rugby is also popular at an inter-provincial level, with the traditional four provinces of Ireland pitted against each other in the Magners League (www.magnersleague .com) and the more prestigious European Rugby Cup (www.ercrugby.com), played by teams throughout the continent; Munster, Ulster and most recently Leinster have won this competition in recent years.

HORSE RACING & GREYHOUND RACING

A passion for horse racing is deeply entrenched in Irish life and comes without the snobbery of its English counterpart. If you fancy a flutter on the ponies you can watch racing around Ireland and England on the TV in bookmakers' shops every day. No money ever seems to change hands in the betting, however, and every Irish punter will tell you they 'broke even'.

Ireland has a reputation for producing world-class horses for racing and other

ꙮ THE FAST & THE FURIOUS

Gaelic games are played by two teams of 15 players whose aim is to get the ball through what resembles a rugby goal. Gaelic football is played with a round, soccer-size ball, and players are allowed to kick it or handpass it, as in Australian Rules Football. Hurling, which is considered by far the more beautiful game, is played with a flat ashen stick or bat known as a hurley, or *camán*. The small leather ball, called a *slíothar*, is hit or carried on the hurley; handpassing is also allowed. Both games are played over 70 action-filled minutes.

Cycle race, County Mayo

equestrian events like showjumping – also very popular, albeit in a less egalitarian kind of way. Major annual races include the Irish Grand National (Fairyhouse, County Meath, April), Irish Derby (the Curragh, County Kildare, June) and Irish Leger (the Curragh, September). For more event information, contact **Horse Racing Ireland** (www.hri.ie).

Traditionally the poor-man's punt, greyhound racing ('the dogs') has been smartened up in recent years and partly turned into a corporate outing. It offers a cheaper, more accessible and more local alternative to horse racing. There are 20 tracks across the country, administered by the **Irish Greyhound Board** (www.igb.ie).

GOLF

Golf is enormously popular in Ireland and there are many fine golf courses. The annual Irish Open takes place in June or July, and the Irish Women's Open in September. For details of venues, contact the **Golfing Union of Ireland** (www.gui.ie). Ireland's best include Rory McIlroy, Graeme McDowell and, of course, the triple Major winner Padraig Harrington – Ireland's only Major winner since Fred Daly in 1947.

CYCLING

Cycling is a popular spectator sport and major annual events include the gruelling **FBD Insurance Rás** (www.fbdinsuranceras.com), formerly known as the Milk Rás, an eight-day stage race held in May that sometimes approaches 1120km (700 miles) in length; and the Tour of Ulster, a three-day stage race held at the end of April. For more information on events see www.irishcycling.com.

ATHLETICS

Athletics is popular here, and the Republic has produced a few international stars, particularly in middle- and long-distance events. Current stars of the track include hurdler Derval

O'Rourke, distance runner Mary Cullen and sprinters David Gillick and Paul Hession. In Ireland, the main athletic meets are held at Morton Stadium, Dublin. The **Belfast Marathon** (www.belfastcitymarathon.com) runs on the first Monday in May; the **Dublin Marathon** (www.dublincitymarathon.ie) is run on the last Monday in October.

BOXING

Boxing has traditionally had a strong working-class following. Irish boxers have often won Olympic medals or world championships. Barry McGuigan and Steve Collins, both now retired, were world champions in their day; the best of the current crop is Dublin boxer Bernard Dunne, who was WBA Super Bantamweight World Champion for a brief time in 2009.

ROAD BOWLING

The object of bowling (pronounced more like *bowel*-ing) is to throw an 800g cast-iron ball along a public road (normally one with little traffic) for a designated distance, usually 1km or 2km. The person who does it in the least number of throws is the winner. The main centres are Cork, which has 200 clubs, and (to a lesser extent) Armagh. Competitions take place throughout the year, attracting considerable crowds. The sport has been taken up in various countries around the world, including the USA, Germany and the Netherlands, and a world championship competition has been set up (see www.irishroadbowling.ie).

⭮THE BEST

HOLGER LEUE

Race day, County Galway

CURRENT SPORTING HEROES

- **Padraig Harrington** (Golf)
- **Brian O'Driscoll** (Rugby)
- **Henry Shefflin** (Hurling)
- **Colm 'Gooch' Cooper** (Gaelic Football)
- **Sea the Stars** (Horse Racing)

IRELAND IN FOCUS

SPORT

THE IRISH PEOPLE

DOUG MCKINLAY

Eating in a snug, Crown Liquor Saloon (p326), Belfast

The Irish may like to grumble – about work, the weather, the government and those *feckin' eejits* on reality TV shows – but if pressed will tell you that they live in the best country on earth. There's loads *wrong* with the place, but isn't it the same way everywhere else?

Traditional Ireland – of the large family, closely linked to church and community – is quickly disappearing as the nation's increased urbanisation continues to break up the social fabric of community interdependence that was a necessary element of relative poverty. Contemporary Ireland is therefore not altogether different from any other European country, and you have to travel further to the margins of the country – the islands and the isolated rural communities – to find an older version of society.

Nevertheless, Ireland's birth rate – the highest in the EU at 17.2 births per 1000 people – grew by a massive 9.4% in 2008, although it's a sign of the times that about a third of the babies born in 2008 were born outside of marriage (even if roughly half of those were registered as having both parents living together). And while the number of couples getting married is down, it is only slightly so, hovering around 5 marriages per 1000 people over the last decade.

The attitude towards gay people has also changed, courtesy of a general liberalisation of the country's mores and the enactment of protective legislation against any kind of sexual discrimination. The passing of the Civil Partnership Act in 2009, which recognised civil unions between same-sex couples but did not grant them full marriage rights, was seen as a further step in the right direction, though not nearly far enough by the LGBT community. Same-sex couples in Northern Ireland do have the rights and responsibilities of full civil marriage, courtesy of the UK's 2004 Civil Partnership Act.

Ireland has long been a pretty homogenous country, but the arrival of thousands of immigrants from all over the world – 10% of the population is foreign-born – has challenged the mores of racial tolerance and integration. To a large extent it has been successful, although if you scratch beneath the surface, racial tensions can be exposed. So long as the new arrivals take on the jobs that many Irish wouldn't bother doing anymore, everything is relatively hunky-dory; it's when the second generation of immigrants begin competing for the middle-class jobs that Ireland's tolerance credentials will truly be tested.

⬎ IRISH NAMES

The most popular names for Irish boys and girls:

- Jack
- Sean
- Conor
- Daniel
- James

- Sarah
- Emma
- Ella
- Katie
- Sophie

THE PUB

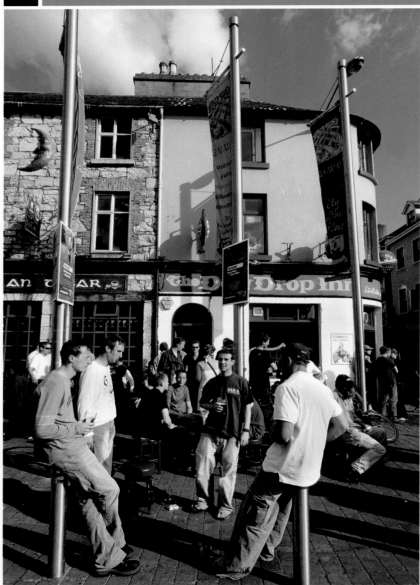

JOHN ELK III

Enjoying a drink outside a pub, County Galway

Simply put, the pub is the heart of Ireland's social existence, and we're guessing the experience of it ranks pretty high on your list of things to do while you're here. But let's be clear: we're not just talking about a place to get a drink. Oh, no. You can get a drink in a restaurant or hotel, or wherever there's someone with a bottle of something strong – the pub is something altogether more than that.

It is the broadest window through which you can examine and experience the very essence of the nation's culture, in all its myriad forms. It's the great leveller where status and rank hold no sway, where generation gaps are bridged, inhibitions lowered, tongues loosened, schemes hatched, songs sung, stories told and gossip embroidered. It's a unique institution: a theatre and a cosy room, a centre stage and a hideaway, a debating chamber and a place for silent contemplation. It's whatever you want it to be, and that's the secret of the great Irish pub.

Talk – whether it is frivolous, earnest or incoherent – is the essential ingredient. Once tongues are loosened and the cogs of thought oiled, your conversation can go anywhere and you should follow it to its natural conclusion. An old Irish adage suggests you should never talk about sport, religion or politics in unfamiliar company. But just be mindful and you needn't restrict yourself too much. While it's a myth to say you can walk into any pub and be befriended, you probably won't be drinking on your own for long – unless that's what you want, of course. There are few more spiritual experiences than a solitary pint in an old country pub in the mid-afternoon.

But remember that banter is the fibre of sociability. 'Slagging', or teasing, is the country's favourite pastime and a far more reliable indicator of the strength of friendship than virtually any kind of compliment: a fast, self-deprecating wit and an ability to take a joke in good spirits will win you plenty of friends.

⇘ PUB ETIQUETTE

As always with somewhere sacred, there are rules. Implicit, rarely explained, but as fast as iron. The rounds system – the simple custom where someone buys you a drink and you buy one back – is the bedrock of Irish pub culture. It's summed up in the Irish saying: 'It's impossible for two men to go to a pub for one drink.' Nothing will hasten your fall from social grace here like the failure to uphold this pub law. The Irish are extremely generous and one thing they can't abide is tightfistedness.

Another golden rule about the system is that the next round starts when the first person has finished (preferably just about to finish) their drink. It doesn't matter if you're only halfway through your pint, if it's your round get them in.

Your greatest challenge will probably be trying to keep up with your fellow drinkers, who may keep buying you drinks in every round even when you've still got a clatter of unfinished pints in front of you and you're sliding face first down the bar.

RICHARD CUMMINS

Outdoor drinks at a pub, County Cork

Aesthetically, there is nothing better than the traditional haunt, populated by flat-capped pensioners bursting with delightful anecdotes and always ready to dispense a kind of wisdom distilled through generations of experience. The best of these have stone floors and a peat fire; the chat barely rises above a respectful murmur save for appreciative laughter, and best of all, there's no music save the kind played by someone sitting next to you. Pubs like these are a disappearing breed, but there are still plenty of them around to ensure that you will find one, no matter where you are.

TRADITIONAL MUSIC

Irish musicians playing at O'Connor's (p263), Doolin, County Clare

Irish music (known here as traditional music, or just trad) has retained a vibrancy not found in other traditional European forms, many of which have lost out to the overbearing influence of pop music. And that's not just because of *Riverdance*, even though that particular show has been a marvellous worldwide ambassador for the more authentic music from whence it came.

Although Irish music has held onto many of its traditional aspects, it has itself influenced many forms of music, most notably US country and western – a fusion of Mississippi Delta blues and Irish traditional tunes that, combined with other influences, such as gospel, is at the root of rock and roll. Other reasons for trad music's current success include the willingness of its exponents to update the way it's played (in ensembles rather than the customary *céilidh* – or communal dance – bands), the habit of pub sessions (introduced by returning migrants) and the economic good times that encouraged the Irish to celebrate their culture rather than trying to replicate international trends. And then, of course, there's *Riverdance*, which made Irish dancing sexy and became a worldwide phenomenon, despite the fact that most aficionados of traditional music are seriously underwhelmed by its musical worth. Good stage show, crap music.

Traditionally, music was performed as a background to dancing, and while this has been true ever since Celtic times, the many thousands of tunes that fill up the repertoire aren't nearly as ancient as that; most aren't much older than a couple of hundred years. Because much of Irish music is handed down orally and aurally, there are numerous variations in the way a single tune is played, depending on the time and place of its playing. The blind itinerant harpist Turlough O'Carolan (1680–1738) wrote more than 200 tunes – it's difficult to know how many versions their repeated learning has spawned.

⬎ THE NUTS & BOLTS

Despite popular perception, the harp isn't widely used in traditional music; the bodhrán (*bow*-rawn) goat-skin drum is much more prevalent. The uillean pipes, played by squeezing bellows under the elbow, provide another distinctive sound, although you're not likely to see them in a pub. The fiddle isn't unique to Ireland but it is one of the main instruments in the country's indigenous music, along with the flute, tin whistle, accordion and bouzouki (a kind of mandolin). Music fits into five main categories – jigs, reels, hornpipes, polkas and slow airs – while the old style of singing unaccompanied versions of traditional ballads and airs is called *sean-nós*.

If you want to hear musical skill that will both tear out your heart and restore your faith in humanity, go no further than the fiddle playing of Tommy Peoples on *The Quiet Glen* (1998), the beauty of Paddy Keenan's uillean pipes on his eponymous 1975 album, or the stunning guitar playing of Andy Irvine on albums such as *Compendium* (2000).

More folksy than traditional, the Dubliners, fronted by the distinctive gravel voice and grey beard of Ronnie Drew (1934–2008), made a career out of bawdy drinking songs that got *everybody* singing along, but their finest moment was a solo performance of *Scorn Not His Simplicity* by band member Luke Kelly (1940–84), surely one of the saddest, most beautiful songs ever recorded. Other popular bands include the Fureys, comprising four brothers originally from the Travelling community (no, not like the Wilburies, but a nomadic Irish people) along with guitarist Davey Arthur. And if it's rousing renditions of Irish rebel songs you're after, you can't go past the Wolfe Tones.

Since the 1970s, various bands have tried to blend traditional with more progressive genres, with mixed success. The first band to pull it off was Moving Hearts, led by Christy Moore, who went on to become the best-loved Irish folk musician ever.

While traditional music remains popular in its own right both in Ireland and abroad, it also continues to provide the base for successful new genres. Think of ambient music with a slightly mystical tinge and invariably Enya will come to mind. As for the stars of tomorrow, the line-up has yet to be finalised, but it will surely include a young piper from Dublin called Sean McKeown and his sometimes playing partner, the fiddler Liam O'Connor.

⬎ THE BEST

DOUG MCKINLAY

Irish musicians at Hughes' Bar (p90), Dublin

TRADITIONAL ALBUMS

- **The Quiet Glen** (Tommy Peoples)
- **Paddy Keenan** (Paddy Keenan)
- **Compendium: The Best of Patrick Street** (Various artists)
- **The Chieftains 6: Bonaparte's Retreat** (The Chieftains)
- **Old Hag You Have Killed Me** (The Bothy Band)

⭨ DIRECTORY & TRANSPORT

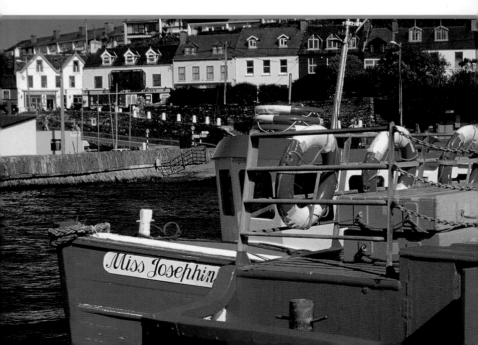

DIRECTORY

ACCOMMODATION

Sleeping entries are categorised by the price of a double room and then ordered by budget. Our favourites are selected because they have a little something – or in some cases, quite a lot of something – that makes a stay there that bit more memorable; we've also endeavoured, where possible, to highlight properties that walk the green walk and are committed to eco-responsibility (see also the GreenDex, p431).

Rates are per *room* per night, unless otherwise stated: budget (under €60/£40), midrange (€60 to €150/£40 to £100) and top end (over €150/£100), and high-season rates are given throughout. Where a range of prices is given, it refers to rates for different rooms during high season. Prices are cheaper online and off-peak. Room prices in Dublin are disproportionately high and can be double what you would pay elsewhere in the country.

Caveat emptor: the global financial crisis has hit Irish tourism very hard and price structuring is not nearly as predictable as it was as recently as 2008. B&B rates have more or less remained steady since 2008 and many hoteliers – particularly at the

upper end of the scale – are in a desperate struggle to stay alive. Consequently, they're doing the previously unthinkable in an effort to sell rooms, slashing rates dramatically and offering a plethora of incentive deals to get you into their hotels: free add-ons like dinners and spa treatments are increasingly standard, as are 'three nights for the price of two' offers.

Rack rates at the top hotels are no longer to be trusted and the standard prices quoted on the brochure or the website have become increasingly pie-in-the-sky – it's quite the norm these days to pay half the quoted rate in some of the country's top properties, particularly out of season. The key, however, is to ask: when making a booking, don't settle for the first rate quoted, and be sure to ask for a better deal. More often than not, you'll get one.

Generally speaking, the majority of accommodation providers will still raise their rates during 'special' weekends – bank holidays or during major sporting events and festivals – when tourist numbers are at their highest and hoteliers can take a breather from worrying about empty rooms. Expect to be charged anything up to 15% to 20% more than usual at these times.

In low season (November to March) you can simply drop in or ring ahead in rural areas. In peak season it's best to book ahead. Fáilte Ireland (Irish Tourist Board) or the Northern Ireland Tourist Board (NITB) will book serviced (€5 to €13 booking fee, depending on the size of your party) or self-catering accommodation (€7 booking fee) through their booking system, **Gulliver Ireland** (☎ **066-979 2030; www.gulliver.ie**).

Much of the accommodation closes during Christmas and New Year, especially in rural areas.

↘ BOOK YOUR STAY ONLINE

For more accommodation reviews and recommendations by Lonely Planet authors, check out the online booking service at www.lonelyplanet.com. You'll find the true, insider lowdown on the best places to stay. Reviews are thorough and independent. Best of all, you can book online.

⇘ PRACTICALITIES

- Ireland uses the metric system for weights, measures, speed limits and most signposting, except for the old-style black-on-white signs which still use miles (as does Northern Ireland).
- DVD players take Region 2 discs, as with the rest of Europe.
- Electrical appliances use a three flat-pin socket and a 220V/50Hz AC power supply.
- Get an insight into Irish life with one of the world's best newspapers, the *Irish Times*, or Ireland's biggest-selling *Irish Independent*.
- Relish Irish political satire in the fortnightly magazine *Phoenix*, or brush up on current affairs in *Magill* magazine.
- Check both sides of Northern Irish current affairs with Loyalist tabloid *News Letter* and the pro-Republican *Irish News*.
- TV addicts should tune into *Questions and Answers* (RTE 1), a hard-hitting current affairs program on Monday nights, or catch a great documentary on TG4, the national Irish-language station (subtitles available).
- Tune into RTE Radio One (88-90 FM or 252 kHz LW) for culture and politics; Today FM (100-102 FM) for pop, rock and alternative music; or Newstalk (106-108 FM) for music, chat and some current affairs.

DIRECTORY

ACCOMMODATION

B&BS

The ubiquitous bed and breakfasts are small, family-run houses, farmhouses and period country houses with fewer than five bedrooms. Standards vary enormously, but most have some bedrooms with private bathroom at a cost of roughly €35 to €40 (£20 to £25) per person per night. In luxurious B&Bs, expect to pay €55 (£38) or more per person. Facilities in budget-range B&Bs may be very limited; TVs, telephones, kettles and the like are the trappings of midrange to top-end establishments, while the hand-held credit card machine is increasingly common (although don't be surprised in remote rural areas if they insist on cash).

GUESTHOUSES

Essentially, guesthouses are much like upmarket B&Bs. The difference lies in their size, with guesthouses having between six and 30 bedrooms. Prices vary enormously according to the standard but the minimum you can expect to shell out is €35 (£22) per person (€40 in Dublin), and up to about €100 (£35) in upmarket places. Unlike hotels, the majority of guesthouses are unlicensed but many have restaurants and good facilities, and can take credit-card payment.

HOTELS

Hotels range from the local pub to medieval castles, and prices fluctuate accordingly. In most cases, you'll get a better rate than the one published if you go online or negotiate directly with the hotel, especially out of season. The explosion of bland midrange chain hotels (many Irish-owned) has proved a major challenge to the traditional B&B or guesthouse: they might not have the same personalised service but their rooms are clean and their facilities generally quite good.

DIRECTORY

ACTIVITIES

⇘ WEBSITE ACCOMMODATION RESOURCES

www.allgohere.com This website lists accommodation in Northern Ireland suitable for travellers with (and without) a disability.

www.corkkerry.ie A useful resource for accommodation and information throughout the southwest.

www.daft.ie Online classified paper for short- and long-term rentals.

www.discovernorthernireland.com Northern Ireland Tourist Board's (NITB) accommodation booking site.

www.elegant.ie Specialises in self-catering castles, period houses and unique properties.

www.familyhomes.ie Lists – you guessed it – family-run guesthouses and self-catering properties.

www.gulliver.ie Fáilte Ireland and the NITB's accommodation booking site.

www.hostelworld.com A useful website for comparing hostels and booking beds.

www.ireland.travel.ie Fáilte Ireland's accommodation booking site.

www.irishlandmark.com Not-for-profit conservation group that rents self-catering properties of historical and cultural significance, such as castles, gate lodges and lighthouses.

www.stayinireland.com Lists guesthouses and self-catering options.

ACTIVITIES

Activities open up Ireland in a way that can be both cheap and relaxing, and offer a unique experience of the country.

BIRDWATCHING

The variety and size of the flocks that visit or breed in Ireland make it of particular interest to birdwatchers. It's also home to some rare and endangered species.

There are more than 70 reserves and sanctuaries in Ireland, but some aren't open to visitors and others are privately owned, so you'll need permission from the proprietors before entering.

More information can be obtained from the tourist boards and from the following organisations:

Birds of Ireland News Service (☎ 01-830 7364; www.birdsireland.com)

BirdWatch Ireland (☎ 01-281 9878; www.birdwatchireland.ie) Offers birdwatching field courses, all of which take place on Cape Clear Island in County Cork.

National Parks & Wildlife Service (☎ 01-888 2000; www.npws.ie)

Royal Society for the Protection of Birds (RSPB; ☎ 028-9049 1547; www.rspb.org.uk; Belvoir Park Forest, Belfast)

Some useful publications on birdwatching are Dominic Couzens' *Collins Birds of Britain and Ireland* and the slightly out-of-date *Where to Watch Birds in Ireland* by Clive Hutchinson.

CYCLING

The tourist boards can supply you with a list of operators who organise cycling holidays. For more on the practicalities of travelling around Ireland with a bike, see p409.

Both **Irish Cycling Safaris** (☎ 01-260 0749; www.cyclingsafaris.com; Belfield Bike Shop,

UCD, Dublin) and Go Ireland (☎ 066-976 2094; www.goactivities.com; Old Orchard House, Killorglin, Co Kerry) organise tours for groups of cyclists in the southwest, the southeast, Connemara and Counties Clare, Donegal and Antrim.

FISHING

Ireland is justly famous for its generally no-fee coarse fishing, covering bream, pike, perch, roach, rudd, tench, carp and eel. Killing of pike over 6.6lb (3kg) in weight is prohibited, so anglers are limited to one pike; killing of coarse fish is frowned upon and anglers are encouraged to return coarse fish alive. Freshwater game fish include salmon, sea trout and brown trout. Some managed fisheries also stock rainbow trout.

Licences in the Republic are available from the local tackle shop or direct from the Central Fisheries Board (☎ 01-884 2600; www.cfb.ie). An all-district licence costs €31.74/£15 while a single district licence costs €15.23/£12; both are valid for one year.

In the North, rod licences for coarse and game fishing are obtainable from the Foyle, Carlingford & Irish Lights Commission (☎ 028-7134 2100; www.loughs-agency.org) for the Foyle and Carlingford areas, and from the Fisheries Conservancy Board (☎ 028-3833 4666; www.fcbni.com) for all other regions. You also require a permit from the owner, which is usually the Department of Culture, Arts & Leisure, Inland Waterways & Inland Fisheries Branch (☎ 028-9025 8825; www.dcalni.gov.uk).

GOLF

There are over 300 golf courses and links in Ireland. Despite the spread of new, American-style parkland courses over the last decade, golf in Ireland is best played on links courses, which can be found along the entirety of its coastline. Contact Fáilte Ireland, the NITB, the Golfing Union of Ireland (☎ 01-505 4000; www.gui.ie) or the Irish Ladies Golf Union (☎ 01-293 4833; www.ilgu.ie) for information on golfing holidays.

Green fees for 18 holes start from around €25 (£15) on weekdays, but top-notch places charge up to €200 (£150). Courses are tested for their level of difficulty; many are playable year-round, especially links.

HANG-GLIDING & PARAGLIDING

Some of the finest hang-gliding and paragliding in the country is found at Mt Leinster in Carlow, Great Sugarloaf Mountain (p119) in Wicklow, Benone and Magilligan Beaches in Derry and Achill Island in Mayo. Check the websites of the Irish Hang Gliding & Paragliding Association (www.ihpa.ie) and the Ulster Hang Gliding & Paragliding Club (www.uhpc.co.uk) for local pilots.

HORSE RIDING

Unsurprisingly, considering the Irish passion for horses, riding is a popular pastime. There are dozens of centres throughout Ireland, offering possibilities ranging from hiring a horse for an hour (from €25/£15) to fully packaged, residential equestrian holidays.

Recommended outfits are Canadian-based Hidden Trails (www.hiddentrails.com) and Ballycumisk Riding School (☎ 028-37246, 087 961 6969; Ballycumisk, Schull, Co Cork).

WALKING

There are many superb walks in Ireland, including 31 'waymarked ways' or designated long-distance paths of varying lengths. The maintenance and development of the ways is administered in the

Republic by the **National Trails Office** (☎ 01-860 8800; www.walkireland.ie) and in the North by **Countryside Access & Activities Network** (CAAN; ☎ 028-9030 3930; www.countrysiderecreation.com).

Some useful guides are Lonely Planet's *Walking in Ireland*, Michael Fewer's *Irish Long-Distance Walks* or *Best Irish Walks* by Joss Lynam.

For mountain rescue call ☎ 999.

MAPS

EastWest Mapping (☎/fax 053-937 7835; www.eastwestmapping.ie) has good maps of long-distance walks in the Republic and the North. Tim Robinson of **Folding Landscapes** (☎ 095-35886; www.folding landscapes.com) produces superbly detailed maps of the Burren, the Aran Islands and Connemara. His and Joss Lynam's *Mountains of Connemara: A Hill Walker's Guide* contains a useful detailed map.

ORGANISED WALKS

If you don't have a travelling companion you could consider joining an organised walking group.

Go Ireland (☎ 066-976 2094; www.goactivi ties.com; Old Orchard House, Killorglin, Co Kerry) Offers walking tours of the west.

South West Walks Ireland (☎ 066-712 8733; www.southwestwalksireland.com; 6 Church St, Tralee, Co Kerry) Provides a series of guided and self-guided walking programs around the southwest, northwest and Wicklow.

ROCK CLIMBING

Ireland's mountain ranges aren't high – Mt Carrantuohil in Kerry's Macgillycuddy's Reeks is the tallest mountain in Ireland at only 1039m – but they're often beautiful and offer some excellent climbing possibilities. The highest mountains are in the southwest.

Adventure centres around the country run courses and organise climbing trips. For further information contact the **Mountaineering Council of Ireland** (☎ 01-625 1115; www.mountaineering.ie), which also publishes climbing guides and the quarterly magazine *Irish Mountain Log*, or check the forums on **Irish Climbing Online** (www.climbing.ie).

WATER SPORTS

CANOEING

Ireland has canoeing for all levels, from novice to expert; winter is the best time, when heavy rains swell the rivers. Check out the **Irish Canoe Union** (☎ 01-625 1105; www.irishcanoeunion.com).

SCUBA DIVING

Ireland has some of the best scuba diving in Europe, found almost entirely off the western coast among its offshore islands and rocks. The best period for diving is roughly March to October. Visibility averages more than 12m but can increase to 30m on good days. For more details about scuba diving in Ireland, contact Comhairle Fó-Thuinn (CFT), also known as the **Irish Underwater Council** (☎ 01-284 4601; www.cft.ie), Ireland's diving regulatory body, which publishes the dive magazine *SubSea* (also available online).

Divecology (☎ 028-28943; www.divecology .com; Cooradarrigan, Schull, Co Cork) is a good dive school, with trips to local wrecks.

SWIMMING & SURFING

Ireland has some magnificent coastline and some great sandy beaches: the cleaner, safer ones have EU Blue Flag awards. Get a list from the government agency **An Taisce** (National Trust for Ireland; ☎ 01-454 1786; www.antaisce.org) or check online with the **Blue Flag Programme** (www.blueflag.org).

Surfers should visit www.surfingireland. net or www.victorkilo.com for beach reports and forecasts. **Donegal Adventure Centre** (☎ **074-984 2418; www.donegal-holidays .com; Bay View Ave, Bundoran, Co Donegal)** is an excellent youth-oriented surf school and **Bundoran Surf Co** (☎ **071-984 1968; www .bundoransurfco.com; Bundoran, Co Donegal)** offers surfing, kite-surfing and power-kiting.

The best months for surfing in Ireland, when the swells are highest, are September (when the water is warmest because of the Gulf Stream) and October. Some of the best locations are on the west and northwest coasts, such as Lahinch (p259) in Clare, Strandhill (p286) and Easkey (p288) in Sligo and Bundoran (p292), Rossnowlagh (p293) and Fanad Peninsula (p302) in Donegal, where you'll also find big surfing schools.

WATER-SKIING

There are water-ski clubs all over Ireland offering tuition, equipment and boats. A full list is available from the **Irish Water Ski Federation** (**www.iwsf.ie**).

WINDSURFING

The windsurfer has plenty of locations to indulge in this popular sport – even on the Grand Canal in Dublin! The western coast is the most challenging and the least crowded. The bay at Rosslare Harbour in County Wexford is ideal for windsurfing, with equipment and tuition available in summer. The **Irish Sailing Association** (☎ **01-280 0239; www.sailing.ie**) is the sport's governing authority and has details of particular activity centres.

CLIMATE CHARTS

Thanks to the moderating effect of the Atlantic Gulf Stream, Ireland's climate is relatively mild for its latitude, with a mean annual temperature of around 10°C (50°F).

The temperature drops below freezing only intermittently during winter, and snow is scarce – perhaps one or two brief flurries a year. The coldest months are January and February, when daily temperatures range from 4°C to 8°C (39°F to 46°F), with 7°C (44°F) the average. In summer, temperatures during the day

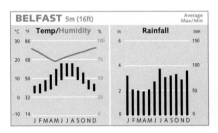

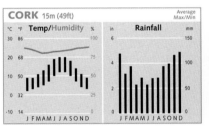

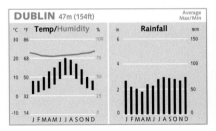

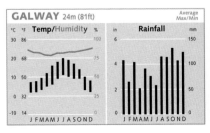

are a comfortable 15°C to 20°C (59°F to 68°F). During the warmest months, July and August, the average is 16°C (61°F). A hot summer's day in Ireland is 22°C to 24°C (72°F to 75°F), although it can sometimes reach 30°C (86°F). There are about 18 hours of daylight daily during July and August and it's only truly dark after about 11pm.

One thing you can be sure of about Irish weather is how little you can be sure of. It may be shirtsleeves and sunglasses in February, but winter woollies in March and even during the summer.

And then there's the rain. Ireland has a lot of rain, with certain areas getting a soaking as many as 270 days of the year. County Kerry is the worst affected. The southeast is the driest, enjoying a more continental climate.

COURSES

There are myriad courses in Ireland, from archery classes to learning how to play the harp. Adventure centres, where you can do everything from hill-walking to raft-building, are increasingly popular; we have listed them throughout the book. Below we have included only guidelines to courses; for greater details, see the relevant sections in the destination chapters or check out www.visitireland.com.

ARTS & CRAFTS

Rockfield Ecological Estate (☎ 043-76024; Rathaspic, Rathowen, Co Westmeath; tour €5, mains €18-25; ☼ by appointment) gives you an inspiring insight into sustainable living as well as traditional Irish culture and crafts. In addition to two-hour tours of the working farm, you can dine on nutritious homemade food made with organic produce from the rambling gardens (while sitting on a chair fashioned from fallen tree branches), and take part in full-day craft courses (€100 per person including lunch) such as spinning, weaving, basket-making, woodcarving and stone-sculpting.

COOKING

Ballyknocken (☎ 0404-69274; www.ballyknocken.com; Glenealy, Ashford, Co Wicklow) Full-day cooking classes given by Ballymaloe graduate Catherine Fulvio run throughout the year.

Ballymaloe (☎ 021-464 6785; www.cookingisfun.ie; Ballycotton, Co Cork) From half-day sessions to 12-week certificate courses.

Berry Lodge (☎ 065-708 7022; www.berrylodge.com; Annagh, Co Clare) Offering in-depth instruction, often over more than one day.

Fiacri Country House Restaurant (☎ 0505-43017; www.fiacrihouse.com; Roscrea, Co Tipperary) Course are run year-round, ranging from one day to five weeks in length.

Ghan House (☎ 042-937 3682; www.ghanhouse.com; Carlingford, Co Louth) Offers hands-on cooking classes and cooking demonstrations.

Good Things Café (☎ 027-61426; www.thegoodthingscafe.com; Durrus, Co Cork) Runs cooking courses year-round, including a two-day 'miracle' program for kitchen beginners.

MEDITATION

Jampa Ling Buddhist Centre (☎ 049-952 3448; www.jampaling.org; Owendoon House, Bawnboy, Co Cavan; self-catering dm/s €20/30, dm/s incl meals €35/40) Offers meditation courses.

MUSIC

In July and August, **Dingle Music School** (☎ 086-319 0438; www.dinglemusicschool.com; Dykegate Lane, Dingle, Co Kerry) offers beginners' workshops in bodhrán (hand-held goatskin drum; from €15; noon Tuesday, Wednesday and Thursday, 11am on Saturday) and tin whistle (€25; 11am Monday). Bodhráns are supplied.

Harp workshops are conducted as part of the O'Carolan International Harp Festival & Summer School (☎ 071-964 7204; www.keadue.harp.net; ☺ late Jul-early Aug).

CUSTOMS

Duty-free sales are not available when travelling within the EU. Goods meant for personal consumption purchased in and exported within the EU incur no additional taxes, if duty has been paid somewhere in the EU. Over certain limits you may have to show that they are for personal use. The amounts that officially constitute personal use are 3200 cigarettes (or 400 cigarillos, 200 cigars or 3kg of tobacco) and either 10L of spirits, 20L of fortified wine, 60L of sparkling wine, 90L of still wine or 110L of beer. There's no customs inspection apart from those concerned with drugs and national security.

Travellers coming from outside the EU are allowed to import duty-free 200 cigarettes, 1L of spirits or 2L of wine, 60mL of perfume and 250mL of eau de toilette.

Dogs and cats brought in from anywhere outside Ireland and the UK are subject to strict quarantine laws. The EU Pet Travel Scheme, whereby animals are fitted with a microchip, vaccinated against rabies and blood-tested six months *prior* to entry, is in force in the UK and the Republic of Ireland. No preparation or documentation is necessary for the movement of pets directly between the UK and the Republic. Contact the Department of Agriculture, Food & Rural Development (☎ 01-607 2000; www.agriculture.gov.ie) in Dublin for further details.

DANGERS & ANNOYANCES

Ireland is safer than most countries in Europe, but normal precautions should be observed. In Dublin, drug-related crime is not uncommon and the city has its fair share of pickpockets and thieves.

Northern Ireland is as safe as anywhere else, but there are areas where the sectarian divide is bitterly pronounced, most notably in parts of Belfast. For the foreseeable future, it's probably best to ensure your visit to Northern Ireland doesn't coincide with the climax of the Orange marching season on 12 July; sectarian passions are usually inflamed and even many Northerners leave the province at this time.

DISCOUNT CARDS
HERITAGE DISCOUNTS

Heritage Card (☎ 01-647 6587; www.heritageireland.com; adult/child & student/senior/family €21/8/16/55) Entitles you to free access to over 75 sites for one year.

National Trust (☎ 0870 458 4000; www.nationaltrust.org.uk; adult/under 25/family £47.50/21.50/82) Entitles you to free admission to its 18 properties in Northern Ireland, but only really makes financial sense if you're touring its British sites too. It's cheaper to join online.

SENIOR CARDS

Senior citizens are entitled to many discounts in Ireland on things such as public transport and museum admission fees, provided they show proof of age. The minimum qualifying age is usually 60 to 65 for men and 55 to 65 for women. In your home country, a lower age may already entitle you to travel packages and discounts (on car hire, for instance).

Car hire companies usually won't rent to drivers aged over 70 or 75.

DIRECTORY

CUSTOMS

EMBASSIES & CONSULATES

IRISH EMBASSIES & CONSULATES

Irish diplomatic offices overseas:

Australia Embassy (☎ 02-6273 3022; www
.embassyofireland.au.com; 20 Arkana St, Yarralumla, Canberra, ACT 2600)

Canada Embassy (☎ 613-233 6281; www
.embassyofireland.ca; 130 Albert St, Suite 1105,
Ottawa, Ontario K1P 5G4)

France Embassy (☎ 01 44 17 67 00; www
.embassyofireland.fr; 4 rue Rude, 75116 Paris)

Germany Embassy (☎ 030-220 720; Frie-
drichstrasse 200, 10117 Berlin)

Italy Embassy (☎ 06 697 9121; www.embassy
ofireland.it; Piazza di Campitelli 3, 00186 Rome)

Netherlands Embassy (☎ 070-363 0993;
www.embassyofireland.nl; Dr Kuyperstraat 9,
2514BA The Hague)

New Zealand Consulate (☎ 09-977 2252;
www.ireland.co.nz; Level 7, Citibank Bldg, 23 Customs St East, Auckland)

UK Embassy (☎ 020-72352171; www.embassy
ofireland.co.uk; 17 Grosvenor Pl, London SW1X
7HR, England); Consulate (☎ 0131-226 7711;
www.irishconsulatescotland.co.uk; 16 Randolph
Cres, Edinburgh EH3 6TT, Scotland); Consulate
(☎ 029-2066 2000; Brunel House, 2 Fitzalan Rd,
Cardiff CF24 0EB, Wales)

USA Embassy (☎ 202-462 3939; www
.embassyofireland.org; 2234 Massachusetts Ave
NW, Washington, DC 20008) There are also
consulates in Boston, Chicago, New
York and San Francisco.

United Kingdom (for Northern Ireland)
diplomatic offices abroad:

Australia High Commission (☎ 02-6270
6666; www.ukinaustralia.fco.gov.uk; Commonwealth Ave, Yarralumla, Canberra, ACT 2600)

Canada High Commission (☎ 613-237
1530; www.ukincanada.fco.gov.uk; 80 Elgin St,
Ottawa, Ontario K1P 5K7)

France Embassy (☎ 01 44 51 31 00; www
.ukinfrance.fco.gov.uk; 35 rue du Faubourg St
Honoré, 75383 Paris)

Germany Embassy (☎ 030-204 570; www
.ukingermany.fco.gov.uk; Wilhelmstrasse 70,
10117 Berlin)

Italy Embassy (☎ 06 4220 0001; www.ukinitaly
.fco.gov.uk; Via XX Settembre 80a, 00187 Rome)

Netherlands Embassy (☎ 070-427 0427;
www.ukinnl.fco.gov.uk; Lange Voorhout 10,
2514ED The Hague)

New Zealand High Commission (☎ 04-
924 2888; www.ukinnewzealand.fco.gov.uk; 44
Hill St, Wellington 6011)

USA Embassy (☎ 202-588 6500; www.ukin
usa.fco.gov.uk; 3100 Massachusetts Ave NW,
Washington, DC 20008)

EMBASSIES & CONSULATES IN IRELAND

If you're even remotely responsible for
any kind of trouble, your country's embassy won't be of any help to you – you're
bound by Irish (and in the North, British)
law. In genuine emergencies you might
get some assistance: a free ticket is exceedingly unlikely but embassies might
assist you with getting a new passport.

The following countries have embassies
in Dublin:

Australia (☎ 01-664 5300; www.ireland.
embassy.gov.au; 7th fl, Fitzwilton House, Wilton
Tce, Dublin 2)

Canada (☎ 01-234 4000; 7-8 Wilton Tce,
Dublin 2)

France (☎ 01-277 5000; www.ambafrance.ie;
36 Ailesbury Rd, Dublin 4)

Germany (☎ 01-269 3011; www.dublin.diplo
.de; 31 Trimleston Ave, Booterstown, Blackrock,
Co Dublin)

Italy (☎ 01-660 1744; www.ambdublin.esteri.it;
63-65 Northumberland Rd, Ballsbridge, Dublin 4)

Netherlands (☎ 01-269 3444; www.nether
landsembassy.ie; 160 Merrion Rd, Ballsbridge, Dublin 4)

UK (☎ 01-205 3700; www.britishembassy.ie; 29 Merrion Rd, Ballsbridge, Dublin 4)
USA (☎ 01-668 8777; www.usembassy.ie; 42 Elgin Rd, Ballsbridge, Dublin 4)

The following countries have consular representation in Northern Ireland:
Germany (☎ 028-9024 4113; Chamber of Commerce House, 22 Great Victoria St, Belfast)
Netherlands (☎ 028-9077 9088; c/o All-Route Shipping Ltd, 14-16 West Bank Rd, Belfast)
USA (☎ 028-9038 6100; Danesfort House, 223 Stranmillis Rd, Belfast)

FESTIVALS & EVENTS

There are literally hundreds of festivals held throughout the year, but the summer months are the most popular; listed here is a thumbnail sketch of the major events. Local tourist offices will have additional information, as will Fáilte Ireland (www.discoverireland.ie). Also, the Association of Irish Festival Events (AOIFE) maintains a very useful website at www.aoife online.com; www.art.ie is worth perusing, too. See the Calendar (p46) for more information.

GAY & LESBIAN TRAVELLERS

Irish laws on homosexuality are among the most liberal in Europe, and the margin of tolerance between the laws and prevalent attitudes is narrowing all the time. Gays and lesbians are a comfortably visible presence on the streets of the bigger urban centres, but even outside of Dublin, Cork and Galway there is a growing acceptance of homosexuality as a fact of life.

Generally the Irish couldn't care less what you do behind closed doors, and neither gays nor lesbians (in the Republic) are excluded from the armed forces. Although the Vatican maintains its position that being gay is a crime against God, the Catholic Church here maintains an air of discreet silence on gay and lesbian issues.

The monthly Gay Community News (www.gcn.ie), found online and in clubs and bars, is a free publication of the National Lesbian & Gay Federation (NLGF; ☎ 01-671 9076; www.nlgf.ie). Aimed at younger members of the gay, lesbian and transgender community, BeLonG To (☎ 01-670 6223; www.belongto.org; 13 Parliament St, Dublin) offers advice and support to people aged 14 to 23 and facilitates support groups throughout the country.

Other online resources and organisations for the gay and lesbian community:
Gaire (www.gaire.com) Message board and info for a host of gay-related issues.
Gay & Lesbian Youth Northern Ireland (www.glyni.org.uk)
Northern Ireland Gay Rights Association (Nigra; ☎ 028-9066 5257; nigra@dnet .co.uk)
Outhouse (☎ 01-873 4932; www.outhouse .ie; 105 Capel St, Dublin) A gay, lesbian and transgender community centre.

The following helplines can be called from anywhere in Ireland:
Gay Men's Health Project (☎ 01-660 2189) Practical advice on men's health issues.
Gay Switchboard Dublin (☎ 01-872 1055; ⏱ 7.30am-9.30pm Mon-Fri, 3.30-6pm Sat)
Lesbian Line Belfast (☎ 028-9023 8668; ⏱ 7.30-10pm Thu)
Lesbian Line Dublin (☎ 01-872 9911; ⏱ 7-9pm Thu)
Mensline Belfast (☎ 028-9032 2023; ⏱ 7.30-10pm Mon-Wed)

HEALTH
BEFORE YOU GO
While Ireland has excellent health care, prevention is the key to staying healthy

while abroad. Bring medications in their original, clearly labelled containers. A signed and dated letter from your doctor describing your medical conditions and medications, including generic names, is also a good idea. If you are carrying syringes or needles, be sure to have a physician's letter documenting their medical necessity. Carry a spare pair of contact lenses and glasses, and take your optical prescription with you.

For information on health insurance, see right.

AVAILABILITY & COST OF HEALTH CARE

Excellent health care is readily available and for minor self-limiting illnesses pharmacists can give valuable advice and sell over-the-counter medication. They can also advise when more specialised help is required and point you in the right direction.

HOLIDAYS

Public holidays can cause road chaos as everyone tries to get somewhere else for the break. It's also wise to book accommodation in advance around these times.

PUBLIC HOLIDAYS

Public holidays in both the Republic and Northern Ireland:

New Year's Day 1 January
St Patrick's Day 17 March
Easter (Good Friday to Easter Monday inclusive) March/April
May Holiday 1st Monday in May
Christmas Day 25 December
St Stephen's Day (Boxing Day) 26 December

NORTHERN IRELAND

Spring Bank Holiday Last Monday in May

Orangeman's Day 12 July
August Holiday Last Monday in August

REPUBLIC

June Holiday 1st Monday in June
August Holiday 1st Monday in August
October Holiday Last Monday in October

St Patrick's Day and St Stephen's Day holidays are taken on the following Monday when they fall on a weekend. In the Republic, nearly everywhere closes on Good Friday even though it isn't an official public holiday. In the North, most shops open on Good Friday but close the following Tuesday.

INSURANCE

Insurance is important: it covers you for everything from medical expenses and luggage loss to cancellations or delays in your travel arrangements, depending on your policy.

If you're an EU citizen, a European Health Insurance Card (EHIC; available from health centres, or from post offices in the UK) covers you for most medical care. Other countries, such as Australia, also have reciprocal agreements with Ireland and Britain, but many countries do not.

If you do need health insurance, remember that some policies offer lower and higher medical-expense options, but the higher one is chiefly for countries that have extremely high medical costs. Ensure that you're covered for the worst possible case, such as an accident requiring an ambulance, hospital treatment or an emergency flight home. You may prefer a policy that pays health-care providers directly rather than having you pay on the spot and claim later.

All cars on public roads must be insured. If you are bringing your own car check that your insurance will cover you in Ireland.

INTERNET ACCESS

Most laptops these days are dual-voltage and should work with just a plug adapter (Ireland uses the same triple flat-pin plug as the UK), but if your computer isn't equipped to handle 220 volts AC, you'll need a universal AC adapter, as well. All hotel rooms have phone lines and you can plug the phone cord into your laptop's modem; although most have direct-dial services, you'll most likely have to dial an outside line access number (usually 9) to get online. Provided you're dialling a local access number you'll be charged the price of a local call (which from a hotel is usually timed and costs 50% more than usual).

Many major internet service providers (ISPs), such as **AOL** (www.aol.com), **CompuServe** (www.compuserve.com) and **AT&T Business Internet Services** (www.attbusiness.net), have dial-in nodes in Ireland. If you access your email account through an ISP based at home, your best option is to open an account with a local ISP provider: the most reliable ones are **Eircom** (☎ 1890 260 260; www.eircom.ie) or **O2** (☎ 1850 200 741; www.o2.ie).

Although Ireland has one of the lowest rates of broadband penetration in Europe (26% in 2009), 60% of Irish households have broadband, including most B&Bs in and around the major towns of Ireland; you'll also find wi-fi (wireless internet) in many midrange and top-end hotels. Most towns also have internet cafes, although many are closing as the rate of household broadband goes up. You can log on for €4 to €10 per hour in the Republic, or about £4 per hour in the North.

LEGAL MATTERS

If you need legal assistance contact the **Legal Aid Board** (☎ 066-947 1000; www .legalaidboard.ie). It has a number of local law centres listed in the phone book. In the North, contact the **Northern Ireland Legal Services Commission** (www.nilsc .org.uk).

The possession of small quantities of marijuana (cannabis) attracts a fine or warning, but harder drugs are treated more seriously. Public drunkenness is illegal but commonplace. Be aware that you will undoubtedly attract police attention if you're way out of line. Fighting is treated more harshly – you could easily end up in a cell for the night, or worse.

MAPS

Many publishers produce some good-quality maps of Ireland. Michelin's 1:400,000-scale Ireland map (No 923) is a decent single sheet map, with clear cartography and most of the island's scenic roads marked. The four maps – North, South, East and West – that make up the Ordnance Survey Holiday map series at 1:250,000 scale are useful if you want more detail. Collins also publishes a range of maps covering Ireland.

For greater detail, map aficionados and walkers should look out for the Ordnance Survey Discovery series, which covers the whole island in 89 maps at a scale of 1:50,000. They're available at the **National Map Centre** (Map p68; ☎ 01-476 0471; www .mapcentre.ie; 34 Aungier St, Dublin), through www.osi.ie and many bookshops around Ireland.

MONEY

To get a general idea of accommodation costs in Ireland, see p388. Tips of around 10% are expected for metered cabs and in restaurants where the service charge isn't included.

ATMS & CREDIT CARDS

Most banks have ATMs that are linked to international money systems such as Cirrus, Maestro or Plus. Each transaction incurs a currency conversion fee and credit cards can incur immediate and exorbitant cash-advance interest rate charges.

Charge cards such as Amex and Diners Club don't have credit limits, but may not be accepted in smaller establishments. Visa and MasterCard are more widely accepted, though some rural B&Bs and some smaller or remote petrol stations still deal only in cash.

Remember to keep a note of the emergency telephone number to ring if your card is lost or stolen.

CASH & TRAVELLERS CHEQUES

Most major brands of travellers cheques are accepted in Ireland. Amex and Thomas Cook travellers cheques are widely recognised and branches don't charge a fee for cashing their own cheques. Travellers cheques are rarely accepted outside banks or used for everyday transactions. Eurocheques can be cashed in Ireland, but special arrangements must be made with your home bank before you travel if you are thinking of using personal cheques.

As for cash, we suggest you arrive with some cash in the local currency (both euros and sterling, if travelling to the North) to tide you over.

CURRENCY

Ireland's currency is the euro (€), which is divided into 100 cents. While the notes are all the same throughout the 12 countries of the euro zone, the Irish coins feature a harp on the reverse side – though of

course all non-Irish euro coins are also legal tender. (Remember that the UK is not a participant, so if you're travelling to Northern Ireland you'll have to change euros into pounds.)

The British pound sterling (£) is used in Northern Ireland, where it is known as the Northern Irish pound. Northern Ireland notes, while equivalent in value to British pound notes, are not readily accepted in Britain, but British banks will swap them for you.

The best exchange rates are obtained at banks. Bureaus de change and other exchange facilities usually open for longer hours but the rate and/or commission will be worse. Many post offices operate a currency-exchange facility and open on Saturday morning. Exchange rates at the time of writing are on the inside front cover of this book.

TAXES & REFUNDS

Value-added tax (VAT) is a sales tax of 21.5% that applies to most luxury goods in Ireland, excluding books, children's footwear and second-hand clothing. Visitors from non-EU countries can claim back most of the VAT on purchases that are subsequently exported from the EU within three months of purchase.

Most shops in both the Republic and Northern Ireland operate a taxback scheme – the most popular are Cashback and Ireland Tax Free – which operate roughly as follows: if you're a resident of a country outside the EU and buy something from a store displaying a Cashback or Ireland Tax Free sticker, you'll be given a relevant voucher with your purchase which can be refunded directly onto your credit card or in US, Canadian or Australian dollars, British pounds or euros at Dublin or Shannon airport; one advantage of Ireland Tax Free is that you can reclaim your tax at the nearest Travelex office, usually Thomas Cook.

If you reclaim more than €250 on any of your vouchers you'll need to get the voucher stamped at the customs booth in the arrivals hall at Dublin or Shannon airport before you can get your refund from the Cashback desk.

In Northern Ireland, shops participating in the Tax-Free Shopping refund scheme will give you a form or invoice on request to be presented to customs when you leave. After customs have certified the form, it will be returned to the shop for a refund and the cheque sent to you at home.

PHOTOGRAPHY

Natural light in Ireland can be very dull, so to capture the sombre atmosphere use faster film, such as 400ASA (though 200ASA should do in most situations). Lonely Planet's full-colour *Travel Photography: A Guide to Taking Better Pictures,* written by internationally renowned travel photographer Richard I'Anson, is full of handy hints and is designed to take on the road. Both film and digital memory cards are readily available in all tourist centres.

In regard to taking photos in Northern Ireland, if you want to take photos of fortified police stations, army posts or other military or quasi-military paraphernalia, get permission first to be on the safe side. In the Protestant and Catholic strongholds of West Belfast it's best not to photograph people without permission: always ask first and be prepared to accept a refusal.

TELEPHONE

You shouldn't have any problems in Ireland making phone calls to anyone, anywhere.

Prices are generally lower in the evenings after 6pm and on weekends. Phone calls made from hotel rooms will cost twice the standard rate. You can send and receive faxes for a fee from post offices or most hotels. Local telephone calls from a public phone in the Republic cost €0.30 for around three minutes (or around €0.60 to a mobile), regardless of when you call.

The number for local and national directory enquiries in the Republic is ☎ 11811 or ☎ 11850; for international it's ☎ 11818. In the North, call ☎ 118118.

Prepaid phonecards by Eircom and private operators are available in newsagencies and post offices, and work from all payphones for both domestic and international calls.

DIRECT HOME CALL CODES

Instead of placing reverse-charge calls through the Irish operator, you can dial direct to your home-country operator and then reverse the charges or charge the call to a credit card. To use the home-direct service dial the codes listed here, the area code and, in most cases, the number you want. Your home-country operator will come on the line before the call goes through.

Australia (☎ 1800 550 061 + number)
France (☎ 1800 551 033 + number)
Italy (☎ 1800 550 039 + number)
New Zealand (☎ 1800 550 064 + number)
Spain (☎ 1800 550 034 + number)
UK – BT (☎ 1800 550 044 + number)
USA – AT&T (☎ 1800 550 000 + number)
USA – MCI (☎ 1800 551 001 + number)
USA – Sprint (☎ 1800 552 001 + number)

MOBILE PHONES

Virtually everyone in Ireland has a mobile phone. Ireland uses the GSM 900/1800 cellular phone system, which is compatible with European and Australian, but not North American or Japanese, phones. SMS is a national obsession, especially with young people (who communic8 mostly by txt).

There are four Irish service providers: Vodafone, O2, Meteor and 3. There are three mobile codes – 085, 086 and 087. All have links with most international GSM providers, which allow you to 'roam' onto a local service on arrival. This means you can use your mobile phone to text and make local calls, but will be charged at a much higher rate. You can also purchase a pay-as-you-go package with a local provider with your own mobile phone. As you use up your airtime, you simply buy a top-up card (€10 to €35) at a newsagency or petrol station. Similar schemes exist in Northern Ireland.

PHONE CODES
When calling the Republic of Ireland from abroad, dial your international access code, followed by 353, then the domestic number including the area code (minus the initial '0').

When calling Northern Ireland from abroad, dial your international access code, then 44-28, and then the local number. To call Northern Ireland from Britain, simply dial 028, then the local number. This changes to 048 when calling from the Republic.

The area code for the whole of Northern Ireland is 028, so domestic callers need only dial the eight-digit local number.

To call UK numbers from the Republic dial 00-44, then the area code minus the initial '0', then the local number. Do the same for international calls, replacing 44 with the country code.

To call Britain from Northern Ireland dial the area code followed by the local number. To place an international call or to call the Republic from Northern Ireland, dial 00 followed by the country code, then the area code (dropping any leading '0') and the local number.

TIME
In winter, Ireland is on Greenwich Mean Time (GMT), also known as Universal Time Coordinated (UTC), the same as Britain. In summer, the clock shifts to GMT plus one hour, so when it's noon in Dublin and London, it's 4am in Los Angeles and Vancouver, 7am in New York and Toronto, 1pm in Paris, 7pm in Singapore, and 9pm in Sydney.

TOILETS
Forget about the few public facilities on the street: they're dirty and usually overrun with drug dealers and addicts. All shopping centres have public toilets – often marked with the Irish *Fir* (Men) and *Mná* (Women); if you're stranded, go into any bar or hotel.

TOURIST INFORMATION
Fáilte Ireland (☎ in the Republic 1850 230 330, in the UK 0800 039 7000; www.discover ireland.ie) and the **Northern Irish Tourist Board** (NITB; ☎ head office 028-9023 1221; www.discovernorthernireland.com) are mines of information.

Both websites include an accommodation booking service; reservations can also be made via the tourist boards' system **Gulliver Ireland** (☎ 066-979 2030; www .gulliver.ie).

Fáilte Ireland has an office in **Belfast** (☎ 028-9032 7888) and NITB has an office in **Dublin** (☎ within the Republic 01-679 1977, 1850 230 230).

In both the Republic and the North there's a tourist office in almost every big town; most can offer a variety of services including accommodation and attraction reservations, currency changing services, map and guidebook sales and free publications. Fáilte Ireland also has six regional offices, which can give more in-depth information on specific areas.

MAIN REGIONAL TOURIST OFFICES IN THE REPUBLIC

Cork & Kerry (☎ 021-425 5100; www.discover ireland.ie/southwest; **Cork Kerry Tourism, Áras Discover, Grand Pde, Cork**)

Dublin (☎ 01-605 7700; www.visitdublin.com; **Dublin Tourism Centre, St Andrew's Church, 2 Suffolk St, Dublin**)

East Coast & Midlands (☎ 044-934 8761; www.discoverireland.ie/eastcoast; **East Coast & Midlands Tourism, Dublin Rd, Mullingar**) For Kildare, Laois, Longford, Louth, Meath, North Offaly, Westmeath and Wicklow.

Ireland North West & Lakelands (☎ 071-916 1201; www.discoverireland.ie/northwest; **Temple St, Sligo**) For Cavan, Donegal, Leitrim, Monaghan and Sligo.

Ireland West (☎ 091-537 700; www.discover ireland.ie/west; **Ireland West Tourism, Áras Fáilte, Forster St, Galway**) For Galway, Roscommon and Mayo.

Shannon Region (☎ 061-361 555; www .discoverireland.ie/shannon; **Shannon Development, Shannon, Clare**) For Clare, Limerick, North Tipperary and South Offaly.

South East (☎ 051-875 823; www.discoverire land.ie/southeast; **South East Tourism, 41 The Quay, Waterford**) For Carlow, Kilkenny, South Tipperary, Waterford and Wexford.

TOURIST OFFICES ABROAD

Outside Ireland, Fáilte Ireland and the NITB unite under the banner Tourism Ireland. More information about offices around the world can be found at its international website, www.discover ireland.com.

TRAVELLERS WITH DISABILITIES

Travelling in Ireland with a disability can be a frustrating experience, as facilities and access are quite poor by European and US standards. Improvements are being made, but progress is quite slow in some areas. If you have a physical disability, get in touch with your national support organisation (preferably the travel officer if there is one) before you go. It often has libraries devoted to travel and can put you in touch with agencies that specialise in tours for travellers with disabilities.

Guesthouses, hotels and tourist sights around Ireland are gradually being adapted for people with disabilities. Fáilte Ireland and NITB's accommodation guides indicate which places are wheelchair accessible.

Public transportation can be a bit hit-and-miss. In the big cities, most buses now have low-floor access and priority space on board, but the number of kneeling buses on regional routes is still relatively small.

Trains are accessible with help. In theory, if you call ahead, an employee of Iarnród Éireann (Irish Rail) will arrange to accompany you to the train. Newer trains have audio and visual information systems for visually impaired and hearing-impaired passengers.

The **Citizens' Information Board** (☎ 01-605 9000; www.citizensinformationboard .ie) in the Republic and **Disability Action** (☎ 028-9066 1252; www.disabilityaction.org) in Northern Ireland can give some advice, although most of their information concerns the rights of Irish citizens with disabilities. Travellers to Northern Ireland can also check out the website www .allgohere.com.

VISAS

UK nationals don't need a passport to visit the Republic, but are advised to carry one (or some other form of photo identification) to prove that they *are* a UK national. It's also necessary to have a passport or photo ID when changing travellers cheques or hiring a car. European Economic Area (EEA) citizens (that is, citizens of EU states, plus Iceland, Liechtenstein and Norway) can enter Ireland with either a passport or a national ID card. Visitors from outside the EEA will need a passport, which should remain valid for at least six months after their intended arrival.

For EEA nationals and citizens of most Western countries, including Australia, Canada, New Zealand and the USA, no visa is required to visit either the Republic or Northern Ireland, but citizens of India, China and many African countries do need a visa for the Republic. Full visa requirements for visiting the Republic are available online at www.dfa.ie; for Northern Ireland's visa requirements see www.ukvisas.gov.uk.

WOMEN TRAVELLERS

Except for the occasional wolf whistle from a building site or a ham-fisted attempt at a chat-up by some drunken guy, women will probably find travelling in Ireland a blissfully relaxing experience. Walking alone at night, especially in certain parts of Dublin, and hitching are probably unwise. Should you have serious problems, be sure to report them to the local tourist authorities.

There's little need to worry about what you wear in Ireland, and the climate is hardly conducive to topless sunbathing. Finding contraception is not the problem it once was, although anyone on the pill should bring adequate supplies.

Rape Crisis Network Ireland (www.rcni .ie) runs a 24-hour helpline at ☎ 1800 77 88 88. In the North, try the **Rape Crisis & Sexual Abuse Centre** (☎ 028-9032 9002).

TRANSPORT
GETTING THERE & AWAY
ENTERING THE COUNTRY

An increase in the number of foreign nationals seeking asylum during the last decade has meant a far more rigorous questioning for those from African and Asian countries or from certain parts of Eastern Europe. The border between the Republic and Northern Ireland still exists as a political reality, but there are few if

---

⌖ CLIMATE CHANGE & TRAVEL

Travel – especially air travel – is a significant contributor to global climate change. At Lonely Planet, we believe that all who travel have a responsibility to limit their personal impact. As a result, we have teamed with Rough Guides and other concerned industry partners to support Climate Care, which allows people to offset the greenhouse gases they are responsible for with contributions to energy-saving projects and other climate-friendly initiatives in the developing world. Lonely Planet offsets all staff and author travel.

For more information, turn to the responsible travel pages on www.lonely planet.com. For details on offsetting your carbon emissions and a carbon calculator, go to www.climatecare.org.

any checkpoints left; for non-EU nationals it is assumed the screening process occurred upon entry to the UK. For information on visa requirements, see left.

PASSPORT
EU citizens can travel freely to and from Ireland if bearing official photo ID. Those from outside the EU, however, must have a passport that remains valid for six months after entry.

AIR
AIRPORTS
There are scheduled nonstop flights from Britain, continental Europe and North America to Dublin and Shannon, and good nonstop connections from Britain and continental Europe to Cork.

Cork (ORK; ☎ 021-431 3131; www.corkairport.com)

Dublin (DUB; ☎ 01-814 1111; www.dublinairport.com)

Shannon (SNN; ☎ 061-712 000; www.shannonairport.com)

Other airports in the Republic with scheduled services from Britain:

Donegal (CFN; ☎ 074-954 8284; www.donegalairport.ie; Carrickfinn)

Kerry (KIR; ☎ 066-976 4644; www.kerryairport.ie; Farranfore)

Knock (NOC; ☎ 094-936 8100; www.irelandwestairport.com)

Waterford (WAT; ☎ 051-875 589; www.flywaterford.com)

In Northern Ireland there are flights to **Belfast International** (BFS; ☎ 028-9448 4848; www.belfastairport.com) from Britain, continental Europe and the USA.

Other airports in Northern Ireland that operate scheduled services from Britain:

Belfast City (BHD; ☎ 028-9093 9093; www.belfastcityairport.com)

TRANSPORT

GETTING THERE & AWAY

↘ FARE GO
Travel costs throughout this book are for single (one-way) adult fares, unless otherwise stated.

Derry (LDY; ☎ 028-7181 0784; www.cityofderryairport.com)

TICKETS
The emergence of the no-frills, low-fares model as the future of European air travel has made cheap tickets the norm rather than the exception. For point-to-point travel, the best deals are almost always available online – indeed, Europe's largest carrier, Ryanair, will penalise passengers who don't avail themselves of the online services (including check-in) – but more complicated travel arrangements are best handled by a real live travel agent, who knows the system, the options and the best deals. Be sure to check the terms and conditions of the cheapest fares before purchasing.

ONLINE BOOKING AGENCIES
Best Fares (www.bestfares.com) American site offering discounted airfares and hotel rooms.

Cheap Flights (www.cheapflights.com) American- and British-based site that lists fare comparisons for discounted flights and travel packages.

ebookers (www.ebookers.com) Irish, web-based internet travel agency.

Expedia (www.expedia.co.uk) Microsoft's travel site.

Opodo (www.opodo.com) Joint booking service for nine European airlines.

Priceline (www.priceline.com) American, web-based travel agency.

STA Travel (www.statravel.com) International student travel agency.

Travelocity (www.travelocity.com) American, web-based travel agency.

AUSTRALIA & NEW ZEALAND

There are no nonstop scheduled air services from Australia or New Zealand to Ireland; generally it's cheapest to fly to London or Amsterdam and continue from there. Most fares to European destinations can have a return flight to Dublin tagged on at little or no extra cost. Round-the-world (RTW) tickets are another good bet and are often better value than standard return fares.

The Saturday travel sections of the *Sydney Morning Herald* and Melbourne *Age* newspapers advertise cheap fares; in New Zealand, check the *New Zealand Herald* travel section.

Recommended agencies:

AUSTRALIA

Flight Centre (☎ 133 133; www.flightcentre .com.au)
Shamrock Travel (☎ 03-9602 3700; www .irishtravel.com.au)
STA Travel (☎ 1300 733 035; www.statravel .com.au)

NEW ZEALAND

Flight Centre (☎ 0800-243 544; www.flight centre.co.nz)
STA Travel (☎ 0508-782 872; www.statravel .co.nz)

CANADA

Air Canada is the only carrier flying directly to Ireland, from Toronto to both Dublin and Shannon. Your best bet for cheaper fares may be to connect to transatlantic gateways in the USA or to fly to London and continue on to Ireland from there. Check the travel sections of the *Globe & Mail, Toronto Star, Montreal Gazette* or *Vancouver Sun* for the latest offers.

Recommended agencies:
Canadian Affair (☎ 1604-678 6868; www .canadian-affair.com) Cheap one-way fares to British cities.
Flight Centre (☎ 1877-967 5302; www .flightcentre.ca)
Travel CUTS (☎ 866-246 9762; www.travel cuts.com)

CONTINENTAL EUROPE

Price wars have cut the cost of flights to Ireland from continental Europe to their lowest rates ever. The two biggest players in the market are the one-time national airline, Aer Lingus (www.aerlingus.com), now a low-frills airline in virtually every respect, offering competitive prices to over 40 destinations; and the king of all low-fares airlines, Ryanair (www.ryanair .com), which serves over 80 European destinations from Dublin and over 100 from its (now) main hub at London Stansted. Ryanair's success is predicated on using secondary airports in or around major cities, which can make for expensive and time-consuming transfers. Check when you book.

UK

There is a mind-boggling array of flights between Britain and Ireland. The best deals are usually available online, and it's not unusual for airport taxes to exceed the base price of the ticket on the lowest fares (generally for early morning or late-night flights midweek).

Most regional airports in Britain have flights to Dublin and Belfast and some also provide services to Shannon, Cork, Kerry, Knock and Waterford.

USA

In the USA, discount travel agencies (called 'consolidators') sell cut-price tickets on scheduled carriers. Aer Lingus is the chief carrier between the USA and Ireland, with flights from New York, Boston, Chicago, San Francisco and Washington, DC, to Shannon, Dublin and Belfast. Heavy competition on transatlantic routes into London might make it cheaper to fly there and then continue on to Ireland. The Sunday travel sections of the *New York Times, San Francisco Chronicle-Examiner, Los Angeles Times* and *Chicago Tribune* list cheap fares.

Some of the more popular travel agencies:

Ireland Consolidated (☎ 212-661 1999; www.irelandair.com)

STA Travel (☎ 800-781 4040; www.statravel .com)

SEA

There are many ferry and fast-boat services from Britain and France to Ireland. Prices quoted throughout this section are one-way fares for a single adult on foot/up to two adults with a car, during peak season.

UK & IRELAND
FERRY & FAST BOAT

There are numerous services between Britain and Ireland but it's definitely wise to plan ahead as fares can vary considerably, depending on the season, day, time and length of stay. Often, some return fares don't cost that much more than one-way fares and it's worth keeping an eye out for special offers. International Student Identity Card (ISIC) holders and Hostelling International (HI) members get a reduction on the normal fares.

These shipping lines operate between Britain and Ireland:

Irish Ferries (☎ in the UK 0870-517 1717, in the Republic 1890 31 31 31; www.irishferries.com) For ferry and fast-boat services from Holyhead to Dublin, and ferry services from Pembroke to Rosslare.

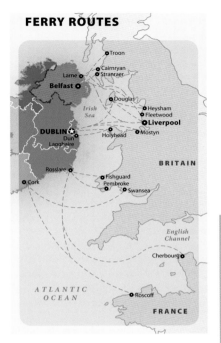

FERRY ROUTES

TRANSPORT

GETTING THERE & AWAY

Isle of Man Steam Packet Company/ Sea Cat (☎ in the UK 1800 805 055, in the Republic 01-836 4019; www.steam-packet.com) Ferry and fast-boat services from Liverpool to Dublin or Belfast via Douglas (on the Isle of Man).

Norfolkline (☎ in the UK 0870-600 4321, in the Republic 01-819 2999; www.norfolkline.com) Ferry services from Liverpool to Belfast and Dublin.

P&O Irish Sea (☎ in the UK 0870-242 4777, in the Republic 01-407 3434; www.poirishsea.com) Ferry and fast-boat services from Larne to Cairnryan and Troon, and ferry services from Liverpool to Dublin.

Stena Line (☎ 0870-570 7070; www.stena line.com) Ferry services from Holyhead to Dun Laoghaire, Fleetwood to Larne and Stranraer to Belfast, and fast-boat services from Holyhead to Dublin, Fishguard to Rosslare, and Stranraer to Belfast.

The main routes from the UK to the Republic include the following:

Fishguard & Pembroke to Rosslare These popular, short ferry crossings take 3½ hours (from Fishguard) or four hours (from Pembroke) and cost around £25/119; the cost drops significantly outside peak season. The fast-boat crossing from Fishguard takes just under two hours and costs around £30/135.

Holyhead to Dublin & Dun Laoghaire The ferry crossing takes just over three hours and costs from £25/95. The fast-boat service from Holyhead to Dun Laoghaire takes a little over 1½ hours and costs £25/130.

Liverpool to Dublin The ferry service takes 8½ hours from Liverpool and costs £25/180. Cabins on overnight sailings cost more. The fast-boat service takes four hours and costs up to £40/240.

The main routes from mainland Britain to the North:

Cairnryan to Larne The fast boat takes one hour and costs £21/170. The ferry takes 1¾ hours and costs £15/120.

Fleetwood to Larne The six-hour crossing costs £122; no foot passengers are carried.

Liverpool to Belfast The 8½-hour crossing costs £40/155 (including meals) during the day and £30/235 (including cabin and meals) at night.

Stranraer to Belfast The fast boat takes 1¾ hours and costs £20/130. The ferry takes 3¼ hours and costs £16/85.

It's possible to combine bus and ferry tickets from major UK centres to all Irish towns on the bus network, which mightn't be as convenient as flying on a budget airline, but leaves less of a carbon footprint. The journey between London and Dublin takes about 12 hours and costs about £43 one way. The London to Belfast trip takes 13 to 16 hours and costs £38 one way. For details in London contact **Eurolines** (☎ 0870-514 3219; www.eurolines.com).

FRANCE
FERRY
Brittany Ferries (☎ in the Republic 021-427 7801, in France 02 98 29 28 00; www.brittany ferries.com) Weekly service from Roscoff to Cork from early April to late September. The crossing takes 14 hours and costs up to €85/490 without accommodation.

Irish Ferries (☎ in Rosslare 053-33158, in Cherbourg 02 33 23 44 44, in Roscoff 02 98 61 17 17; www.irishferries.com) One to three times a week from Roscoff to Rosslare from late April to late September; the crossing time is 17½ hours. Ferries from Cherbourg to Rosslare sail two to four times per week year-round, except in late January and all of February; crossing time is 20½ hours. Both services cost up to €150/625 without accommodation.

GETTING AROUND
Travelling around Ireland is short, simple and sweet – or maddeningly long and infuriatingly complicated. Distances are relatively short and there's a good network of roads, but public transportation can be infrequent, expensive or both and – especially with trains – does not reach many of the more interesting places.

Having your own transport is a major advantage and it's worth considering car hire for at least part of your trip. The growing network of motorways have cut journey times considerably, but the huge network of secondary and tertiary roads is much better if you want to 'experience' Ireland as you travel – although it is still true that smaller, rural roads can make for difficult driving conditions.

If you opt not to drive, a mixture of buses, the occasional taxi, plenty of time, walking and sometimes hiring a bicycle will get you just about anywhere.

AIR

Ireland's size makes domestic flying unnecessary unless you're in a hurry, but there are flights between Dublin and Belfast, Cork, Derry, Donegal, Galway, Kerry, Shannon and Sligo, as well as a Belfast–Cork service. Most flights within Ireland take around 30 to 50 minutes.

The only domestic carriers are the following:

Aer Árann (☎ 1890-462 726, in Dublin 01-814 5240, in Galway 091-593 034, in Cork 021-814 1058; www.aerarann.com) Operates flights from Dublin to Belfast, Cork, Derry, Donegal, Galway, Knock and Sligo; and a Belfast-to-Cork route.

Aer Lingus (☎ information & bookings 01-886 8844, flight information 01-705 6705, in Belfast 028-9442 2888; www.aerlingus.com) Operates flights between Dublin and Shannon.

Ryanair (www.ryanair.com) Budget airline runs flights between Dublin and Cork.

BICYCLE

Ireland is a great place for bicycle touring, despite bad road surfaces in places and inclement weather. If you intend to cycle in the west, the prevailing winds mean it's easier to cycle from south to north. Both **Irish Cycling Safaris** (☎ 01-260 0749; www .cyclingsafaris.com; Belfield Bike Shop, UCD, Dublin 4) and **Go Ireland** (☎ 066-976 2094; www.go visitireland.com; Old Orchard House, Killorglin, Co Kerry) organise tours for groups of cyclists in the southwest, the southeast, Clare, Connemara, Donegal and Antrim.

Bicycles can be transported by bus if there's enough room; the charge varies. By train the cost varies from €4 to €8 for a one-way journey, but bikes are not al-lowed on certain train routes, including the Dublin Area Rapid Transit (DART); check with **Iarnród Éireann** (☎ 01-836 3333).

Typical bicycle hire costs are €20 to €25 per day or €60 to €100 per week plus a deposit of around €100. There are many local independent outlets, but several dealers have outlets around the country:

Irish Cycle Hire (☎ 041-685 3772; www .irishcyclehire.com; Unit 6, Enterprise Centre, Ardee, Co Louth)

Raleigh Ireland (☎ 01-626 1333; www .raleigh.ie; Raleigh House, Kylemore Rd, Dublin) Ireland's biggest rental dealer.

Rent-a-Bike Ireland (☎ 061-416 983; www.irelandrentabike.com; 1 Patrick St, Limerick, Co Limerick)

BOAT

There are many boat services to islands lying off the coast, including to the Aran and Skellig Islands to the west, the Saltee Islands to the southeast, and Tory and Rathlin Islands to the north. Ferries also operate across rivers, inlets and loughs, providing useful short cuts, particularly for cyclists.

Cruises are very popular on the 258km-long Shannon-Erne Waterway and on a variety of other lakes and loughs. The tourist offices only recommend operators that are registered with them. Details of non-tourist-board-affiliated boat trips are given under the relevant sections throughout this book.

BORDER CROSSINGS

Security has been progressively scaled down in Northern Ireland in recent years and all border crossings with the Republic are now open and generally unstaffed. Permanent checkpoints have been removed and ramps levelled. On major routes your only indication that you

↘ FERRY, BUS & TRAIN DISCOUNT DEALS

FOR TRAVEL ACROSS EUROPE

Eurail (www.eurail.com) passes are for non-Europeans who have been in Europe for less than six months. They are valid on trains in the Republic, but not in Northern Ireland, and offer discounts on Irish Ferries crossings to France. Passes are cheaper when purchased outside Europe. In the USA and Canada phone ☎ 1888-667 9734. In London contact Rail Europe (☎ 0870-584 8848; 179 Piccadilly).

InterRail (www.interrail.com) passes give you a 50% fare reduction on train travel within Ireland, as well as discounts on Irish Ferries and Stena Line services. Passes can be purchased at most major train stations and at student travel outlets.

FOR TRAVEL WITHIN IRELAND

Holders of the new Student Travel Card (www.studenttravelcard.ie) are entitled to a 40% discount on Irish trains and 25% off Bus Éireann services. The card is available at branch offices of USIT (www.usit.ie).

UNLIMITED-TRAVEL TICKETS FOR BUSES & TRAINS

The Open-Road Pass covers bus-only travel within the Republic, allowing for a variety of travel options, from three days' travel out of six consecutive days (€54) to 15 days' travel out of 30 (€234).

Irish Rover tickets combine services on Bus Éireann and Ulsterbus. They cost €83.50 (for three days' travel out of eight consecutive days), €190 (eight days out of 15) and €280 (15 days out of 30).

Iarnród Éireann Explorer tickets cover train travel in the Republic. They cost €160 (for five days travel out of 15 consecutive days). The Irish Explorer rail and bus tickets (€245) allow eight days' travel out of 15 consecutive days on trains and buses within the Republic.

Freedom of Northern Ireland passes allow unlimited travel on NIR, Ulsterbus and Citybus services for £15 for one day, £36 for three out of eight consecutive days, and £53 for seven consecutive days.

Children aged under 16 pay half price for all these passes and for all normal tickets. Children aged under three travel for free on public transport. You can buy the above passes at most major train and bus stations in Ireland. Although they're good value, many of them make economic sense only if you're planning to travel around Ireland at the speed of light.

have crossed the border will be a change in road signs and the colour of number plates and postboxes.

BUS

Bus Éireann (☎ 01-836 6111; www.buseireann .ie; Busáras, Store St, Dublin) is the Republic's bus line and offers an extensive network throughout the South. Private buses compete – often very favourably – with Bus Éireann in the Republic and also run where the national buses are irregular or absent.

The larger bus companies will usually carry bikes for free but you should always check in advance to avoid surprises. Ulsterbus (☎ 028-9066 6600; www.ulsterbus .co.uk; Milewater Rd, Belfast) is the only bus service in Northern Ireland. In Belfast, the bus service is operated by Metro (☎ 028-9066 6630; www.translink.co.uk).

BUS PASSES
Details of special deals and passes are given in the boxed text, left.

COSTS
Bus travel is much cheaper than train travel, and private buses often charge less than Bus Éireann. Generally, return fares cost little more than a one-way fare.

See the table below for some sample one-way bus fares.

RESERVATIONS
Bus Éireann bookings can be made online, but you can't reserve a seat for a particular service.

CAR & MOTORCYCLE
Ireland has more cars than ever and the building of new roads and the upgrading of existing ones just hasn't kept pace. Be prepared for delays, especially at holiday weekends. AA Roadwatch (☎ 1550 131 811; www.aaroadwatch.ie) provides traffic information in the Republic.

In the Republic, speed-limit and distance signs are in kilometres (although the occasional older white sign shows distances in miles); in the North, speed-limit and distance signs are in miles.

You'll need a good road map and a sense of humour to deal with the severe lack of signposts in the Republic, and on minor roads be prepared for lots of potholes.

Petrol is considerably cheaper in the Republic than in the North. Most service stations accept payment by credit card, but some small, remote ones may take cash only.

BUS FARES

SERVICE	COST (ONE-WAY)	DURATION (HR) (MON-SAT)	SERVICES PER DAY
Belfast-Dublin	£13	3	7
Derry-Belfast	£10	1¾	10+
Derry-Galway	£26.10	5¼	4
Dublin-Cork	€11.70	4½	6
Dublin-Donegal	€17.60	4	5
Dublin-Rosslare	€16.70	3	12
Dublin-Tralee	€23	6	12
Dublin-Waterford	€12.20	2¾	7
Killarney-Cork	€15.30	2	12
Killarney-Waterford	€21.20	4½	12

All cars on public roads must be insured. If you are bringing your own vehicle in to the country, check that your insurance will cover you in Ireland.

BRING YOUR OWN VEHICLE

It's easy to take your own vehicle to Ireland and there are no specific procedures involved, but you should carry a vehicle registration document as proof that it's yours.

Automobile Association members should ask for a Card of Introduction entitling them to services offered by sister organisations (including maps, information, breakdown assistance, legal advice etc), usually free of charge.

Automobile Association (AA; www.aa ireland.ie) Northern Ireland (☎ 0870-950 0600, breakdown assistance 0800-667 788); Republic (☎ Dublin 01-617 9999, Cork 021-425 2444, breakdown assistance 1800 667 788)

Royal Automobile Club (RAC; www .rac.ie) Northern Ireland (☎ 0800 029 029, breakdown assistance 0800-828 282); Republic (☎ 1890-483 483)

DRIVING LICENCE

Unless you have an EU licence, which is treated like an Irish one, your driving licence is valid for 12 months from the date of entry to Ireland, but you should have held it for two years prior to that. If you don't hold an EU licence, it's a good idea to obtain an International Driving Permit (IDP) from your home automobile association before you leave. Your home-country licence is usually enough to hire a car for three months.

You must carry your driving licence at all times.

HIRE

Car hire in Ireland is expensive, so you're often better off making arrangements in your home country with some sort of package deal. For travel in July and August it's wise to book well ahead. Most cars are manual; automatic cars are available, but they're more expensive to hire.

The international hire companies and the major local operators have offices all over Ireland. **Nova Car Hire** (www .rentacar-ireland.com) acts as an agent for Alamo, Budget, European and National, and offers greatly discounted rates. In the Republic typical weekly high-season hire rates with Nova are around €150 for a small car, €185 for a medium-sized car, and €320 for a five-seater people carrier. In the North, similar cars are marginally more expensive.

When hiring a car, be sure to check whether the price includes collision-damage waiver (CDW), insurance (eg for car theft and windscreen damage), value-added tax (VAT) and unlimited mileage.

If you're travelling from the Republic into Northern Ireland, it's important to make sure that your rental insurance covers journeys to the North. People aged 21 years and under aren't allowed to hire a car; for the majority of hire companies, you have to be aged at least 23 and have held a valid driving licence for a minimum of one year. Some companies in the Republic won't rent to you if you're aged 74 or over; there's no upper age limit in the North.

Motorbikes and mopeds are not available for rent in Ireland.

PARKING

Ireland is tiny and the Irish love their cars; the numbers just don't add up and parking is an expensive and difficult nightmare. Parking in towns and cities is either by meter, 'pay and display' tickets or disc parking (discs, which rotate to display the time you parked your car, are available from newsagencies).

ROAD RULES

Copies of Ireland's road rules are available from tourist offices. Here are some of the most basic rules:

- Drive on the left; overtake to the right.
- Safety belts must be worn by the driver and all passengers.
- Children aged under 12 aren't allowed to sit in the front passenger seat.
- Motorcyclists and their passengers must wear helmets.
- When entering a roundabout, give way to the right.
- Speed limits are 120km/h on motorways, 100km/h on national roads, 80km/h on regional and local roads and 50km/h or as signposted in towns.
- The legal alcohol limit is 80mg of alcohol per 100mL of blood. Driving while over the limit can lead to a fine of up to €5000 and/or a jail term of up to six months. Your liver can eliminate the effects of one standard drink per hour, roughly equivalent to a half-pint of beer.

LOCAL TRANSPORT

There are comprehensive local bus networks in Dublin (Dublin Bus), Belfast (Metro) and some other larger towns. The Dublin Area Rapid Transport (DART) line in Dublin runs roughly the length of the city's coastline, while the Luas tram system has two very popular lines.

Taxis tend to be expensive – for daytime rates, flagfall is €4.10 and fares start at €1.03 per kilometre after that (night-time rates are a bit higher).

TOURS

If your time is limited, it might be worth considering an organised tour, though it's cheaper to see things independently, and Ireland is small enough for you to get to even the most remote places within a few hours. Tours can be booked through travel agencies, tourist offices in the major cities, or directly through the tour companies themselves.

Bus Éireann (☎ 01-836 6111; www.bus eireann.ie; 59 Upper O'Connell St, Dublin) Runs day tours to various parts of the Republic and the North.

CIE Tours International (☎ 01-703 1888; www.cietours.ie; 35 Lower Abbey St, Dublin) Runs four- to 11-day coach tours of the Republic and the North, including accommodation and meals. The Taste of Ireland tour (five days) takes in Blarney, Ring of Kerry, Killarney, Cliffs of Moher and the region around the River Shannon (€715 in high season).

Grayline Tours (☎ 01-872 9010; www .irishcitytours.com; 33 Bachelor's Walk, Dublin) Located in Dublin, it offers half- and full-day tours (€25) from Dublin to Newgrange, Glendalough and north Dublin, and three- and four-day trips to the Ring of Kerry (€219 to €369).

Paddywagon Tours (☎ 01-672 6007; www .paddywagontours.com) Activity-filled three- and six-day tours all over Ireland with friendly tour guides. Accommodation is in IHH hostels.

Ulsterbus Tours (☎ 028-9033 7004; www .ulsterbus.co.uk) Runs a large number of day trips throughout the North and the Republic.

It's worth checking **GoIreland.com** (☎ 1800 668 668; www.goireland.com) for holiday packages.

For train enthusiasts, **Railtours Ireland** (☎ 01-856 0045; www.railtoursireland.com)

organises a series of one- and two-day train trips in association with Iarnród Éireann. A three-day trip from Dublin to Cork, Blarney Castle and Kerry costs €339.

TRAIN

Iarnród Éireann (Irish Rail; ☎ 1850 366 222; www.irishrail.ie; 35 Lower Abbey St, Dublin) operates trains in the Republic on routes that fan out from Dublin. The system is limited though: there's no north–south route along the western coast, no network in Donegal, and no direct connec-

tions from Waterford to Cork or Killarney. **Northern Ireland Railways (NIR; ☎ 028-9089 9411; www.nirailways.co.uk; Belfast Central Station)** runs four routes from Belfast. One links with the system in the Republic via Newry to Dublin; the other three go east to Bangor, northeast to Larne and northwest to Derry via Coleraine (see the map below).

COSTS

Train travel is more expensive than bus travel and one-way fares are particularly poor value – a midweek return ticket is

TRAIN ROUTES

TRAIN FARES

SERVICE	COST (ONE WAY)	DURATION (HRS)	SERVICES PER DAY (MON-SAT)
Dublin-Belfast	€38	2	half-hourly
Dublin-Cork	€66	3¼	8
Dublin-Galway	€34.50	3¼	5
Dublin-Limerick	€50	2½	13
Dublin-Sligo	€32	3	3
Dublin-Tralee	€68.50	4½	8
Dublin-Waterford	€27	2½	7

often about the same as a one-way fare. First-class tickets cost around €5 to €10 more than the standard fare for a single journey.

See the table above for some sample one-way fares.

RESERVATIONS

Iarnród Éireann takes reservations for all its train services. You need to fax your details (name, number of passengers, date and time of service, credit-card number and expiry date) to ☎ 01-703 4136.

↘ GLOSSARY

An Óige – literally 'the Youth'; Republic of Ireland Youth Hostel Association
An Taisce – National Trust for the Republic of Ireland

bailey – outer wall of a castle
beehive hut – see *clochán*
Black & Tans – British recruits to the Royal Irish Constabulary just after WWI
Blarney Stone – sacred stone perched on top of Blarney Castle; kissing it is said to bestow the gift of gab
bodhrán – hand-held goatskin drum
Bronze Age – earliest metal-using period, around 2500 BC to 300 BC in Ireland
bullaun – stone with a depression, probably used as a mortar for grinding

caher – stone-walled circular area
cairn – mound of stones heaped over a prehistoric grave
cashel – stone-walled *ring fort*
céilidh – session of traditional music and dancing; also called 'ceili'
Celtic Tiger – nickname of the Irish boom economy of the 1990s
chancel – eastern end of a church, where the altar is situated
chipper – fish 'n' chips restaurant
cill – literally 'church'; Irish place name; also known as 'kill'
cillín – literally 'little cell'; a hermitage
Claddagh ring – traditional ring with a crowned heart between two hands
clochán – circular stone building, shaped like an old-fashioned beehive
Connaught – one of Ireland's four ancient provinces, sometimes 'Connacht'; see also *Leinster, Munster* and *Ulster*
craic – conversation, chit-chat, gossip, fun, good times; also known as 'crack'

crannóg – artificial island made in a lake for habitation
currach – traditional rowing boat of tarred canvas over a lath framework

Dáil – lower house of the parliament of the Republic of Ireland; see also *Oireachtas* and *Seanad*
DART – Dublin Area Rapid Transport train line
diamond – town square
dolmen – tomb chamber of vertical stones topped by a huge capstone
Dúchas – Republic department of parks, monuments and gardens
dún – fort, usually made of stone

Éire – Irish name for *Republic of Ireland*
esker – raised ridge formed by glaciers

Fáilte Ireland – literally 'Welcome Board'; Irish Tourist Board
fir – men (singular 'fear'); sign on men's toilets; see also *mná*
fleadh – festival

GAA – Gaelic Athletic Association; promotes Gaelic football and *hurling*
Gaeltacht – Irish-speaking
garda – Irish Republic police

HINI – Hostelling International of Northern Ireland
hurling – Irish sport similar to hockey

Iarnród Éireann – Republic of Ireland Railways
IRA – Irish Republican Army; the largest Republican *paramilitary*, founded 1919
Iron Age – metal-using period after the *Bronze Age*

jaunting car – Killarney's traditional horse-drawn transport

Leinster – one of Ireland's four ancient provinces; see also *Connaught, Munster* and *Ulster*
lough – lake or long, narrow bay
Loyalist – see *Unionist*
Luas – Dublin's light-rail transit system

marching season – *Orange Order* parades, celebrating Protestant William III's victory over Catholic James II
mesolithic – time of the first human settlers in Ireland, about 8000 to 4000 BC
mná – women; sign on women's toilets; see also *fir*
motte – early Norman fortification of a raised, flattened mound with a keep
Munster – one of Ireland's four ancient provinces; see also *Connaught, Leinster* and *Ulster*

Nationalist – see *Republican*
neolithic – a period of settled agriculture lasting from around 4000 to 2500 BC in Ireland; followed by the *Bronze Age*
NIR – Northern Ireland Railways
NITB – Northern Ireland Tourist Board
North, the – political entity of Northern Ireland, not used geographically
NUI – National University of Ireland

Ogham stone – a stone etched with the earliest form of writing in Ireland
Oireachtas – Parliament of the Republic of Ireland; see *Dáil* and *Seanad*
Orange Order – Northern Ireland's largest Protestant organisation

Palladian – style of architecture developed by Andrea Palladio (1508–80), based on ancient Roman architecture
paramilitaries – armed illegal organisations, either *Loyalist* or *Republican*

Partition – division of Ireland in 1921
passage grave – Celtic tomb with a chamber reached by a narrow passage
Plantation – settlement of Protestant migrants in Ireland in the 17th century
poitín – illegally brewed whiskey
PSNI – Police Service of Northern Ireland

ráth – *ring fort* with earthen banks around a timber wall
Republic of Ireland – the 26 counties of *the South;* also just 'the Republic'
Republican – supporter of a united Ireland
ring fort – circular habitation area surrounded by banks and ditches
RTE – Radio Telefís Éireann; the Republic's national broadcasting service
RUC – Royal Ulster Constabulary, now the *PSNI*

Seanad – upper house of the parliament of the Republic of Ireland; see also *Oireachtas* and *Dáil*
seisiún – music session
Sinn Féin – literally 'We Ourselves'; *Republican* political party
snug – partitioned-off table in a pub
souterrain – underground chamber usually found in hill forts and *ring forts*
South, the – the Republic of Ireland

Taoiseach – Republic of Ireland prime minister
Tricolour – green, white and orange Irish flag symbolising a united Ireland

uillean pipes – Irish bagpipes
Ulster – one of Ireland's four ancient provinces; sometimes inaccurately used to describe *the North*; see also *Connaught, Leinster* and *Munster*
Unionist – person who wants to retain Northern Ireland's links with Britain

GLOSSARY

↘ BEHIND THE SCENES

THE AUTHORS
FIONN DAVENPORT

Coordinating author, This is Ireland, Ireland's Top 25 Experiences, Ireland's Top Itineraries, Planning Your Trip, Ireland In Focus, Dublin, County Dublin, Counties Kildare & Wicklow, Directory & Transport

Born and partly bred in Dublin, it took Fionn years before he understood that though part of the same nation, Ireland beyond the pale was often a different country. Which made for some great exploring, but in the end he settled for the bits he knew best – and discovered a whole bunch of stuff on his doorstep he didn't know about. Which makes writing about his country year after year never get boring. Over the years he's also expanded his travel bag to include TV and radio – catch him on Newstalk 106-108FM (www.newstalk.ie).

Author thanks My thanks to all of the Lonely Planet staff who helped with the book: Clifton Wilkinson, Eoin Dunlevy, Herman So, Mark Griffiths and Ali Lemer. Thanks to Neil Wilson for his help on Northern Ireland; cheers also to the 10 who contributed to the chapter highlights. Finally, thanks to Caroline, who helped me soldier on with cups of tea and patient smiles.

CATHERINE LE NEVEZ
Ireland's Top 25 Experiences, Counties Donegal, Kilkenny, Mayo, Sligo, Waterford & Wexford

Catherine's wanderlust kicked in when she roadtripped across Europe aged four, and she's been hitting the road at every opportunity since, completing a Doctorate of Creative Arts in Writing, Masters in Professional Writing, and postgrad qualifications in Editing and Publishing along the way. Her Celtic connections include Irish and Breton heritage, as well as Irish mates who warned her that Ireland would be a grand country if it had a roof (and that the Guinness tastes better there than anywhere else on earth). She's since crisscrossed Ireland for several Lonely Planet gigs, discovering that the Guinness tastes so much better it more than makes up for the rain.

ETAIN O'CARROLL   Counties Meath, Louth & Offaly

Born and bred in the boggy hinterlands of rural Ireland, it was almost inevitable that Etain's youthful quests for more exotic pastures would translate into a career as a travel writer and photographer. Although work often takes her far from home, Etain has written about Ireland's landscape and culture for a wide variety of publications, and the lure of untouched pubs, meandering rivers and genuine craic never quite goes away. Work on this guide provided a cherished opportunity to traipse around her own backyard searching for hidden treats, revisit some of her favourite places and quiz friends and family on the best spots in the country to eat, drink and be merry.

RYAN VER BERKMOES   Ireland's Top 25 Experiences, Counties Clare, Cork, Galway, Kerry & Tipperary

From Galway to Cork, with plenty of diversions in between, Ryan Ver Berkmoes has delighted in this great swath of Ireland. He first visited the latter in 1985, from when he remembers a grey place where the locals wandered the muddy tidal flats for fun and frolic. Times have changed! From lost rural pubs to lost memory, he's revelled in a place where his first name brings a smile and his surname brings a 'huh?' Catch up with him at www.ryanverberkmoes.com.

NEIL WILSON   Ireland's Top 25 Experiences, Northern Ireland

Neil's first visit to Northern Ireland was in 1994, during the first flush of post-ceasefire optimism, and his interest in the history and politics of the place intensified a few years later when he found out that most of his mum's ancestors were from Ulster. Working on recent editions of the Ireland guidebook has allowed him to witness firsthand the progress being made towards a lasting peace, as well as enjoying some excellent hiking on the Causeway Coast and in the Mourne Mountains. Neil is a full-time travel writer based in Edinburgh, Scotland, and has written more than 45 guidebooks for half a dozen publishers.

CONTRIBUTING AUTHORS

Content for the section on Health was originally written by Dr Caroline Evans.

THIS BOOK

This 1st edition of *Discover Ireland* was coordinated by Fionn Davenport, and researched and written by Catherine Le Nevez, Etain O'Carroll, Ryan Ver Berkmoes and Neil Wilson. This guidebook was commissioned in Lonely Planet's London office, and produced by the following:

Commissioning Editor Clifton Wilkinson
Coordinating Editor Ali Lemer
Coordinating Cartographer Mark Griffiths
Coordinating Layout Designer Nicholas Colicchia
Managing Editor Bruce Evans
Managing Cartographers Alison Lyall, Herman So
Managing Layout Designers Sally Darmody
Assisting Editors Anne Mulvaney, Kirsten Rawlings
Assisting Cartographers Anthony Phelan

Cover research Jane Hart, lonelyplanetimages.com
Internal image research Aude Vauconsant, lonelyplanetimages.com
Project Manager Eoin Dunlevy

Thanks to Sasha Baskett, Glenn Beanland, Lucy Birchley, Yvonne Bischofberger, Ryan Evans, Suki Gear, Joshua Geoghegan, Mark Germanchis, Chris Girdler, Michelle Glynn, Brice Gosnell, Imogen Hall, James Hardy, Steve Henderson, Lauren Hunt, Laura Jane, Chris Lee Ack, Nic Lehman, John Mazzocchi, Jennifer Mullins, Wayne Murphy, Darren O'Connell, Naomi Parker, Piers Pickard, Howard Ralley, Lachlan Ross, Julie Sheridan, Jason Shugg, Caroline Sieg, Naomi Stephens, Geoff Stringer, Jane Thompson, Sam Trafford, Stefanie Di Trocchio, Tashi Wheeler, Juan Winata, Emily K Wolman, Nick Wood

Internal photographs p4 Shepherd with flock, County Donegal, Simon Greenwood; p10 Eightercua Stone Row, County Kerry, Richard Cummins; p12 Kilkenny city, Richard Cummins; pp31–2 Custom House, Dublin, Richard Cummins; p39 Derreen Tower, Achill Island, County Mayo, John Elk III; p3, p50 Temple Bar, Dublin, Micah Wright; p3, p97 Powerscourt Waterfall, County Wicklow, Richard Cummins; p3, p139 Kilkenny Castle, Richard Cummins; p3, p179 Slea Head, County Kerry, Richard Cummins; p3, p225 Galway city, Richard Cummins; p3, p271 Mt Errigal, County Donegal, Gareth McCormack; p272 Slieve League, County Donegal, Stephen Saks; p3, p307 Giant's Causeway, County Antrim, Martin Moos; p342 Rock of Cashel, County Tipperary, Sean Caffrey; p387 Baltimore, County Cork, Gareth McCormack.

SEND US YOUR FEEDBACK

We love to hear from travellers – your comments keep us on our toes and help make our books better. Our well-travelled team reads every word on what you loved or loathed about this book. Although we cannot reply individually to postal submissions, we always guarantee that your feedback goes straight to the appropriate authors, in time for the next edition. Each person who sends us information is thanked in the next edition and the most useful submissions are rewarded with a free book.

To send us your updates – and find out about Lonely Planet events, newsletters and travel news – visit our award-winning website: **lonelyplanet.com/contact**.

Note: we may edit, reproduce and incorporate your comments in Lonely Planet products such as guidebooks, websites and digital products, so let us know if you don't want your comments reproduced or your name acknowledged. For a copy of our privacy policy visit **lonelyplanet.com/privacy**.

BEHIND THE SCENES

THIS BOOK

NOTES

⬎ INDEX

INDEX

C-F

INDEX

F-I

000 Map pages
000 Photograph pages

INDEX

T-Z